"Misfits" in Fin-de-Siècle
France and Italy

"Misfits" in Fin-de-Siècle France and Italy

Anatomies of Difference

Susan A. Ashley

Bloomsbury Academic
An imprint of Bloomsbury Publishing Plc

B L O O M S B U R Y
LONDON · OXFORD · NEW YORK · NEW DELHI · SYDNEY

Bloomsbury Academic

An imprint of Bloomsbury Publishing Plc

50 Bedford Square
London
WC1B 3DP
UK

1385 Broadway
New York
NY 10018
USA

www.bloomsbury.com

BLOOMSBURY and the Diana logo are trademarks of Bloomsbury Publishing Plc

First published 2017

British Library Cataloguing-in-Publication Data
A catalogue record for this book is available from the British Library.

ISBN: HB: 978-1-3500-1339-1
        ePDF: 978-1-3500-1340-7
        eBook: 978-1-3500-1341-4

Library of Congress Cataloging-in-Publication Data
Names: Ashley, Susan A., 1943- author.
Title: "Misfits" in Fin de siècle France and Italy: anatomies of difference / Susan A. Ashley.
Description: London; New York: Bloomsbury Academic, an imprint of Bloomsbury Publishing Plc, 2017.
Identifiers: LCCN 2016047249 | ISBN 9781350013391 (hardback) |
ISBN 9781350013414 (ePub) | ISBN 9781350013407 (PDF)
Subjects: LCSH: France–Social conditions–19th century. | Italy–Social conditions–1870-1918. |
Marginality, Social–France–History–19th century. | Marginality, Social–Italy–History–19th century. |
Deviant behavior–Social aspects–France–History–19th century. | Deviant behavior–Social aspects–
France–History–19th century. | Social medicine–France–History–19th century. | Social sciences–
France–History–19th century. | BISAC: HISTORY / Europe / France. | HISTORY / Europe / Italy. |
HISTORY / Modern / 19th Century. | HISTORY / Social History.
Classification: LCC HN425 .A87 2017 | DDC 306.0944–dc23
LC record available at https://lccn.loc.gov/2016047249

Cover image © Bibliothèque Nationale, Paris, France Archives Charmet/Bridgeman Images

Typeset by Integra Software Services Pvt. Ltd.
Printed and bound in Great Britain

To find out more about our authors and books visit www.bloomsbury.com.
Here you will find extracts, author interviews, details of forthcoming
events and the option to sign up for our newsletters.

To
Robert, William, and Matthew

Contents

Preface

Some years ago, I agreed to teach some English to my son's first-grade class in Florence, Italy. The school district required nothing more than a certification of my sanity from a medical doctor. I turned to the college physician, a person I had known informally for years. She faxed this terse assessment: "she falls within the limits of the normal." The nature of these limits would, she assumed, be clear to anyone. And she was right; the superintendent accepted the verdict without question. Evidently she felt confident that they both knew what normal meant. On a superficial level, they surely did, but as an historian I knew that definitions of sanity differ depending on the time and the place. Several years later, I took up the question of what counts as normal and who says so in earnest, choosing the two countries and the period I knew best, Italy and France in the fin de siècle. I began with criminologists and moved as they did into other realms of social and psychological difference. They saw affinities among them that I did not. Intrigued, I've tried to map those singular connections and to uncover the logic behind them.

Over the years invested in this project, I've profited immensely from the advice and encouragement of colleagues and friends. Fellow members of the Colorado College History Department Peter Blasenheim, Anne Hyde, Bill Hochman, Doug Monroy, Carol Neel, Tip Ragan, and John Williams read pieces of the manuscript and asked provocative questions not likely to occur to a modern Europeanist. I am indebted to colleagues at meetings of the Western Society for French History and the Society for French Historical Studies, whose suggestions helped to broaden the scope of the inquiry and to reinforce the argument. Special appreciation goes to K. Steven Vincent and Dennis Showalter who read the final draft of the manuscript and offered reassuring assessments. The reviewers for Bloomsbury Academic offered perceptive and constructive observations. I hope I have done them justice. Other colleagues, including Robin Walz, Steven Hause, Torbjörn Wandel, Michael Wilson, Kathy Giuffre, and Jean Blondel, inspired and challenged me, sometimes unwittingly. Two Colorado College students, Evie English and Erik Laitos, offered assistance along the way, as did History Department administrative assistants Sandy Papuga and Joanna Popiel. They and others deserve credit for enriching this study. Responsibility for the remaining defects falls to me.

The exceptional resources and capable staff at the Bibliothèque Nationale of France and the Biblioteca Nazionale Centrale in Florence made this project possible. Thanks to Peter Kennealy, I also had the privilege of using the well-curated collection of recent work in the social sciences at the European University Institute Library in Florence. Colorado College provided funding for travel and for the leaves indispensable to this research.

Research can be a lonely enterprise, but it is hardly a hardship when conducted in Florence and Paris. I appreciated the fellowship of friends in both cities, particular that of Janet Smith, Giovanni Tonarelli, Gail Solberg, Martina Ghiandelli, and Tess Blondel. The most constant inspiration and support came from my family, to whom I dedicate this effort.

1

In Spite of Evolution, Because of Modern Life

Looking behind them, late nineteenth-century French and Italian liberals congratulated themselves on the evident decline of ignorance and autocracy. The unification of Italy and the establishment of the French Third Republic gave them particular reason for satisfaction. Installing parliamentary institutions, they believed, secured liberty and diminished the obstacles to continued progress. Looking beyond Europe enhanced their sense of superiority by displaying the distance between the primitive beginnings of the human species and modern civilization. Scientists took the disciplined, hardworking, and law-abiding citizens they saw around them as evidence of the latest stages of human evolution. Just as in nature, they pointed out, some groups developed more rapidly than others, and those best able to adapt to conditions flourished, while those less well equipped to survive vanished. It appeared, then, that society moved in directions ordained by the laws of nature. With free institutions reinforcing biological progress, those on top expected civilization to triumph over savagery, reason to prevail over ignorance, self-control to suppress impulse, and hard work to win out over indolence. And yet statistics confirmed what personal experience, the press, and the experts made clear: the abundant presence of misfits. Increases in crime, vagrancy, suicide, insanity, and neuroses disrupted confident assumptions about the benefits of liberty and the results of evolution. Too many people fell out of line. They did not obey the law, hold a job, settle down, or practice monogamy. Too many misfits showed signs of deficient or twisted reason and of confused and lightly held values. Such surprising and troubling evidence required an explanation and a response.

This study reconstructs efforts at the time to understand and to deal with the gap between expectations and disconcerting realities. It explores how specialists and observers grappled with aberrant behaviors. The aspiring experts addressed the anomalies from a variety of backgrounds and perspectives. Jurists, politicians, doctors, and educators joined advocates of emerging specialties, including psychiatry, neurology, sociology, and criminology. With few exceptions, they claimed to set aside metaphysics for science, and they earnestly embraced what they understood as empirical methods. Some patterns worth noting emerge. Contemporary sources, whether written by medical practitioners or social scientists, confirm what historians emphasize: the importance of biological determinism. But that is not the whole story. Investigators, including doctors, took pains to distinguish between very serious and less serious forms of deviance based on their assessment of the causes. For each category of misfits, they distinguished between external and internal drivers. In the first case, circumstances provoked ordinary people to do what they otherwise would not do. In the second and rarer category, the acts resulted from organic abnormalities, leaving these people powerless to change the roots of their behavior. The distinction between accidental and born deviance left a large space for normality and a small one for innate aberrations. When neither circumstances nor biology explained actions, experts recognized a third possibility: willful deviance. That possibility retained the once significantly larger space assigned to vice and to original sin.

This analysis focuses on six categories of misfits. Some old problems—vagrancy, crime, and madness—received renewed scrutiny in the decades on either side of the turn of the century, because they alarmed people and because they challenged the confident equation of advanced society with reason and self-control. New problems, including nervous disorders and sexual perversions, also provoked great interest and a flurry of studies. Among long-recognized but little-studied anomalies, genius and idiocy (their label) drew fresh attention. Vagrancy, crime, and sexual perversions, surfeits and deficits of intelligence, insanity, and neuroses all appeared as disturbing examples of difference. They attracted notice because they surprised and threatened, and because taken together they produced an apparent storm of extra-social behavior. Fascination about them also came from what these misfits indicated about progress. Perhaps evolution had left them behind, but maybe they announced the future, one of decline.

These experts sought to explain the apparent plague of misfits, and they believed that they found the answers. Playing on their credibility as empiricists, they urged lawmakers to take their discoveries seriously. They pressed for changes informed by their analyses of deviance, and in some measure they succeeded. But the effects of their theories go beyond their practical applications. Investigators dealt with evolution and progress, the body and mind, and the self and morality, and they meant to get closer to the truth about these grander matters. Their answers raised more questions, and great alarm. Taking an empirical look at the laws of nature and history, they issued an alert against overconfident predictions about progress. They detailed evidence that demonstrated the vulnerability of the fully evolved body, and they described the mental and physical toll that modern life took. Their observations helped to explain misfits, but their warnings did not just apply to them. Successful people also invited problems. As they tracked down the roots of organic abnormalities, experts reorganized the body, and they did it in ways which made everyone a potential misfit. What they discovered about the brain's structure, for example, raised questions about its unity, and with that about the unity of the self—anyone's self. Their studies also disrupted established ideas of something as basic as sexual identity. The results of their inquiries, then, applied not only to misfits but to ordinary people as well.

The phenomenon of deviance is by no means uncharted territory. It engages the interest of scholars from several disciplines, including historians, because it commanded so much attention at the time and because it indicates a great deal about society, politics, and values. Michel Foucault's work, including his analyses of criminality, mental illness, and sexuality, influenced a generation of historians. He played an important role in defining issues and setting a research agenda. In his work, Foucault singled out areas of deviance for scrutiny and turned attention to how those in power inculcated norms and managed deviants. By insisting that in free societies power seeks to impose conformity, he inspired a fresh appraisal of deviance in the period. In his view, the dominant groups, particularly the liberals, focused on deviance and normality in order to maintain control in a context of political and social change. Determined to manage freedom and equality, he argues, they perfected mechanisms of restraint and conformity which maintained the appearance of freedom while gutting it of its substance. His position coincided with that of Marxist historiography where it remained influential, as it did in Italy, and it turned attention to elites and their use of power where it did not.

While recognizing Foucault's importance, recent historians and their allies in disciplines including literature, sociology, and anthropology take some distance from his conclusions. Generally, they call for further research and for more subtle and complex arguments. With that in mind, they reconsider the motives of experts and lawmakers, and they broaden the analysis of what produced antisocial behavior and what determined the elites' responses to it. Historians no longer see constructionism either as a perspective they need to defend or as an approach to apply to the exclusion of essentialism. The latest studies fill the gaps, reinforce the interpretations with different evidence, challenge Foucault's perspectives, or offer new approaches.

Like Foucault, scholars interested in deviance have found it a compelling path to understanding end-of-the-century European values and structures of power. Robert Nye and Jan Goldstein, among many others, follow the shift from religion to science, from moral to medical, and from misplaced reason to pathology in approaches to those identified as "other."[1] Particular types of deviance draw different constellations of scholars, and their perspectives, especially those of historians, informed this study. Historians emphasize the expanding role of biology in explanations of deviance. Scientists, they argue, traced antisocial behaviors to the body and transformed deviants into the unwilling victims of organic defects and damage. Increasingly, studies of deviance report, specialists saw the glitches and flaws as evidence of the progressive degeneration of families and eventually of the entire race. That diagnosis, historians show, led experts to recommend treatment rather than punishment for victims of degeneration and, if dangerous, to call for their confinement in hospitals or asylums. Either they joined or they leant their authority, Foucault and others argue, to elite efforts to sideline antagonists and non-conformists. That goal, in some cases, extended to advocating eugenics to secure the future, they point out.

Explanations of the appeal of biological explanations, and in particular of *dégénérescence*, differ. Contending that knowledge manifests power, Foucault sees these theories as extensions of the interests and values of those in charge. Historian Alberto De Bernardi applies this assessment to insanity. Attributing mental illness to innate defects rather than to social conditions, he argues, justified putting the mentally ill in asylums and administering therapies centered on compliance. By this optic, such tactics conformed to the elites' larger goal of pushing aside and burying the underclass.[2]

A variant of this approach connects the theories to the personal and professional interests of the investigators themselves. In the late 1850s and 1860s, Janet Oppenheim argues, psychiatrists faced something of a crisis of public confidence. Having publicized the benefits of individualized treatment in asylums, they found themselves unable to deliver results, and they sought a scientifically respectable excuse. "The hypothesis of a morbid hereditary process, worsening with each generation, possessed unique value for them in this embarrassing situation, as they quickly realized.... Degeneration theory helped alienists out of a professional impasse."[3] Ian Dowbiggin develops a similar argument, stressing the challenge psychiatrists faced convincing followers of the Church, other doctors, lawyers, and an increasingly skeptical public of their credentials to diagnose and to treat. Their defensiveness and insecurity, he argues, caused them to accept the theory of degeneracy.[4] These assessments imply, if they do not assert, that self-interest drove scientists' conclusions. Unconsciously or not, they let legitimizing their disciplines and enhancing their reputations shape their theories. That investigators sought to validate their specialties and aligned their findings with their professional interests rings true. At the same time, end-of-the-century literature on deviance shows the fluidity and permeability of disciplinary boundaries. Especially by modern standards, investigators appear singularly versatile in their own research and catholic in their collaborations. If they adjusted their theories to mark out their specialties, they did so in a less clear and rigidly divided scientific landscape than ours. The idea that they responded to their professional interests invites another explanation of the new theories. As scientists, they valued empiricism and touted their ability to ferret out the truth. They took pride in seeking different hypotheses when current therapies failed and in matching them to the evidence before them. The nature of their discoveries doubtless coincided with their ambitions, but it also conformed to their identities as empiricists.

Another explanation of the new theories of deviance centers on class. There is merit in this view when applied to how authorities defined "abnormality." People got classified as misfits when they did not or could not conform to what the middle class, in particular, considered important to society. In their strictures against lawbreaking, vagabondage, and idleness, lawmakers mainly targeted the lower classes. Although public alarm about vagrants and criminals extended beyond the elites, the powerful took the lead in combating social dissonance, as Foucault and others argue. A look at mental misfits, however, shows that class applied differently. Mental illness, epilepsy, and hysteria affected individuals across society, scientists revealed, while hard-driving establishment types seemed especially susceptible to neurasthenia. Abnormal sexual behaviors presented a more complex picture. Pederasty, according to observers, paired social and economic unequals, while sexual inversion seemingly ignored class lines. Widening the lens of class to take in mental and nervous disorders shows that those on top recognized their vulnerability to unfortunate biology as well.

Historians have seen the effects of class bias more sharply in how authorities dealt with misfits. This approach contends that politicians cut them down primarily in order to secure their own domination. If science helped them make the case, so much the better. Especially important in the 1980s, and in Italian historiography, this optic argues that the middle class embraced positivism as a weapon of class warfare. For example, Vincenzo Accattatis contends that in the 1870s and the 1880s, the middle class used anthropology and sociology to legitimize "the systematic and brutal violence applied to the marginalized ... and to the representatives of the lower classes."[5] Similar motives inspired Italian criminologists Raffaele Garofalo and Cesare Lombroso and their followers, according to this view. Applying "the logic of class violence," these experts urged the elimination of criminals, an impulse evident later in Fascism and Nazism, according to this argument.[6] The Italian system of *ammonizione* and the 1885 recidivism law in France offer examples of the alignment of public order goals with those of science, Accattatis observes. The record supplies ample evidence that governments did invoke the dangers of born deviants to take action against troublemakers in the name of defending society. Medical and social scientists fed, if they did not inspire, the association of born delinquents with strategies of sequestration and repression. However, using danger as a standard for policy also contributed to scientists' successful call for "alternative punishments" such as fines and suspended sentences for occasional offenders. From this perspective, social danger cut both ways: it marginalized serious offenders and aimed to reintegrate others.

Other scholars see the effects of class distinctions and biases in the theories themselves. Doctors and criminologists looked to prisons, asylums, and public hospitals to supply the subjects to probe, measure, and count. As a result, the case studies so important to the development and illustration of their ideas often featured patients and inmates. Cesare Lombroso's (1835–1909) research strategies offer one example. He documented his profile of the criminal man with anatomical and physiological data collected from prisoners, reinforced by photographs to illustrate their distinctive facial features. As critics at the time pointed out, prisoners and patients came largely from the lower classes and represented a very small minority of that large group. Skeptics also noted that law-abiding citizens, especially Southerners, looked a lot like Lombroso's born criminals. His sample skewed his results, but as Mary Gibson and Nicole Rafter observe, he also doctored the evidence, using the same photos in different editions of *Criminal Man*, but making them uglier.[7] Other empirically minded investigators examined individual misfits where they found them: in asylums, prisons, and hospitals. When they generalized from that narrow group, they created a biological basis for existing social and ethnic distinctions. It is also true, however, that investigators directly addressed the effects of class on deviance and called for social reforms. They described a large subgroup of misfits of every type as victims of economic and social circumstances they did not control and urged lawmakers to attack the problems responsible for marginalizing them.

Recent studies look more at the mind-set and culture of the political and intellectual elites than to their individual ambitions and class interests. In his influential study of degeneration, Daniel Pick compares French, Italian, and English versions of degeneration theory, attributing the differences to national conditions. Taking Henry Maudsley, Cesare Lombroso, and Bénédict Augustin Morel's definitions of *dégénérescence* as examples, he discerns a logic which corresponds to contemporary anxieties.[8] In France, Pick argues, degeneration registered an unsettled response to the recent past; it conceptualized "a felt crisis of history."[9] Toward mid-century, when Morel wrote, the sequence of recent revolutions had produced a perplexing legacy. The Revolution of 1848 resembled 1830 and 1789 in some ways but not others so that "it seemed to demonstrate the radical unpredictability of change, the irreducibility of new social phenomena to earlier models."[10] Grasping this ambiguity, Morel saw degeneration as a set of aberrations from an original ideal type which produced a predictable sequence of increasingly drastic anomalies across generations, Pick suggests.

According to Pick, Lombroso's twist on degeneration registered Italian worries about division and disorder rather than about the course of history. Optimistic about the Risorgimento's promise for unification but well aware of the obstacles, Italian leaders searched for ways to account for problematic regions and individuals. Lombroso's equation of degeneration with atavism reduced the problem to backwardness. That theory appealed to liberals who believed that unification put Italy among the advanced nations and who worried when resistance to their project challenged that ranking. The idea that biology held some citizens back provided a convincing explanation why some people violated norms while normal, responsible citizens did not.[11] As Pick explains it, Lombroso's ideas "did indeed 'make sense'"; they spoke powerfully to a particular crisis and provided "a new language of social representation" which related to post-Unification politics and to socialism.[12]

The interplay between politics and conceptions of deviance figures prominently in Martine Kaluszynski's narrower study of criminology in the French Third Republic. She argues that the application of science to deviance created a "bio-political" construct which "crystallized the issues, the fears, the values" of the end-of-the-century Third Republic.[13] She stresses that industrialization and urbanization, the economic crisis, political unrest, and a ferment of new ideas caused unnerving social dislocation and cultural confusion. Preoccupied with installing and legitimizing the Republic, leaders put a high premium on stability and order. In that context, the sharp reactions to violence and criminality reflected "the worries, the fears of a society in movement" and more than other issues, they engaged "the values, founding principles, and the balance of society."[14] Crime bothered politicians, and when they approached it as a science, they could see it as an object of inquiry and a target for action. They turned to criminology, whose growing influence she carefully chronicles, because it corresponded to their political principles and moral values. Criminologists shared the public's near obsession with lawlessness, a phenomenon that Dominique Kalifa examines in his study of crime and culture. He argues that the press and other transmitters of culture made crime more visible and "accessible." They "also contributed to diffusing an integrated image of norms, of common and shared perceptions of the tolerable and the intolerable."[15]

Looking at mental deviance, historian Mark Micale discerns a similar preoccupation with change. As pioneering French neurologist Jean-Martin Charcot and his followers worked out the symptoms of newly discovered traumatic disorders, Micale argues, they medicalized change, just as doctors did other social phenomena. Making change into a pathology, he observes, gave the French a way of dealing with their anxieties. "Individually and collectively, French men and women construed social, political, and economic modernization as a shock that was best accounted for by medical science and best ministered to through clinical therapeutics."[16] While the invention of traumatic disorders extended doctors' reach, it also provided "a kind of social and cultural commentary on the troubled, traumatized world of the early French Third Republic," he concludes.[17]

While this study of misfits owes a good deal to Foucault's argument that deviance proved useful to the powerful, it owes more to his contention that very basic ways of thinking define epochs. What it is impossible to think and not to think, he argues, defines the limits of knowing. Less conscious, accessible, and changeable than what Marc Bloch and the *Annales* school described as modes of thought and perception, these structures underlie the systems of thought fundamental to cultures. Foucault describes this bedrock as subject to occasional seismic shifts, evident only after one system replaces another. Developed in *The Archaeology of Knowledge* and *The Order of Things*, his identification of the substrata of knowledge, of epistemes, provides useful insight into why experts adopted some conclusions and dismissed others or paid no attention to still other apparent (to us) possibilities.[18] A variant of this approach, laid out by philosopher Ian Hacking, pulls epistemological structures out from under and makes them visible. He talks in terms of "ecological niches" defined by vectors.[19] Constructed from distinct yet interrelated components, these recesses exist to contain specific ideas. Unlike epistemes, which rarely change and then for no discernible reason, a crack in one wall can break these niches down. That piece of the framework then disappears, or its elements recombine with others to enclose a different proposition. Hacking develops the image of niches and vectors in an effort to understand transient mental illness, the diseases that come and go from the repertoire of pathologies. His example, fugue, interested scientists at the turn of the century, and then it slipped away. Now an obscure ailment, its former prominence appears misguided or quaint. Fugue's fate points to a common trajectory of ideas, Hacking suggests. What appears very real, urgent even, in one period, disappears, causing later observers to belittle the methods or marvel at the ignorance of those once captivated and convinced by an illusion. Hacking insists that what scientists saw in fugue was real given the context, and he describes what made it appear that way to them.

Hacking's topography of knowledge differs from Foucault's. For Hacking, even passing ideas grow out of a subsoil deposited by cultural and social conditions, while Foucault attaches them to a bedrock invisible to those who stand on it. They agree, however, that concepts do not appear from nowhere; they respond to the realities of the time. While individuals and groups refine and apply these ideas to achieve their own agendas, they work with a set of prescribed pieces. Understanding what promoted particular ideas involves, then, not only scrutinizing their authors' aims but also locating the foundations that permitted their thinking. Examining what scientists and social theorists said in order to identify patterns and to excavate the structures supporting them is the driving purpose of this study. The investigation shows that at the turn of the century, medical practitioners, criminologists, and sociologists identified several new disorders, fugue among them. They noticed pathologies unique to evolved humans such as abulia and moral insanity, and some, such as neurasthenia, that modern life aggravated if it did not spawn. In other cases, including fetishism and sexual inversion, they uncovered and named what they assumed had always existed. They also redefined long-recognized illnesses, including epilepsy, changing them virtually beyond recognition. This list of pathologies grew out of a dynamic and contentious mix of theories that aimed to make sense of the profusion of misfits. The number of fields involved and the volume of research produced repeated shifts in thinking, as one element or another no longer made sense. At the same time, some theories survived scrutiny and secured broad agreement; they occupied sturdier niches. These compelling ideas cast the evidence one way, and what did not fit either got framed differently or discarded as irrelevant. In the longer term, some of what experts took to be real disappeared, and some did not. Epidemic diseases of the day—neurasthenia, hysteria, and general abulia—faded after the First World War, their symptoms subsumed into other illnesses or ignored. Epilepsy, a weighty and capacious disease at the end of the century, returned to its former and more discrete contours.

Misfits starts with what medical and social scientists said and looks to the social and cultural givens and contingencies behind their words. It aligns with studies interested in ideas and with the cultural matrix that shaped them. It differs from most of them, however, in its scope. Most analyses focus on one type of deviance. Dominique Kalifa and Martine Kaluszynski, for example, contribute substantially to conceptions of crime in France. Other historians single out juvenile delinquency, homosexuality, or hysteria, focusing on the nature and the extent of these phenomena. Or they emphasize how the public, governments, the police, and the courts reacted to antisocial behaviors. Some historians turn the target of analysis from misfits to those who studied them. They investigate the development of psychiatry, neurology, criminology, sociology, and sexology, or they develop intellectual biographies of influential specialists. All these approaches acknowledge the importance assigned to the biological explanations of deviance at the time. In that context, they address theories of *dégénérescence* and broader conceptions of abnormality.

In the main, scholars explore deviance in a national context. The literature on England and France is extensive, that on Italy somewhat less so. For example, Jean-François Wagniart studies vagrants in France, Bruno P.F. Wanrooij analyzes sexuality in Italy, and Ann Jefferson reviews French conceptions of genius.[20] As Kaluszynski does with responses to crime, Jefferson identifies a distinctively French approach to genius. In his study *Italy's Margins: Social Exclusion and Nation Formation since 1861*, David Forgacs connects marginalized groups to the construction of Italian national identity.[21] He considers five cases, including slums, asylums, and nomad camps, stressing the role that writers and photographers played in creating and populating spaces on the margins, particularly after the Second World War. Other treatments of broader themes add to the country-focused studies. Although he privileges French sources, Foucault's examination of mechanisms of power and normalizing strategies refers to middle-class and liberal power holders beyond France. A different approach, one represented by Roy Porter and Edward Shorter's histories of medicine, addresses one aspect of deviance in the European context.[22] Among the nationally focused and thematic treatments, the few explicitly comparative studies stand out. Daniel Pick's comparison of the allure of degeneration theory in England, Italy, and France is an unusual and an effective one. Comparing social reform policies at the end of the century in Germany, Britain, and Italy allows Enzo Bartocci to highlight the peculiarities of each, and Chiara Beccalossi's recent study of female inversion in Italy and England grasps patterns evident only in a comparative context.[23]

Despite the relative scarcity of cross-national studies, the subject of deviance invites such treatment, because contemporaries saw the problem of misfits not only as their own. They recognized similar patterns of dissonance elsewhere and looked for causes in factors familiar to all of them: the human body, evolution, and modern life. Because they assumed that they were not alone, investigators and public officials looked outside their national precincts to gauge the gravity of the challenges they confronted. They routinely cited statistics from other countries to put their own numbers in perspective, and they referred to policies debated elsewhere as they shaped their response to misfits. Even more evident in the contemporary literature, medical and social scientists communicated and organized across borders and across disciplines. They made themselves familiar with the work of their counterparts and generated a strikingly polyglot effort to address deviance. Interconnecting conversations influenced theories and through them policies on a European, and even transatlantic, scale. At the same time, investigators and lawmakers processed and applied what they borrowed in ways defined by the personalities involved and by the circumstances they confronted. In understanding conceptions of deviance, examining national contexts bears fruit, and confronting more than one, as Pick, Bartocci, and Beccalossi do, helps separate the unique from the common.

Italy and France provide the terrain for this study. In both countries, new governments sought to establish their authority. In Italy, that meant not only creating the nation but establishing its place among other European states. French liberals installed the Third Republic almost by accident, and they confronted the disappointed advocates of failed regimes and citizens stunned by defeat in the Franco-Prussian War and still skeptical about untried institutions. Taking power with high hopes but little practical experience governing, politicians in both countries tried to build convincing parliamentary institutions. They did so in a context of rapid and uneven economic and social change. Italy industrialized slowly at the end of the nineteenth century, and then mainly in the North; France developed more rapidly, but lagged behind England and Germany. In both countries modernization generated social tensions, and political unrest added to the urgency governments felt about establishing their legitimacy and securing public order. To succeed, they counted on citizens adapting to the demands of life in advanced societies and paid attention when they lagged behind or deviated from expectations. National priorities, then, provide potentially constructive grounds for comparison. If reinforcing power put a premium on conformity in France, as Foucault suggests, the same should hold, and for greater reason, in Italy. Similarly, the effects of economic growth and performance on the treatment of misfits invite a common look. Moreover, those who framed the debate over misfits in both countries communicated with each other as part of an international scientific network. In certain areas, such as criminology, and with certain theories and personalities, the French and Italian investigators directly influenced each other. A comparative look at their views reveals more commonalities than differences, just as it puts the work in each country in sharper perspective.

Because the study focuses mainly on ideas, it builds on contemporary writings. Each category of misfits generated profuse commentary and analysis. Several factors, including growing literacy rates, influenced the stream of publications. With an expanding readership and sharp public interest, publishers provided a ready outlet for specialized treatises and more popular treatments. They also responded to a moment of unusual fluidity in the study of the human body and society. In this period, investigators commanded areas of inquiry that specialties later divided up and claimed as their own terrains. The parallels thinkers drew between biology and society and their use of umbrella concepts like degeneration also encouraged investigations which by later standards crossed disciplinary lines. Typically individuals researched several, and sometimes what appear in retrospect to be widely divergent, subjects.

That intellectually cacophonous scene included both established and newly emerging specialties, all of them touting their scientific credentials. The novelty of the fields and methods meant that experts rarely settled anything. The more data and theories they proposed, the more replies they inspired. There is, then, plenty of material for evaluating thinking about unconventional behaviors; the problem is selection. The experts read each other's work and widely referred to key articles and treatises and to influential colleagues. Those sources joined the list used in this study along with less-widely diffused texts that prominent experts singled out as important. A comprehensive examination of the works of major figures such as Cesare Lombroso further illuminates the context for the ongoing debates. Less noticed and more randomly selected specialized treatises as well as books published for popular audiences extend the research beyond the better-known authorities.

According to theories that won agreement in this period, understanding misfits depended first on distinguishing those who got that way by accident from those who did not. Temporary misfits did not present the enigma or the threat that habitual types did. They reacted to situations in comprehensible ways, and they usually returned to normal when the pressures on them eased. Investigators concentrated more on biologically induced abnormality. They needed to make the case that there was such a thing, describe what forms it took, and determine the underlying causes. Scientists worked from the outside in, beginning with telltale actions and with physical marks that they believed indicated internal anomalies. From there the terrain darkened as they tried to pinpoint the changes inside the body that produced criminals, geniuses, and neurotics. As a result of their investigations, they discovered properties of the body undetected before and developed new theories about how the body operated. For example, they saw that rational people—those who knew better—nonetheless committed vile acts. Reason enabled them to recognize the good but apparently did not compel them to do it. Wanting to do good must result, they hypothesized, from a recently evolved property of the brain, an element they called moral sensibility. Because it emerged late, they surmised that it was especially fragile, and when it weakened or when it did not fully develop, they concluded that moral insanity resulted. Not all commentators latched on to the idea of moral insanity, but they did accept the proposition that structural or operational anomalies in the brain accounted for unusual behaviors.

They also agreed on the possible sources of these abnormalities: a congenital condition, either inherited or developed during gestation, or a problem acquired as a result of illness, trauma, or aging. Of those, most agreed that heredity played the largest part, by either directly causing the defect or by predisposing the body to react negatively to outside conditions. Neurasthenia fit this pattern. It affected people born with defective nervous systems or with latent weaknesses activated by overwork and overstimulation. A trauma might also inflict neurasthenia, usually temporarily. Other variants of abnormality responded to the same range of causes, they believed.

Several influential thinkers pushed the analogies among the six types of difference further, arguing that they stemmed from a single source and appeared interchangeably generation to generation. They lumped some or all of the abnormalities together as "degenerative disorders," a term much disputed and sharply redefined at the turn of the century. In the broadest and most widely accepted use of the term, *dégénérescence* referred to inherited developmental irregularities. Looking beyond individuals to their families revealed enough defects to convince investigators that heredity could disrupt normal development and produce the anomalies believed responsible for abnormal behaviors. According to some scientists, the specific disorder often passed to the next generation in a different but allied form, so that alcoholism in the father appeared as genius or criminality in the child. In the view of key scientists, then, developmental glitches served as the mother lode for a group of related conditions that took people out of the mainstream. Among those progenitors, experts saw epilepsy at work in vagrancy, crime, sexual excess, and genius.

Investigators also tried to identify what caused the defects behind antisocial behavior. Some proposed that heredity transmitted sudden reversions or unexpected mutations from generation to generation. Others argued that habits, both the useful and the pernicious ones, got ingrained in the organism as reflexes. In the first model, change just happened, and in the second, it resulted from human actions. Both scenarios played on key mechanisms of evolution–mutation and heredity. Another common assessment focused on the disruptive effects of the milieu, as toxins and exertions damaged the organism in ways that parents passed to their offspring. These biological costs added to the evidence that the pressures of modern life increased petty crime, vagrancy, neuroses, and sexual excess or impotence. Society, then, caused some organic abnormalities, and it also accounted for the large numbers of people pushed temporarily to the margins by drastic circumstances.

Typically doctors and social theorists went beyond diagnosing the problem and proposed solutions. What they recommended, and how effectively, shaped their status at the time and influenced later appraisals of their work. Scholars tend to emphasize the negative effects of their recommendations. They point out that criminologists and doctors stressed the danger born misfits posed to society and urged confinement as well as the establishment (Italy) and the maintenance (France) of the death penalty. Because scientists believed that heredity damaged future generations, they urged those with degenerative disorders not to have children, and a few campaigned for sterilization. Contending with heredity's role in perpetuating organic defects explains what historian Mary Gibson calls the "hard" approach promoted by criminologists.[24] However, the experts on deviance also campaigned for reform. More than historians acknowledge, they also took a constructive approach to solving the problem of misfits. They urged reform because social conditions loomed so large in their explanations of antisocial behaviors. In describing their "soft" approach, Gibson points to their humanitarian impulses.[25] Some did invoke social solidarity, but more often they detailed the practical benefits of the policies they championed. Reforms would, they argued, reduce the number of misfits. To make the case, they documented juvenile crime, unemployment, or the effects of overwork, and then called for initiatives to address the problems they publicized. A few militated from the benches of parliament or from within political parties; others called for change in their writings and lectures. While they sought to influence decision and opinion makers, some of them also hoped to educate the public. How much they affected popular understanding and attitudes is hard to determine. Judging from the multiple new editions of their work, some treatises reached beyond the circle of specialists. Publishers also recruited well-known authorities to contribute to collections designed for the reading public. Their theories also circulated through the press, novels, and reports of expert testimony at well-publicized trials.

The problem

As the new governments took hold, a host of bad things seemed to be happening all at once. Diomede Carito lamented that "the number of the weak grows every day" as heredity multiplied defects and contagion spread infections. The stigmata of degeneration appeared in the voice and the eyes, he said, delivering striking evidence to observers of the exhaustion of the mind and the body. Everyone, including the rich, showed signs of flagging and failing. How, he asked, to address this problem when God sought and evolution led to the full development of humans?[26] According to conventional thinking, progress promised to reduce ignorance and enhance reason, but the unsettling spread of madness suggested otherwise. Losing one's mind struck some contemporary experts as a particularly modern scourge, since insanity did not seem to occur in primitive societies and rarely in the ancient world. "Madmen have multiplied, increased hundreds of times over with civilization, so much so that whereas a few years ago one insane asylum sufficed, now five or six are necessary," observed doctor and criminal anthropologist Cesare Lombroso.[27] While madness appeared in recognized forms such as melancholia, hallucinations, and delusions, different symptoms indicated the appearance of new or previously unnoticed illnesses such as psychic epilepsy, moral insanity, and abulia. Offering his readers evidence of insanity's rapid spread, Pasquale Penta noted in 1893 that in France between 1836 and 1869 the general population grew by 11.23 percent and the asylum population by 530.87 percent, a factor of 1 to 47.[28] In Italy estimates counted 51 insane for every 100,000 inhabitants in 1874 and 74.1 in 1888. England also experienced a significant increase, as the number of insane expanded by 250 percent and the population by 45 percent.[29] That the figures might result from more asylums, improved record keeping, changes in medical practices, or redefinitions of insanity seemed less plausible to contemporary experts than a real increase in insanity.

Just as troubling to those who expected reason to flourish, evidence registered a growth in nervous disorders. Especially in the last thirty years, an Italian doctor proclaimed, more people succumbed to an expanding array of neuroses, creating a "nightmare for humanity."[30] The problem, he observed, affected many countries, particularly the most economically developed, as well as every social group. Three diseases reached epidemic proportions, according to observers: hysteria, epilepsy, and neurasthenia. Diagnoses of epilepsy increased in number and in scope. According to influential authorities, it affected the psyche as well as the motor-sensory system, leaving people irritable, impulsive, and potentially very dangerous. When gripped by an attack, they might act with uncharacteristic immodesty, turn violent, and even commit bloody murders. Less menacing but no less disturbing, hysteria affected growing numbers of women and men, causing them to lose control over their bodies and at times to surrender to a second subterranean self. More pervasive and insidious than epilepsy, the medical literature claimed, neurasthenia left people, especially ambitious achievers, prostrate and morose. As with mental illness, civilization appeared to stimulate both the variety and the gravity of neuroses. They spread so widely that the author of a popular book on training the will, Paul-Émile Lévy, concluded that "almost everyone recognizes some neurasthenia in themselves."[31]

These pathologies dramatized the fragility of reason and self-restraint. Similar issues of control applied to society and generated equivalent alarm. Free institutions, liberals believed, encouraged citizens to respect the law, but escalating crime rates challenged that assumption. The numbers indicated an upsurge throughout Europe in the last decades of the nineteenth century, with variations according to the type and severity of the crime. "It is very certain," concluded French criminologist Henri Joly, "that crime is on the rise everywhere." In France, in the fifty years between 1838 and 1888, the general crime rate increased by 133 percent, he noted.[32] There and in Italy, fewer cases reached the higher courts, but more came to the lower courts, a pattern evident in Germany, Austria, and England as well. These crimes got noticed, but experts feared that many more continued to go unreported and undetected.

Within these broad patterns, the numbers showed oscillations in certain crimes, in the number of cases heard, and in conviction rates. Overall, crimes against persons decreased, while property crimes increased. Subsets of these categories also registered some ups and downs, observers reported. For example, Joly noted that offenses against morals and sexual attacks on children reached "enormous proportions" in France.[33] Sometimes, experts continued, changes in criminal codes, judicial procedure, the competencies of courts, and the organization of the police accounted for spikes in the numbers. They also evaluated the impact of immediate economic and political conditions on sudden surges or reductions in crime. But they did not believe that these contingent factors accounted fully for the elevated crime rates. To complete the picture, they looked at economic and social structures, moral values, and the mental and physical health of criminals.

Earnest efforts to turn the ever-expanding number of criminals into law-abiding citizens produced disconcertingly poor results, as recidivism rates rose markedly in Italy and France. In Italy, reported one analysis, 15 percent of the prisoners in 1870 had criminal records, whereas 41 percent did in 1893–1894.[34] Recidivism rates for France suggested similar patterns, as they steadily rose from 36 percent for men and 16 percent for women in the half-decade 1851–1855 to 53 and 21 percent, respectively, between 1876 and 1880.[35] Judging from these statistics, it appeared that a group of hardened criminals flouted social norms systematically and without regret. Observers saw them as a challenge to the efficacy of the prison system and a threat to society, and they sought to understand why this group proved so resistant to correction and deterrence. Circumstances, they concluded, might motivate some repeat offenders, but it seemed likely that something deeper explained their intransigence.

The public appeared even more alarmed about crime than the troubling statistical evidence warranted. They got plenty of exposure to crime in the press. Journalists chronicled petty crime, reported on society murders, and followed the gruesome work of a spate of serial killers. Joseph Vacher admitted to killing eleven people and mutilating some of the corpses between May 1894 and June 1897. The Bluebeard of Gambais, Henri Desiré Landru, it was thought, lured women to his house, killed them, chopped them up, and burned the pieces in his oven.[36] A woodcutter from Calabria, Giuseppe Musolino, galvanized Italy as he methodically killed seven people and eluded the police for three years. Across the channel, Jack the Ripper, the elusive assassin of at least five women in 1888, terrified the public. Another sensational case featured Dr. Thomas Cream, a Scotsman convicted in Chicago for plotting murder and released in July 1891. He moved to London and between October and April dispatched four women, all of them prostitutes, with lethal doses of strychnine. One who only pretended to take the proffered pills lived to testify against him.[37] Serial murder, with grisly twists, fed concerns about the direction of society. So did the eruption of types of criminality that seemed to be spawned by modern life. For example, Dominique Kalifa describes the gangs of juvenile delinquents from the outskirts of Paris who terrorized citizens in the early twentieth century.[38] Known as "the apaches," the name indicated the unease of those who expected better of modernity.

Spectacular crimes riveted public attention, but more run-of-the-mill lawlessness also drew notice at the time. Especially in France, crime sold copy, and journalists capitalized on readers' interest, describing the acts and following the efforts of detectives to track down the guilty. Authors of popular fiction rode the wave of public interest, marketing crime stories and detective novels in newspaper serials and books. As Kalifa's analysis indicates, crime reporters and writers fed the fears that they exploited. The usual suspects—the down and out, habitual offenders, and perverse individuals—fed the crime wave. But women and the well-established also entered the annals of crime, reinforcing the unsettling impression of an epidemic of lawlessness. Public anxiety encouraged the authorities to crack down on crime, and their success in bringing the criminals to justice confirmed the magnitude of the problem. To manage crime, the police extended and added investigative services, giving substance to the idea of the hardworking and wily detective featured in fiction. The specialists in crime detection also used new techniques such as photography and fingerprinting to identify criminals and profited from improved communication among local districts and between the police and the courts. In one notable example, the results allowed local authorities to develop and to share Vacher's identikit and eventually to link him to murders committed in remote spots at widely separate locations.

To add to the concern about public safety, people without jobs or a place to live appeared to be multiplying. "Every morning in Paris," commented Italian sociologist Napoleone Colajanni, "there are 50,000 people who don't know where they'll find food or where they'll sleep. In London 100,000 abandoned children wandered the streets, while in Vienna in 1880 shelters received 90,000 homeless people."[39] The public imagined and the crime statistics confirmed that vagabonds lived by crime. According to reports, many criminals started out as vagrants, and vagrants committed a significant percentage of thefts.[40] Beyond their tendency to steal and beg, the fact that they lacked work and a stable home challenged basic values and made them look like outcasts and parasites. Their defiance of the expectation that people live in the same place, work to earn their keep, and observe the laws made a disconcerting commentary on civilized society.

A more delicate and unmentionable matter also preoccupied the public in these years. In fact, according to Foucault, despite the apparent reticence of proper Victorians, people thought obsessively about sex. The experts did too, and they produced a stream of studies which analyzed unusual practices. Given the publicity surrounding criminals like Vacher and Jack the Ripper, it would have been hard to avoid learning something about sadism. Sargent François Bertrand, the "vampire of Montparnasse," supplied memorable details about necrophilia. Someone was profaning graves in the Montparnasse cemetery, and Bertrand turned out to be the guilty one. A soldier with an excellent record, he explained that periodic excruciating headaches produced morbid impulses, and he felt compelled to carry them out. A military court sentenced him to a year in prison, acknowledging, according to Dr. Benjamin Ball, the medical diagnosis of insanity while satisfying an outraged public.[41]

Exceptional examples such as these highlighted extreme sexual behavior and reinforced efforts to expose its roots. They took their place in the catalog of perversions along with nymphomania and satyriasis. Other less dramatic but more familiar practices drew expert attention, none more than same-sex attraction, which investigators saw as more widespread and more mystifying than other aberrations. Although they found it difficult to dismiss vice as an explanation, they applied the analytical frame they used to explain crime and vagrancy and found answers that attributed pederasty to organic anomalies and social conditions.

Yet another scourge of modern life gave the lie to notions of ever-broadening well-being and happiness: the "constant, rapid, general" increase in suicides.[42] Another appraisal observed the "terrifying upward march" of suicides, explaining that over fifty years the suicide rate in France rose from 5 in every 100,000 Frenchmen to 18. Only Hamlet's Denmark registered higher numbers. No surprise, commented Albert Bournet, "in a society preoccupied with gain, that is with pleasure, where the philosophy of nothingness reigns, man curses life, sees death as an advantage and becomes criminal."[43] While Italy registered rates among the lowest in Europe, figures showed the Italians catching up. United Italy experienced "a real epidemic of suicide," according to historian Ty Geltmaker, especially in the north and among the young, a situation which prompted soul searching among scientists and educators.[44]

All these signs of trouble in expected paradise occurred in a context of rapid social change. Historians have analyzed the longer-term structural changes which accompanied industrialization and modernization in both countries. From early in the century, France began to industrialize, and the resulting change in the workforce along with migration into the cities produced social dislocation and unrest. In Italy, iron and steel production increased in the 1880s, with state encouragement, and the textile industry expanded as a result of larger and more accessible markets and the adoption of more efficient production techniques. But these developments occurred primarily in the northwest.[45] At the turn of the century, more intense industrialization, partly stimulated by the development of hydro-electric power, caused what historians characterize as an "industrial take-off." This sudden and regionally concentrated surge of industrialization favored the emergence of a radical syndicalist movement which competed with the Socialist Party for working-class support. In the South, in contrast, industrialization lagged, and the persistence of latifundia obstructed agricultural modernization and fed political turmoil.

Shorter-term pressures produced by the worldwide depression of prices between 1870 and 1896 undercut markets for emerging industries and affected rural areas in both countries. Localized crises, such as the effects of phylloxera in France and a series of bad harvests in Sicily in 1892 and 1893 and there and in Lombardy in 1898, magnified hardship. The exodus of Italians from the South to the North and beyond to northern Europe and the Americas dramatized the desperate nature of conditions there. A less obvious but no less pointed commentary on the dire levels of poverty in some rural areas in Italy, the law passed in 1873 to regulate children's work in the itinerant trades included a provision prohibiting parents from selling their children. Even though emigrating provided an acknowledged safety valve, misery led to endemic violence, especially in the South, and to sharp outbreaks of unrest in 1894 and 1898.

Novice governments found themselves managing the detritus left by these crises. The shift from the Second Empire to the Third Republic maintained the infrastructure, legal system, and administrative base. At the same time, the Republic began in uncertainty and continued to deal with anti-system groups and a generally skeptical polity. Manhood suffrage put a premium on generating support for the Republic, just as the instability of prior regimes set an unenviable precedent for failure. Italy needed to construct what France already possessed—a national system of transportation and communication, a state bureaucracy, and a uniform set of laws—and do it in a country with a tradition of autocratic rule, low literacy rates, an underdeveloped economy, as well as hostility, especially in the South, to unification. Until 1912 when the legislature adopted almost-universal manhood suffrage, only educated and propertied males voted.[46] This group shrunk further after the new state seized Rome in 1870, and the Church ordered the faithful to boycott elections and public office. Thus a slim legion of voters earnestly preached the benefits of liberal, united Italy to a population excluded from power.

Liberals in both countries brought a combination of idealism and pragmatism to politics. Commitment to the idea of an educated citizenry inspired legislators to approve compulsory primary education, but in both countries belief in the low-profile state and in free enterprise made every social reform initiative contentious and slow. Still, after delays and false starts, lawmakers passed child labor laws, state-supported maternity leave funds, accident and sickness insurance, and unemployment insurance. They also took steps to protect abandoned and neglected children. Defending public order encountered fewer obstacles, even though the conflict between protecting individual rights and curbing dissent troubled French and Italian liberals alike. Despite some reservations, governments took aggressive measures. Especially in Italy, governments of the Left empowered the police to prevent disorder and used repression when those measures failed. The expectation that freedom, and in Italy's case, independence, would eliminate the obstacles to progress and happiness encouraged liberals to take strong measures in order to make things work.

In the charged inaugural decades of united Italy and the Third Republic, something took individual citizens out of an imagined and expected mainstream. Some combination of political change, modernization, and shifts in values explained the dissonance, at least for certain observers. For example, Catholic moralists and Marxists looked at conditions and predicted disharmony, although for different reasons, and they did what they could to magnify it. Another explanation, and the one at issue here, came from those who claimed to take an objective scientific approach. They exchanged metaphysical for material explanations, and in the realm of the material, they reorganized the role of biological and social conditions. Their reasoning depended on a collection of factors which coincided at the time, but not for long. These factors included the investigators themselves and their shared assumptions especially about how the body developed and what kept it running.

The investigators

By the end of this period, social sciences, including criminology and sociology, and medical specialties such as psychiatry and neurology established themselves. They based their claims to legitimacy on their empiricism, by which they meant basing theories on statistics, tests, and case studies. Analyzing the data they collected caused them to make comparisons and to invent categories to organize the results. They centered their investigations around description and explanation, and their classification systems used both nosology and etiology to identify types and subtypes. Whether they studied insanity or criminality, experts recognized and named gradations and differences; they divided and subdivided, and divided again. For example, Giovanni Bovio, Italian philosopher and literary critic, published a well-regarded study of genius. In it, he distinguished among geniuses, the clever-minded, pseudo-geniuses, and evil geniuses. Doctors divided epilepsy into motor, sensory, visceral, and psychic forms, and sexologists separated inverts from pederasts, and subdivided the latter into the true and the pseudo. Thus, variations acquired labels and their own spots on grids, tables, and scales marked off by fine lines or gaping fissures. The schemas became a central part of theories and of scholarly exchange, constructions subject to continuous challenge and adjustment.

Not only did investigators share an approach, they based their work on similar assumptions as well. That is, they saw the body as an integrated system, society as composed of interdependent elements, and society and the body as linked. They supplied multiple examples of the body's interconnections. For example, overusing the brain could affect the nervous system and leave the person unable to work, eat, sleep, or have sex, problems which in turn produced irritability and depression. They pointed to latent criminality to prove the ties between society and the body. A defect in the mechanism responsible for moral feeling went undetected until activated by circumstances. When that happened, a law-abiding citizen turned into an antisocial force, observers claimed. The connections, whether in the body or society, occurred in dynamic and even volatile conditions, they believed. That idea drew on a notion of change that only magnified alarm.

Bénédict-Augustin Morel's (1809–1873) work on *dégénérescence* influenced a generation of French and Italian physicians, anthropologists, and sociologists. It provided a framework for understanding abnormality that they challenged and adjusted but found difficult to dismiss completely. His *Traité des dégénérescences physiques, intellectuelles et morales de l'espèce humaine* (Treatise on the Physical, Intellectual, and Moral Degenerations of the Human Species), published in 1857, described two contrasting currents of biological change, one healthy and the other degenerate. In the first type, reasonably benign environmental conditions modified the original human type in positive ways. In the second, poor diet, toxic substances, drugs or alcohol, and harsh social circumstances could produce unhealthy changes in the body. Heredity carried both the constructive and destructive changes to the next generation. In the negative scenario, the pathologies became more and more serious as individuals passed them to their offspring and then to the race as a whole. Describing this pattern, Morel indicated that "immorality, depravity, binge drinking, general paralysis" might affect the first generation and "hereditary drunkenness, maniacal fits, and general paralysis" the next. These defects then turned into "depression, persecution complexes, homicidal tendencies" and after that into "stunted intelligence, the first signs of insanity … stupidity, a move toward idiocy, and the likely definitive extinction of the race."[47] These and related pathologies drew from a similar degenerative base, he argued, and they could combine differently as they progressively destroyed the group. Because responses to the environment produced either pathological or healthy changes, two radically different groups of people existed—the tainted and the sound; when they intermarried and reproduced, dramatic, cumulative degradation usually occurred.[48]

Sharing basic premises meant that inquiries about misfits intersected and that medical and social scientists knew and used each other's work. By later standards, they moved quite freely among established and emerging fields. The new specialties had flexible and overlapping boundaries, and until they gained recognition as distinct disciplines, they operated within existing university and hospital structures. Establishing a field's autonomy took concerted effort. It involved pushing names such as "criminal anthropology" and "psychiatry" and inventing hybrid labels such as "neuropsychiatry" and "psychophysiology" to claim terrain. To rally adherents, individuals also founded professional organizations, created journals, and called meetings of colleagues.

Contemporaries credited Cesare Lombroso with founding criminal anthropology. His medical colleague Alexandre Lacassagne built the discipline in France. Both of them established journals, and Lombroso organized an initial international meeting of criminal anthropologists, attended by Lacassagne. They proved to be indefatigable and successful champions of the scientific study of crime. Their efforts and those of their counterparts in other fields led to the creation of university chairs and departments and cohorts of students who with time expanded and reinforced the specialty. Professorial appointments indicated the permeability of the disciplines. Lombroso taught forensic medicine at the University of Turin, adding appointments in psychiatry and later criminal anthropology to his official duties, while Pasquale Penta served as professor of psychiatry and criminal anthropology at the University of Naples. Théodule Ribot, a pioneer in establishing psychology in France, earned degrees in philosophy from the École Normale Supérieur and the Sorbonne, and then accepted appointment to the first chair in experimental and comparative psychology at the Collège de France.[49]

Societies and journals served to define and publicize the emerging disciplines, according to recent studies. Martine Kaluszynski makes the point in her detailed analysis of *Les Archives d'anthropologie criminelle* (The Archives of Criminal Anthropology) established by Lacassagne in 1886. This and other new journals cast a wide net. Their large editorial boards represented diverse professional backgrounds and, often, countries. They served audiences with what looked to later specialists like distinctly eclectic interests. But by the standards of the period, the journals addressed a coherent set of related topics. A look at the titles of the journals, the collaborators, and their contents demonstrates a noticeable convergence of professional interests.

The *Archivio di psichiatria, antropologia criminale e scienze penali per servire allo studio dell'uomo alienato e delinquente* (Archives of Psychiatry, Criminal Anthropology, and Penal Science to Support the Study of the Insane and Criminals), established by Lombroso and criminologist Raffaele Garofalo in 1880, changed its title to Archives of Psychiatry, Neuropathology, Criminal Anthropology and Legal Medicine in 1904 and again in 1910 to Archives of Anthropology, Psychiatry and Legal Medicine.[50] The original editorial board included prominent collaborators from elsewhere in Europe such as Maxime du Camp, French writer and photographer; Franz von Liszt, a prominent German criminologist; Moritz Benedikt, Austrian psychiatrist; Lacassagne; and Paul Brouardel, a leading French specialist in legal medicine.[51] Physicians, anthropologists, criminologists, jurists, and forensic experts published in the journal. A typical issue of the *Archives* presented feature articles on the body hair of normal people and degenerates, new cures for pellegra, hereditary criminality, Christopher Columbus's mental health status, and crime victims' right to retaliate in addition to briefer communications on subjects such as the lingo of Mafia types and case studies of an epileptic murderer and a retarded rapist.[52] Reviews of journal articles and books completed the volume.

Other journals announced their range with descriptive lists or with broadly synthetic titles. There was the *Rivista sperimentale di freniatria e medicina legale*

(Experimental Review of Mental Illness and Legal Medicine) established in 1875 and *La Revue philosophique pour France et l'étranger* (The Philosophical Review for France and Foreign Countries).[53] The latter, established in 1876 by Théodule Ribot, drew science into philosophy. It welcomed all schools and doctrines, Ribot wrote in the inaugural issue. That initial volume featured articles on habits, ancient Indian philosophy, the cause of pain and pleasure, and on aphasia, among others. Since the time of the ancients, Ribot observed, psychology belonged to philosophy; now students of psychology and philosophy recognized "the direct and immediate utility of anatomy, physiology, mental pathology, history, [and] anthropology."[54] Publishers also sponsored monograph series that drew wide-ranging sets of disciplines together. For example, Fratelli Bocca of Turin produced the well-regarded *Biblioteca Antropologica-Giuridica* (Anthropological-Juridical Series), which listed titles from prominent international researchers on subjects such as crime, sexual perversion, the brain, epilepsy, and hypnotism.[55]

Individual investigators also claimed expertise in a striking array of topics. Lombroso, admittedly an exceptionally prolific and versatile scholar even for the time, published works on genius, criminal man, cretinism, female criminality, and political crime, among others. Although less remarkable for the amount they wrote, other authorities ranged as widely and combined social thought and medicine as naturally. Doctors thought nothing about dealing with vagrancy or anthropologists with epilepsy. The French psychiatrist Charles Féré, for example, produced influential studies of epilepsy, degenerative disorders, criminality, and the sexual instinct; Havelock Ellis, British psychologist, wrote important studies of sex, criminality, and genius. Moreover, in studies focused on one type of deviance, experts routinely referred to several other variants. Thus, French physician Armand Pagnier's study of vagrancy analyzed its roots in neuroses, psychoses, and psycho-neuroses, and Silvio Venturi's study of psycho-sexual disorders linked sexual function to mental retardation, criminality, and genius.

The networks of exchange among investigators and the ease with which they moved in and through specialties help to explain the commonalities in their approach to misfits. The connections also suggest that collaboration accompanied, if it did not overshadow, the territoriality historians have ascribed to the new disciplines. Until the lines separating disciplines hardened and training got more specialized, experts sought out and responded to each other's ideas. As Ribot suggested, they continued to see the utility in other perspectives and to share basic theories about the human and social bodies. This convergence of interests and assumptions characterized the study of deviance. The problem spanned fields, and social and medical scientists alike felt equipped to deal with it. They also found it profitable ground for gaining attention and influence and for establishing their professional bona fides.

Methodologies—names and stories

Making distinctions enabled investigators to order and then to interpret what they observed. When their initial rough classifications did not incorporate the evidence, they subdivided a category or established a new one. How to categorize cases or make room for exceptions played a significant role in how investigators s.. their arguments and responded to each other's work. Part of what they did involveα developing a nomenclature understood and agreed upon by other investigators. Because they realized the importance of a common technical language, scientists took pains to describe and defend new labels. For historians, recovering the meaning of the terms involves a meticulous process of reestablishing the context of their use. This is especially so when the words persist but take on different meanings. Such is the case with "sexual inversion" and homosexuality, for example. Fetishism, in contrast, means much the same now as it did when Alfred Binet coined it in the late 1880s.

Using language meaningful to current readers to describe past phenomena avoids approximate translations, but it can also promote anachronistic associations. For example, to describe difference, modern historians and sociologists deploy a vocabulary which includes terms such as "deviants," "outsiders," and the "excluded" based on factors including legal status, social opportunities, and popular attitudes. The meaning of the labels generates debate, as does their use to describe particular situations and groups. The word "misfit" seems less controversial as a term and still sufficiently descriptive. It is not too confined by modern associations, yet its meanings now match conceptions of difference then. But these labels, including misfit, are not the ones that contemporaries typically employed. In both France and Italy, people out of the ordinary got labeled with their problem: "born criminal," "neurasthenic," "epileptic," "vagabond," "invert," "idiot," "genius," "melancholic." The adjectives real, professional, born, or innate distinguished them from their accidental or occasional equivalents. For the category as a whole, contemporaries used abnormal and degenerate and more rarely monster, meaning unnatural. Terms like "unbalanced," "ill-adjusted," and "primitive" referred to the root problem, while "dangerous" and "anti-," "extra-," and "a-social" described how difference manifested itself.

What amounted to a frenzy to classify or niche build and to label stemmed from a continuously growing stock of data as well as from the proliferation of categories and subcategories. Empirically minded medical and social scientists obtained their data using certain favored methodologies. These included statistics, laboratory experiments, and the study of selected groups. The latter required observation, interviews, measurements, and tests according to protocols developed by leading doctors and social theorists and followed by their colleagues and students. In reporting the data, they relied on graphs and charts, photographs, and case studies. From each case, they sought to draw general observations. Adding to their own case files and exchanging and comparing cases with colleagues enabled them to identify patterns and from patterns to determine prototypes. Conversely, noticeable differences called for the refinement of the existing subcategories or the invention of new ones.

The literature is, then, full of stories, told by subjects and retold by investigators. Whether criminologists or doctors, they started with what the subjects said and what tests and observation said about them. Based on that information, scientists crafted and published narratives intending to contribute to the running catalog of variants and to provide evidence to support their hypotheses. The subject's story followed a script shaped by the interlocutor's questions, just as the case report conformed to a customary outline. From the many stories, especially those cited again and again by specialists, we know something about the lives of people who came under scrutiny, because their actions qualified them as abnormal. It is a second hand picture. Investigators controlled the interviews and the tests, and they authored the reports. Sometimes, patients or inmates themselves described their condition and their lives either at the behest of the specialist or on their own initiative. These confessions got incorporated into the case study, or more rarely took their place alongside the specialists' assessment. Those who were not the subjects of study did not usually volunteer information, except for homosexuals. Inspired by research on sexual inversion, some sent the experts their autobiographies and these joined the repertoire of case studies.[56] Occasionally, observers turned the examining eye on themselves, offering their own experience as evidence.

Because they depended on direct evidence, case studies figured prominently in analyses of difference. At the same time, judging from how much they worried about being taken in by fakers, investigators realized that their subjects could manipulate the facts. They imagined that at least some of those whom they evaluated knew the score, that an accused criminal, for example, realized that feigning epileptic seizures could get him acquitted. Subjects might, then, say or do what they believed necessary to achieve a desired result. At least the examiners regularly entertained that possibility. They did not, however, express concern that their questions limited the information they received or that they served a prescribed set of conclusions. Nor did the researchers seem to suspect that the subjects might begin to see themselves through their eyes, as Carlo Ginzburg discovered occurred in Inquisition trials.[57]

Attentive reading of the cases confirms the use of standardized ways of collecting and communicating information. In an often-referenced thesis on compulsive vagrancy published in 1892, Henri-Barthélemy Géhin, a student of Albert Pitres, professor of clinical medicine at the University of Bordeaux, compiled a list of cases which included his own and those he selected from published sources. He used them to support his argument that different neuroses produced distinct variants of fugue. Taking a case from Jules Voisin, a doctor at Salpêtrière and an authority on epilepsy, Géhin described 27-year-old Julien L... who owned a dry goods store.[58] Occasionally L... took off, the last time for five weeks, without arranging for his customers or letting his parents know. He wandered the roads, eating and sleeping where he could, sometimes working at odd jobs. His flights began when he was ten years old and left school to go to the fair without permission. At thirteen, he disappeared and turned up at his uncle's house some distance away in Poitiers. During his military service, he requested a twenty-four-hour leave and when denied, he left anyway. Once he settled down to run his store, these flights became a pattern. L... knew that he worried his parents and risked his business, but he did not care. He experienced an irrepressible urge to travel, and when on the road he reported feeling happy and free.

A person from a healthy family, making a decent living who acted this way required medical attention, the people around him believed. When the doctor examined him, he noted that L... seemed haggard and that his hands and tongue trembled. Asked to describe the flights, L... recalled them in detail. He remembered that he knew he wanted to leave, and when he did, his actions appeared entirely normal to any observer. Before the fugues, however, L…reported that he felt distracted, empty, and sad; he had headaches and felt sexually aroused. On the basis of the available information, Géhin concluded that L… was not epileptic or hysteric. Rather, the physical and psychological signs combined with his inability to suppress his desire to travel, despite knowing the consequences, indicated that he suffered from neurasthenia. What clinched the diagnosis of neurasthenia was that he fled despite having a good job and stable home. The doctor, Géhin reported, prescribed hydrotherapy, bromide of sodium, and other medicines which helped to relieve the symptoms.

Julien L…'s case captures salient features of how experts imagined deviants. It indicates what sort of behavior counted as aberrant and how scientists went about uncovering its causes. Because vagabonds aroused great alarm at the time, Julien L… likely attracted attention, and if he did not have his papers, the police detained him and then sent him back home. Unlike the unemployed or the derelict, he had a family, residence, and business, and when he bolted, he not only ignored his duties, he risked self and social respect. The incongruity of his actions pointed either to a rebellious nature or to a medical problem. The second seemed far more likely than the first to experts. What Géhin found when he looked is revealing. He readily accepted Julien L…'s report that an overpowering force seized him. Drawing on an understanding of the body common at the time, Géhin came to logical conclusions. When a respectable citizen yielded to impulse, it meant that the will had faltered, and that event pointed to disturbances of the nervous system. Géhin's careful analysis of the origins of L…'s problem depended on an emerging consensus about the symptoms of the most common neuroses: epilepsy, hysteria, and neurasthenia. He established that unlike epileptics and hysterics, L… was fully aware throughout the episodes, and he easily remembered what he did during his absences. Before leaving, however, he experienced a mounting restlessness along with a set of physical signals, and at a certain point his will yielded to the imperious desire to get moving. That the balance of the evidence pointed to neurasthenia makes sense, given the frequency of the diagnosis at the time. But within three decades, what appeared as an overwhelming menace had virtually vanished from the annals of medicine. Géhin's confident diagnosis of neurasthenia derived from a set of interlocking assumptions about normality. Events and the adjustments they incited researchers to make in their arguments later challenged these initial givens.

Who, then, counts as a misfit at a given moment reveals something about the uncertainties of mainstream citizens. Ordinary people felt rattled in the decades before the First World War as industrialization, urbanization, and secularization altered how many worked, where they lived, and what they believed. They sought to confirm their place, and they did it in part by delineating the boundary between what passed as ordinary and what did not. It may be that, as medical historian Roy Porter argues, all societies think some people are mad. They do not, though, think that only the mad are different. Porter describes the marginalization of the mad as part of a process that stigmatizes certain groups by giving them "a spoiled identity." Projecting what they see as "inferior, repugnant, or disgraceful" onto individuals, they "translate disgust into the disgusting and fears into the fearful, first by singling out difference, next by calling it inferiority, and finally by blaming 'victims' for their otherness."[59] In Porter's view, the process fulfills needs at the psychological and anthropological levels, mainly the needs to gain identity by creating an opposite and to feel whole by defining some as sick.[60] While that binary reflex may characterize all societies, its terms and targets vary. So do, and arguably more so, the explanations of the gap and the profile of those who determined who belonged where. In the period studied here, the body separated ordinary people and misfits. Its level of development and its integrity determined where people stood, biologically and socially. Full development meant adapted, balanced, and normal. Abnormal meant unrestrained and morally dull as a result of organic defects and deficiencies.

The operative binary distinguished between those who fit and those who did not, but the nature of those distinctions also built bridges across the gap. The bridges were of two kinds. One resulted from the separation of real and accidental misfits. It drew many whose behavior made them outliers into the embrace of the normal. When crises opened a cruel parenthesis in otherwise routine lives, ordinary citizens could see themselves in the other. The second bridge tied everyone together as moderns. Their bodies followed similar paths to reach similar destinations; they began simple and grew more complex, began primitive and became civilized. Although heredity destined some not to mature fully or to revert to an earlier edition of man, modern life exposed everyone to disruptive traumas and illnesses. Paradoxically, basing difference on the body made reliable, clear distinctions between ordinary and odd, normal and abnormal difficult.

Defining misfits in this fashion registers contemporary anxieties about change. Experts set aside the image of misfits as mistaken, ignorant, or villainous individuals. Instead, they explained them as the products of biological and social forces largely beyond their control. As their studies of misfits demonstrated, these forces generated widespread, disruptive, and increasingly unpredictable change, change that affected people unevenly. Because of their organic makeup, misfits fell back, fell short, or surged ahead, while normal people developed properly. For that reason, the fit managed to meet advanced society's demands, whereas misfits failed or struggled and paid a price. What they learned about change in abnormals they applied to defining and understanding what passed as normal. Misfits not only illuminated the process of change, they indicated its direction. Increasingly apprehensive about the future, observers looked at misfits to read the tea leaves.

Deviants focused the uncertainties generated by modernization. They drew attention to the patterns inherent in change at the same time that they dramatized its contingency. Because misfits challenged confidence in ordered change, how the experts explained them carried high stakes. Their understanding of evolution helped investigators frame the answer. Especially the Darwinian strand combined predictability and unpredictability; it operated according to laws but depended on accident. Mutations occurred, but then natural selection took over and determined their fate according to their utility to the species. Applied to the future, these laws favored constructive change but gave no hint of its exact form. Looking back, what appeared chaotic or outlandish gained purpose as part of a necessary sequence of favorable adjustments. That chain laid out the path for the development of societies and individuals as they matured. It contained change in regulated and positive movement and clarified the abnormality of disruptions to the process. To avoid conceding that the disruptions just happened, investigators worked to identify plausible causes and pointed to defects and damage. These they constrained by emphasizing the role of heredity and the effects of trauma and of certain illnesses. In normal people, entrenched physical protocols directed the change inside their bodies as well as their bodies' reaction to outside stimuli. But when they looked more closely, scientists discovered chaos at the core of everyman. The layers of the self deposited as humans evolved coexisted uneasily, as intellect competed with reflexes and instincts for control. Channeled by specialized internal mechanisms, the agitation and tension authored the self.

Looking to misfits for a glimpse of the future, scientists stressed the relative rarity of those born out of step. Those deviants showed at once the complexity and fragility of advanced stages of evolution, but, concluded most investigators, they did not forecast the decline of the race. Biological defects and damage resulted from faulty heredity, the side effects of illness, or a shock to the system. They were, stressed the experts, aberrations and anomalies. A normal bloodline and healthy habits ensured that most people developed as nature dictated and adapted fully to their milieu. For the same reasons that born criminals or neurotics did not promote the decline of the race neither did geniuses propel it forward. The mechanics of evolution, whether based on variation and the struggle for life or on the inheritance of acquired characteristics, reinforced order and channeled change. Like nature, liberal societies deployed laws to corral and direct change for the benefit of citizens. As for the random, they saw it at work in variation, but they emphasized that nature ferreted out what did not serve and kept what did. Unexpected events also happened in modern societies, as conditions exposed normal citizens to hardship as well as to surprising jolts and shocks. In both cases, observers took pains to name and to contain the negative effects of sharp and temporary dislocations. They diagnosed neurasthenia and identified therapeutic and preventive strategies, for example, and they demonstrated the connection between unemployment and vagrancy, aiming to reassure politicians and the public. When they considered the implications of their conclusions, some end-of-the-century thinkers had second thoughts. If natural and social laws favored adaptation, then normality locked in the status quo. Some, at least, realized that they had disciplined change to the point of stasis. In that light, they began to see misfits as the progenitors of novelty, and even progress.

Part I

Mental Misfits

2

Geniuses

Genius is a type of degenerative neurosis.

Cesare Lombroso[1]

Genius is nothing more than an extreme degree of cerebral superiority.

Edouard Toulouse[2]

Antisocial behavior defined criminals, vagrants, and pederasts as misfits; mental abnormalities drew a line around others. Superior or inferior intelligence, lucid insanity, and nervous collapse generated as much interest as crime, vagrancy, and sexual eccentricities did. According to observers, mental and nervous disorders appeared to be on the rise. More and more people took to their beds exhausted by their efforts to succeed or to just hold their own. They struggled to do their schoolwork, hold down jobs, and maintain households. Or their willpower failed and they fell prey to wild passions and irresistible impulses. In the worst cases, obsessions, hallucinations, and dementia pulled them off course, or neurasthenia brought them to a standstill. Since many people showed signs of mental disarray and neurosis at some stage or in some area of their lives, doctors and sociologists found it hard to draw the line between eccentricity and insanity and between ordinary fatigue and pathological apathy. To determine who required treatment meant identifying illnesses and creating reliable standards for diagnosis.

The preoccupation with mental and nervous collapse offers special insight into modernity, according to some scholars. In his recent study, *Cult of the Will*, Michael Cowan dubs the period around 1900 the "age of nervousness."[3] He argues that modernity with its constant changes left Europeans feeling uncertain and insecure. As their self-confidence waned, their nerves failed and their willpower faltered, leaving them inert and inept. Cowan describes the efforts of German reformers to counter the alarming growth of neurasthenia and abulia. In what Cowan sees as a paradoxical and tellingly modern approach, they focused on reinforcing the will by disciplining the body. *Cult of the Will* intersects with Anson Rabinbach's earlier and deservedly influential study *The Human Motor: Energy, Fatigue, and the Origins of Modernity*.[4] Modern Europeans discovered fatigue, Rabinbach argues, and then worried mightily about its effects. Seeing the laws of thermodynamics at work in the human body revealed energy's importance as well as its limits. Increasingly concerned about everything from weariness to pathological fatigue, scientists and reformers sought to manage work in order to conserve energy and maintain productivity. Like the reformers Cowen describes, they blamed fatigue on overwork at the same time as they advocated work as the path to recovery.

Scientists interested in the mind reached similar verdicts about the strains imposed by modern life. They observed patterns, identified them as abnormal, diagnosed them as illnesses, and proposed treatments and prophylactic strategies. Cowan acknowledges the influence of French doctors, in particular, on the strategies that Germans developed to combat the paralyzing insecurities of modern life. While Rabinbach refers to the research of psychologists and neurologists, he pays more attention to the influence of physicists and of biologists interested in body mechanics and fatigue. Clearly, their work contributed to the unusually complex and vibrant contemporary debate about the human body. Those more interested in the brain and nervous system saw energy as an animating force and will as a key agent in directing it, and they investigated how they functioned and why they sometimes failed. Fatigue made their list of the unfortunate by-products of civilized life, but it had company, and they thought they saw connections among these abnormalities and wanted to know why.

In the realm of mental misfits, one category proved less difficult to identify, but no easier to explain: those with an unusual complement of intelligence. Textbooks on mental illness commonly devoted a section to intellectual disability. They distinguished between "idiots," "imbeciles," and the "feeble-minded," described symptoms, and outlined therapies. Doctors typically did not include genius in their lessons and textbooks, but the profusion of special studies suggests intense interest in the subject. Marvelous misfits, geniuses offered clues to the mechanics of the intellect. To understand them, doctors and social theorists used the methods and typologies they applied to other sorts of misfits, and as they did so, they recognized some disconcerting affinities.

Whether they looked at genius or idiocy, experts differed over definitions and classification schemes. Although they might include idiocy in texts on mental pathologies, doctors came to see it as the result of a structural defect present since birth rather than as an illness. The less drastic category of weak-mindedness or imbecility, on the other hand, registered an operational glitch produced by another illness or by external conditions. Genius proved more slippery both to discern and to explain. Some observers judged genius in terms of singular achievements. Analyzing genius and insanity for the *Annales médico-psychologiques* in 1898, Albert Regnard (1836–1903) accepted Thomas Carlyle's identification of geniuses as "heroes of humanity."[5] According to others, the only mark of real genius was innovation, whatever the field of action. Very few shared Italian alienist Eugenio Tanzi's minimalist assessment. Not the least bit marvelous, he asserted, geniuses were intelligent men, who benefited from strong wills and the good fortune of achieving fame.[6] Or, turning the criteria from accomplishments and quality of mind to the sources of mental acumen, observers contended that effort produced talent, while nature made geniuses.

The debate over mental misfits showed uncertainty about the sources of intelligence, even though the experts shared considerable common ground. They rejected the idea that divine grace or wrath accounted for levels of mental acuity and looked instead to biological factors for explanations. Both superiority and deficiency resulted, they believed, from some anomaly in the brain's structure or operation just as habitual criminality and vagrancy and most irregular sexual behaviors did. The nature and exact cause of the abnormality eluded them, however, especially when it came to genius. Social scientists and psychiatrists easily accepted the idea that intellectual disability indicated an organic problem, although appropriate treatment strategies left them divided and unsure. That genius might stem from a flaw provoked significantly more debate. Some saw morbid defects or illness at work, while others attributed genius to a special enhancement of the standard mental equipment. Whichever side they took, their answers affected their assumptions about abnormality.

The sublime anomaly

Genius drew more attention at the end of the century than idiocy did. Books devoted to the topic began to appear in France and Italy in the 1870s and 1880s. The subject attracted writers and philosophers to a discussion which also involved doctors and social thinkers. In some cases the same individuals who studied insanity, criminality, vagrancy, and prostitution also addressed genius. Havelock Ellis added an investigation of famous English geniuses to books on criminality and homosexuality, and Cesare Lombroso worked on the subject over the span of his career. They treated genius in the same way they dealt with other types of difference. Those, like Italian literary critic Adolfo Padovan (1869–1930) and philosopher Giovanni Bovio (1837–1903), who used a more humanistic lens accepted the basic premises adopted by medical and social scientists. Arguably, they speculated with more abandon and gave their theories more rhetorical spark than scientists did, although they could not claim a monopoly on lush language. Nor did their theories seriously transgress the boundaries of the possible. No one understood how the brain worked, so even scientists used their imaginations when explaining superior intellect. But unlike novelists or philosophers, scientists embraced the constraints of empiricism, even though they admitted that something as ineffable as genius tested that commitment.

French and Italian investigators focused on reputed geniuses, using autobiographies and reports of people who knew them to reconstruct their lives and medical profiles. For the most part, scientists and social thinkers drew conclusions from data gathered at a distance. In a few cases, they managed to convince living examples to submit to the same sorts of physical, physiological, and psychological tests imposed on criminals and mental cases. In making sense of this data, they applied what they knew about the development and the operation of the brain and the nervous system. They also drew heavily on recent discoveries about mental illness and neurosis, using one kind of anomaly to shed light on another.

Interpreting the information proved to be troublesome, because it exposed the limits of their logic. They knew that exceptional minds existed, and just as they did with other kinds of difference, they attributed them to organic anomalies. They understood other anomalies as inherited or acquired defects or deficiencies that produced an innate disposition to crime, vagabondage, aberrant sexuality, neuroses, and psychoses. In contrast, genius enhanced rather than weakened the brain, and it seemed to result from unusual profusion rather than deficiency. Geniuses also differed from other deviants in their effects on society. They lifted it up rather than pulled it down. At the same time, commentators recognized affinities between genius and folly, just as the ancients had. They also discerned evidence of neuroses and wanderlust in geniuses, troubles which many believed indicated degeneration. Either, then, geniuses belonged with other misfits, or they counted as anomalies among anomalies and occupied a category of their own. Whether investigators extended *dégénérescence* to include genius or redefined abnormality to exclude it, they needed to rethink difference.

Where they looked to learn more about genius depended on how they defined it. Lombroso took a sweeping view, labeling as "a genius" virtually anyone who achieved prominence in politics, science, or the arts, a sign of his optimism according to a recent study.[7] Havelock Ellis (1859–1939) added intellectual ability to prominence as a criterion in his study of British geniuses. Taking a systematic approach to selecting his sample, Ellis chose the 1,030 citizens important enough to merit three pages of text in the *Dictionary of National Biography*. If beauty, or the accident of their birth, or circumstances rather than ability won them mention, he eliminated them, and he added to the list those who achieved little but whose intellectual prowess distinguished them.[8] Max Nordau (1849–1923), eclectic social observer and student of degeneration, gave that combination a distinctive twist. Geniuses were "human phenomena who change the course of world history." At the top of a hierarchy based on the "dignity of the tissue" involved, Nordau put men such as Alexander the Great, Mohammad, Cromwell, and Napoleon.[9] When perfect judgment and willpower coincided, they produced "men of action who make the history of the world, who give material and cultural formation to peoples and who dictate their destinies over a long span of time, great lawmakers, founders of States, revolutionaries … captains and conquerors."[10] Because they lacked sufficient will, Nordau excluded most highly intelligent and prominent achievers. Artists, he assigned to another realm entirely. Their work depended on acute sensibility rather than on extraordinary cognitive abilities. His dismissal of artists, or "emotional geniuses," as he labeled them, challenged what others thought. So did his conviction that genius required above all exceptional judgment and volition.

Other observers set geniuses apart from the rest based on a scale of superior intellect. Accepting the common distinction between innate and acquired difference, they separated genius and talent, arguing that achievements based on hard work did not define genius. Another approach looked at qualities of mind rather than the causes of genius. Talented people pushed existing knowledge to its limits, while geniuses came up with entirely new ideas. Or, geniuses possessed powers of intuition beyond the reach of the talented. Specified Padovan, "Caesar is a genius, Wallenstein is intelligent…; Columbus a genius, Vespucci intelligent…; Pitt a genius, Thiers intelligent; Luther a genius, Calvin intelligent."[11] Erudite people had talent, Bovio explained, but geniuses made connections. By taking great creative leaps, geniuses put together concepts no one else thought to connect. They achieved "that supreme degree of synthesis that brings an original and a distantly related idea together to discover 'the Truth.'"[12]

Whatever their criteria, investigators wanted to know how geniuses' minds worked. They offered two contrasting images. According to one, geniuses developed their ideas over long periods of conscious and deliberate thinking. Their creativity required the kind of broad knowledge and close observation and analysis that took years of effort. Their superiority might also depend on a "hyperconsciousness" to intensify concentration and focus.[13] The other approach theorized that genius came on unexpectedly. It operated mainly behind the scenes, unconsciously, and then erupted into outbreaks of feverish creativity. Sporadic, momentary, and all-consuming, these fits put geniuses in another zone, out of their minds, absent. Whichever model they adopted, investigators concluded that geniuses thought differently, for intriguing and, they discovered, illusive reasons.

When Lombroso looked at Christopher Columbus he saw an unlikely candidate for great achievement. An ignorant but determined and ambitious man, Columbus mastered obstacles daunting to a person of "normal intelligence," because he believed that God inspired and directed him. His religious faith, excessive even by the standards of the time, bordered on delirium and paranoia. "What psychiatrist wouldn't see that he's a religious, ambitious, and hallucinating paranoic?" Lombroso asked.[14] Only because of his paranoid illusions could he believe himself to be an instrument of God, ignore obvious problems, and latch on to such a dubious hypothesis as Toscanelli's. His paranoia, contended Lombroso, spurred him to heights that only the greatest geniuses reached. Columbus's mental imbalance, he concluded, "sharpened his intelligence and especially his love of novelty ... making the intense commotion in his brain silence the voice of prudence, the objections of critics, uncertainties and inertia, carrying his talent to the point of genius, at least in the area of his will power."[15]

Adolfo Padovan, who wrote extensively on genius, also examined Columbus. He focused on his "unlimited force of will" and his "blind and absolute faith in his own genius."[16] Padovan, like Lombroso, argued that religious faith explained Columbus's determination. "Bigots," he commented, "are naturally dogged and intransigent."[17] The belief that he had God's backing actually stemmed from his sense of inferiority in the presence of the royal court of Castile, Padovan surmised. That single-mindedness inspired Columbus to venture forth, but his genius told him where to go. He owed his intuition about the passage to the east not to his psychoses but to his physiological good fortune. Like all geniuses, he possessed "a nervous system rich in cells" especially well adapted "to receive, assimilate, connect, and transmit sensations."[18]

These assessments of Columbus point to the basic issues involved in the debate over the roots of genius. While both assigned it to physical sources, Lombroso and Padovan disagreed markedly over their nature. Padovan attributed unusual ability to cellular perfection, while Lombroso believed it resulted from pathologies. In a number of key works published between 1877 and 1902, Lombroso announced, developed, and refined his position. His approach recalled the work of Jacques-Joseph Moreau (de Tours) (1804–1884) who laid the basis for a new appraisal of the roots of genius in a study published in 1859. Moreau traced all the differences among humans to variations in the formative "material *substratum*" of the organism.[19] Mental capacity, or, as he termed it, "psycho-cerebral vitality," developed from the inside. Education and other external factors could work within these innate limits, but they could not change them.[20] Moreau traced the main mental pathologies to one "primordial lesion" in the reservoir of nervous energy that animated every process and moved from generation to generation. That, he argued, "is why you see them in members of the same family, in their descendants, in their ancestors and among their relatives."[21] The matrix contained the seeds of idiocy and madness as well as their transcendent contrary, genius, Moreau argued. Two decades earlier, in a study of moral insanity, he had asserted that genius developed not despite or along with but because of the factors that promoted mental imbalance. "It is absolutely and strictly by the same psychological mechanism that the mental elements that create illustrious talents, great, generous or evil passions, ... and all the disorders of insanity take form and grow."[22]

Lombroso began there, and his views along with Moreau's framed the discussion in Italy and in France. Genius, Lombroso contended in *L'Uomo di genio* (Man of Genius), resulted from the "intermittent and significant irritation of a large brain." In somewhat smaller brains, with less area for stimulation, talent rather than genius emerged, while normal people "simply worked and ate."[23] He traced this intense "stimulation of the cortex" to morbid conditions in the nervous system. "Genius," he concluded, "is a neurosis."[24] Even a cursory look at the evidence indicated a high incidence of mental illness and epilepsy among geniuses, Lombroso added. That they exhibited abnormalities commonly associated with degeneration put geniuses in surprising company.

Lowering the "most sublime manifestations of human [activity] to the most foul and most sadly degenerate, to idiots and madmen" made him feel uneasy, Lombroso admitted.[25] But, he noted, the association of brilliance and insanity went back to the ancients, and popular lore as well as scientific evidence confirmed the reality of the connection. Lombroso pointed to Baudelaire, Rousseau, Newton, and Schopenhauer as examples of mad geniuses and argued that the flashes of creative genius shown by anonymous inmates in asylums confirmed the association. He described in more detail the geniuses who suffered from mental and nervous diseases in his *L'Uomo di genio*. By their own admission and according to the reports of others, "the majority of geniuses" experienced melancholy and "an enormous" number killed themselves.[26] Lombroso also found evidence of megalomania and its opposite, pathological self-doubt, in their works and their autobiographical reflections. In some cases, they struggled with tenacious, long-term insanity; in others, they experienced occasional episodes of imbalance. Whether these problems promoted creativity depended, he suggested, on their nature. Depression, for example, had no direct link, whereas hallucinations and impulsiveness formed the very "nucleus" of an individual's genius.[27] Clearly, then, insanity and brilliance coexisted, and in some cases the first fed the second. The evidence did not, however, support a necessary cause and effect connection between them, Lombroso insisted.[28]

The association of genius with nervous disorders, especially epilepsy, was even more apparent, he argued. Pointing to exceptional men with confirmed or suspected cases, Lombroso claimed that epilepsy constituted one of the "fundamental bases" of genius.[29] For example, Napoleon, Caesar, Dostoevsky, Petrarch, Flaubert, Charles V, Saint Paul, and Marlborough displayed the symptoms of epilepsy. Even those such as Darwin, Galileo, da Vinci, and Michelangelo who appeared free of the disease on closer scrutiny actually showed its telltale stigmata, Lombroso contended.[30] In addition to those with epilepsy's classic sensory-motor symptoms, "many" geniuses had strange tics and jerky movements, while even more displayed the "loss of moral sense" common in psychic epilepsy.[31] Although Lombroso did not believe epilepsy necessarily accompanied genius, the two conditions shared common elements.[32] Clinical and experimental studies indicated that epilepsy resulted from a "localised irritation of the cerebral cortex" either inherited or environmentally induced. Similarly, genius occurred when an organic anomaly intensified the brain's receptivity to stimuli. Moreover, Lombroso saw striking parallels between epileptic seizures and the flashes of intuition or creativity that geniuses reported. They described moments of brilliance "as a very sweet fever, during which their thought involuntarily and rapidly becomes fertile, and explodes like a spark from a violently-struck brand."[33] Epileptics reported similar sensations, indicating that the two experiences possibly stemmed from the same aberration in the brain, Lombroso concluded.

The frequent incidence of epilepsy and insanity in geniuses pointed to the presence of degeneration, and additional signs compounded the evidence. A remarkable number of geniuses bore the characteristic physical marks of *dégénérescence*, Lombroso observed. They were abnormally short, tall, or thin; they were hunchbacked, lame, and stunted; their heads were too large, too small, or misshapened. Note, for example, Petrarch and Manzoni's receding foreheads and Foscolo and Descartes's unusually small heads, Lombroso urged.[34] Adding to the evidence, exceptionally intelligent men matured too early or too late; they stammered; they hated change. Sterility also affected great geniuses, Lombroso contended. Either they did not marry, of if they did, they had few children and their children's children died prematurely.[35] Confirming that heredity played a role, as it did with other degenerative anomalies, Lombroso claimed that "a very large number of talented men had epileptic, criminal, idiot or maniacal parents and children, or vice versa." He offered examples: "Carlyle had a crazy mother. Kant a sister. Victor Hugo a daughter. Wollstonecraft a drunkard father, maniacal mother, insane sister. St. Theresa had an insane brother. Vanderbilt had an epileptic son."[36]

Echoing Moreau de Tours, Lombroso concluded that in terms of their psycho-physiological profile, little distinguished geniuses from criminals, madmen, or idiots. They all showed signs of degeneration and its characteristic abnormalities. Numerous critics lambasted the association of degeneration and genius as outrageous and wrong, and Lombroso himself admitted how difficult he found it to accept such an idea. He introduced this "most paradoxical part" of his theory in *L'Uomo di genio* and presented it in greater detail in a later study *Genius and Degeneration*, first published in 1897. Used in the broadest sense, he reminded his readers, degeneration referred to an aberration, a departure from the norm. According to this definition, geniuses must qualify, since normal people lacked whatever produced the originality at the core of genius.[37] In a narrower construction of the term, one Lombroso supported, degeneration involved developmental quirks. It halted or reversed the usual course of maturation, leaving its victims steps behind. In this sense, too, geniuses displayed signs of degeneration.

To counter the objections, Lombroso pointed to similar combinations of opposites in the natural world and society. In nature, advances in one area caused a halt or regression in another, and what appeared as a step backward actually could promote adaptation and development. Simplification, for example, sometimes served evolution by enhancing the capacity of organisms to adapt and survive. In societies, too, the most advanced institutions and practices combined with backward ones, he contended, and the same held true in individuals. Idiots, for example, could display prodigious abilities along with dramatic voids in intellect.[38] According to this pattern, more primitive qualities might well accompany genius, and, Lombroso suggested, they might even promote it. Under a kind of "law of compensation," gifts in some areas carried afflictions in others. "Just as giants pay a heavy ransom for their stature in sterility and relative muscular and mental weakness, so the giants of thought," surmised Lombroso, "expiate their intellectual force in degeneration and psychoses."[39]

That degenerative aberrations and genius coexisted Lombroso found perfectly natural, even necessary, almost "fated." So highly developed in some areas, it stood to reason that geniuses experienced regression or arrested development in others and "often" in the same organ that inspired their brilliance.[40] Recognized forms of degeneration could approximate or merge with genius, but Lombroso specifically denied that they always caused it. He did not, as French doctor and critic Edouard Toulouse said he did, see "a nervous disorder as the immediate cause of the marvelous faculties of genius."[41] He did speculate that epileptic seizures explained the flashes of creativity which some geniuses reported experiencing. But for the most part genius derived from a very specific anomaly in the brain. Using his broad definition of the term, that fact alone qualified genius as degenerative.

Lombroso's ideas provided the lodestone for the debate over the nature of genius in and outside Italy. He found considerable support for different elements of his thinking.[42] Commenting on the pathology of genius in 1892, Augusto Tamburini, director of the Asylum of Reggio-Emilia, agreed that high development in one area led to compensatory weaknesses and illnesses in others. In Tamburini's view, a "hereditary, degenerative, neuropathic" condition "undoubtedly" caused an anomaly in the brain which produced genius. Because the body favored balance, the resulting spike in the brain's capacity left the rest of the organism vulnerable to disease.[43] Taking stock of the debate in 1900, Italian anthropologist Giuseppe Sergi (1841–1936) argued that genius involved eccentricity and produced imbalance, and like every such disruption in the organism, it derived from degeneration. The same basic mechanism caused criminality, insanity, and genius, but why it produced one or the other neither he, Lombroso, nor anyone else understood.[44]

Establishing that mental illnesses and neuroses accompanied genius, or caused it, or developed from it dominated studies of the subject. Research built on some key examples, including Columbus, Napoleon, and Emile Zola. Napoleon offered an especially appealing test case. Writing in 1895, Augusto Tebaldi, professor at the University of Padua, compiled a careful "psycho-physical" portrait of the man. From his family, especially his mother, he inherited nervous problems, and circumstances aggravated them over time. His nervous system's extraordinary sensitivity to stimuli accounted for his energy, his capacity for hard work, and his mental quickness, but it left him with a raft of physical problems including "migraines, constipation, rashes from which he sought relief by deep scratching; weak digestion, nausea and recurring colic."[45] Napoleon also suffered from several nervous disorders but probably not from epilepsy in its classic sensory-motor form, Tebaldi concluded. He did, however, show signs of latent or psychic epilepsy, in particular in his quickness to anger and his dubious morals.[46] Without entirely endorsing Lombroso's arguments, Tebaldi conceded that when "the epileptic germ" spread into the mind, the chances for the combination of "outbursts of genius along with deficiencies in moral sense" increased.[47]

As to his mental properties, Tebaldi concluded from reports that Napoleon thought rapidly, held a lot of ideas in his head, and concentrated unusually well for long periods. Capable of generosity and passion for his family and friends, Napoleon nonetheless centered his relationships, as he did all else, on himself. His character showed the effects of his nervous makeup; he angered easily and acted impulsively, exactly as "neurotics, geniuses, hysterics, [and] epileptics" did.[48] As circumstances aggravated these inborn propensities, Napoleon exhibited sharper signs of disequilibrium. The Revolution, Tebaldi argued, brought out the best in Napoleon, but it also increased his egotism and sense of superiority until in the Russian campaign imagination and delusion took over. Tebaldi did not think Napoleon qualified as a "crazy genius," but he certainly resembled the numerous "reforming, politicizing, scheming megalomaniacs" confined in asylums.[49] When present in insanity and genius, the "unhealthy and paradoxical logic" of the delusions looked the same although how much power the victims possessed made the consequences quite different. In the last years of Napoleon's rule, concluded Tebaldi, rampant egotism held sway, making him not completely mad but "certainly very unbalanced."[50]

Two years later, Lombroso published a more categoric diagnosis of Napoleon. No one demonstrated the connection between epilepsy and genius better than he did, Lombroso contended. "One of the most complete examples of genius," Napoleon, as everyone knew, suffered from convulsions which caused him to lose consciousness or fall into a coma.[51] He possessed other characteristic symptoms of psychic or larval epilepsy as well: impulsiveness, boundless egotism, cynicism, and especially a "complete lack of morals."[52] While clearly of immense intelligence, Napoleon, like other epileptics, had moments of "noteworthy obtuseness" and late in his life episodes of "genuine imbecility."[53]

Critics attacked theories that linked genius and illness. Some rejected any association of pathology with something as sublime as genius. It came, they argued, from brains which reached the highest levels of development and operation. Far from pathologies or defects, genius indicated organic perfection. Others accepted the general idea that cerebral abnormalities accounted for superior intelligence, but refused to admit the association of genius with degeneration. Still others saw degeneration at work but discounted the role Lombroso assigned to epilepsy.[54] A good deal of the debate revolved around definitions—of genius, degeneration, and epilepsy, in particular. But it also involved, even for the most adamant opponents of the pathology of genius, explaining why people with exceptional mental gifts experienced mental, nervous, and physical disorders. Did these problems and genius come from the same source, as Moreau contended, or did genius cause those illnesses? Or did they develop along with genius as nature's way of balancing a surfeit in one area with defects in others?

The attacks on Lombroso's theory commonly took issue with his methods. For one thing, he relied too heavily on unverifiable reports about dead geniuses. Scientific evidence required close clinical study or at least more careful use of secondhand information, critics asserted. If they accepted the value of historical evidence, his opponents often accused him of distorting and exaggerating the record to support his theories. Padovan, for example, chided Lombroso for "exposing the slightest flaw to make genius look like a psychosis."[55] In an article he called "What Is Genius?" Italian neurologist and anthropologist Paolo Mantegazzo mocked Lombroso for drawing "puerile and make-believe" conclusions from the evidence. "Does one suffer from *insomnia, amenomania,* from *anosphrasia,* from *battology,* from *bradyphrasia,* from *dysphasia,* from *graphomania,* from *claustrophobia,* from *neophilia,* from *neophobia,* from *gynophilia,* from *misogyny,* from *hypersensitivity,* from *hypergeusia,* from *hyperosmia,* from *rhotacism,* from *vagabondage*?" If the answer is no, then at most you have a man of talent; if yes—and preferably in combination, then a genius.[56]

Edouard Toulouse (1865–1947), head doctor at the Villejuif asylum and director of the Laboratory of Experimental Psychology at the École des Hautes Études in Paris, took direct aim at Moreau and Lombroso for their unscientific approach. They used "unreliable and unverified testimony, or drew on isolated, poorly established, badly interpreted pathological facts, on dubious diagnostic deductions, so that many of these documents do not stand up to serious analysis and few leave the impression of accuracy."[57] He scoffed at the idea of basing any theory of genius on examples from the past. That approach exchanged analysis for anecdote, gave credence to wild facts, and invited the casual use of evidence, as Lombroso's writings amply demonstrated. Better, Toulouse asserted, to use established clinical methods to achieve the objectivity that empiricism required.

Different commentators addressed the substance of the theory more directly. In a study of the physiology of genius, initially published in 1889, Italian neurophysiologist Giovanni Gallerani (1860–1940) dismissed the connections between degeneration and genius. Not many geniuses exhibited signs of degeneration, he argued, just as few degenerates counted as geniuses. In response to Lombroso's examples, he disqualified them as geniuses or claimed that they were healthier than Lombroso thought. For example, Lombroso described Heine, Byron, Petrarch, and Cervantes, among others, as compulsive fugueurs. A closer look revealed that circumstances kept them on the run, or they practiced "sublime vagrancy" as they traveled "in search of the absolute."[58] That geniuses often appeared to be ultrasensitive and highly emotional he took as a by-product of metaphysical searching and constant thinking. Heredity could, he admitted, predispose geniuses to diseases, but when that happened, the problems undermined rather than fed their intellectual powers. Napoleon, he asserted, inherited his father's disposition to epilepsy and his mother's "serious, resolute, imperious and intelligent nature." As long as his "notable cerebral-psychic structures and operations" commanded, he showed his mother's genius, but once epilepsy developed, he became impulsive and made fatal mistakes.[59] Real or "perfect" geniuses, such as Galileo, Michelangelo, Darwin, and Voltaire, showed no signs of illness. Their brains had reached the highest point on "the path to perfection and evolution," and nothing else compromised the superior structure, development, or the "exquisite operation of the brain's cells."[60]

Gallerani, then, minimized the incidence of *dégénérescence* in geniuses, and when it occurred, he banished them from the ranks of perfect geniuses. Giovanni Bovio took a similar approach in his influential study of genius published a decade later (1899). Like Gallerani, Bovio objected to Lombroso's identification of genius with degeneration. According to Bovio, genius-level originality required an exceptional ability to synthesize and a high degree of wisdom, and nobody achieved those prerequisites without robust mental health.[61] When the ancients associated genius and folly, they mistook the ramblings of mentally imbalanced people for originality.[62] More precise definitions of genius would have dispelled their confusion, just as it would among his own contemporaries. Ingenious people, he pointed out, just interpreted the works of geniuses; pseudo-geniuses stole and distorted their ideas; and evil geniuses applied the distortions to nefarious ends. They all thought of themselves as geniuses, and they deceived others, including Lombroso, into thinking so too. But because of their "congenital neurasthenia and poorly developed gray matter" pseudo geniuses could not seek new truths.[63] They and evil geniuses were degenerates whose defects blocked rather than opened the route to genius. Those he described as ingenious lacked the mental stuff for real genius. Women, for example, might be ingenious, but never real or even pseudo geniuses given the limited quality of their brains.[64] Thus, in contrast to Lombroso whose expansive definition encompassed even the talented, though not females, Bovio's restrictions, like those of Gallerani, imagined a category where only "perfect" and untainted intellectual giants resided.

French critics also took aim at Lombroso's theories. Militant socialist and former Communard, Albert Regnard (1836–1903) offered a detailed and insistent denunciation of the pathological nature of genius. Put madmen, criminals, and great men in the same sack, as Moreau did? He found the idea "shocking" and "anti human."[65] Modern science claimed to demonstrate beyond doubt that criminals and the insane suffered from degenerative illnesses, but including geniuses in the mix, as Lombroso and his followers did, went too far. Regnard promised to dismantle the "structure of sophisms" which served as apparent proof of the "monstrous affinity" between genius and insanity.[66] Singling out those "heroes of humanity" whose impact on society depended more on their mental capacity than their will, he identified a group of 409 confirmed geniuses in the areas of politics, philosophy, and aesthetics. Of them only 11 or 2.68 percent qualified as degenerate by Moreau de Tour's and Lombroso's measures.[67] Among those, Pascal, Comte, Rousseau, Tasso, Schumann, and Joan of Arc "were really and radically insane," while Mohammad, Luther, Socrates, Schopenhauer, and Caesar suffered from less obvious problems, he contended.[68]

Regnard, like Gallerani, claimed that brain cells that functioned at "the highest degree of wholeness and perfection" produced genius.[69] In the few verifiable cases of mad geniuses, the cellular damage responsible for the insanity affected entirely different sections of the brain than those responsible for their stellar intelligence. The positivist philosopher Auguste Comte provided a telling example, Regnard argued. Comte undeniably experienced episodes of mania and depression and displayed suicidal instincts. His problems landed him in an asylum in 1826, and he suffered two more crises in 1838 and 1842 in the course of writing the six volumes of his masterful *Cours du philosophie* (Course on Philosophy), written between 1830 and 1842.[70]

Evidently, Regnard concluded, one part of his brain functioned at optimal levels at the same time that another threw him into certifiable madness. As to Rousseau, a favorite example for those who claimed the pathological roots of genius, Regnard detailed his physical and psychological problems but insisted that despite his "deplorable mental state," he managed to write very good literature, if bad philosophy.[71] Because madness and genius inhabited different zones of the brain, the first could not inspire the second, but like Gallerani, Regnard thought insanity could corrode the luster of genius. Among the eleven mad geniuses whom he identified, only in the cases of Mohammad and Luther whose madness produced religious visions, did it enhance their contributions. But, cautioned Regnard, these two did not really count as heroes of humanity since the negative effects of their work outweighed the positives.[72]

In this diatribe against Moreau de Tours and Lombroso, Regnard demonstrated that the great majority of geniuses enjoyed mental health, and the few who did not nonetheless possessed highly perfected cells in the areas of their brains responsible for genius. Because he accepted the model of the functionally divided brain, he, like Gallerani, could argue that one area could operate at its peak while another misfired. As Regnard saw it, the undamaged gray matter of geniuses put them on one end of a scale, and the tainted equipment of idiots, imbeciles, the morally insane, and criminals put them on the other. To bring the extremes together not only confounded logic; it contradicted the evidence. In making his case, Regnard turned Lombroso's method against him, offering a meticulous review of individuals Lombroso identified as geniuses, and then dismissing any indications of degeneration as irrelevant.

Gallerani, Bovio, and Regnard all minimized or excluded connections between genius and insanity or any of the wider set of degenerative disorders. Defects could not produce and did not characterize the superior or perfect brains of geniuses. Genius, though, might itself cause other disorders. Toulouse made this case in a medico-psychological study of intellectual superiority which he published in 1896. Because it featured a thorough clinical profile of Émile Zola, it attracted a lot of attention. Toulouse proposed that repeated overstimulation of the brain "very probably" made it more susceptible to damage.[73] Or, more likely, neuropathic activity accompanied both thought and nervous disease, and too much of the first enhanced the possibility of the second. "Who uses the sword dies by the sword; in the same way it's dangerous to overuse the brain," he remarked. "To summarize, nervous disorders seem to me to be parasites of genius; in the same way mistletoe grows on the oak without aiding its development, because it finds it a favorable place to live."[74] Zola's case confirmed his theory.

Toulouse exposed Zola to a battery of psychological and physiological tests whose results he included in his investigation. He found no evidence of mental illness, epilepsy, or hysteria, but the data did indicate "numerous nervous disorders," including "muscle spasms, nervous bladder, heart palpitations, chest spasms, false angina, hypersensitivities, allergies, obsessive and impulsive ideas."[75] Zola also possessed pathologically intense emotions which caused "disorderly and painful reactions" when triggered by the "slightest stimuli."[76] His ultra-strong feelings pointed to psychic lacunae of the sort sometimes found in "superior degenerates," as French alienist Valentin Magnan defined them, but they did not interfere with the operation of Zola's mind. Rather, mental overwork acted on latent hereditary weaknesses and "little by little destroyed the delicate health of the nervous tissue."[77] Taking Zola as the example, he concluded that genius wore down the nerves and the brain, bringing to the fore hidden pathologies.

Read differently, the same data supported the opposite theory, and not surprisingly Lombroso spelled out the contrasting implications in his *Genio e degenerazione* ("Genius and Degeneration"), first published in 1897. Zola, he asserted, affirmed the link between genius and neurosis. The son of mixed parentage, his mother suffered from physical and nervous disorders, and so did Zola.[78] The tests revealed a number of the conventional signs of degeneration, including his unusually long-arm span, highly developed sense of smell, and his abnormally keen memory and imagination.[79] His novels reinforced the clinical evidence of degeneration, with their "use of slang, obscenities, the abuse of images of smell." All in all, Lombroso concluded, Zola showed strong signs of hysteria and epilepsy.[80]

Padovan joined the chorus of objections, flat out rejecting the links to pathologies, arguing that most geniuses exhibited no signs of psychosis. The prototypical, undisputed genius, Galileo, did not. Neither, he asserted, did "Leonardo, Machiavelli, Titian, Columbus, Goethe, Michelangelo, Spinoza, Manzoni [or] Volta."[81] He admitted that some geniuses suffered from various defects and illnesses. None of these were unique to geniuses; all appeared in ordinary people as well. Like Toulouse, he thought that geniuses might be unusually susceptible to certain disorders, because they overworked their brains, and brain strain produced "chemical, molecular, and cellular degeneration which led to nervous and psychological deterioration."[82] The process did not, however, work the other way; psychoses did not spawn genius. Nor did serious analysis bear out the theory that geniuses created in a flash of sudden inspiration or psychic seizure, according to Padovan. They arrived at their ideas only after long preparation and conscious deliberation.[83]

Havelock Ellis, the British physician and sexologist, did a more comprehensive analysis of his sample of geniuses. In most areas, their mental and physical health indicated no unusual patterns.[84] His geniuses suffered strokes, consumption, and other maladies as often as ordinary people did. Insanity did occur somewhat more frequently, but not so much as to establish a special connection between genius and insanity or to see genius as a form of insanity.[85] Thus, although worth noting its presence, the incidence of mental illness did not warrant the conclusions others drew, Ellis argued. Cases of serious nervous disorders, including epilepsy, he found "strikingly rare" among his sample. He found no evidence that the parents of geniuses suffered to an unusual degree from mental or nervous diseases either. When mental illness did occur, Ellis concluded that it compromised intellectual ability, because it required "intense cerebral energy," so much that it could reduce the reserves required for sustained, high-level thought.[86]

Critics read Lombroso selectively and, as a result, they oversimplified his theories. He offered a convenient target and taking aim helped them clarify and position their own ideas. The dynamic and eclectic aspects of Lombroso's thinking also contributed to the misunderstanding. Which ideas people assigned to Lombroso depended on which work and sometimes which edition they read or on whose account of his views they used. The response to Moreau and Lombroso also occurred in a wider context, one in which degeneration played a central role. As they themselves pointed out, investigators used *dégénérescence* in different ways at the end of the century, and competing meanings fed the confrontation over pathology and genius. Those who associated genius and degeneration used these terms more broadly than their critics did. According to Sergi, for one, anything in the organism's operation or makeup that differed from "normal nature" qualified as degenerative. Using the term this way, he confidently concluded that "one fact is by now established, degeneration as an immediate cause of genius, that is that genius depends on a pathological condition. But what produces the different varieties of genius and what ultimately causes it is still unclear."[87] Lombroso also defined degeneration broadly, and he insisted that it had a positive dimension. Ordinary, mediocre people, well-adapted to their milieu, he pointed out, lacked the "crazy anomalies" responsible for the "fertile originality" essential to genius. As a result, Lombroso insisted, "degeneration…rather than destroying reinforces the diagnosis and the extent of genius."[88] Toulouse, in contrast, followed Benedict-Augustin Morel's original conception of degeneration more closely. He reminded his readers that it involved anatomical and physiological defects which led to the extinction of the race. From the benign nervous complaints at the beginning of the process to idiocy at its end, *dégénérescence* involved diminution and imbalance, conditions incompatible with intellectual superiority. Equating degeneration and abnormality made room for genius, but looking at degeneration as Morel did made genius an uncomfortable fit.

No matter how sharp their differences over its nature, observers from Lombroso to Regnard gave genius organic roots. They took the next step and imagined the sort of physical anomaly likely to produce genius, pointing to the size of the brain, the capacity of its cells, or the intricacy of its operation. Gallerani attributed genius to the superior composition of the brain, particularly the cells' perfect development and finely tuned activity.[89] Regnard used similar terminology, instructing his readers that the most solid and well-formed cells in the brain's gray matter produced thinking at the highest levels.[90] Bovio also gave considerable credit to size and capacity: "below a certain weight, a certain quantity of scintillating blood cells and of phosphorus, and without an appropriate structure you can't think."[91] The heavier and larger the brain, the higher the quality of the thinking, he asserted. The need for the right sort of brain explained why males and Caucasians enjoyed a monopoly on genius, Bovio argued; it also explained why degenerate families and races did not produce geniuses.

Padovan acknowledged that the weight of the brain and the complexity of its folds played a role, but he especially emphasized the intricacy of its connections to the nervous system.[92] For unknown reasons, some people were born with more complex and better connected nerve cells, with that "physiological state of refined, exceptional nervous sensitivity" which answered the question, "What is genius?"[93] Because of their "numerous protoplasmic, physical, and collateral expansions," these cells "received, assimilated, associated and transmitted sensations" exceptionally actively and effectively.[94] As a result, geniuses stood out from even highly talented people for the originality and the impact of their achievements. Caesar, Columbus, Pitt, and Luther overshadowed their merely talented counterparts Wallenstein, Vespucci, Thiers, and Calvin, thanks to the "exquisite perfection" of their nervous systems.[95]

Others, including Lombroso and Toulouse, thought that exceptionally intense bursts of energy from the nervous system galvanized the cerebral cortex and sparked inspiration. The irritation of the cortex also occurred in sensory-motor epilepsy, and the commonality explained why Lombroso compared flashes of genius to seizures.[96] Toulouse, for one, insisted that unlike epileptics, geniuses at their most creative did not black out or experience amnesia. And yet, the literature offered examples which confirmed the kinetic image of genius and possibly its alliance with epilepsy. The composer Gaetano Donizetti, reported Italian psychiatrist Giuseppe Antonini (1874–1938), said that he created when he experienced an overwhelming urge. Relying on witnesses' accounts of such "attacks," Antonini described one instance where Donizetti returned from a walk looking pale and sad. He complained of a headache and went to bed, but shortly after he rang and asked for paper and pen. In a flash, he wrote the music for *Tu Che a Dio Spiegasti L'Ali* and said he felt better and fell asleep. Donizetti usually worked this way, friends reported. He had days when he got irritable, turned silent, wanted to be alone, and experienced "ambulatory automatism." Then he recounted that he felt ill, often with an acute headache, and suddenly he began to write without stopping. But he also had periods of "creative impotence" and "almost psychic arrest."[97] The mood swings, fugue, and the misanthropy looked like epilepsy, Antonini observed, and he expected that further examination would confirm the connection.[98] Reports of this kind reinforced the idea that a surge of energy stimulated the cortex and produced exceptional creativity, a description of inspiration that invited comparisons with psychic epilepsy.

Max Nordau advanced a more eclectic theory of the organic bases of genius. Calling him "one of the best minds of our time," Lombroso credited Nordau with stimulating his thinking and applying his doctrine in useful ways.[99] Nordau returned the admiration, dedicating his work *Degeneration* to Lombroso. Like others in the business of studying genius, he insisted that it had a physiological and anatomical base, one he identified with the two laws that governed the species: heredity and primitive vitality. That "vital force" generated endlessly different organisms, and heredity linked each variant to the species. Geniuses possessed an extra dose of primordial vitality and that explained their originality. The keyboard of their minds, he said, had "in some way an extra octave."[100] But no one knew why, he said.

Like Nordau, experts at the time admitted their ignorance when it came to explaining what produced the organic anomalies behind genius. They looked where they usually did to account for abnormal behavior: external and internal factors, that is, the milieu and society on the one hand, and biology on the other. As they did with other misfits, they weighed the role of circumstances and acquired conditions against innate determinants. Especially for those who ascribed genius to organic perfection, evolution appeared to play a role, while the association with degeneration pointed to heredity. Both avenues raised questions. Darwin's theory of variation corresponded to the idea that genius just happened, but it was not clear whether natural selection preserved the changes. If heredity played a role, it did not seem to be a direct one. That is, geniuses did not father geniuses. However, some analysts, including British psychiatrist Henry Maudsley, believed that as one of a group of inherited degenerative disorders, genius cropped up in the progeny of alcoholics, epileptics, consumptives, and born criminals.

The shaky nature of their evidence—imprecise statistical correlations, autobiographical information, and secondhand reports—made it especially difficult to zero in on what actually provoked changes in the brain or nervous system. Seen as a pathology, genius could result from other defects or illnesses or itself constitute a morbid abnormality. In the latter case, it could be congenital or develop later in life. In line with this reasoning, Lombroso examined the possible effects of fever, cranial trauma, and spinal diseases on genius, and he concluded that the evidence better supported a connection with mental and nervous diseases, especially epilepsy. The presence of an organic substratum favorable to disturbances that included hallucinations, seizures, and genius seemed a plausible hypothesis to Lombroso. Ellis did not find significant connections to these illnesses or events in his sample, but he did find a signature disease. Gout occurred so often, he reported, and "in such extreme forms, and in men of such pre-eminent intellectual ability, that it is impossible not to regard it as having a real association with such ability."[101] Whether gout promoted genius or genius encouraged gout required further exploration, he concluded.

Another possible explanation of what produced the organic anomaly behind genius looked to Darwin. His theory fit the description of geniuses as those who moved society forward, and it explained physiological shifts which seemed to come from nowhere. Padovan, for example, explained that in the earliest societies the need to be clever, to synthesize sensory information, and to share knowledge caused the brain to develop.[102] A few people somehow endowed with superior brains led the way. When they invented tools and thought to appeal to the gods to gain control of nature, they showed a unique human capacity to innovate. Unlike the discoveries that occurred by accident or imitated what appeared in nature, devices such as the potter's wheel and the barbed spear came entirely from the mind.[103] These first glimmers of genius related to science, but when survival no longer commanded all their attention, people became capable of artistic thought as well. At each stage, a few geniuses appeared at the forefront, exhibiting the innovation which later became the norm. In their case, the embryo happened to develop the more complex network of nervous cells requisite for genius, and that richness could, like any other physiological property, pass to the next generation.[104]

The uncertainty surrounding the basic biological wellspring of genius inspired investigators to look at circumstances as well. At the most, they concluded that social factors played a contributing role in genius. Tebaldi's analysis of Napoleon, for example, combined inborn propensities and outside circumstances. The Revolution provided outlets for the intense nervous energy and ultra-sensibility that he inherited from his parents. But at the same time, the very conditions that allowed him to maximize his abilities also aggravated his neuroses, turning fruitful egotism into ruinous delusions of grandeur. While Bovio attributed genius mainly to fortunate anatomy, he also thought that the milieu mattered. Genius did not appear, he said, "in icy reaches or flaming sands," in desolate regions unfit for human habitation.[105] It required, he implied, engagement in society, since geniuses gave words to what others felt but could not express.[106] Thus, Napoleon's genius could not be explained without reference to the Revolution, and Bovio chided Lombroso for barking up Napoleon's family tree while ignoring the charged events that surrounded him.[107]

Lombroso, in *L'Uomo di genio*, offered a somewhat more systematic review of possible external determinants, beginning with the impact of the weather. Putting together what geniuses themselves said and the months of their discoveries, Lombroso observed that certain kinds of creativity flourished according to the season. Thus spring favored discoveries in the arts, physics, and astronomy, and he urged further investigation of these connections.[108] He continued by examining the possible impact of climate. A study of the regional incidence of genius in Italy and Europe suggested the positive effects of moderate climate and an urban environment. Topography also discouraged or permitted genius. Mountainous regions clearly fell in the first category, Lombroso concluded, because the rarefied air reduced the amount of oxygen in the blood and impaired thought.[109] Lombroso also examined the role of race, arguing that race and climate appeared to operate together. Shifting to social variables, he argued that poverty, political conditions, and demographic patterns seemed to promote changes in the brain more than they actually did. Nonetheless, certain external factors likely mattered on the level of the individual. The circumstances of conception, for example, seemed to promote the anomalies related to genius. Noting that a large number of geniuses were illegitimate, Lombroso concluded that their conception occurred in moments of "violent passion," and such electricity affected the fetus. That "Newton was conceived after two years of forced chastity on the part of his parents" sealed the case for Lombroso who observed that the same pattern applied to degenerates, the insane, and the depressed.[110]

Toulouse evaluated a number of variables, including the weight of the brain, the role of heredity, the effects of upbringing, and the contributions of the general milieu. And while he stressed that genius, like criminality, vice, and madness, took root where the ground permitted, he avoided definitive judgments on particulars. He termed genius a "psycho-social fact" and proposed a list of possible conditions worth further investigation. Ellis came to the same conclusion after a thorough search for patterns in his sample of geniuses. Among other things, he looked at the county of their birth, their social class, heredity and parentage, childhood and youth, marriage and family, life span, and appearance. He pointed out that disproportionate numbers came from aristocratic families, and in particular the minor aristocracy and the clergy. They showed their superiority early; they were usually the first born in larger than average families, mostly of boys; many were handsome according to reports and had "unusual brilliancy of the eyes."[111] They lived longer than average, but selecting famous geniuses skewed his sample, he admitted, since genius came at birth, but it took time to gain fame.[112] Intellectual ability "frequently tended to run in families," making heredity a "real" though not "omnipresent" factor. Sons most likely inherited ability from their fathers, who took it from either their paternal or maternal grandfathers.[113] On the basis of the patterns he identified, Ellis concluded that a number of elements came together to produce the biological anomaly responsible for genius. He singled out parents' interests, the circumstances surrounding conception, pregnancy, and birth, and the child's upbringing, and urged further research to determine their specific impact.[114] Even though his examples reinforced the weight of social factors, including gender and class, Ellis attributed genius to an organic abnormality.

Intellectual disability

Although they entered the fray over genius, philosophers and writers left its opposite, mental deficiency, to doctors, psychiatrists, anthropologists, and sociologists. Families kept the mentally disabled at home, or for want of specialized facilities sent them to mental asylums or wards in hospitals for care. Even more than in the case of genius, impaired reason seemed to resemble folly. That association, however, came under attack in the nineteenth century, as experts looked more closely at insanity. Andrea Verga (1811–1895), the father of Italian psychiatry, for example, emphasized the difference between mental disorders and mental deficiency in an article he wrote in 1877. His call for the establishment of special institutions for the care of the mentally deficient met with general indifference until the late 1880s, as did the condition itself.[115] Those affected remained in asylums, and the particular nature and source of their problems attracted less attention than mania and depression or impairments of the senses such as deafness and blindness. When psychiatrists and other investigators did address mental deficiency, they found it a good deal easier to label its victims as "abnormal" and as "degenerates" than they did geniuses.[116]

As with mental disease, and to a lesser extent genius, efforts to develop a typology took precedence early in the discussions of intellectual disability. Keeping records, standardizing clinical studies, exchanging information, and testing treatment strategies all depended on developing agreed-upon categories and terminology. Generally these efforts followed the lines adopted for nervous and mental disorders. That is, researchers tried out classifications based on severity, symptoms, and causes, and they came up with a mixed system subject to a good deal of debate. Using normal children as the standard, they commonly maintained the two principal variants identified by the French alienist Jean-Étienne Dominique Esquirol (1772–1840) in the early part of the nineteenth century: "idiocy" and "imbecility." Morel added a third category, deficiency or feeble-mindedness, one frequently used by Italian medical experts as well. By general agreement, cretinism belonged in a category by itself. It referred to a disorder common in certain areas characterized by physical deformity and intellectual disability. As research about child development and studies of patients institutionalized in asylums or, more rarely in special wards or institutes, added evidence, they tried to update these terms.

In a compendium of the lessons he presented at the Faculty of Medicine in Paris in 1875 and 1876 and after 1879 at the Sainte-Anne Hospital, Benjamin Ball addressed "morphological forms of insanity" or idiocy and imbecility in one lesson and cretinism in another.[117] Idiocy, in contrast to dementia or folly, came from an absence rather than a decline or perversion of mental powers. In the worst cases, idiots lacked even the instincts necessary to survive, forcing them to depend on others to meet their basic needs. Those with low levels of intelligence and with enough willpower to exercise some self-control he classified as "imbeciles." Like Esquirol, then, Ball saw a spectrum of intellectual deprivation marked by idiocy on one end and imbecility on the other. "Feeble-mindedness" he found too general a term to be useful. In addition to the quotient of mental ability, evident physical signs separated idiots from imbeciles. Imbeciles looked normal—attractive even—and they enjoyed good health, he noted, whereas idiots had misshapen skulls, irregular facial features, various tics and grimaces, and nervous diseases such as epilepsy and Huntington's disease.[118] In terms of anatomy, the brains of idiots were abnormally small and light or larger than normal, atrophied in some areas, or affected by cellular irregularities. Heredity, especially involving parents with epilepsy, excessive libido, alcoholism, or syphilis accounted for most cases of idiocy and imbecility, Ball instructed. Problems during gestation or delivery or "blows, falls, violent emotions or fright" in early childhood could also bring normal intellectual development to a halt.[119]

Paul Sollier (1861–1933), a French neuropsychologist whose theories of memory inspired Marcel Proust, took a stand in 1894 against the conventional assessment of idiocy and imbecility as manifestations of the same problem. He saw them as fundamentally different conditions, and his argument drew considerable attention and support in France and Italy. He traced idiocy to lesions in the nervous system produced either by negative heredity or by a serious interruption of development. The same abnormalities that disrupted the development of intelligence in children provoked its decline in the aged, he believed. In senile dementia and in idiocy, reduced intelligence stemmed from an underlying pathology which altered the brain's structure. Mental incapacity was not, then, the illness itself, but a symptom of it.[120] Imbecility, in contrast, resulted from a functional glitch in the nervous system rather than an anatomical defect. His examination of the brains of 350 idiots, imbeciles, and epileptics from the museum at Bicêtre confirmed his theory; he always found lesions in the brains of idiots, but not in imbeciles.[121] These differences, he concluded, explained why idiots experienced more physical problems and died younger than imbeciles did.

The nature of the two conditions dictated different responses, Sollier argued. Idiots, he insisted, could not function in society, and the anatomical basis of their condition permitted no hope for improvement or cure. Out of the mainstream, with no possibility of integration, idiots were "extra-social." Imbeciles were also "incapable and useless," he observed, but they possessed some intelligence, and it could be considerable in certain domains. This combination of obtuseness, particularly in the areas of moral sensibility, will, and judgment, with acumen in others made imbeciles potential troublemakers. The dangers they posed to society made them "anti-social" in Sollier's view.[122]

Sollier's distinctions did not win complete support, but they clearly informed conceptions of mental deficiency. Sante de Sanctis (1862–1935), an Italian who worked with mentally disabled children, in particular, argued that Sollier oversimplified. He called for a more complicated set of categories based not only on the root physical problem but also on the links between motor and mental dysfunction.[123] He agreed, though, that all but the most seriously incapacitated presented a threat to society. The well-known fact that criminals and the morally insane were often imbeciles or semi-imbeciles underscored the danger, he said, and how medical and public authorities currently dealt with the problem only exacerbated it. His work with children in clinics and asylums showed that training improved social responsibility and even abilities such as language and powers of concentration. But the treatment stopped too soon, and adolescents returned to society at precisely the moment of greatest danger for any person: far better for society to send them to agricultural colonies or special institutions for further training once they completed educational programs at age twelve or fourteen.

Cretinism, experts agreed, constituted a distinct condition, even though it resembled idiocy in key ways. Complete cretins offered the full panoply of degenerative signs, beginning with the shape of their skulls and faces. Ball specified: "the nose is flattened; the tongue hangs outside the thick and fleshy lips; the neck is thick and short, and yet the child has trouble holding up his head, which jerks every which way."[124] In every area, they developed slowly, looking like old people as children and children as adults. Even though they ate voraciously, physiological problems left them sterile and weak.[125] Look-alikes shared the facial features of cretins but not all the symptoms. Semi-cretins, for example, often had enlarged thyroid glands, whereas cretins always had goiter. Ball noted the concentration of cretinism in high mountain valleys and speculated on its connection to intermarriage, to social conditions, or to environmental factors.[126] Gradually experts traced it and goiter to the water supply, a factor universally recognized, according to Ball, either as the primary cause or one among several. When bringing water from a town unaffected by cretinism to one with a high incidence of the condition caused the condition to disappear, experts understood the cause and the cure.

It proved considerably easier to explain, and therefore to deal with cretinism, than with idiocy and imbecility. Morel proposed one influential explanation. According to his theory, the worsening string of aberrations produced by toxic agents in the environment escalated by heredity ended with imbecility and idiocy.[127] Seen in the context of Morel's theory of degeneration, idiocy and imbecility resulted from the cumulative effects of hereditary disorders. That schema influenced thinking, but by the end of the century, medical experts and social thinkers kept some of it and discarded some of it. They generally accepted heredity as the key cause. Many also identified idiocy as degenerative, applying a broad definition of the narrower variant articulated by Morel. In their gloss on Morel, later thinkers recognized that an interchangeable mix of nasty conditions, including idiocy, passed along in certain families although not in a predictable downward spiral.

Just as they did with insanity and neurosis, criminality, vagrancy, and abnormal sexual behaviors, experts made room for external conditions such as emotional or physical trauma and the side effects of certain illnesses. Outside pressures could damage the brain itself or negatively affect its operation. Epilepsy in particular appeared to be closely related to mental deficiency, but the nature of the link produced the usual controversies. Exactly as they did with genius, some doctors traced both epilepsy and idiocy to abnormalities in the same part of the brain. Or, they theorized that epileptic seizures damaged the brain, producing a progressive decline in intelligence. As they learned more about both epilepsy and idiocy, doctors identified distinctive types of epileptic retardation. For example, G.B. Pellizzi, director of Mental and Nervous Diseases in Pisa, described two major variants of idiocy in an article published in 1900: the "essential" and the "symptomatic." In the first, heredity or a disease that affected the brain during gestation and infancy produced non-motor convulsions and intellectual disability. Inflammation or infection in the brain early in life brought on the second, which combined motor seizures and serious mental weakness.[128] Epilepsy itself, Pellizzi argued, followed a similar pattern. Extreme levels of hereditary degeneration in the brain cells caused the essential variant, and a chemical imbalance in the cortex caused by fatigue, intoxication, illness, or trauma triggered the symptomatic form. The cellular disruption could produce born criminality as well as intellectual disability and epilepsy, he concluded.[129]

Nothing seemed further apart than idiots and geniuses. The first, according to most descriptions, existed beyond the margins of society, adding absolutely nothing to it. Geniuses, in contrast, set themselves apart because of their stellar contributions. Their brains were livelier, larger, denser, better connected to the nervous system, or more complex than normal, while deficiencies, absences, and aborted development damaged the brains of idiots. An absence of will and the inability to break free from instinct, Ball claimed, distinguished idiots from ordinary people, and even from imbeciles. Strength of will and judgment made geniuses, in Nordau's view, while others stressed geniuses' ability to synthesize and to innovate. In these respects, genius constituted the exact reverse of idiocy.

Despite these evident differences, both groups exceeded norms, and studies applied similar analytical frameworks and methods to understand why. They traced superior and inferior intelligence to aberrations in the body. They saw these anomalies as primarily innate in idiots and geniuses and mainly acquired in imbeciles and acquired or absent in the talented. The same line that divided born and occasional criminals, inveterate and accidental vagrants, inverts and pederasts, genuine and temporary neurasthenics put real geniuses and idiots in classes of their own. Propitious social circumstances or hard work produced mental distinction, but not the breathtaking innovation of the genius. Similarly, disease or trauma jolted children from the normal course of development and made them imbeciles. With training, they could develop areas of weakness and exploit areas of strength to good ends. Idiots, however, arrived on earth with defective mental equipment; rarely did external factors reduce people to that level of intelligence. Similarly, signs of exceptional intelligence appeared early. That both genius and idiocy seemed to be inborn reinforced the case for heredity and encouraged the link of both to degeneration.

Some investigators saw genius and idiocy as even more closely related and, according to some, as virtually interchangeable. Moreau de Tours argued that "the most transcendent intellectual qualities, genius, and the reverse," originated in the same organic substratum.[130] The identical basic anomaly produced the best and the worst, a position many students of genius found outrageous, in part because they saw its logic. Regnard followed Moreau and made geniuses the perfect counterpart of the damaged—of idiots, imbeciles, the morally impaired, and criminals.[131] For Sergi, any abnormality in the brain—any degenerative disorder at all, for that matter— produced imbalance so that geniuses exhibited the same sort of disharmony that idiots did, despite their very different contributions to society.[132] In another variant of the argument, Ellis recognized a "real affinity" between genius and "congenital imbecility" based on a common "organic inaptitude" resulting from a change in the nervous system. The same alteration could favor extraordinary abilities, or it could take the opposite course. The contrasting outcomes, he specified, defined a spectrum with "idiot savants, the wonderful calculators, mattoids, and 'men of one idea'" populating the area between genius and idiocy.[133]

Predictions

Idiocy and genius both raised troubling questions about their longer term consequences. They appeared to pull in opposite directions, with geniuses advancing human progress and idiots contributing to retrogression or decline. Did natural selection save the organic changes responsible for genius, pushing humans along to greater perfection? Did idiocy transmit to the next generation, feeding or, as Morel supposed, concluding a downward spiral? To what extent, then, did genius and idiocy forecast the prospects of the human species? Which would prevail? The same issue shadowed discussions of criminality, vagrancy, neuroses, and insanity. How did the unmistakable increase in these forms of abnormality square with evolution and adaptation? Was it just individuals who slid backwards or leaped ahead on the sharply inclined scale of biological and social advancement? Or did they stand at the forefront, pulling others backwards or forward or announcing a shift in direction? The discussion of genius and idiocy gave particular focus to these issues.

Those such as Padovan, Gallerani, and Regnard who saw the anomaly responsible for genius as healthy easily linked it to theories of adaptation and to evolution. Just such sudden variations, in a welcoming social context, caused the primitive brain to develop and society to advance as a result. According to other sources, especially those who attributed genius to pathologies, it did not appear to transmit at all, or it appeared only sporadically within a family. Logically, then, either the cerebral lesions resulted from unrepeatable variations or, as appeared plausible to those such as Lombroso and his followers, the abnormalities recurred but took on different forms from one generation to the next. According to the first approach, genius resulted from glitches in the makeup of the brain which left no biological trace. By the second, it constituted one of several possible interrelated inherited abnormalities.

The argument that evolution both produced and favored genius had its naysayers. Said Sergi for one, those who argued that natural selection preserved changes in the brain either misunderstood Darwin's theory or distorted genius. Because natural selection accepted what equipped the organism to deal with present conditions, and genius by definition ran counter to them, it did not expand the population of geniuses, Sergi argued. What they achieved might advance civilization, but the organic anomalies responsible for their creativity did not permanently improve the brain itself, whatever Padovan and the like might think. Lombroso put the same argument somewhat more simply: "Nature, a fatal and ferocious leveler, just like ordinary people, does not admit genius."[134] In the context of evolution, genius qualified as a mutation, but not one likely to transform the species.

Seeing genius as pathological, and especially as degenerative, also challenged evolutionary explanations. Lombroso, like Féré, argued that the germ of degeneration manifested itself differently as it moved through generations. His studies revealed that a disproportionate number of geniuses descended from alcoholics, epileptics, and other obvious degenerates. By identifying genius with degeneration and developmental irregularities, especially atavism, he linked genius to regression. Genius, then, flowed with backward currents against the forward momentum of evolution. Lombroso, however, argued that regression did not always reverse evolution; it could accompany it and sometimes stimulate it. Atavistic accidents could promote advance, and when that happened what looked like a step backward actually produced a leap forward. As evidence he pointed to variations which by simplifying organisms allowed them to adapt more effectively. In the same way, degeneration could secure progress, he insisted.[135]

Enrico Ferri (1856–1929), a prominent Italian criminologist, developed this idea more explicitly. Degenerates or by his definition abnormal people fell into two categories: the "retrogressive" and the "progressive." The first, a small minority, included the "cretin, the idiot, the most backward imbecile, the atavistic, inhuman, and egotistical criminal, the deleterious and useless refuse of the social organism," and the second, "the mystic or religious or political fanatic and the scientific or artistic genius."[136] While members of the first group lived for themselves, those in the second aimed to enhance human life. Degeneration, then, appeared as a "double-faced monster: horrible, dehumanized, and dehumanizing on one side, and magnificent, rebellious, and productive on the other."[137] Every improvement in social relations, every conquest of the unknown, every liberation from prejudice sprung, he said, from the degeneration characteristic of progressive abnormals.[138] With his idea of productive abnormality, Ferri saved genius for progress without denying its association with degeneration. That particular twist held no weight with Padovan who saw genius as a departure from the primitive, although it resonated with Nordau's argument that geniuses possessed extra doses of the primitive vital force.

The role that idiocy played in the destiny of groups or the species also received attention. It seemed to reappear in families more often than genius did, but not often enough to conclude that it weakened the brains of ever-expanding numbers of people. In part, sterility limited its hereditary effects (and those of genius), experts believed. Idiocy did seem, they agreed, to appear in the company of other types of deviance, reinforcing the idea of an interconnected group of anomalies springing from a similar organic matrix. These abnormalities pulled individuals rather than groups or the species off the normal course of development. Given their nature, they returned people to a more primitive state or prevented their full evolution, and for that reason, they contributed nothing new. Their deviation could not, then, serve progress as it might with geniuses. It was not a step backward which permitted a move forward; it was a step backward, full stop.

In investigating genius, Padovan said he proceeded without "preconceived ideas," "slavishly" applying the experimental method to the human psyche.[139] The same allegiance to science informed the conclusions of Lombroso, Sergi, Gallerani, and Toulouse, or at least they said so. Vaunting their objectivity, they insisted that they used empirical criteria to assess other theories and to legitimize their own. Because the mentally disabled populated hospitals and asylums, doctors found it reasonably convenient to observe and to evaluate them. It was more difficult to convince geniuses to lend themselves to study. But when possible they ran tests to read from the outside in. More often, they relied on what geniuses said about themselves or on what others reported about them. The profiles of famous men stood in for the case studies so important to their analyses of other types of misfits. Chosen for their notoriety, they served as examples whose authority gained force from familiarity. The indirect nature of the evidence left space for interpretation, or invention, as skeptics and critics readily pointed out. Occasionally, investigators did autopsies on known geniuses and idiots, but when they detected structural abnormalities as they reported they did with idiots, they could not confidently connect them to any particular mental characteristic. The difficulty of using visible signs to read invisible reality explains why Toulouse and Lombroso reached opposite conclusions using exactly the same evidence. Both agreed that Zola suffered a series of debilitating ailments, but Toulouse felt sure that Zola's illnesses resulted from mental exhaustion, while Lombroso took them as proof that degeneration produced genius.

Certainly what they sought directed them to what they found. They assumed that the capacity to think resided in the brain. Voids in intelligence pointed to defects in the brain's makeup or in its operation caused by faulty development or the effects of illness or aging. In the same way, exceptional creativity or unusual willpower indicated an aberration in the brain's structure or activity. Sure as they were about the organic anomalies, they did not get too far in identifying what caused them. In that regard, genius proved harder to pin down than idiocy. With genius, they remained in the domain of hypothesis, even if they offered their conclusions as truth. The exact mechanisms at work and the precise zones of the brain responsible for genius remained elusive. In the case of limited intelligence, they examined the effect of organic anomalies and of trauma and aging with more confidence. Except for cretinism and senility, what they discovered supported a variety of theories, as it did with dementia and other forms of insanity and neurosis. Their inability to see inside a living brain and their abiding uncertainties about its structure left them to proceed by inference and by the accumulation of examples and of clinical profiles in hopes of discerning patterns which might reveal the hidden sources of aberrant intellect.

Despite facing the same opaqueness, investigators felt more confident about deficiency, because it so closely fit their framework of analysis. No other abnormality demonstrated the equation of biology with anomalies more clearly. Whether they defined degeneration as a downward spiral, or as obstructed development, or as organic anomalies of any sort, the rubric included idiocy. It confirmed what they felt sure occurred in the species and in individuals: the psyche evolved from reflexive, to impulsive, to disciplined. It also provided evidence for the equally convincing theory that disease or aging reversed the developmental process beginning with the latest layer. When scientists described fully evolved examples of the species, they simultaneously presented the identikit of their opposites: volatile, unable to work, and sterile. These alien behaviors settled the borders of normality. Appearance provided a similar dividing line. Even skeptics observed that idiots gave unmistakable evidence of internal asymmetries in their features and expressions. That eloquent testimony reinforced the idea that normalcy and health depended on internal balance and harmony.

The ease with which they applied current theories of deviance to idiocy and imbecility explains why investigators found genius so hard to characterize and to explain. Anomalies usually appeared as defects, and defects as antisocial. They indicated regression, arrested development, or illnesses. Rather than enhance, they subtracted; rather than advance individuals, the group, or the species, they restrained or reversed forward movement. To incorporate genius into this model of deviance meant squaring high intelligence with defects and seeing defects as positive in their results. Either that or genius stood alone, an unexpected and evanescent display of perfection. Other possible approaches appeared too. Silvo Venturi, an expert on sexual perversions, offers an example. He put regressive deviations in one category, those resulting from arrested development in another, and the rest he called accidents or "monstrosities." In that last group, he included "mind monsters" or geniuses.[140] Accepting genius as an anomaly among others, or as in a category of its own, classified it but did not explain it.

3

Lunatics

No matter how similar in so many regards to other men, the insane person is nonetheless essentially different! From the moment that he is marked with the official sign of decline, he no longer belongs to the community, he is eliminated from society, he is outside the law.

Benjamin Ball[1]

Caught between the habits that render it useless and the illnesses that mutilate or destroy it, the will is ... a happy accident.

Théodule Ribot[2]

Insanity came in many guises and from many different sources. Toward the beginning of the nineteenth century, it looked to observers as if the mad were not born that way; they turned mad. The few born with defective intellects belonged in a different category, one defined by deficiency rather than by derangement. Madness affected reason as delusions alienated the diseased mind from the world. Over the course of the century, psychiatrists and neurologists moved away from the equation of insanity with distorted reason. Their work on the brain and the body revealed that will and moral feeling, once seen as components of reason, were distinct operations, subject to defects and damage of their own. When the moral sense faltered, scientists recognized a condition they called moral insanity or moral imbecility, while diseased will in its most pronounced form they labeled "abulia." While the usual types of mental illness put people out of touch with reality, these disorders did not affect the intellect. Rather, they struck the centers of action and self-restraint, making normal life difficult to impossible. Even more directly than unreason, they intersected with criminality and vagabondage so that they turned mental into social misfits.

In the grip of hallucinations, manias, and delusions, people could turn violent or take flight, but usually their odd ideas took a more benign form. Disturbances of the will and moral feeling provoked sharper concern, because they reduced the normal restraints against antisocial instincts and impulses. Moral insanity helped criminologists and forensic doctors explain lucid killers, while weak will figured prominently in analyses of habitual vagrancy and fugue. Extreme abulia ruined people's lives by making the most mundane activities impossible, while its lighter versions appeared to weaken the discipline and focus of widening swaths of the population, according to observers. These and other mental illnesses called for medical treatment or if considered dangerous or incurable for confinement for the patients' and for society's benefit. Because of the importance of accurate diagnoses, medical practitioners, especially psychiatrists and neurologists, moved to the fore as they classified and described illnesses. They gathered data on symptoms, causes, and therapies and reported it in scientific journals and treatises and at meetings. As they did so, new professional labels, professorships, professional associations, and journals registered both the extension and the growing fragmentation of the field.[3] Experimental psychologists looked at how the mind operated; alienists or psychiatrists concentrated on its illnesses; neurologists examined disorders of the nervous system and their effects on the brain. The territories they claimed overlapped, so that emerging specialists took care to explain the body's structure and operation in ways that justified their expertise.

By paying attention to mental disease, these authorities gave scientific weight to amorphous yet increasingly intrusive problems. Just as elites define crime to serve their interests, so what passes as lunacy varies considerably according to a society's preoccupations and values. In the nineteenth century, more behaviors attracted notice as bizarre or threatening, and more fell under the scrutiny and the authority of physicians. What might earlier have passed as bad judgment, a surly phase, poor upbringing, or a nasty character increasingly qualified as pathological. Similarly, distraction, flagging energy, moral indifference, and impulsiveness pointed to mental disturbance. Peculiar behavior, doctors discovered, meant something more than eccentricity; it manifested a disorder of some kind, possibly treatable, possibly not. Similarly, the inability to keep up with the demands of work and family and a yen to flaunt rules indicated congenital abnormalities, they asserted. Their diagnoses made discordant actions and attitudes more obvious and more threatening, just as they made the mentally ill seem inferior and somehow to blame for their condition. As difference became deviance, historian of medicine Roy Porter points out that the few positive qualities once associated with folly disappeared.[4]

As hospitals and asylums treated more mentally ill patients, doctors paid increasing attention to their cases. Out of public view and under the professional examining lens, mental illness lost little of its horror. Like prisoners having done their time, patients sent home from asylums after successful therapies met a cold reception even from their families. The recovered patient, observed one Milanese psychiatrist in 1875, "finds … society deaf and mute to his appeals for help and support, because unfortunately the old prejudice that the madman never gets well and therefore must always be treated as a useless and dangerous being persists."[5] That attitude helps explain why the apparent increase in insanity in civilized countries aroused such concern. Recalling that civilization bred insanity, Lombroso estimated a hundredfold increase, noting the effort to add asylums to take care of the rush.[6] Claimed Italian doctor Pasquale Penta (1859–1904) early in the 1890s, never so much and such serious madness existed as in present-day Europe.[7] For every 10,000 inhabitants, 18.15 were insane in Norway; 14.63 in France; 17.80 in Great Britain and Ireland; 8.81 in Germany, and 7.41 in Italy, Penta reported.[8]

The problem

As new theories of the topography of the mind emerged, medical and social scientists moved front and center to explain the bewildering evidence of uncivilized behavior in contemporary society. Scientists unveiled the layers of the developed mind which allowed ordinary moderns to function. When adults went awry, shirked, left town, broke the law, or engaged in unconventional sexual behaviors, the status of their mental equipment provided one ready explanation. Building on that insight, investigators tried to understand how reason, morality, and willpower worked so that they could get to the roots of aberrant behavior. As they did so, they exposed the complexity and fragility of the brain and nervous system. The more they learned, the more authority they proclaimed, just as the more they knew, the more sharply they disagreed about categories of mental illness. The relative simplicity of equating folly with tainted reason disappeared into the rush of cases and contesting hypotheses. In that confusion, a vision of a fragile and divided mind and self took form, increasing the threat of insanity just as doctors admitted both its dangers and the limits of their answers.

Organic immorality

Judging by the frequency with which other doctors referred to them, Benjamin Ball's lectures, published in 1876 and again in 1890, provided an influential point of reference about the nature and range of mental disease, particularly in France. Ball (1834–1893) discussed a full range of mental aberrations, including the latest work on the defects of reason and of other components of the mind. In one session on irresistible impulses, he presented the case of B..., a Creole whose father died insane and whose brother suffered from severe epilepsy. His niece, despite a gentile upbringing, became a prostitute, and several other family members killed themselves. B..., Ball reported, "was a vigorous, intelligent, hardworking, iron-willed man." As a child, he was highly competitive, ultrasensitive, and given to extremes in everything. He showed an early fascination with guns and killing and liked to visit morgues and witness trials and executions. Later, he learned to shoot and to fence, and went out at night, Ball continued, "wrapped in a dark cloak, a dagger in his hand, wandering dangerous streets in search of adventures."[9] When he discovered that one of his lovers sold herself to another man, he went to her house and shot her twice in the back, expecting to convince a jury that he acted in a fit of passion. Sentenced to ten years at hard labor, he served his time and returned to Paris, where Ball met him by accident and pronounced him "absolutely the same man as before."[10]

In Paris, B... got caught up in his work and began courting a respectable young woman. He was, Ball observed, "entirely constant, sophisticated, and correct in his social relationships, and won the respect and the sympathy of everyone around him." And yet, Ball insisted, he harbored "deep inside this horrible need to kill which was the main, or rather, the true foundation of his life."[11] When riots broke out in Paris in February 1848, B... immediately joined the fight, and he took to the barricades again that June and at the moment of Louis Napoleon's coup d'etat, not out of idealism,

Ball explained, but because he enjoyed killing soldiers. He fought the Indians in California, returned to France in 1853, and took up archeology, publishing many books and articles and securing a government position. Along with his brilliant mind and admirable social skills, B… displayed, Ball insisted, a stunning yen for bloodshed. He "seemed absolutely without moral sensibility when it came to his many murders: he spoke about [killing] easily, without the least reserve, and as if it were the most natural thing in the world. He seemed to believe that on this subject his listeners must think exactly as he did."[12] Ball concluded that B… suffered from "homicidal insanity" or "homicidal monomania," a "blind instinct, a particular impulse, which orders murder and seeks blood."[13] He attributed B…'s condition to hereditary defects that disrupted the operation of his brain.

B… demonstrated that intelligence and social respectability could coexist with the basest instincts. By commonly accepted standards, B…'s delight in killing qualified him as crazy, while his intelligence, including the fact that he understood the difference between right and wrong, defined him as sane. Such cases challenged ordinary diagnostic categories, forcing the experts to admit difficult possibilities: that the most fully developed intellects could be morally perverse and, conversely, that those with weak reason might be quite moral.[14] To explain intelligent patients who acted as if they were crazy, doctors pointed to what they called reasoning folly. One variant was moral insanity. "Not a day passes," noted Italian psychiatrist Francesco Bini in 1881, "in which in casual conversations, in the press, and especially in trial reports, there isn't talk of moral, lucid, and rational insanity seen by some as a tactic of defense attorneys based on scientific exaggeration [and] by others as insanity of the worst kind, a real and extremely serious misfortune."[15]

The notion of reasoning folly gained credence in the early part of the nineteenth century with the work of Philippe Pinel (1745–1826), Jean-Etienne Esquirol, and the English physician and ethnologist James Cowles Prichard (1786–1848).[16] Separating will from reason, Pinel identified a category of mental illnesses which left judgment, memory, perception, and understanding untouched. Even when free of hallucinations or delusions, he argued, people could turn vicious and commit acts they recognized as evil but could not resist doing. Because they remained lucid and because they distinguished between right and wrong, Pinel labeled their condition "reasoning mania" or "mania without delirium."[17] Esquirol built on and clarified Pinel's theory in his identification and description of monomania. A person who was rational except for an isolated compulsion or fixation or someone who rationally pursued irrational ends qualified as a monomaniac. When impulses partially overpowered reason, Esquirol suspected defects in the will, and when lucidity accompanied brutal actions, he saw diseased morality and, more broadly, defective character at work. As they reviewed the idea of reasoning folly later in the century, Italian and French medical practitioners credited Prichard with narrowing the scope of reasoning insanity still further to diseased moral sensibility. He simplified lucid folly, and he gave it a stronger clinical basis by demonstrating that fevers and traumas could affect the capacity to act morally.[18]

Almost fifty years later, prominent Italian alienist Cesare Agostini (1864–1942), in a handbook on clinical psychiatry, reviewed the principal characteristics of moral insanity. These abnormalities appeared early: the victims "are stubborn, capricious, self-centered, cruel, violent, [and] arrogant children, intolerant of any control, who show no affection for their parents or their friends. They display a precocious tendency to lie, steal, play, and run away. They can be intelligent or not so intelligent." In puberty the problems escalated as their precocious sexuality led them to perverted behavior and uncontrolled masturbation. They used obscene language and got involved in the world of prostitutes and pimps, Agostini specified. Indifferent to discipline, they continually attacked their friends and parents, could not or would not work, and refused to change their vile attitude. When their parents or the authorities dispatched them to reformatories, the miscreants found "a favorable environment for developing their criminal instincts and refining their antisocial aptitudes," Agostini reported.[19]

Such detailed descriptions notwithstanding, moral insanity was not an easy disorder to pin down or identify, French and Italian doctors warned. Because its victims appeared entirely normal, it could be diagnosed when it did not exist and ignored when it did. What did clearly mark the morally insane—traits such as egotism, volatility, and aggressivity—characterized other conditions as well, so that a diagnosis of moral insanity required additional indicators.[20] According to Eugenio Tanzi (1856–1934), consistently antisocial behavior without obvious social justifications or evidence of other mental disorders, especially if it began in childhood, pointed to moral insanity,[21] while Francesco Bini linked it to a combination of moodiness, abnormal feelings and emotions, and insensitivity to social norms.[22]

These symptoms resulted from a specific defect, scientists theorized. It did not affect reason, since the morally insane often learned fast, argued cogently, answered questions clearly, and defended their choices logically. Nor did it involve their ability to make ethical distinctions, since they understood the difference between right and wrong. Rather, it damaged ethical sensibility or the capacity to value moral action. It was, Agostini clarified, an inherited "anomaly of the psyche, characterized by the absence, or by the perversion of affect" and by assertive egotism and unbridled immorality.[23] Other doctors explained the disorder the same way. When the sixteen-year-old Antonio Sbro … murdered his father and brother, he understood "the laws of morality"; he just didn't care about them, Augusto Tamburini and Giovanni Guicciardi contended. He explained that his father fought with his mother and mistreated him, and he admitted that he went a little crazy when he killed him.[24] If only the authorities had arrested him right away, he would not have killed his brother, he complained. With his youthful impetuosity behind him, he felt he had paid the price for his crimes in the asylum, and he wanted his freedom. But based on his confident and terse responses, the doctors judged him cold, heartless, egotistical, and intellectually rigid, and they resisted releasing him.[25] Another case reinforced the pattern. Geo … understood right and wrong, the examining physician concluded, but his "pathological psychic make-up" prevented him from doing good.[26] According to contemporary thinking, these and other victims of moral insanity lacked the capacity to appreciate the moral imperative enough to avoid self-serving and antisocial behavior.

The very idea of lucid folly and its expression in moral insanity aroused the ire of critics who objected both on principle and on clinical grounds. They bridled at

Ball's conclusion in the case of B ... that "perfectly healthy mental faculties can coexist with insanity so extreme it leads to crime."[27] Lucid insanity assumed a divided and compartmentalized mind, in which one faculty might malfunction without affecting the others. This theory did not win full consensus, and in an interchange in 1866 and 1867 which attracted a good deal of attention, Jules Falret (1824–1902) and Louis Delasiauve (1804–1893), two high-profile French doctors, laid out the issues. Speaking to the Société Médico-Psychologique (Medical-Psychological Society), Falret rejected lucid folly, including moral insanity, although he conceded that imagining the existence of distinct faculties might facilitate study of the brain. However useful as a construction, the mind actually operated as a single unit, a fact which made lucid folly a physiological impossibility.[28] Any defects in the feelings or instincts, therefore, inevitably affected the intellect. For his part, Delasiauve riposted that mental illnesses selectively affected pieces of the mind and should be classified according to the processes they affected.[29]

Falret also dismissed the clinical evidence, arguing that what others called lucid folly was "only an arbitrary and artificial collection of disparate factors."[30] Every sign of lucid folly characterized other well-known diseases until practically nothing remained that might define reasoning insanity itself. Thus, for example, the maniacal exaltation identified with reasoning folly more likely indicated circular insanity (now bipolarism), general paralysis, or hysteria.[31] Pressed by Delasiauve, Falret admitted that Bénédict Augustin Morel described something that looked like lucid insanity when he singled out people with compromised heredity who exhibited "a complete absence of moral feeling" beginning in childhood. Consistently disruptive and changeable, they lived "in open revolt against their families and all of society; they everywhere inspire repulsion and hatred." Sent to asylums, they wangled their way free and resumed their irregular and perverse lives.[32] Such cases existed, Falret admitted, but to classify them as a form of hereditary insanity, as Morel did, he found too general, while to call them reasoning folly defied known facts about the brain.

Falret registered reservations shared by others, but he did not manage to dismantle the category or erase the assumptions about the structure of the mind that supported it. Rather, these gained widespread support in the closing decades of the century. Agostini's clinical profile of the disorder in 1908 conformed to what Morel had described as a subcategory of hereditary insanity decades before. Those symptoms, at a minimum, described moral insanity, and some doctors kept it at that. However, especially when taken as a synonym for lucid folly, moral insanity became a more flexible, open category. The profusion of symptoms and their presence in other conditions caused later doctors to repeat Falret's reservations about its distinctive nature. Complained Ernesto Bonvecchiato, an Italian expert on the subject, in 1884, moral insanity became a "nebulous, monstrous illness without real boundaries or limits of its own."[33] He, like Falret, believed that the symptoms existed but that they did not constitute a separate condition, a position that found some support among doctors.[34] Notwithstanding these reservations, which also applied to hysteria, epilepsy, and neurasthenia, most doctors agreed that the presence of certain symptoms and the absence of others, such as delirium, indicated a real condition, probably an anatomical defect, possibly a physiological flaw.

They and others also accepted the underlying premise: the divided mind. They identified distinct mental faculties, working in concert but individually prone to damage, and some went further and assigned the various functions to specific locations in the brain. Efforts to pin down these sites and to determine how the will, emotions, and intellect operated reinforced the view of the mind as a complex system of interconnected but distinct elements. Those who recognized separate faculties might or might not include moral feeling among them. When they did not, they believed that reason controlled moral action. The more generally accepted theory, however, assigned knowing the good to reason and doing it to other faculties. According to this view, reason identified the good, moral sensibility valued it, and will enabled ethical actions.

Those who recognized moral sensibility debated its location and nature. According to one idea, people learned as children to restrain their impulses in order to avoid punishment, later they did so to please others, and finally as adults they did good to satisfy themselves. The morally insane never got beyond routine obedience, because they could not disdain immoral behavior enough to avoid it. Another theory, one articulated by Herbert Spencer, saw moral sensibility as an attribute of the species which emerged as society developed. Behavior useful for surviving in a group turned from necessity into habit, from habit to instinct, and from instinct to an innate mechanism of feeling.[35] By the first argument, moral insanity affected a learned attitude; by the second, it damaged the equipment of fully evolved humans.

Noticeable indifference to morality pointed to the condition but revealed little about how it worked or what caused it. If doctors assumed a "lesion in the moral sense," they still could not establish its exact physical site, and their best chance of seeing inside the body—autopsies—proved of limited value. Moreover, doctors couldn't be sure that what they found in autopsies caused or resulted from a disorder, if it related to it at all. They turned, then, to clinical observation for more concrete data. Most cases appeared in childhood, although adults sometimes contracted it as the side effect of other illnesses or trauma. The fact that it usually erupted early and resisted treatment made it the likely result of an inherited defect or a problem occurring during gestation, authorities surmised. Investigations of other family members routinely turned up an array of mental and nervous defects and diseases, although not always moral insanity itself: "they have in their families either others with their type of degeneration or with all sorts of mental illnesses, or epileptics or victims of other nervous disorders," proclaimed Bini. In addition to their family medical histories, these patients and their relatives looked like degenerates, Bini argued, noting "defects in the shape of the skull, stubby fingers, flat feet, genital anomalies, strabismus, sterility."[36] On the basis of such evidence, other doctors included moral madness among the group of degenerative disorders.[37] While degenerative heredity usually explained moral insanity, it could also result from other illnesses or brain injuries.

For all the uncertainty about moral insanity, and perhaps because of it, it loomed large in asylums and in courtrooms at the end of the century. Lombroso shaped the discussion of the reach of moral insanity by advertising its connections to born criminality and to epilepsy. His theories demanded attention in France as well as in Italy and, as usual, they proved contentious. Moral insanity came in many forms,

Lombroso specified, so by no means all those afflicted by it were criminals. Neither were all born criminals morally insane, but judging from their physical features and especially their personalities and behavior patterns, many appeared to be, he noted.[38] The two conditions could blend together, Lombroso contended, and when they did, moral insanity exacerbated inborn criminal drives. The more depraved a criminal's actions, in fact, and the more unrepentant their attitude, the more likely that moral insanity played a role.[39]

Others supported the combination of born criminality and moral insanity with clinical evidence. Agostini, for example, reviewed the distinctive physical characteristics of "real" or born criminals, and then described a patient with a long criminal record, also diagnosed as morally insane. "Physically," Agostini explained, "one sees…the small head, the receding forehead with a very pronounced brow, eyebrows that join, the large and square jaw, the prominent cheekbones, the notable development of muscle mass, swollen breasts, the slight development of the hair follicles." In addition to these telltale features, the patient's cold, hard gaze and morose look betrayed his abnormal personality.[40] Moreover, like born criminals, he had various tattoos, including a cross and a hymn to anarchy. The patient exhibited somewhat limited intelligence and "a complete absence of moral sensibility."[41] Occasional intense seizures completed the clinical profile. This case, Agostini observed, indicated the presence of both innate criminality and moral insanity, a pattern he credited criminal anthropologists, such as Lombroso, with identifying.

The patient he described also suffered from epilepsy which resembled moral insanity, but was, Agostini insisted, a distinct illness. Here he parted company with Lombroso who theorized that the similarity of symptoms indicated close connections between the two diseases. Acknowledging the influence of German psychiatrist Richard Krafft-Ebing's work on his thinking, Lombroso argued in an article published in 1885 that photographs of epileptics and the morally insane revealed similar irregularities of the skull and facial features. Physiological tests also produced parallel results in agility, reflexes, and senses. But the most striking similarities related to their psychological profiles, he asserted. Irritability, sporadic outbursts, emotional instability, and coldness likened epileptics to the morally insane.[42]

To confirm the link between moral insanity and epilepsy, Italian doctors Celso Sighicelli and Ruggero Tambroni recorded an especially noteworthy case. From early childhood, E.C. of Ferrara was "strange, disobedient, and violent."[43] He mistreated animals, stole things, and showed precocious and deviant sexual behavior. As an adolescent, he drank, gambled, and fought, supporting himself by theft and extortion. His doctors described him as "a liar of the first order, a very skilled dissimulator, highly undisciplined, and finally a person with a strong conspiratorial and rebellious bent." They noted unmistakable marks of physical degeneration: "lots of hair, a heavy jaw, asymmetrical face, precocious sexual development and epilepsy."[44] He landed in jail for stealing, but the first of numerous epileptic seizures opened a period of confinement in asylums, the last time under their care. They reported that E.C. alternated between periods of calm and rebellious behavior and suffered several severe seizures, including a cascade of especially violent attacks that led to his death at age twenty-two. Doctors labeled him a "mixed" type and concluded that at a minimum epilepsy exacerbated the consequences of moral insanity by weakening his centers of inhibition.[45]

While E.C. experienced violent and eventually fatal motor seizures, Lombroso observed that the morally insane usually exhibited the dizziness, trances, and unstable personality that French doctors identified with the psychic form of epilepsy.[46] The commonality of the symptoms indicated, he argued, that moral insanity and epilepsy came from the same source, and he followed the French doctor Valentin Magnan in tracing epilepsy to the cerebral cortex, and in the case of the psychic type, to discharges from the frontal lobes, the same area affected in moral insanity and born criminality. Moral insanity, then, came out of the same organic matrix as epilepsy, and the two diseases resembled each other so much that one could be taken for the other. Lombroso speculated that psychic epilepsy "might be none other than the acute form of moral insanity and congenital criminality."[47] But Lombroso also joined psychiatrist Enrico Morselli in cautioning against confusing the two. Either one, they believed, likely contributed to what judges condemned in court as violence or brutality or as instinctive nastiness or perversity.[48] Most of Lombroso's interlocutors agreed that epilepsy, especially in its traditional sensory-motor form, differed from moral insanity.[49]

Lombroso was not alone in pursuing connections between insanity and crime.[50] Criminologists such as Enrico Ferri took a more reserved and, for most investigators, a more sensible position. Although Ferri emphasized the social roots of lawlessness, he came to understand murder primarily as the result of psychological factors, mainly the absence or impairment of moral sensibility. Killers, he argued, did not feel the visceral revulsion ordinary people did at the prospect of murder. Even occasional crime, he suggested, pointed to abnormal moral sensibility, since stealing did not appeal to honest people no matter how bad their situation.[51] In his view, weak moral sensibility also explained other antisocial behaviors, especially precocious sexuality and unrestrained masturbation.

Difficult to diagnose, moral insanity proved even harder to cure, because it typically resulted from an inherited, organic defect, doctors believed. When illness or trauma disrupted moral feeling or will, removing the irritant gave some hope for improvement. But when it resulted from an anatomical defect, trying to reinforce moral sensibility through education produced marginal to no results. Doctors and criminologists praised judges and juries for recognizing that the morally insane could not be held legally responsible for their actions, but they urged that the courts confine them permanently, because they threatened society. Too deranged for prisons and too lucid for regular asylums, they recommended sequestering them in special wards or institutions.

Diseases of the will

Of all mental disorders, moral insanity posed the greatest dangers to society, particularly when it existed in tandem with epilepsy or congenital criminality, experts warned. It turned people into long-term social misfits, incapable of accepting authority, of getting along with other people, and of putting in a normal day's work.

Their unruly temperaments turned them to crime, and their precocious sexuality encouraged unacceptable personal habits. Most unsettling, they understood the antisocial nature of their deeds, and they retained enough intelligence to lie and cajole convincingly. In fact, the ability to fool naive lawyers, judges, and even doctors stood out as a distinctive feature of their disorder. Other forms of insanity also affected morality, usually when they weakened the will so much that it could not resist antisocial impulses.

The will emerged as a, even the, key to civilized living, scientists realized. In 1847, Eugène Billod (1818–1886) published an influential analysis of its disorders. Doctors knew they existed, Billod said. They encountered them all the time, but they paid little attention because they understood them so poorly. A closer look at these pathologies revealed a good deal about how the will normally worked, Billod contended. He presented a case, often repeated in subsequent literature, of a 65-year-old notary, M.P... who desperately tried to perform routine tasks but could not. Asked to sign a document, he lifted the pen, tried again and again to write, and after great effort managed a rough approximation of his signature. On a therapeutic trip to Italy, accompanied by Billod, he decided he wanted to see the sights, put on his hat, and approached the door but could not get himself to go through it. When he finally managed to leave, he returned after a few minutes, sweating and exhausted. Billod observed that M.P... could make decisions, and he could carry out instinctive movements without hesitation. Seeing nothing wrong with M.P...'s intelligence or motor system, Billod traced the problem to defects in the will itself, a diagnosis confirmed by the patient's complaint that "he *could not will*."[52] "When I gave him advice, my patient often answered: 'You're right, it would be a good thing, I should do it, I want to do it; but how to will it?'"[53] "So," ventured Billod, "this who knows what [*je ne sais quoi*] constitutes the essential core of volition, it is volition itself and in its purest physiological form."[54]

Subsequent work on the physiology and the pathology of the will extended Billod's reasoning. French doctors and educators published studies on the operation of the will and judging by the popularity of their work, they attracted a good deal of professional and public interest. Théodule Ribot's *Les maladies de la volonté* (The Diseases of the Will), first published in 1883, reached its 37th edition in 1936 and educator Jules Payot's *L'éducation de la volonté* (The Education of the Will) went through seventy-one editions in fifty-three years.[55] British psychiatrist Henry Maudsley also shaped the discussion with his work *Body and Will*, published in 1884.[56] Italians writing on the subject looked to Ribot and Maudsley, in particular, as they described volition and cataloged its malfunctions. All these studies insisted on the organic nature of the will. It is, philosopher and psychologist Frédéric Paulhan clarified in 1903, "a psychic act which is, like all psychological phenomena a complex of physiological factors of which we can know, in a general way and up to a certain point, the constituent parts."[57] According to the majority of experts, the will functioned mostly unconsciously, and it came into play much less often than reflex and habit did in determining ordinary actions.

In his widely read study, Ribot (1839–1916) began with abulia, a pathological weakness of the will. Reviewing the case of M.P... thirty-six years after Billod presented it, he concluded, "What we have here is the sickness of the will, in the strictest sense."[58] Abulia came primarily from a weak drive to act, according to Ribot. He, like Billod, broke voluntary action into three parts: deliberation, will, and motion.[59] According to Billod, abulia infected only one of these, the will, making it difficult for M.P ... to transmit his intellect's decisions to his motor centers. Ribot broadened the site of the problem, arguing that the apathy typical of *abouliques* resulted from their flaccid, dull emotions. Unless invigorated by feelings, ideas did not translate into movement, he asserted. "Any decline in the vital *tonus*, slight or pronounced, fugitive or durable, has an effect."[60] Thus, M.P ... lacked the emotional energy required by the will to transform decisions into action.

Pierre Janet (1859–1947), director of the Psychological Laboratory at Salpêtrière, traced abulia to the physiology of the will itself. In 1898, he presented the case of Marcelle, a young woman he identified as "almost completely without what one calls *volonté*," an *aboulique*.[61] Asked to accomplish a simple but unfamiliar task, she agreed, tried again and again, and then gave up. If she managed to do it once, he noted, she hesitated less the next time. Like Billod and Ribot, he concluded that the obstacle lay in what brought decision and action together, the will. Janet, however, rejected Ribot's theory that abulia stemmed from the inability to generate strong feelings. Marcelle exhibited plenty of emotion, but she lacked the ability to organize new perceptions into ideas. When she did succeed in processing perceptions, the new associations remained and permitted her to act the next time.[62]

Janet attributed abulia to weak ideas, Ribot to weak emotions, and both of them to the will's inability to process stimuli and produce directives. This form of abulia affected the execution of actions. M.P. and Marcelle knew what they wanted to do but could not do it. Another variant of abulia affected the ability to make decisions. In this case, obsessive doubt or endless second guessing stymied action.[63] "Devoured by ceaseless hesitations," Ribot observed, "these unfortunates don't write any more, don't listen any more, don't speak anymore."[64] In a third version of the disorder, the will foundered when unusually strong urges overpowered it. Seized by a sudden overwhelming impulse, the subject usually acted "like an animal with its head cut off or at least without the lobes of its brain."[65] Obsessives, epileptics, and hysterics fell in this category, as did patients too scattered or distracted to concentrate, Ribot observed. When the will struggled against the wild impulses and lost, patients watched themselves do what they did not want to do. In these cases, abnormally weak or strong impulses or ideas affected the will, but the will itself could also malfunction. Sometimes the will did not develop, or it developed poorly, and then caprice reigned, as it did in hysterics, Ribot contended. Sleepwalkers, ecstatics, and epileptics exhibited such a loss of control, while other people experienced a slower dismantling of the will as a result either of conditions such as neurasthenia and alcoholism or of aging.[66]

Defective will slowed people down or it caused them to cut loose from normal restraints. It could also disturb their ability to concentrate and to follow through on tasks. Based on medical descriptions of the will, social critics and educators drew dramatic conclusions about the state of modern society. In treatises intended to alarm, they detailed the price of the "general failing of wills ... the great illness of our age."[67] A healthy will gave individuals "complete self control" or, said Payot

(1859–1940), rector of the Academy at Aix-en-Provence, "complete self possession."[68] Without it, they surrendered to their natural nomadic and lawless tendencies. Observers such as Paulhan, Payot, and Dr. Paul-Emile Lévy lamented that young people got up late and spent what little energy they possessed on entertainments, often of a dubious sort. When they sat down to work, they quickly lost interest and fell to daydreaming. Bureaucrats and politicians also showed signs of abulia in their passivity and lackluster performances. They might struggle against their inertia, as M.P … did, but if the will faltered, then they yielded to the dictates of reflex and habit. By depriving them of what it took to succeed as students, lawmakers, and factory workers, a weak will made misfits.

Identifying pathologies of the will assumed that it worked within "the framework of biological processes" and as "a pyschophysiological mechanism."[69] Advocates of this approach all dismissed free will as a metaphysical construction and generally echoed Billod's identification of volition with the *je ne sais quoi* which occurred between a decision and its execution. Billod saw that something as a distinct faculty, one on par with deliberation and movement.[70] Later doctors distinguished between willing and will (*volition* and *volonté*). Ribot, for example, recognized the conscious decision to act (volition or willing) and the underlying physiological mechanisms—he called them the will—that either permitted or restrained action. Neither reflexive actions nor abstract ideas activated the will. Only when ideas required deliberation, Ribot argued, did the will engage, and depending on how it balanced the push to do or not to do, volition then permitted or inhibited action. Unlike Ribot, Professor of Legal Medicine at the University of Bruxelles, Jules Dallemagne (1858–1923) did not separate will and willing. He believed that the entire nervous system operated on the basis of reflexes.[71] Dallemagne did, however, distinguish unconscious vegetative reflexes from more complex "voluntary reflexes," including volition.

In a study published in a series on experimental psychology in 1903, Fréderic Paulhan (1856–1931) seconded and extended Ribot's conception. People began, he argued, with a set of inherited instincts and reflexes which produced spontaneous responses to most situations. But the "growing complication of instincts and the violent conflict of ideas and desires" interfered with automatic reflexes. One impulse countered another, or unfamiliar situations triggered no response, leaving the self confused and adrift. In response to both the profusion and the dearth of reflexes and instincts, the will developed. It acted to synthesize and coordinate the multiple, fluctuating, and conflicting elements of the personality and to manage novelty. Once the will determined the appropriate response, that course of action settled into the realm of habit and reflex. If it operated efficiently, the will harmonized all the pieces within the self and the self with the outside world, but that never happened, Paulhan argued. "Always the psychic element, that combination of urges, ideas, desires and actions, tends to become independent, to live for itself," and new situations always challenged the "acquired personality" so that everyone depended on the will but never achieved a unified self.[72]

This model proved to be a common one among doctors who described the physiological will. Distinct yet interdependent evolutionary stages linked sensation, desire, idea, decision, and action in a chain or path. Automatic reflexes short-circuited will, as did familiar sensations which prompted ingrained responses. Novel stimuli, in contrast, stirred up a volatile mixture of conflicting desires and inhibitions, and they activated the will to manage and direct them. What triggered action grew in complexity as humans evolved. Ribot, for example, proposed that primitives and infants reacted to reflexes; later, desires developed; and finally intellect appeared, and with it will and volition. In Dallemagne's scheme, as cells in the nervous system multiplied and formed more intricate interconnections, reflexes grew more complex, finally producing conscious and voluntary acts.[73] Will, doctors believed, brought and held the pieces together. It existed, Dallemagne pointed out, to "combine, adapt, associate" the energies of myriad distinct but connected cells, "with an eye to a common integrated action."[74] Or, as Janet succinctly put it, "will is the power of mental synthesis."[75]

Underneath the synthesizing activity of will and the volition that it permitted, doctors saw the brain and nervous system at work. Dallemagne claimed that neurons, the stuff of the nervous system, formed distinct "reflex arcs" tied to each other in patterns of increasing complexity. All physiological activity involved the neurons' reflex actions, operating by themselves or in groups. The neurons accomplished separate small functions, and then transmitted their energy to associated neurons that performed more complex operations.[76] A somewhat similar conception, advanced by the English psychiatrist and "gloomy genius" Henry Maudsley (1835–1918), held that the brain contained "a countless multitude of inter-connected nerve-centers, of high and low dignity, arranged in the same layer and in superimposed layers, functionally differentiated, and ready to be stirred into action by suitable stimulation, to increase, to combine, to restrain, to neutralize, to modify in unknown ways one another's function."[77] Stimuli caused energy to flow from the motor nerves to the muscles, and then to movement. When the resulting action provoked a negative response, a nerve center stored the memory, and the next time, the stimulus triggered competing stop and go responses, whose conflict the will resolved. Turning to the will's operation, neuropathologist Leonardo Bianchi (1848–1927) explained that it discharged energy through circuits with older circuits satisfying individual instincts and the newer and larger ones managing the social *self*.[78] British psychiatrist Alexander Bain (1818–1903), who influenced Ribot's thinking, also suggested that electricity powered the nervous system and will. Networks of cells and fibers, he concluded, stored and discharged surplus nervous energy or "vital force" which produced both instinctive and voluntary actions.[79]

With so many elements of the body engaged, no wonder scientists stressed that the will foundered or failed so frequently. Will was, Ribot contended, "a perpetually unstable product [of human development], always on the verge of falling apart."[80] The last functions to develop, will and volition lacked the stability of reflexes and habits. By a law first identified by James Prichard and widely accepted at the end of the nineteenth century, what emerged last fell apart first, so that age or disease eroded the layers deposited by evolution beginning with the highest and least entrenched.[81] The complexity of the elements that the will managed also compromised its operation, as an abnormality in one piece risked to affect the entire process. "Organic problems" disorganized the personalities of hysterics, Ribot argued, causing the will to give way to caprice. "A stable character on such shifting foundations would be a miracle," he noted.[82] In epilepsy, in contrast, disruptions of the motor system froze the will and let impulse take over.

The number of potential sources of weakness made it difficult to pin down what exactly disrupted the will. Problems could result from emotional shock, the effects of drug or alcohol abuse, or exhaustion. In the absence of these conditions, doctors looked to heredity, but if the case history did not indicate neuroses or arthritis in the family, and if the person had no previous episodes, then something situational likely caused the problem. For example, Marcelle, Janet's patient at Salpêtrière, showed the effects of a family tainted by heredity. She inherited a weak will, and illness and emotional shock triggered her attacks of abulia. Typhoid fever brought on the first episode at age fourteen, Janet pointed out, and her father's death and a failed romance the next.[83] M.P... fell victim to the negative effects of retirement. As Billod noted, upsetting established rhythms often provoked "congestion, strokes, mental illness."[84]

Doctors detected impaired will in mental patients, neurotics, hardened criminals and vagrants, lackadaisical students, and listless professionals. In the form of abulia, it appeared in patients diagnosed with hysteria, neurasthenia, and degenerative disorders. Faltering will did not affect only mental patients and neurotics; it also struck ordinary people. "Who hasn't experienced," asked Ribot, "hours of collapse where all the external and internal impulses, sensations, and ideas, do not inspire action, [but] leave us cold?"[85] Benign enough when it flagged momentarily, serious deficits had far more troublesome consequences as the number of vagrants, criminals, and mental patients diagnosed with defective wills indicated. When the will faltered, delusions, hallucinations, and obsessions worsened, and the crazy impulses that normal people repressed or channeled into innocuous eccentricities took over, scientists asserted. Without a manager, the self reverted to basic instincts or got caught up in the surging impulses associated with attacks of hysteria and with epileptic seizures.

Aberrant social behavior could also result from defective will, according to experts. Ribot offered homicidal mania, kleptomania, pyromania, and suicide as examples of crimes likely affected by fixed ideas or unrestrained urges. The will also figured prominently in explanations of habitual vagabondage. Without the discipline and focus fostered by the will, people found it harder to hold a job and easier to surrender to the primitive instinct to roam, studies concluded. Investigators also thought that malfunctions in the will explained some sexual perversions, especially masturbation. While low quotients of will brought on the gamut of mental and social problems, surplus will empowered men to change the world. Caesar, Michelangelo, and St. Vincent de Paul, Ribot contended, showed "a life always in accord with itself, because in them everything conspires, converges, and consents."[86] The unique synthesizing power of their will enabled them to pursue their goals with single-minded intensity and exceptional success.

If deficient will helped account for the alarming rise of social deviance and personal apathy evident at the turn of the century, its vigor secured the civilized self. Because it commanded "the exercise of intelligence, memory, and concentration," Billod argued, it created "what is truly personal, really human in man."[87] Ribot concurred, observing that will sprung from "the deepest recesses of our tissues" and constituted "we ourselves."[88] As the organizing force of the many-sided and chaotic self, these scientists made the will more central to managing life than reason. It constituted the necessary prerequisite for "the exercise of *duty*, for the respect of others, for abnegation," proclaimed Eugenio Tanzi and his collaborator Ernesto Lugaro (1870–1940). If their will operated normally, people achieved "complete self control" and with that they gained what mattered most: a livelihood and social acceptance.[89]

When will malfunctioned, doctors proposed therapies whose effectiveness depended on the precise nature of the problem. Removing the conditions that disrupted the will could bring improvement, but in the case of hereditary weakness, little could be done, doctors believed. Serious cases of situational abulia such as M.P...'s sometimes responded to treatment. He returned home from his excursion to Italy slightly improved. Janet used conventional therapies, including bromides, cold showers, and electrical shocks to the brain to treat Marcelle, and when those failed he used hypnosis to peel away her obsessions layer by layer. She left the hospital, got married, and apparently managed her daily life, although Janet expressed some skepticism about the solidity of her recovery.[90] Another case, that of 27-year-old businessman M.X..., responded to a battery of treatments. Business reversals and family problems threw him "into a state of extreme depression," according to Dominique-Joseph-Bertrand Rivière, who published a clinical study of abulia. Unable to eat or sleep and experiencing palpitations, M.X... went to bed unable to move. Rivière detected no physical problems and no delusions, hallucinations, or suicidal thoughts; nothing indicated hereditary weaknesses. Hydrotherapy, electrical treatments, diet, tonics, isolation, and changes of scenery produced improvement, but any emotion or stress caused him to turn red, sweat, and become upset. In this state, he could not lift his pen, get dressed, or concentrate. When the episode passed, he had no trouble accomplishing what he could not get himself to do before. The last barrier to a full recovery was putting on his socks, an effort that was completely beyond him, Rivière reported. For a time he managed to get one on and to carry the other around on his belt. When at last he overcame that obstacle, the hold of the illness loosened and he returned to all his former activities.[91]

Dealing with what Payot called generalized *aboulie* permitted greater optimism. Self-help tracts advised normal people how to shore up their will and improve their powers of concentration. Payot counseled his readers to practice focused thinking; leave no minute unscheduled; repeat unpleasant tasks to entrench them in routine; pay attention to diet; avoid prostitutes and self-abuse. Vigorous physical exercise, Payot argued, turned young people into "unrefined fighters" and intellectual dullards. The great human victories, he warned, "are no longer won with muscles, they are won with discoveries, with great feelings, with fruitful ideas." Following a schedule, completing tasks, getting fresh air, Payot insisted would restore energy and bring happiness.[92] Another tactic, suggestive therapy, disciplined the will and allowed people to become the masters of their bodies, promised Dr. Paul-Emile Lévy. He instructed that before going to sleep and when they woke up, people should review who they were, what they sought, and what they had done that day and would do the next in order to achieve their goals. By repeating desirable actions, they would soon turn them into habits.[93]

Understanding mental abnormalities

Identifying moral feeling and volition as distinct functions of the brain changed notions of insanity. Troubled reason disrupted lives, but defects in will and moral sensibility turned rational adults into social misfits. Lucid but mentally impaired, they witnessed their own paralysis or knowingly committed mayhem. Benjamin Ball reminded his students of the material nature of mental processes, a fact "universally admitted in our time."[94] By the end of the century, scientists had "pulled psychiatry from the nebulous ontological heights" and planted it in the physical realm of the brain, commented Lorenzo Ellero, assistant at the psychiatric clinic at the University of Padua.[95] They left the soul to the metaphysicians, collapsed the mind into the brain, and the brain into the cerebral cortex. Reason, feelings, and volition developed as the human species adapted to the environment, and they emerged one by one as individuals moved from gestation to adulthood. Just as elsewhere in the body, defects, deficits, and disease affected the brain's structure and operation. These abnormalities, in turn, subjugated people to their impulses, producing the eccentric behaviors that indicated insanity. Treating mental illness depended on understanding the brain and nervous system, a goal psychiatrists and neurologists such as Ball set for themselves.

However, the difficulty of seeing inside the body to uncover its operation complicated this experimental approach. To deal with the difficulties, doctors refined laboratory techniques, but a good deal of that work remained preliminary and its conclusions highly disputed, particularly when it came to the biology of reason and will. Seeking additional, concrete, empirical data, they relied on clinical investigation. Taking themselves as subjects worked only to a point since, as leading physiologists reminded them, a lot went on in their heads without them realizing it, and consciousness itself likely depended on invisible physical processes. But looking at other people, especially at the apparently abnormal, gave them telling information about normality, they asserted. That knowledge, in turn, enabled them to classify and treat the disorders.

Just as they did with genius and idiocy, investigators focused on individuals and tried to generalize from their profiles. As they examined each case with the idea of constructing types or of refining already existing diagnostic categories, they objectified the distinct and slippery aspects of difference. They sought, first of all, to identify variants of insanity and to catalog their characteristics in order to facilitate diagnosis. Their continuous and almost frantic efforts to develop a reliable taxonomy of mental and nervous disorders demonstrated the extreme fluidity of the field. As they generated different theories of how the body worked, some well-known diagnostic categories disappeared, others emerged, and still others recombined pieces of known ailments, as doctors invented other more rational configurations. Henry Maudsley explained the challenge: "it frequently happens that [different symptoms] blend, combine, or replace one another in a way that confounds our distinctions, giving rise to hybrid varieties intermediate between those which are regarded as typical."[96]

What constituted the mental part of "mental" illness remained hotly disputed territory, particularly as doctors explored the connections between the brain and the nervous system.[97] Associating symptoms assigned to insanity with other diseases also raised questions about the "mental" in mental illness. For example, epileptics typically experienced amnesia and often hallucinations after seizures, but most doctors did not define motor-sensory epilepsy as a mental disorder. Rather, they saw it as a nervous disease that affected the mind. Evidence also indicated that disturbances in the digestive and nervous systems caused extreme depression and exceeding anger. To clarify the brain's involvement, alienists divided mental illnesses into idiopathic and sympathetic. In the first case, the disorder originated in the brain, and in the second, the psyche registered problems elsewhere in the body. The distinction proved as difficult to apply as it was convenient to enunciate.

What the "illness" in mental illness meant also generated confusion, particularly when the causes of insanity remained so obscure. An illness followed a discernible course; it appeared and it responded to treatment, with varying levels of success depending on its origins and its gravity. A defect or absence was not dynamic, and it did not disappear or improve. Idiocy, for example, resulted from a congenital deficiency in reason, whereas, for those who accepted the distinction, imbecility resembled an illness. French neuropsychiatrist Gilbert Ballet (1853–1916) clarified these distinctions for the benefit of his students. He instructed them to collect all the symptoms, including physical troubles, and then consider the source of the mental or nervous affliction. Either it derived from a malformation, lesion, or abnormal hardening or softening of the brain or, more often, it resulted from a functional abnormality located at the cellular level. Like other psychiatrists, Ballet stressed operational anomalies, while recognizing that anatomy accounted for some disturbances. Using the term loosely, Ballet called both types "illness."[98] Others distinguished between structural defects and illness and classified insanity as the second. Applying this perspective, moral insanity or organic immorality did not qualify as insanity, a point Lombroso underscored. Describing insanity as illness invited treatment under the direction of psychiatrists, and according to some historians, led to a new emphasis on the hereditary and congenital bases of insanity when psychiatrists found so many cases incurable.

Because psychiatrists and neurologists kept discovering variants and variables, they kept refining their systems of classification. Without those, they could not organize the data, situate and compare cases, keep statistics, assign patients to the appropriate physician, or evaluate therapeutic strategies.[99] But the fluidity of the field, the differences in expertise, and conflicts over interpreting the data made categorizing immensely contentious. The systems used varied a good deal depending on who developed them and why. And virtually anyone who presented a system, and many did, admitted it was arbitrary and abstract and therefore of dubious accuracy and utility.

On the most general level, doctors increasingly distinguished between disorders related to the nervous system and those directly affecting the brain. From the perspective of neurologists, such as Jean-Martin Charcot, the nerve centers commanded the brain, so that nervous disorders encompassed mental problems. By this optic, the sensory and motor functions lodged in the nervous system registered stimuli and transferred them to the brain for processing, and then received them back for action. Psychiatrists, on the other hand, acknowledged the interchange between the two areas, but made the mind a distinct zone of activity with its own problems.[100]

More precise classification required an organizing principle, and the one commanding the greatest allegiance changed. One approach used by psychiatrists organized dysfunctions around symptoms; another grouped disorders on the basis of the function affected. Using the latter approach, Ribot examined disturbances of the personality, will, memory, and attention. But as they learned more about insanity, doctors increasingly based categories on causes. Agostini offered an example in his textbook on mental illness. He divided diseases into acquired, latent, and hereditary. In the first set, he put mania, melancholy, alcohol or drug-induced psychoses, and senile dementia. Disorders that affected people with congenitally weak characters, including frenastenia, moral insanity, and sexual perversions belonged in the second group. In the third category, that of hereditary illnesses, he collected all the neurasthenic, hysteric, and epileptic psychoneuroses.[101] His approach edged out one widely used in Italy in the 1880s, that of Krafft-Ebing, which created categories for degenerative disorders, psychoneuroses, brain pathologies, and abnormalities related to arrested psychic development. Instead, Agostini drew on a system pioneered by the German psychiatrist Emil Kraepelin and used by many asylums in and outside of Italy. Kraepelin used categories based on etiology (infections, exhaustion, poisoning, thyroid conditions, encephalitis, arrested development) and symptoms (types of dementia, manic depression, paranoia, general neuroses, psychopathic states, and regressive disorders).[102] These efforts to name, describe, and classify mental disease provided a framework for professional exchange.

Another key element in understanding mental disease involved research on the structure and the operation of the brain.[103] Two basic theories directed the debate. In 1908, Agostino spelled out the results of recent research to doctors and students. Certain areas, in particular the cerebral cortex, served as a site for motor, sensory, and associative activity, he explained. The remaining parts of the brain, labeled "latent zones," seemed to host psychic functions such as forming ideas and making connections. This view, Agostini explained, made "intelligence the result of the work of the entire brain functioning in harmony" rather than assigning intellectual work to one site in the brain.[104] The alternative approach broke down and localized the brain's functions still further, arguing that each part of the brain commanded a distinct function. Intellect, according to this view, centered in the prefrontal lobes.

In addition to figuring out the topography of the brain, investigators examined the cellular basis of its activity. They accepted as fact that struggle and adaptation made the brains of civilized moderns different from the primitive brain. The more evolved the body, the more specialized, complex, and delicate its elements and operation. Thus, only in fully developed adults did reason prevail over the impulses commanded by instinct and reflex. In images evoking the modern factory, Leonardo Bianchi noted the division of labor and the coordination of tasks in the efficient production of movement, speech, thought, and memory. As an example, he noted that, thanks to their brain's dense motor cells, modern warriors gracefully wielded their swords, while primitives could only brandish clubs.[105] The latest research identified the sensory centers that received and transmitted data, Tanzi and Lugaro reported in the updated edition of their textbook on mental diseases. Different zones in the nervous system processed and filed that data away. Similarly, at the cellular level some cells registered and sent information and others sorted and stored it.

Medical science agreed that the evolved brain also connected in ways as yet imperfectly understood to the nervous system. Neurologists, in particular, tried to work out how the external stimuli registered by the nervous system turned into ideas and then actions. The brain, they theorized, operated as one element in a complex network of nerves, ganglia, and neurons, and its health depended on the vitality of nerve cells and their connections. Charles Richet (1850–1935), professor at the Faculty of Medicine in Paris, applied that view specifically to the will. Like all other mental processes, the will "depends on the state of the nervous cells; it is a psychic function, which, like all psychic functions, has a physiological origin."[106]

Based on what they discovered about the brain, doctors claimed to understand what caused mental illness and, with that, the roots of recalcitrant social disobedience. According to Tanzi and Lugaro, scientists agreed that outside agents caused some disorders, while inherited or congenital abnormalities caused others. Ball, for example, saw mental illness as something "installed in the flesh and blood," as a part of a person's nature. He addressed his students in the mid-1870s: "And if you were to ask me to reduce, to a single word, all that we know about the origins of insanity, I would willingly answer: 'There is only one cause of mental illness, it is heredity.'"[107] Rather than pass directly from parents to their children, insanity appeared in families with histories of neuroses, eccentricities, vice, crime, and sometimes genius. Other doctors took much the same position. In cases such as idiocy and moral insanity, an inherited or congenital structural defect directly affected how the brain functioned.[108] More often, heredity predisposed the body to mental illness by weakening the nervous system and brain, especially in families disposed to degenerative disorders.

External causes explained mental misfits as well, physicians stressed. Agostini used language familiar in the analysis of crime, vagrancy, and sexual perversions to express distinctions between innate and situational factors. Accidental mental illness, he argued, resulted mainly from social conditions. But the side effects of illnesses, addictions, and traumas as well as overwork, surges of passion, and the power of suggestion could also trouble the brains of healthy people, he contended.[109] Infections and toxins, including the abuse of alcohol and drugs, and physical strain of the sort produced by pregnancy, delivery, and lactation explained some mental troubles. Emotional jolts and intense, persistent passions could also weaken the brain. Such shocks and taxing emotions often resulted from such things as unhappy marriages, poverty, and the rapid pace of modern life. According to most psychiatrists, these social factors usually affected brains already vulnerable to disruption from the outside. Ball cautioned his students: "But I especially wanted to get out of your minds the common notion that insanity is an accidental storm that blows through existence." Almost always mental illness needs "favorable ground," and heredity constitutes the most important of the predisposing conditions.[110] Or in Tanzi's words, "behind every external cause there is the shadow of an internal cause."[111]

Implications

When they explained mental pathologies, then, doctors identified a combination of biological and social causes, exactly as criminologists did when they analyzed social deviance. They both laid out a continuum stretching from biological fatality to social contingency and assigned mental and social misfits a place according to what appeared to be responsible for their condition. Like inborn criminality and vagabondage, a congenital disposition to madness affected a tragic and growing minority. On the other end, social factors produced folly just as they led occasional criminals to break laws and the unemployed to take to the roads in search of work. "Accidental" events such as a love affair gone wrong, financial loss, an injury, an infection, or sickness led to mental illnesses that temporarily or permanently pushed unfortunates to the margins. More often than inborn defects, circumstances explained mental illness, medical experts believed. It looked, then, as if anyone might suffer a bout of madness or become a temporary delinquent in certain situations. The possibility of turning abnormal, if only briefly, closed the gap between ordinary people and misfits. At the same time, the experts emphasized that romantic disappointments did not invariably plunge people into melancholia, just as poverty did not always lead to crime. Perhaps life's blows just came harder, or possibly they triggered a latent vulnerability. In the view of investigators, the second explanation made more sense than the first, making inherent weakness the divide between those who fell and those who did not.

The strategies promoted for dealing with mental illness depended on what caused it, as it did for criminality and vagabondage. Mental problems brought on by personal crises or traumas usually responded well to treatment. These causes had a recognized beginning and that implied a possible end. In many cases, it sufficed to remove the conditions that disturbed the normal operation of the brain. Often, though, doctors prescribed a range of additional, more aggressive treatments, including electrical stimulation. Psychological therapies, particularly in the form of work, provided the "most important and effective cure," in Agostini's view.[112] When organic anomalies played a role, doctors offered little hope for a solution. Agostini concluded that inborn defects and the "physical and psychological stigmata of degeneration" made it difficult to avoid or to arrest insanity. When madness affected neuropaths, epileptics, hysterics, or neurasthenics, the prognosis improved, because it occurred only episodically, he argued. If, however, the attacks recurred, their cumulative effects led to chronic and incurable mental illness.[113] In other innate forms of insanity, aggressive treatment could sometimes attenuate the symptoms, but when the illness produced antisocial behavior, as it did with moral insanity, the patients, like born criminals and inveterate vagrants, required confinement. Ball laid out the risks: "The insane person constitutes, in fact, above all else, a public peril, and one can take as a general thesis that of four mentally ill there are at least three who are dangerous in varying degrees."[114]

Historians interested in mental illness emphasize the increase in the number of asylums and asylum patients during the nineteenth century.[115] In 1838, the French required departments to establish asylums and specified procedures for committing those mentally ill considered dangerous to others. As a result, the number of patients increased from 10,000 to 43,000 between 1834 and 1874 and reached 95,000 by the end of the Third Republic.[116] Italy saw the number of patients grow by a factor of five between 1881 and 1907.[117] In addition to asylums, Italians set aside special sections in prisons for the criminally insane and subsequently established separate facilities administered by doctors and prison officials to house them.[118] The Criminal Code of 1889 reinforced the initiative by empowering judges to commit criminals ruled not guilty by reason of insanity to regular or special asylums for as long as the authorities deemed necessary.[119] Legislation approved in 1904 specified that the mentally ill who presented a danger to themselves or others and who could not be cared for in any other way be institutionalized. Judges and in emergencies the police authorized confinement, and they and the asylum director determined the length of the stay.

The use of asylums to segregate potentially dangerous people shifted their role from cure to control, a change evident in both Italy and France. Unable to deal with the mentally ill any other way, liberals took steps to manage them, historian Robert Castel argues. Lawmakers established the right of the mentally ill to support and treatment, while taking those diagnosed as dangerous out of circulation. Thus, Castel contends, liberal politicians allied with medical specialists to turn a perceived source of disorder into a technical and administrative problem.[120] Other historians explain the move more in terms of psychiatrists' professional interests.[121] Earlier in the century, alienists touted their ability to cure mental patients, particularly when given the sustained individual attention that asylums allowed. But the growing number of incurables collecting in hospitals caused psychiatrists to emphasize the role of heredity in producing mental illness, these historians argue. In such intractable cases, doctors could hope to ease the symptoms but could not be expected to eliminate the source of the problem. Because of its role as a harbor for dangerous madmen, the asylum, according to Roy Porter, "underlined the Otherhood of the insane and carved out a managerial milieu in which that alienness could be handled."[122] In his view, the campaign for asylums responded to a broad range of issues and interests and not just to the professional goals of psychiatrists. If anything, Porter points out, asylums created psychiatrists, not the reverse.[123]

While doctors and social thinkers discussed treatment, they also focused attention on prevention, particularly in light of the connections between mental illness and factors such as diet, environmental toxins, and alcoholism. Just as reformers urged measures to increase jobs and reduce poverty in order to curb occasional crime, so doctors proposed aggressive political initiatives to fight certain mental and nervous illnesses. For example, they urged better nutrition to minimize pellegra and cretinism and campaigned to keep youth from falling into nasty habits. Aggressive measures to eliminate syphilis and alcoholism would reduce the number of the mentally ill by a quarter overall and by a half in the cities, Agostini, for one, claimed.[124] When life itself seemed at fault, doctors typically invoked still broader solutions. "The consequences of Malthus's law," preached Penta in his popular treatise on mental illness, "are made more serious and inevitable by the organization of modern society."[125] Some attributed the troubles to the extremes of wealth and poverty and called for a redistribution of wealth. Others, noting the absence of insanity in primitive societies, saw insanity as a condition inherent to modernity, bound to stay until evolution and history removed it.

Heredity's role in mental disease also encouraged attention to prevention. Those influenced by Morel's predictions issued the call with particular urgency, asserting that nothing less than the future of the race was at stake. The string of worsening diseases disabled families and threatened to undermine society, doctors such as Diomede Carito warned. "From a generation of creatures suffering from carebaria [sensation of heaviness in the head] and migraines, follows another which includes hysterics and epileptics, and in the end proceeds to idiocy, to insanity."[126] Better, Penta urged his readers "to see to it that close relatives, the insane, the semi-insane, imbeciles, epileptics, criminals, neurasthenics, the strange, the eccentric, the neurotic, the tubercular, diabetics, syphilitics … don't get married."[127] In his textbook, Agostini emphasized the doctor's duty to look beyond individual patients to the mental health of the general population in order to keep "the number of those antisocial beings from increasing." They compromised the interests and progress of the community, in addition to requiring public resources for their maintenance, he proclaimed.[128] With such issues in mind, doctors urged people to take care in choosing their partners. But, especially in France they frequently cautioned against any legal prohibitions against marriage. Such an intrusion on individual rights exceeded the proper reach of the law and offended tradition. The weight then fell on doctors, they said, to use persuasion to exhort the most vulnerable to celibacy.

Such apocalyptic predictions and prophylactic schemes measured how much insecurity mental illness generated. Like criminality and vagrancy, it seemed to be on the rise, and the fact that specialists committed to explaining it and institutions designed to treat it proliferated confirmed that impression. The explanations of mental illness, in fact, tended to universalize the risk. Psychiatrists and neurologists mapped the evolved mind, locating its many functions and intricate connections and confirming the fragility of its highest properties. At the same time, they compiled a long list of all the conditions which led to mental and nervous disorders. As if that did not suffice to alarm, they traced some mental deficiencies to the family, arguing that one disease led to another. If they read popular medical treatises or listened to doctors, people whose uncle suffered from tuberculosis or alcoholism might well worry about their or their children's vulnerability to insanity.

Discovering that the brain had distinct facets accompanied a developing medical disassembling of the self. It and everything in it, Richet pointed out, "has varieties, degrees, illnesses, anomalies."[129] Separating knowing from valuing and doing good underlay the idea of diseased morality; the difference between ideas, decisions, and actions explained why the will existed and what could go wrong with it. These distinctions reduced the reach of reason and made it the captive of other functions in the brain. Thus, the intellect depended on the will and the motor centers to transform deliberation into action, and when those functions were defective or weak, reason felt the effects, just as the will registered the impact of a perturbed intellect. Even when completely healthy and collaborating effectively, reason and will exhibited limited power since reflexes and habits produced most actions without them. All these functions developed independently and together they made up the piecemeal self.

What defined individuals—their feelings, ideas, and actions—boiled down to an accumulation of stimuli and responses lodged in networks of cells and neurons, according to physiologists and neurologists. Ribot's telegraphic summary—"That organism, that personality"—resumed the theory of the self that lay behind the ideas of moral sensibility and will and their pathologies.[130] An individual represented nothing more than generations of cellular development shaped by the demands of survival. Experience also contributed to their character but only through the mediating influence of internal organic processes. The self was, Ribot asserted, "as small, simple, incoherent or complex and unified as it [the organism] is."[131] The fully evolved organism and self, then, contained multiple layers deposited by evolution and held in precarious balance by the operation of the will. Italian Silvio Venturi (1850–1900?), director of Girifalco asylum and a deputy, agreed. Humans began as pre-individuals, added individuality, and finally developed a social self, with each successive dimension subject to alteration and damage.[132] As they matured, modern individuals retraced that route, so that adults possessed affective and moral feelings, ideas of justice, an understanding of appropriate conduct, language and writing, and a clear sexual identity. When alcohol, anger, illnesses, and dementia weakened the mature self, the person went socially AWOL. According to this construction, normality involved equilibrium, and it sounded complex harmonies rather than a monotonous mechanical hum.

The mentally fit, then, achieved an effective balance of the disparate components of the self. How close individuals came depended on the perfection and the resilience of their mental equipment. Judging from the medical literature, it did not come complete or undamaged very often, and even when all appeared in order, what went wrong later suggested that concealed weaknesses had promised problems from the start. The grim image did conform to doctors' professional interest in identifying and treating pathologies, but it also reflected how they thought the body worked. Their views, in turn, responded to social and cultural values and concerns. As they squeezed the self into the viscera, scientists displaced the deranged souls of bedlam to make room for defective, dysfunctional, unbalanced, and exhausted brains and nerves. The idea that madness conferred special powers and that madmen saw beneath the surface or that they reached exceptional creative heights thanks to their folly belonged largely to the past. Lombroso did argue that geniuses went mad and that inmates in asylums exhibited streaks of creative insight, but in his view, the affinity stemmed from a common pathology and not a gift. Rather, when mental illness attacked reason, the will, or moral sensibility, it disrupted what allowed people to manage the demands of modern life.

Liberals valued reason too highly to take its aberrations lightly. For one thing, political life put reason at its core, as liberalism traced the formation and survival of the state to the rationality of its citizens.[133] The rule of law, guarantor of individual freedom, presumed rational action, and the punishments meted out by law courts aimed to restore reason to those who misused it. Order, then, and the freedom it guaranteed, depended on using reason, and it followed that weak or twisted reason caused shock and anxiety. It demanded explanation and treatment by those who claimed to know.

When reason worked but the will failed, the effects proved even more troubling. Defective will caused people to stop in their tracks, to try in vain to act on their decisions and desires. Or it subjected them to the tyranny of impulse, its weakness turning them into willful children and savages. A robust will, in contrast, permitted the self-restraint considered essential to life in modern society, and by managing new stimuli, it allowed people to operate in a context charged with sensations and continual change. It followed that deficiencies of the will left people confused, unfocused, lazy, or if their worst impulses took charge, landed them in an asylum or prison. It also happened that moral insanity accompanied normal reason and will, creating a potent source of antisocial behavior. The combination made children unmanageable and adults extremely dangerous misfits. More than other mental disorders, moral indifference threatened society, according to medical and social scientists.

The mental disorders that psychiatrists and neurologists discovered in the last decades of the nineteenth century helped to explain increases in crime, vagrancy, and suicide; they also accounted for disturbing evidence that ordinary citizens were losing their grip. Attributing social maladjustment to mental disorders ostensibly offered a scientific diagnosis of pressing problems. It reinforced the conclusions of neurologists, criminologists, and sociologists about the weight of heredity and the milieu in explaining dissonant social behavior. The solutions that they proposed depended on what they learned about the body from case studies, experimental physiology, and autopsies. To interpret the data, they applied the theories of evolution and degeneration. They also drew on their understanding of civil society to analyze the body. Dallemagne, for example, explained that neurons existed for themselves, but they also combined in a dizzying array of neural arcs to fulfill larger organic functions. The number, the solidity, and the integration of these connections determined an individual's stability. Liberals believed that the same dynamic occurred in civil society, as individuals pursued their private interests in ways that promoted the common good. As the social tensions at the turn of the century proved, the more advanced the society, the more complex its structure and the more volatile the interactions of individuals and groups. Looking to laws and lawmakers to manage the chaos and finding them ineffective, social critics called for reform, deploying words such as "control," "channel," "integrate," "balance," "unify," "mediate," and "coordinate." Medical descriptions of the will and its role used exactly the same language.

In explaining activity inside the nervous system, doctors seemed to draw on the incessant change evident around them. Energy flow dominated physiological processes, they argued, and good health depended on its effective collection, maintenance, and dispersion. As they described how energy moved, doctors referred to pathways, circuits, networks, and transmission centers, mapping the inside of the body as they did the boulevards and commuter railway lines of late nineteenth-century Paris and London. "The cells," asserted Alexander Bain, "are the Grand Junctions or Crossings where the fibers extend and multiply their connections."[134] In the modern metropolis crowds circulated in intricate weblike patterns, prompting contemporaries to see the throng, according to art historian Renzo Dubbini, as "a multiform mass characterized by compactness, fluidity, and dynamism."[135] Doctors described the organic bases of action, desire, and ideas in similar ways. What agents regulated the flow also mirrored the logic of liberal politics.[136] Will, not reason, policed the connections. It did what fell to effective governments in pluralistic societies on the edge of chaos; it coordinated, managed, and adjudicated. As they touted strategies for reinforcing the will, doctors echoed the widespread demands for more vigorous and focused government. Reformers exhorted politicians to bring society together and to give it direction by using suggestion, reinforcing connections, and attaching the social base to the decision-making centers. Medical advice to individuals seeking self-mastery followed similar lines.

Thus, knowledge of the social and the physical bodies proved mutually reinforcing. The functions of one shed light on the functions of the other; the dysfunctions of one explained the weaknesses of the other. The exact correspondences reflected a logic determined to a large degree by conditions in society and in the field of medicine. It stands to reason, then, that changes in society would alter medical understanding of the brain and nervous system and their pathologies. In fact, hysteria, neurasthenia, and larval or psychic epilepsy largely disappeared from the medical lexicon, the symptoms gone or reassigned to other diseases. As to the will, it ceased to be "a fashionable concept" by the end of the First World War, as doctors took their distance from what one commentator called its "unsavory history."[137] Abulia rarely occurred, psychiatrists noted, and then only with schizophrenics.[138] To the extent that they did look at the problems once associated with volition, psychiatrists focused on motivation and on ways of changing addictive behaviors.

Already in the early decades of the twentieth century, debate over the nature of the will figured less prominently in setting the agenda for psychiatry.[139] The move away from the will "as a descriptive and explanatory concept" indicated changes in the science of the mind and in the understanding of the nervous system.[140] Some psychiatrists contended that the idea of the material will made little sense. Others, particularly those influenced by Sigmund Freud, viewed the mind and self in ways that excluded the mediating properties of the will. Social changes also affected definitions of mental health and social adjustment. In the aftermath of the First World War, the equation of personal happiness with work and of joy with self-abnegation lost legitimacy. So did reliance on the will to pull the self together. No longer did medical practitioners and citizens put such confidence in the therapeutic power of self-mastery. Anxious to confront the crisis and flux of the end of the century, Payot had claimed in 1894 that "any feeling, deliberately chosen, can, by the intelligent use of our psychological resources, take control of all of life."[141] Circumstances in the interwar period made that promise an exceedingly audacious one.

4

Neurotics

And, today, neurasthenia has become a very complex neurosis, almost as proto form as hysteria.

Jules Dallemagne[1]

Those [neurasthenics] who are seriously affected… are extra-social; they are outside normal behavior. They are fearful, discouraged, incapable of taking care of themselves; they obey for their whole lives.

Auguste Vial[2]

Epilepsy has acquired an extraordinary quantity of forms and types beyond what anyone imagined before.

Cesare Lombroso[3]

Three illnesses stormed through Europe at the end of the nineteenth century: epilepsy, hysteria, and neurasthenia. Neurasthenia sent hard-driving professionals, leisured women, and striving schoolchildren to their beds to brood over their terrifying and debilitating symptoms. Clinics and hospital wards treated patients, mostly female, who howled, jerked, writhed, and froze in the contorted positions typical of hysteria. Among their patients, doctors saw the traditional symptoms of epilepsy, but they identified other variants including a form that affected the psyche and created a distinctive epileptic temperament characterized by irascibility and impulsiveness. In the view of many doctors and criminologists, this type of epilepsy could explain the actions of lucid killers and of the habitual criminals who filled the prisons.

These diseases took their victims out of the mainstream. Neurasthenia produced devastating apathy in ambitious, vital people and in obedient and hardworking children. Those who exerted themselves to meet society's expectations found themselves paralyzed and overwhelmed by symptoms that seemed to signal their imminent death. Unlike neurasthenia which left people listless but aware, hysteria and epilepsy provoked uncharacteristic episodes of mindless behavior. Victims lost control of their bodies and, in the case of psychic epilepsy, nasty second selves submerged the better sides of their personalities. The medical literature reported cases where epileptics took flight without a reasonable destination, appeared naked in the streets, set things on fire, or gave in to other vile impulses during attacks. They broke social rules, but unlike neurasthenics who wanted to do their duty and could not, they did not know what they were doing.

The apparent increase in these disorders aroused both interest and concern. One commentator observed a "really surprising" expansion of nervous disorders in the last thirty years. The ranks of the ill grew, and the number of recognized variants continued to multiply.[4] It would take "as many pages as there are leaves in a huge forest" to record all the forms of neurasthenia, commented Paolo Mantegazza.[5] The experts were not sure whether greater awareness and improved statistics brought long existing patterns to light, or whether the number of cases actually rose. Neurasthenia appeared along with modern life, some doctors believed, while others argued that it had existed since ancient times but hardly at the current high levels. Nervous diseases got attention from neurologists, psychiatrists, social theorists, and, in the case of epilepsy in particular, from criminal anthropologists and forensic doctors. They published their discoveries, exchanged information at professional meetings, and presented cases in clinical lessons and lectures. Their research on the big three—neurasthenia, epilepsy, and hysteria—found its way into works intended for a popular audience and into collections devoted to social problems. High-profile trials also alerted the public to connections between neuroses and crime.

The work on nervous disorders generated controversy and confusion among experts, just as investigations of mental disease did. The differences between neuroses and madness remained a contentious issue, partly because theories about the nervous system and brain changed so rapidly and partly because emerging medical specialties staked out overlapping realms of expertise. Neurologists, psychiatrists, and physiologists all showed interest and claimed authority, and their use of hyphenated combinations of these specialties indicated disciplinary imperialism as well as a good deal of shared knowledge and collaboration. Depending on their perspective, they emphasized neuroses or psychoses, psycho-neuroses, or neuro-psychoses, as they cataloged symptoms, named diseases, identified causes, and tried out therapies. How they understood the nervous system complicated the task of classifying its dysfunctions. According to theories current at the time, nerves connected the body to the outside world by registering sensory data and transmitting it to the brain and motor system. Nerves also coordinated internal processes as different as thought and digestion so that any nervous disorder resonated widely in the body, just as problems in any part of the body readily affected the nerves. To animate the body's dynamic and interlocking elements, the nerves required steady supplies of energy, and any surges or deficits disrupted their operation. The system's complexity and delicacy made it especially vulnerable to congenital anomalies and to the effects of illnesses, infections, traumas, and excesses, investigators contended.

As it did with mental illness, their exploration of neuroses depended largely on clinical evidence. Typically attached to hospitals with special sections for hysterics and epileptics and active outpatient clinics, and with patients of their own, medical specialists studied these diseases firsthand. Criminologists and forensic doctors encountered neurotics among the prison population and in asylums. They developed theories based on individual profiles, ones they compiled and others that they drew from the literature. The practice of giving public clinical sessions, used with such success by Jean-Martin Charcot (1825–1893) at Salpêtrière, helped standardize diagnostic procedures and added to the collection of widely known cases. However, relying on cases proved particularly problematic when it came to nervous disorders. During epileptic seizures and episodes of hysteria, the patient remembered little to nothing, and when attacks lasted only moments or happened at night, no one witnessed them. Neurasthenics, in contrast, tended to be overly alert to their ailments; in fact, exaggerating symptoms indicated the disease's presence. These factors made it difficult for observers to get a reliable reading on what the patient experienced. What they did observe often fit uneasily into existing diagnostic parameters, tempting investigators to add another subcategory to an already rich array.

Close observation and questioning in addition to tests and measurements and, when possible, autopsies aimed at uncovering what caused the neuroses. Despite their efforts, doctors and psychiatrists found it difficult to assign the symptoms to a specific site or lesion. Lacking that information made detecting the underlying causes problematic. Some doctors drew on the laboratory study of animals to understand the nervous system, or they built on cellular research. While these experiments generated information, they produced little clarity, because the evidence itself commanded different levels of confidence, and its interpretation left plenty of room for contention.

Neurasthenia, hysteria, and epilepsy demanded and received a great deal of attention from medical and social scientists. Neurasthenia, commented George Beard, the American expert on the subject, was "the Central Africa of medicine—an unexplored territory into which few men enter, and those few have been compelled to bring reports that have been neither credited nor comprehended."[6] After the Great War, the trio of psychic epilepsy, neurasthenia, and hysteria virtually disappeared. They passed out of sight in the same way that abulia and moral insanity did, and for similar reasons. Ian Hacking's analysis of transient mental disorders, those that flame intensely then vanish, applies to these diseases. They filled, to use his words, an "ecological niche" defined by specific social and cultural factors, and when the "vectors" changed, the niche fell apart and its contents dispersed.[7] While neurasthenia and psychic epilepsy largely vanished as distinct disorders, elements of them reappeared in combination with other symptoms in frameworks carrying different labels and explanations.

Neurasthenia

The spread of neurasthenia made it "one of the greatest, inescapable problems of our time," declared Italian Diomede Carito in a study of the disease.[8] Its victims, "frighteningly normal in their variety," came from all professions, ages, and social classes, but many experts said that neurasthenia favored adults (twenty to fifty years old) and hit some groups, such as the French, Russians, Americans, Italians, and Jews, and some occupations harder than others.[9] It did not just attack the upper classes, Charcot specified, but workers as well.[10] Many doctors believed it affected men more than women, but some commented that menstruation, pregnancy, and women's greater emotivity made them especially prone to neurasthenia.[11]

Toward the end of the 1880s, neurophysiologists and psychiatrists joined forces to nail down its symptoms, causes, and boundaries. Articles and treatises described the disease and its victims, detailing troubling variants such as sexual and gastric neurasthenia and "railway spine." Neurasthenia also found its way into textbooks on mental illness and into popular medical tracts designed to inform the worried and warn the unwitting. This attention increased the public's awareness of its presence in others or in themselves since fairly common complaints, including listlessness, indigestion, and sexual dysfunction, accompanied it. Neurasthenia became, in the words of commentators, "the disease of the day," or more dramatically, "the malady of the century," or the "disease of our time."[12]

Europeans credited the American doctor George Miller Beard (1839–1883) with alerting them to the existence of neurasthenia. In works first published in 1880 and 1881, Beard described a new illness caused by the competitiveness and intensity of civilized life and characterized by exhaustion of the nervous system. The disease appeared first in America, he argued, "and no age, no country, and no form of civilization, not Greece, nor Rome, nor Spain, nor the Netherlands, in the days of their glory, possessed such maladies."[13] His work attracted attention in the United States and in Europe where other doctors recognized the symptoms that he described. Sometimes referred to as "Beard's disease" or more commonly the "American disease," Europeans insisted it was not unique to the United States. It was, most French and Italian doctors agreed, a disease "as old as the world, or at least as medicine," known by the ancient Greeks as hypochondria or hysteria, some said.[14] Old or new, they believed that the disease was spreading at unprecedented rates in modern society, especially in urban areas. One-fourth of the patients hospitalized at Salpêtrière and a twelfth of its outpatients suffered from neurasthenia, estimated doctors practicing there. These figures surely underestimated the incidence of the disease, they believed, since it favored the upper classes, and they usually received care at home or in private clinics.[15] Moreover, most people diagnosed as nervous, hypochondriacs, or eccentrics actually suffered from neurasthenia, according to Léon Bouveret (1850–1929), a colleague of Alexandre Lacassagne, the prominent French specialist in forensic medicine.[16]

Although it took different forms and shared symptoms with other diseases, neurasthenia was, experts on the matter asserted, a syndrome or an illness with a profile sufficiently distinct and clear to permit diagnosis. Fernand Levillain made the following case: neurasthenia was "a limited clinical type, characterized by special symptoms which are almost always linked and are the same and reasonably specific."[17] Whereas Beard provided a convincing and long list of disparate signs, Jean-Martin Charcot urged simplification, and his proposed set became the standard among medical practitioners. A core group of clinical signs, when present together, indicated the disease, while several others often accompanied them. Neurasthenics felt heaviness in their heads, or a sense of constriction, as if a tight helmet pressed in on them.[18] Similar sensations of pressure or of burning occurred along the spine or in the lower back. They commonly suffered from insomnia, struggling to fall asleep then waking with a start in the middle of the night. Sluggish digestion caused discomfort after eating and in serious cases a loss of appetite. Victims also complained of terrible lassitude. Their muscles refused to work, and they found that the smallest physical tasks exhausted them. They also experienced disturbing mental and emotional problems. Their minds strayed, their memories faltered, and they found themselves quick to anger and prone to bouts of sadness and weeping.[19] In neurasthenia, claimed Levillain, "it is always the same play being performed: the main characters and the central scenes do not ever change, only the secondary roles and stage sets vary in importance and command more or less of our attention."[20]

Among the less common troubles that plagued some victims, the most disturbing and one of the most studied, was male impotence.[21] Sufferers also reported dizziness, motor problems, and circulatory and respiratory disturbances. These patients, summarized Paul Blocq (1860–1896), head of Anatomical-Pathological Research at Salpêtrière, "suffered all over; all their organs could be involved one by one and yet without any physical changes in them."[22] Struck down by a combination of afflictions, the victims took to their beds and imagining the worst, they organized their lives around their condition. Their worries sometimes turned into pathological obsessions, making neurasthenia a frequent precursor of insanity or, as many doctors specified, neurasthenic folly.[23] Their health became a pathological fixation; self-doubt paralyzed them; they lost all willpower; they felt sad. Neurasthenia's effects could lead to drug addiction and suicide and to additional illnesses associated with anxiety or sedentary living. However, no matter how serious this retinue of complaints, neurasthenia itself did not kill patients, doctors insisted.

As with mental illness, treating neurasthenia depended on understanding its etiology. Investigators looked for anatomical anomalies, but autopsies uncovered nothing out of place in the brain, spine, nerves, or the meninges, even at the cellular level. That they could not find any defects did not mean they were not there, some doctors argued.[24] After all, no symptom appeared without there being "some organic change, macroscopic or microscopic" behind it, asserted Italian psychiatrist Egisto De Nigris.[25] An early theory, advanced by Frantz Glénard in France, helped to crystallize doubts about the existence of a neurasthenia-specific lesion or defect. He assigned neurasthenia to a prolapsed intestine. Taking up the idea, the Italian Sante De Sanctis urged doctors to recognize intestinal neurasthenia, but he also argued that "primitive" or "essential" neurasthenia stemmed not from a localized problem but from a condition that affected the whole body.[26] In the first case, wearing a pelvic belt promised relief, but the second required more aggressive and varied treatment. Despite neurasthenics' complaints about gastric distress, doctors, especially in France, came to believe that diagnosing intestinal neurasthenia mistook effects for causes.[27]

The lack of convincing evidence that structural defects produced neurasthenia led doctors to see it as a functional problem as Beard contended and the name itself suggested. The trouble did not seem to involve a flaw, glitch, or breakdown but a general decline in operational effectiveness displayed in a loss of vitality or energy. The characteristic signs, they increasingly believed, suggested a "dynamic lesion."[28] The fact that neurasthenics reported serious symptoms yet continued to move and to think, though in slow motion, and that they suffered but did not die, reinforced the theory that neurasthenia involved a loss of nervous energy. That the nervous system as a whole slowed down also made sense, because so much of the body registered the effects. The arduous pace of modern life and the disease's virulence in urban areas and in the most advanced countries added to the evidence that fatigue caused neurasthenia.

The main blame for flagging energy fell on toxins and overexertion. Constant effort and recourse to coffee, tea, absinthe, wine, tobacco, and brandy produced what Mantegazza described as "a state of electric phosphorescence, that consumes us, that burns us alive, that transforms us into the most delicate and the most sensitive of galvanometers."[29] Doctors pointed to a "shocking turbine" driving people to improve their lot in life, and social commentators agreed with that analysis.[30] Mantegazza blamed the principle of equality, because it fed ambition and greed, enticing people to overreach to get ahead.[31] Leonardo Bianchi added to the chorus: "certainly the mental efforts, the worries, the anxieties, the multiplicity of objects, the steamroller of activity that expanding needs require, the unlimited desires … explain not a small number of neurasthenics, especially when one is predisposed to it."[32] To succeed in an ever more complex world required doing, getting, knowing, and feeling more, and the incessant reach for something else overloaded the nervous system. Adults triggered neurasthenia by overworking their brains or by trying to sate their insistent and bottomless desires, just as schoolchildren easily succumbed to "scholastic neurasthenia." "All these precocious Pico della Mirandolas rapidly sink below the horizon if death does not strike them down first," warned Carito.[33]

Modern-day citizens worked and played too hard or worried too much, and, noted several doctors, most of them displayed some signs of neurasthenia. Albert Mathieu (1855–1917), professor at the Faculty of Medicine in Paris, insisted, "There is no one, among those who are engaged in mental work who has not at certain moments experienced some transitory neurasthenic phenomenon…". The same thing happened to people who spent the evening "drinking and smoking," he asserted. "The next morning, there's a general achiness, headache, lack of appetite; work is impossible or at least very difficult."[34] Lamented Mathieu in 1892, "We overexert ourselves to create a profession…. We overexert ourselves to make a name for ourselves, to eclipse our rivals. We overexert ourselves on the pretext of enjoying ourselves or relaxing."[35]

Even in the absence of such frenetic activity, the rapid pace imposed by wrist watches, streetcars, trains, and the telegraph sapped the nervous system's reserves, observers insisted. So did the barrage of stimuli typical of modern life. An unprecedented clash of extremes assaulted the more refined sensibilities of the civilized mind. "Excessive wealth coexists with boundless poverty; sweet relaxation with brutal work; crass and primitive ignorance, with supreme culture."[36] Such contrasts along with unrelenting demands, observed De Nigris in his handbook on the disorder, "create in man … a continual tension in the nervous system, incessant doubts about the future, a state in other words, in which the nerves gradually lose their energy, creating in this way a condition more favorable to the development of neurasthenia."[37] Without fresh energy supplies, the nervous system gradually wound down and eventually collapsed.

Some people managed the daily pressures and constant stimulation but succumbed to sudden, intense assaults on their nerves. A surge of activity or emotion too strong for the established nerve connections to handle, as Beard explained it, forced the nervous system to forge new paths. That effort could lead to nervous collapse. As a clinical example, Léon Bouveret described a young woman whose husband died two months after their marriage. She fell into a state of "profound prostration with headaches, tenacious insomnia, nervous stomach, constipation, weakness in her lower limbs" and after six years still showed no signs of improvement.[38] Carito presented another case. A young woman whose mother married her fiancé ended up in a clinic, possessed by visions and wasting away from lack of sleep. He diagnosed neurasthenia.[39] Infectious diseases, especially the flu and syphilis, childhood illnesses, or child birth and nursing could also overtax the nerves and bring on attacks of neurasthenia.[40] A number of experts noted that sexual abuses, in particular excessive or prolonged masturbation, that "scourge of humanity," could produce similar results.[41]

Medical practitioners also began to connect neurasthenia to trauma despite some initial discomfort with that formula. Falling out of a window, being caned, or getting stepped on by a horse could provoke an emotional reaction strong enough to bring on neurasthenia, they reported.[42] More than these random incidents, railway accidents drew attention to what looked like traumatic neurasthenia. A medical examiner at the Paris Faculty of Medicine, Charles-Albert Vibert (1854?–1918), described a case in 1888, one other doctors included in their studies. It involved Monsieur D..., age 45, an herbalist by trade. A "skillful and intelligent businessman ... affectionate and devoted to his wife and daughters," he enjoyed excellent health. He had no bad habits, did not drink, and displayed no evidence of hereditary problems according to the medical report. That comfortable normality changed on September 5, 1881. M. D.... was in the fourth car from the end of a train stopped at the Charenton station when an express train rammed into it at full speed. He felt a violent jolt but suffered only a few bruises. M. D.... helped other victims and then took the tram home. Shortly after, his behavior changed and he began to experience serious and debilitating physical problems. They worsened, causing the examining physician to conclude "that the physical and mental decline of Monsieur D... has reached such a point that it is no longer possible to hope for improvement."[43] Just the day before the doctor completed his report, M. D. ..., apparently overwhelmed by his condition, poisoned himself, but impatient with its slow effects, he "seized a knife and after stabbing himself seven times in the chest, died instantly."[44]

It made sense that physical injuries resulting from accidents might, like infectious diseases, overtax the nerves and provoke nervous collapse. But M. D.... and others walked away from the accidents unharmed only to exhibit symptoms days, weeks, and even months after. Vibert examined eighty-six victims of the Charenton collision in the eight to ten days following it. Most of them complained of nightmares and headaches; they trembled and felt tremendous anxiety, but symptoms such as these usually disappeared in a few weeks, he observed.[45] Other victims of the accident returned to work immediately as if nothing had happened, and after a period of time began to experience increasingly disturbing physical and mental difficulties. Writing five years later, Albert Blum (1844–1914), doctor at Saint-Antoine hospital in Paris, specified that this group felt "violent pains in the bruised areas, in the head, in the spine, couldn't sleep, moved with difficulty.... The patients become taciturn and they want to be alone. They can't ... leave their bed or their chair, they are obsessed with dark thoughts which can even include suicide. An indifference to everything around them … takes over."[46] That people in good health who suffered no obvious physical injury in the accident nonetheless developed such devastating symptoms intrigued doctors.

They also got interested because accident victims increasingly invoked railway brain or spine in damage claims against the railway companies. Medical testimony for both plaintiffs and the defense revolved around the nature of a disease whose delayed effects struck healthy people with no serious injuries. When tests failed to uncover problems, it made diagnosis more difficult especially because fakery promised lucrative awards. "It must be abundantly obvious," a British expert on the subject noted, "how largely the reality of many of the symptoms, lacking all vestige of objective sign, depends upon the veracity and good faith of the patients themselves."[47] Some doctors doubted their good faith. "G," Albert Blum reported, received damages of 10,000 francs plus annual payments of 2,500 francs. As a result of this "metallic therapy, his paralysis, visual problems, memory loss, and brain softening disappeared as if by magic."[48] Improvement was to be expected after settlements, argued others, because worry over the damage suit exacerbated the symptoms. Doctors also observed that neurasthenia produced a tendency to exaggerate, so that the stories that seemed fabricated actually confirmed the presence of the condition. Attentive medical examination, they asserted, would unmask the malingerers.

Early evaluations of railway brain tried to localize the source. It must derive, experts argued, from real though undetectable damage. Vibert, for one, attributed the complaints of the eighty-six victims he studied to the physical effects of the accident. An abrupt motion—too slight to cause a bruise or lesion—still produced a shock sufficient to provoke the headaches, insomnia, memory loss, and character changes that he observed in these patients. He also suggested that the powerful emotions provoked by the accident could cause the physical and mental troubles.[49] But in most cases, he concluded, the jolt produced an inflammation that then triggered a gradually developing sequence of serious physical and psychological problems. Vibert noted that the symptoms presented by the victims looked strikingly similar to those described by John Eric Erichsen, in his study of the effects of accidents published in 1866. Erichsen argued that although the impact did not produce a rupture or fracture, it did resonate through the spinal membrane. The disturbance caused an infection which, in turn, affected the nervous system and "doomed the sufferer to a life of pain, misery, and uselessness."[50]

Others doubted that the delayed symptoms resulted from localized shocks to either the brain or the spine. In 1883, Herbert W. Page, doctor for the London and North Western Railway Company, dismissed the idea of spinal concussion, arguing that the spinal column protected the cord from vibrations. The slight physical damage to the spine evident in autopsies usually resulted from general muscle and ligament strain, he argued. To account for the late appearance of incapacitating ailments in uninjured accident victims, doctors needed to look elsewhere than damage to the brain or spine. Page thought they resulted from "general nervous shock," an effect distinct from the emotional collapse that often immediately followed the accident. Instead, fear and emotional backlash could trigger an aggravated and prolonged disturbance of the nervous system characterized by insomnia, vascular-motor troubles, headache, nervousness, trembling, despair, excessive sweating, visual problems, and the inability to concentrate.[51]

By 1889, remarked Salpêtrière intern Adolphe Dutil, everyone understood railway brain as a functional disorder that affected the nervous system, not just the spine or the brain. German doctors identified it as a separate illness which they called traumatic neurosis, but Italian and French doctors noted the similarities with neurasthenia and classified it as a form of that disease.[52] Or they accepted Jean-Martin Charcot's argument that neurasthenia preceded hysteria, in a condition he called *hystéro-neurasthénie.* Some argued that the two conditions occurred simultaneously in accident victims.[53] Whatever the niche or name, the shock to the nerves caused by the sharp emotion provoked by an accident produced the telltale signs of nervous exhaustion. "Railway brain" or "railway spine" became "railway neurasthenia."

The trauma of a collision or a fall, a sudden surge of emotion, the burden of an illness or an infection, and the cumulative effects of hard work could vitiate the nervous system and launch the collection of symptoms identified with neurasthenia, experts concluded. Unlike mental illness and other neuroses, neurasthenia appeared, then, to result from social conditions or as a secondary effect of an illness or accident. This conclusion did not, however, satisfy investigators for the same reasons that they found social explanations of insanity, crime, or vagrancy wanting. Stress and overstimulation, accidents and illnesses did not affect everyone in the same way, and that pattern demanded explanation. Either the pressures and shocks were not really as serious, or something protected some people and exposed others. Beard attributed the differences to variations in personal allotments of nervous energy and in the demands on it. Those key variables depended primarily on good fortune, in his view. According to most Italian and French doctors, not luck but heredity explained the susceptibility of some and the resistance of others.

They identified two distinct types of neurasthenia. There was, insisted Georges Gilles de la Tourette (1857–1904), professor of the Faculty of Medicine in Paris and doctor at the Saint Antoine Hospital, "truc" neurasthenia and a "radically different" look-alike.[54] In the first, circumstances played the primary role, and in the second, heredity dominated. Treatment worked in the first; in the second, it did not. Just as they emphasized the difference between occasional and inborn criminality, vagrancy, and sexual perversions, so they drew an etiological line between two strains of neurasthenia. The French labeled the occasional variant "true" or "simple neurasthenia," and the second "hereditary" or "organic." Italians accepted those terms but also referred to "little" and "big," to capture the difference in gravity.

As happened with bouts of mental disease, healthy people unexpectedly got neurasthenia. In the railway accident cases he reviewed, Albert Blum reported that "I rarely noted the existence of personal or hereditary antecedents."[55] Overwork or overstimulation could also bring on neurasthenia in normal people. Invoking "multiple observations made on infinite cases," Carito concluded that alone among all known neuroses, this one could "develop all of a sudden, accidentally."[56] And Levillain explained that "individuals born absolutely healthy, with no evident nervous defects, can become neurasthenics by accident as a result of nervous overexertion or from other causes."[57] This was certainly the case when people pushed themselves too hard and temporarily experienced headaches, indigestion, and lassitude. The effects passed, but if the situation recurred, they invited more serious bouts of neurasthenia.

Other investigators proved considerably more cautious about entirely accidental or occasional neurasthenia. If external conditions sufficed to cause it, anyone might develop neurasthenia. To give so much room to contingency made no sense to them, especially since people reacted to overwork and accidents so differently. Those who succumbed must inherit an undetected, dormant weakness brought to the fore by trauma, emotional strain, illness, or exertion. Even those who believed that circumstances alone could cause nervous collapse admitted that hereditary factors might hasten or exacerbate it.[58] But they agreed with Beard that if heredity played any role, it acted only in conjunction with the negative effects of modern civilization.

The "radically different" type of neurasthenia resulted directly from heredity. Influenced by Charcot, French doctors tended to insist on the organic or the hereditary forms. They took root in a congenitally unhealthy nervous system whose neuropathic elements appeared early or remained latent until exacerbated by circumstances. A number of doctors argued that neurasthenia belonged to the group of degenerative diseases, keeping company with epilepsy, hysteria, hypochondria, insanity, and idiocy. "The neurasthenic can be the son of a diabetic, or an eccentric, or an imbalanced or an insane person, to give some concrete examples," explained Albert Mathieu.[59] Charles Féré, in his often-quoted study on the neuropathic family, confirmed the pattern and expanded the list, observing that special connections linked neurasthenia to arthritis, gout, obesity, and diabetes.[60] That neurasthenia did not appear to pass from parents to children but cropped up in families showed the effects of transformative heredity. That is, neurasthenics received and transmitted a degenerative disorder but not the same one.

Symptoms of occasional and organic neurasthenia looked a lot alike, and doctors made an effort to distinguish between the two.[61] "True" or occasional neurasthenia appeared suddenly and for clear reasons, and it primarily affected the mind, specified Fernand Veuillot in his thesis on neurasthenic disorders.[62] With proper treatment, the patient improved and for sustained periods of time. In hereditary neurasthenia, in contrast, the symptoms took a much more severe form, causing victims to "lead a miserable existence, always suffering, always obsessed with their disease," Gilles de la Tourette explained.[63] This type led to more numerous and more serious mental troubles and did not respond to treatment, lasting "as long as the patients themselves did."[64]

Whether inherited or acquired, neurasthenia could pass to the next generation. As Mathieu put it, it could be the "daughter," the offspring of neuropathic relatives, or it served as the "mother" in the degenerative family. "The son of a neurasthenic can be an eccentric, a hothead, suffer from gout, from epilepsy, from migraines, and be a neurasthenic."[65] Extending the image, Levillain observed that neurasthenia was "the true mother of the whole neuropathic family!"[66] Féré also argued that neurasthenia gave other pathologies their chance. Summarizing the bleak views advanced by others, Auguste Vial claimed that neurasthenia was the "well spring of all degenerative states."[67]

If neurasthenia provided a, and even *the*, breeding ground for other degenerative disorders, then it not only ruined the lives of individuals and their families but also threatened to compromise the health and effectiveness of future generations. Some doctors applied Morel's dynamic of escalating gravity to neurasthenia as well. "A generation of creatures suffering headaches or migraines, leads to another, including hysterics and epileptics, and finally you arrive at idiocy, at madness." A couple made neurotic by modern life "can easily become the founders of a neuropathic family."[68] The more apocalyptic among the authorities urged their colleagues to counsel neurasthenics to avoid marriage or refrain from having children. Marrying, pronounced Émile Laurent, is "a bad action, almost a crime; to a young woman who brings him [the neurasthenic] her youth and her beauty, he only offers an inert soul in a ravaged body."[69]

Those whose family histories made them vulnerable might stave off the worst by protecting their health and husbanding their energies. But in true or classic neurasthenia, heredity played no part or took the backseat to the pressures of modern life, making everyone vulnerable. In order to function, normal people risked railway and streetcar accidents, falls, and infections, but in other areas, they could take preventive measures. They could moderate their ambitions, pace themselves better, reduce their use of stimulants, and avoid sexual excesses. Parents and lawmakers could protect children by limiting homework and by letting more light and air into the classroom. Doctors' manuals directed at the public also urged vigilant monitoring of young males, because masturbation could bring on neurasthenia.[70]

Because of its varied symptoms and its elusive causes, neurasthenia proved difficult to classify. Early descriptions of the disease assigned the problem to a specific site such as the stomach, the genitals, or the spine; in later versions, the disease originated in the nervous system and affected the entire body. Because of its reach, its symptoms overlapped with those of other diseases, raising questions about its limits. It mimicked several serious organic illnesses, including general paralysis and anemia, but unlike them neurasthenia did not result from perceptible damage or defects. All the pieces were in place; they just functioned poorly. Neurasthenia should not be confused with insanity either, they argued. While it could lead to madness, and particularly to obsessive disorders, it did not originate in the mind. By the current understanding of the term, neurasthenia qualified as a neurosis. It involved the nervous system but "without any known anatomical lesion," taking the form of "a kind of pathological fatigue," Levillain clarified.[71]

Doctors specified, however, that it not be confused with other neuroses such as hysteria, hypochondria, or epilepsy. At the same time, they recognized its affinity with these conditions, and their ready use of hyphens maintained distinctions while calling attention to connections. The Salpêtrière school, in particular, clarified the relationship between neurasthenia and hysteria.[72] Using his public lessons to address the diagnostic nuances, in 1887 Charcot introduced a patient who complained that he experienced something pressing in on his head, a feeling of dizziness, a prickling sensation, lower back pain, and minor indigestion. Charcot noted that his mental faculties were intact but slowing down, which explained why any mental effort increased his headaches. He concluded that the patient suffered from "accidental neurasthenia" brought on by his lifestyle. The same thing could happen to anyone with important duties and, referring to Beard's initial study, he noted that it occurred frequently in the United States where people worked all the time at full throttle. Reassuring the patient that he did not have a serious illness, he recommended that he ask for a leave and continue to take potassium bromide and cold showers directed at his lower limbs.[73]

Another lesson that year featured a brakeman whose symptoms indicated both neurasthenia and hysteria. His job, Charcot observed, demanded continual alertness and carried great responsibility, a key factor in his nervous troubles. Sexual problems, pressure headaches, indigestion, dizziness, and his fear of being left alone all indicated neurasthenia; a sensation of weakness in his limbs, blurred vision, and small convulsions pointed to hysteria. Neurasthenia was not uncommon among railway workers, Charcot told the audience, and this case showed that hysteria and neurasthenia existed together, probably the result of the same underlying condition. When trauma induced the problem, Charcot reported that neurasthenia appeared first, and then hysteria, in a condition that he called *hystéro-neurasthénie*. The case of 42-year-old Claw…Louis supported that diagnosis. He worked for the Compagnie International des Wagons-lits and enjoyed good health until his train derailed and was hit by an express train at full speed. He lost consciousness briefly, then finding he had minor bruises and scratches, he helped the injured, and then returned to Paris. Hours after the accident and for several days he trembled and slept badly, and then began to lose his appetite and have headaches and lower back pain. He returned to work, but the symptoms worsened, and he became forgetful, worried, and morose. Two months after the accident, he lost consciousness, fell to the floor, writhing, trembling, and crying out. The same thing happened again and again, and he entered Salpêtrière about a year after the accident. Initially he showed the signs of Beard's disease, but the sensory-motor attacks indicated the onset of hysteria.[74] Based on this and other cases, trauma's role in unleashing this special combination became widely accepted.

Hysteria also occurred by itself, and Charcot credited his clinic with clarifying that it affected males as well as females. Poverty, unhealthy occupations, alcoholism, shock, and hereditary weakness encouraged its development. Bar…, a 24-year-old male, repaired casks and barrels, a profession that encouraged drinking. By age nineteen, he averaged 5–6 liters of wine a day with four glasses of brandy in between. When he was twenty, a huge pile of barrels crashed down on him. Fellow workers pulled him out, trembling all over but with no injuries or bruises. After a few hours, he returned to work, but he continued to sleep badly and have nightmares. After two months, he experienced his first "hystero-epileptic" attack, and when he joined the army four months later, a fall provoked facial paralysis. Charcot concluded that the earlier accident left him in "an indescribable nervous state." But he also surmised that alcohol played a role since the serious attacks stopped in the army and returned when he left it and resumed drinking. While trauma and alcohol precipitated the hysteria, at bottom Bar… suffered from weaknesses passed to him by his parents, both of them high strung, irascible, and given to drink, Charcot concluded.[75]

In Bar...'s case, the presence of seizures, without the tongue-biting typical of epileptics, and of paralysis pointed to full-fledged hysteria provoked by a trauma so terrifying that he could not talk about it even four years after the event. Had his nerves been stronger from the start, he would have escaped the psychic and nervous aftermath of the accident, despite his drinking, in Charcot's view. The symptoms associated with neurasthenia, in contrast, involved a set of complaints including upset stomach, headaches, listlessness, sexual dysfunction, and insomnia. Because hysteria and neurasthenia both involved the nerves and both responded to energy-sapping trauma and illnesses, they shared common ground. Especially in cases of trauma, they occurred at the same time, as in the brakeman's case, or sequentially, as they did in *hystéro-neurasthénie*. When heredity produced either complaint, one or the other might appear as part of the degenerative package of inherited disorders.

A deficit, not a defect, affecting the nerves, not the brain, produced a distinctive neurosis. Lacking sufficient energy to operate, the nervous system wound down, causing multiple mundane symptoms that debilitated and frightened the victims. The prognosis necessarily depended on the variant. Hereditary neurasthenia resisted treatment, because of the inherent weakness of the nervous system and the greater severity of the symptoms. In the absence of a cure, doctors could only try to make the patient's life less difficult, Clodomiro Bonfigli advised.[76] Accidental or "true" neurasthenia offered greater hope, particularly when overexertion or another illness brought on the disease. Rest and a change of scene sometimes sufficed, but doctors also recommended mild exercise, a moderate diet, hydrotherapy, little or no alcohol and tobacco, sexual restraint, and certain tonics and medications. Émile Laurent specified a maximum of half a liter of light wine a day and at most sex once a week.[77] He and other self-appointed experts touted a variety of other medicines and tonics to revive energy and manage the symptoms. While clearly a scourge at the time, some experts felt optimistic about eliminating neurasthenia in the future. Beard predicted that it would disappear as Americans adjusted physiologically to the demands of modern life. Paolo Mantegazza echoed that view, arguing that the effort it took "to open the door to the promised land" produced neurasthenia. Just as naturally as it came, it would go, since the brain would gain the resilience required to manage modernity.[78] According to another perspective, the elements of the civilized body most vulnerable to fatigue would become more robust as time entrenched them. Thanks to adaptation, subsequent generations would better resist the assault of hard work and intense stimulation on their nerves.

Combining disparate symptoms to construct a disorder shows a particular logic at work. To begin with, the idea of neurasthenia corresponded to how scientists understood the body. Assigning numb feet, lassitude, temporary paralysis, and indigestion, among other signs, to the nervous system confirmed the importance assigned it at the time. Their idea that overworking the brain affected the nerves and that nervous fatigue produced morbid fears and memory loss indicates that they saw the brain and nerves as interdependent. As scientists learned more about the nervous system, they imagined a complex network of nerves, ganglia, and neurons absorbing and transmitting sensations throughout the body. Carito, for example, explained that the sympathetic nerve, composed of ganglia linked by nerve filaments, ran down the sides and the front of the spinal column and linked to ganglia in the chest, abdomen, and intestines. According to this design, nerves reached out to all the organs, creating a single unit based on multiple connected parts.[79] The nerves also opened the body to the outside world, registering sensations and transmitting them to the brain and other organs. De Nigris added that "all the activities, all the functions are in direct relationship with the nervous centers, which support and animate them; once their energy is spent or about to be, all acts, like thought, memory, feeling, movement, the circulation of the blood, digestion, etc. will register the consequences."[80]

To power its continual movement and exchange, the network of nerves needed energy. According to scientific thinking, everyone received a quotient of energy or vital force at birth, an amount that varied according to the fortunes of heredity and gestation. Judging by their warnings against too much work or pleasure, the normal stock of energy just sufficed to support a well-modulated lifestyle. Excess demands drained the supply as did harsh living conditions, illness, emotional shock, and trauma. In normal people, eliminating the source of strain as well as rest and restorative tonics brought the system back in balance, but those who suffered from congenital deficiencies or permanent energy loss could not expect such positive results. The theory that the nervous system evolved also led doctors to neurasthenia. They reasoned that the brain and nervous system adapted to conditions but not fast enough to manage rapid and intense change. The very elements that separated civilized men and savages made matters worse, they believed. The highly evolved senses and intellect absorbed too many stimuli, causing the nervous system to founder under the load. Compounding the problem, the principle "late to come, first to go," meant that the most intricate nerve connections, those linked to willpower and moral feeling, faltered first.

Their assessment of civilized society also made neurasthenia possible as a disease and an idea. Neurasthenia developed, all the experts agreed, in direct response to specific aspects of modern life, mainly, Beard said, "steam power, the periodical press, the telegraph, the sciences, and the mental activity of women."[81] These features accelerated life's pace and invaded even traditional sources of refuge, such as the home. Add to these pressures the confusion of elections and changing governments and the ambitions unleashed by principles of equality, and the most touted achievements of civilization appeared to exact a physical price. The seamier sides of modern life also widened the niche occupied by neurasthenia as cities encouraged the insatiable search for pleasure and the mindless surrender to forbidden delights. Uncurbed masturbation, evidently rampant among civilized youth, taxed the body, and it made sense to experts that the body retaliated with sexual and general neurasthenia.

The more actively people tried to meet society's expectations, the greater the likelihood of becoming neurasthenic, according to studies. Thus schools ruined the health of earnest children; inspired writers suddenly encountered blocks provoked by their traitorous nerves; fine-featured women who found brightly colored clothing unbearably stimulating chose pastels or suffered the consequences. Civilized life bore down on the evolved body, taking out those given to nasty excesses but mostly affecting citizens who followed the rules and who excelled at what society favored. This response to modernity indicates ambivalence about rapid change and discomfort with the sorts of lives they understood it to permit, if not to require.

Looking at modern life in this way associated common complaints with a pathology and laid out the drastic results of crossing certain lines. It seemed clear that ordinary citizens, especially in the cities, occasionally found it hard to eat, sleep, love, think, or work. Attributing their problems to the pace of their lives made sense to the medical community and to social observers. In a study written for a series on medical sociology in 1905, Dr. Lucien Angelvin reminded his readers that normal people with normal parents could experience a touch of arthritis or an occasional migraine, "and who does not?" They might eat poorly, have digestive troubles, and feel out of sorts and down on things. When that happened they had a bit of neurasthenia, nothing to worry about, he said. But, he cautioned, if they got too excited or too disturbed, if they overdid pleasure, or worked too hard, then serious neurasthenia could result. He told them, on the one hand, to expect some aches, pains, and moodiness, and on the other, he gave them strong reasons to avoid self-indulgence, to practice moderation, and to seek balance in their lives.[82]

Insisting on the difference between light and heavy variants, or situational and innate neurasthenia, followed the established approach to abnormalities. A biological barrier, it seemed, separated temporary neurasthenics from hopeless cases just as it did talent from genius, occasional from congenital criminals, and men looking for work from drifters. Experts understood that people under duress broke the law or left home to look for work while inveterate criminals and vagabonds responded to organic codes that deprived them of a moral compass and set them adrift. From this perspective, good health and solid parentage put ordinary people on the safe side and moderate habits kept them there. However, the logic that drew the dividing line in the first place also made it both flexible and permeable. To many experts, it looked as if circumstances led to occasional criminality and vagrancy only when they triggered latent tendencies. Similarly, some observers challenged the idea that external conditions alone could cause neurasthenia. Even when something as random as a railway accident provoked the problems, heredity crept in as a necessary though not sufficient cause.

Investigators applied the same reasoning to other types of abnormality that they did to neurasthenia. They used a similar analytical approach, but substantive connections also bound neurasthenics to other sorts of misfits. Especially for researchers who added neurasthenia to the group of degenerative disorders, it came from the same matrix and transmitted within families along with the others. Neurasthenia also directly caused other abnormalities, particularly those involving weak will and low energy. Doctors invoked neurasthenia to explain impotence, and they saw it at work in obsessions such as hypochondria and paranoia. It also explained a common variant of fugue identified by Charcot and others.

The case of Klein, presented by Charcot in February 1889, became a standard example of neurasthenia's tie to habitual vagrancy. The 23-year-old Hungarian Jew arrived at Salpêtrière "tattered, dirty, pale, thin, falling from fatigue, and confused."[83] Klein was, Charcot began, a veritable descendent of Ahasvérus or Cartaphilus, the two legendary Wandering Jews. Pushed by the irresistible need to move, always looking to make his fortune, Klein stopped when he found work as a tailor, and then moved on. He belonged to the category of neurotic travelers, a group that included hysterics and neurasthenics but not epileptic-like ambulatory automats. On his way from Brussels to Paris, Klein fell asleep in a heavy rainstorm and woke up with sharp pains and an uncomfortable sensation of numbness on his right side. His arm was twisted and the hand cramped closed at an angle, a posture associated with hysteria. He showed no signs of physiological problems or any disturbance of his vision or hearing, but he had no taste on the right side of his tongue, a symptom fairly common in male hysterics. Charcot diagnosed hysteric-traumatic paralysis provoked by sleeping on the wet ground. That trauma, he hypothesized, caused a psychological reaction which triggered the contraction of limbs on the right side. Because Klein was Jewish, he was predisposed to hysterical neurosis, an observation Charcot felt no need to explain. He added that Klein's impulsive wandering and his plans to set off again after his release confirmed his neurosis.[84] Others built on these cases and on their own experience to recognize neurasthenic fugue. These fugueurs felt an irrepressible urge to travel, and they did so fully aware of their actions from the beginning to the end of their wanderings.

In the cases of fugue, paranoia, melancholy, and impotence, neurasthenia caused the problems, but the cause-effect pattern worked in reverse as well. Other abnormal behaviors, especially excessive or unnatural sex, fostered neurasthenia.[85] Experts saw these habits quite literally as draining energy from the body. The same effects held for hardworking intellectuals and especially for geniuses. According to some authorities, geniuses operated with abnormal nervous systems in the first place, and the effort required for creativity exposed them to neurasthenic collapse.

Epilepsy

Epilepsy seized attention in the last decades of the nineteenth century as much for its social repercussions as for its medical interest. It appeared in unlikely places: the creative spark of genius, the mental voids of imbeciles, the identikits of outrageous killers, the psychic baggage of the tramp, and the imbalance of the insane. Jules Voisin (1844–1920), doctor at Salpêtrière, urged his colleagues to check for epilepsy if they encountered "any unusual nervous or psychic condition" in their patients.[86] Doctors appointed by courts to report on the capacity of accused criminals to stand trial routinely looked for and frequently found epilepsy. When they inspected prisoner populations, forensic doctors and criminologists also discovered that an unusual number of inmates exhibited epileptic symptoms. Although temperamental children, contentious adolescents, and curmudgeonly adults stayed on the right side of the law, their toxic behavior also aroused suspicions of epilepsy. In fact, even in the absence of any of the classical physical symptoms, traits such as selfishness and impulsiveness suggested the psychic variant.

Unlike neurasthenia, no expert proclaimed the novelty of epilepsy, a disease described since ancient times. Public hospitals treated epileptics in separate wards or along with the insane, and doctors also received them as outpatients. In France, the law of 1838 admitted epileptics into the asylum system and brought them under the scrutiny of alienists. These patients then became objects of study for doctors committed to the increasingly popular clinical approach to medical knowledge. Doctors brought to this work more refined and standardized clinical procedures as well as new data on the nervous system and brain. And because they believed that epilepsy involved the motor, sensory, and psychic systems, a range of medical specialists made it their territory. Its social repercussions brought criminologists and social scientists into the study of epileptics as well. As a result of the scrutiny, epilepsy grew in range and complexity, and it became a standard suspect in many categories of abnormal behavior recognized at the time.

As with neurasthenia and hysteria and with mental illnesses, the greater sophistication of clinical methods and the new information about the body complicated more than it clarified. The more neurologists and psychiatrists learned, the more they extended the limits of the disease to reflect patterns that they observed in their patients. They had significant help in this enterprise from criminologists and sociologists who enlarged the array of symptoms, added parts of the body involved, and extended the likely causes, creating a massive disease and a debate to match. "A protean psycho pathology," Salvatore Ottolenghi, doctor and student of Lombroso, observed, one with ever-expanding and enormous boundaries.[87] As happened with other mental and nervous illnesses, the profusion of examples invited the creation of subcategories for different combinations of symptoms and causes. These classifications, in turn, provoked debate, because until they agreed on what belonged where, experts lacked the basis for diagnosis and treatment.

Consensus came hard. Investigators spoke of different forms of a single disease or used epilepsy in the plural, or argued that the types added up to a syndrome or syndromes rather than a sickness.[88] They also debated which groups of symptoms indicated epilepsy and which a different epileptic-like disease. In an often-cited study of epilepsies, Charles Féré (1852–1907) addressed the types as well as the look-alikes or what he and others called epileptic equivalents. He accepted the existence of four major variants based on the area of the body affected. Epilepsy, in its classic and pared down form, affected the motor system. To that variety Féré and others added sensory, visceral, and psychic types of epilepsy. "Larval" or "latent epilepsy," terms commonly used but not always in the same way, indicated one type, usually the psychic; the presence of one or two variants indicated incomplete epilepsy; all four in the same patient, complete epilepsy. In any of these forms, the symptoms commonly varied in extent and intensity, so that when seizures occurred on one side of the body and not the other, for example, the doctors recognized Jacksonian epilepsy.

Despite the extensive range of possible symptoms, even in the same patient, doctors identified certain basic signs: a sudden attack, loss of consciousness, and no memory of the episode. Physical and psychic disturbances generated an aura which announced the onset of a seizure.[89] The characteristics of the aura and the shape, duration, and frequency of the attacks varied considerably according to the individual, but in almost all cases they appeared unaware during the attack and exhibited amnesia after it. When the seizure subsided, patients usually felt drained, and they could experience tremors and paralysis, sensory disturbances, or forgetfulness. In some cases, obsessions and hallucinations followed the attack, at times so intense and terrifying that they drove victims to murder, arson, or suicide. In these cases, the residues of nervous energy provoked "impulses of extraordinary violence; or an attack of mania which lasts several days," reported Féré.[90] An irresistible impulse might prompt victims to take off, and on these occasions, too, they could give in to homicidal drives. When they returned to themselves, as with the seizures, the victims usually did not remember where they'd been and what they had done or felt.

Within this general rubric, the four variants displayed different patterns, investigators observed. In motor epilepsy, troubles such as indigestion, melancholy, tics, disturbed sleep, and flashbacks inaugurated the process. The seizure itself took hold quickly; the muscles stiffened then jerked spasmodically and finally relaxed as the patient awoke with a sense of profound lassitude and no recollection of the event. Sometimes the seizures affected a single limb or one side of the body; sometimes they progressively moved from one part to another. In visceral epilepsy, similar spasms might grip the lungs or heart, causing an asthma attack or racing pulse, Féré explained.[91] Sensory epilepsy produced sudden buzzing or roaring noises, bright flashes, and migraine headaches.

Epilepsy settled in the psyche more often than in the limbs, organs, or the senses, medical practitioners contended. Féré detailed the effects. Sometimes the person got dizzy, blacked out, woke up, then proceeded as if nothing had happened. Or epilepsy produced a trancelike state. Victims froze, turned pale, appeared disconnected even though they retained some measure of awareness and memory. A third and more disturbing type took the form of odd or violent impulses which drove the person to undress, steal, strike people, even to kill. They might run off in the course of the attack, but they knew where they were going, organized their escape, and responded to people reasonably along the way. But when the attack ended and they came to, they could not remember where they had been or why they had left. In these cases, attacks directly affected parts of the brain in addition to or instead of the senses, muscles, or organs.

Epilepsy's many varieties and symptoms tempted investigators to see it everywhere, and yet the ubiquity of its signs made it an oddly elusive disease. Similar symptoms accompanied other diseases, most strikingly hysteria, and those considered most typical of epilepsy did not all occur or occur always in certified epileptics. The absence of the standard symptoms—seizures, loss of consciousness, and amnesia—did not disqualify the complaint as epilepsy. But the appearance of the signs often associated with epilepsy did not guarantee its presence either. Thus by no means all outbursts of violence, racing pulse, tremor, or trance came from epilepsy. Even motor epilepsy, a condition with relatively clear signs, sometimes eluded doctors, because the seizures came abruptly, sporadically, and often at night and because of the patient's amnesia. Just as with neurasthenia, the possibility that patients might imagine or feign the symptoms increased the importance of reliable diagnostic techniques. To that end, doctors and psychiatrists looked for other predictors of the disease in the body and in the conditions that seemed to promote the disease.

Students of epilepsy constructed, in effect, an epileptic type based on a set of biological and social indicators, just as they did with neurasthenia and hysteria.

The profile helped doctors narrow their diagnostic sights and enabled them to turn possible into likely epilepsy with greater confidence. It also served to single out people with no evident signs of the disease and label them "epileptic-prone" on the basis of their medical records and their family histories. Forewarned, the vulnerable, and there were many, could avoid situations and behaviors that might precipitate seizures. Because of their potential for dangerous behavior, identifying possible epileptics could also be socially useful, investigators thought. As one component of the diagnostic profile, doctors looked for physical irregularities that might indicate epilepsy. Lombroso, for example, thought that epileptics were taller and better developed than average. But Féré argued that Lombroso's own statistics did not support his claims about stature. Féré did note that epileptics very frequently had abnormally large fingers, irregular skulls and faces, and genital anomalies.[92] Testing muscular strength and flexibility and the acuity of the senses also revealed telling abnormalities.

Although supported by tests and numbers, telltale anatomical and functional signs seemed less conclusive than the far more impressionistic descriptions of an "epileptic temperament." Most doctors and criminologists endorsed the idea that epileptics behaved in recognizably aberrant or eccentric ways, and that even in the absence of seizures, these features sufficed to indicate the presence of the disease.[93] The signature elements often appeared during childhood, in capricious behavior, temper tantrums, uncontrollable crying, physical violence, and difficulty getting along with others. As the children grew up, they displayed the same characteristics that the victims of moral insanity did, contended Leonardo Bianchi in his textbook on psychiatry.[94] Above all, volatility and instability characterized the personality and behavior of epileptics. They were, Féré observed, "sometimes gentle and generous, sometimes violent and of squalid rapacity; sometimes polite and disturbingly obsequious, sometimes insolent and crude; sometimes gay and expansive, sometimes sullen and silent."[95] Aware of their lack of self-control, they felt resentful, "hating without reason and without measure," Féré observed.[96] Any of these characteristics, particularly in combination, suggested and sometimes secured a diagnosis of epilepsy. And since immoderate or eccentric behavior of this kind could appear in criminals, vagrants, and mental patients, experts often suspected that epilepsy drove their actions.

Understanding what caused epilepsy promised to clarify the range of the disease, but in fact it achieved the opposite. Unable to uncover a convincing source, doctors identified a range of possibilities, all of them difficult to disprove. Those committed to anatomical explanations looked for evidence of lesions but found nothing certain. Others looked for physiological or functional anomalies in the nervous system. Jules Voisin imagined that toxins affected the nerves and disrupted the brain cells, causing convulsions, and Féré thought that surplus energy overloaded the cortical centers and provoked an "explosion" which shook the nervous system or the brain.[97] Leonardo Bianchi agreed with Féré, proposing that the nerves overstimulated the brain, creating excessive energy which spilled into the motor system.[98]

Although unsure of the exact defect or mechanism responsible, studies usually asserted that weakness in the nervous system provided the ground for epilepsy. The abnormality could develop at the moment of conception or during gestation, but as with other nervous diseases, unhealthy heredity, and for most experts, degenerative heredity, more frequently caused it. More often than his fellow experts acknowledged, Féré thought, epilepsy passed directly from parents to children, although typically it appeared as one of the interchangeable set of degenerative disorders. Its companions included, specified Voisin, tuberculosis, alcoholism, insanity, and other nervous ailments.[99]

Environmental factors could activate and sometimes cause epilepsy, investigators commented. The list closely resembled the conditions that could provoke neurasthenia. An emotional shock or a serious illness, especially an infection, the flu, syphilis, or rheumatism, could irritate the nervous system and spark seizures. Drinking or using other stimulants, immoderate and unnatural sexual practices, especially masturbation, a poor diet, and even overwork and sleepless nights precipitated attacks in people vulnerable to epilepsy. A blow to the head or other physical trauma might also bring epilepsy to the fore.[100] These conditions did not produce epilepsy in people of sound stock and robust nervous equipment, nor did they matter much in those born with more than a proclivity to epilepsy. In the most serious cases, the disease cropped up early and inevitably.

For people thought likely to develop epilepsy, disciplined commitment to a well-modulated lifestyle, including moderation in work, rest, pleasure, diet, and emotion, might reduce the risks. Since it took getting epilepsy to reveal a vulnerability to the disease, the provident citizen, like the good Calvinist, imagined the worst and conducted life accordingly. If it did appear, and nothing indicated that it was hereditary, then bolstering the nervous system through medication and curative regimens and leading a subdued life could prevent further trouble. Particularly when trauma, drug and alcohol abuse, or general paralysis brought on attacks, Voisin noted, careful treatment could produce a cure. But when family history pointed to heredity, then as with neurasthenia, the prognosis worsened. Epilepsy in that form, Voisin observed, "unfailingly led to dementia if the individual had not already died."[101] Medication and shielding the patient from situations likely to provoke attacks promised little, and the more frequent and intense the attacks, the more marked the decline in intellectual ability and the more certain the onset of mental illness, making confinement in asylums or hospitals the recommended option. Moreover, unlike neurasthenia which developed slowly and paralyzed the victims with lassitude, epileptic attacks came on so suddenly and at such unpredictable intervals, and with potentially such devastating consequences that confinement proved a tempting preventive option even at the first sign of trouble. To provide that choice, many doctors argued for special facilities for epileptics who were in full possession of their mental faculties.

Doctors acknowledged that some epileptics managed to lead reasonably normal lives. Still their seizures exposed them to serious accident or to death as a result of a fall or asphyxiation. Even with rare attacks following a predictable course, the disease could push victims to the edges of society. The physiological weaknesses accompanying epilepsy led to indolence and indifference, observers noted, and these factors in turn spawned poverty and ignorance, and then crime and vice. If epileptics escaped these negative effects, they could not avoid others. Attacks wore down the brain, leading over time to intellectual deterioration and dementia. In addition to or in lieu of these problems, the physical stigmata, including misshapen heads, asymmetrical facial features, tics, tremors, and paralysis, marked the epileptic as different, according to studies.

Because serious cases ended up in hospitals and asylums, doctors based their clinical studies primarily on them. Armed with new medical data, criminal anthropologists as well as doctors examined prison populations and made epilepsy an element of their search. As a result, the experts stressed frightening and dangerous aspects of the disease largely absent in milder and less noticeable cases. Voisin reminded his students at Salpêtrière that "all forms of this terrible nervous disorder expose the persons afflicted to a more or less great risk of death or to the dangers of madness, confinement, and crime."[102] The fact that, as some experts believed, epilepsy also sparked the creativity or produced the exceeding tenacity of geniuses hardly compensated for its role in crime and other unacceptable actions. There wasn't an epileptic in a hospital who didn't suffer from mental problems, Féré contended, "and among those who live in society, there are very few who do not show a permanent or temporary mental weakness, or abnormally volatile character and conduct."[103]

During attacks, epileptics clearly lost their moral grip, and driven by hallucinations or their impulses they engaged in antisocial behaviors, some shocking but harmless, some extremely dangerous. When they returned to "normal," their angry, hateful, unpredictable personalities meant nothing but trouble. And, judging from studies of criminals, many crossed the line to illegal actions. Convicted criminals, Lombroso asserted, had anywhere from ten to thirty times the incidence of epilepsy that law-abiding citizens did.[104] When the born criminals among them suffered from epilepsy, Lombroso contended, they exhibited greater ferocity. To colleagues at the fifth annual meeting of the Società Freniatrica Italiana in 1886, he observed: "These individuals are extremely cruel; they are often cannibals; everyone knows of cases of cannibalism among epileptics."[105] The coincidence of congenital criminality, moral insanity, and epilepsy suggested deeper affinities among these three sources of difference. Claimed Lombroso in an article published in 1885 in the *Archivio di Psichiatria, Scienze Penali, ed Antropologia Criminale* (Archives of Psychiatry, Penal Science, and Criminal Anthropology): " it is certain that born criminality and moral insanity are none other than special forms of epilepsy."[106] Other criminologists and doctors protested that Lombroso went too far and suggested that epileptics acted as if they were morally insane without necessarily being so. They did resemble born criminals, Bianchi agreed, because both conditions resulted from degeneracy, but epileptics fell into crime periodically, whereas for born criminals it was the very essence of their lives.[107]

The apparent links of epilepsy to crime brought forensic doctors into the courtroom. As more work appeared about the epileptic temperament and about the hallucinations that accompanied seizures, more crimes seemed driven by the disease, a pattern emphasized by criminologists. Impulsive and inexplicably cruel crimes or evidence that the accused acted in a rage or a daze and remembered and regretted nothing pointed to epilepsy. Since the criminal codes in both countries based legal responsibility on awareness and intent, judges had to declare the accused mentally unfit if the crime occurred during a seizure. Whether impunity also applied to epileptics whose actions resulted from their volatile and irascible personalities aroused much more debate. Defense lawyers had reason to emphasize these connections to obtain acquittal, as did the accused who might feign well-known symptoms and lie about their medical histories. Doctors worried about deception, particularly since the worst criminals often fit the epileptic profile. The need to separate fact from fabrication, and then to prove that the crime actually occurred during a seizure, or that the accused operated under the dictates of a diseased character, made epilepsy a major issue in forensic medicine in the late nineteenth and early twentieth centuries.

The case of Luigi Rizzetti illustrates the interest in epilepsy. When his fiancée fell from a window to her death, the authorities accused Rizzetti of pushing her. One expert found Rizzetti "brainless" but not criminal and concluded that she probably jumped.[108] Called as a witness by the prosecution, Lombroso considered Rizzetti an epileptic and born criminal who likely pushed her, possibly in the throes of a seizure. Resuming the evidence, Guglielmo Ferrero (1871–1942) concluded that Rizzetti was probably an epileptic and "like all epileptics extremely irritable and egotistical" and lacking in "moral sense."[109] He was, Ferrero asserted, the quintessential born criminal, with additional signs of criminal insanity. Ruled guilty, he received an eight-year prison sentence, but Rizzetti jumped bail and fled.

Treatises at the time explored the possible role of epilepsy in forms of social deviance other than crime. They saw its tie to vagrancy in the "ambulatory automatism" that could occur during a seizure or in its immediate aftermath. Between attacks, the restlessness characteristic of the epileptic personality sometimes provoked sudden flight or constant wandering. Epileptics' indolence and inability to concentrate could, according to experts, also turn them into vagrants. Sexual deviance figures less prominently in medical discussions of the effects of epilepsy, but in the view of authorities such as Féré, epilepsy could alter sexual behavior because it affected the instincts. Sexual perversions and in particular same-sex attraction seemed linked to epilepsy, Féré suggested, especially when the behavior appeared suddenly and occurred intermittently.[110] Other studies observed that sexual precocity announced epilepsy, general paralysis and masturbation promoted it, and sexual activity triggered seizures.

As with neurasthenia, the more doctors learned about the disease, the wider its definition and the less certain its origins became. The borders between hysteria and epilepsy perplexed doctors since hysterical attacks sometimes bore remarkable resemblance to epileptic seizures. Many doctors diagnosed and treated these as epilepsy, especially in males. However, the Salpêtrière group insisted that hysteria was a distinct disease. Patients could, of course, exhibit symptoms of both either sequentially or mixed together, a condition Paul Richer, student and later colleague of Charcot, identified as *hystéro-épilepsie* ("grand hysteria").[111] In attacks of *hystéro-épilepsie*, the first phase looked very much like epilepsy, Richer observed, but unlike epilepsy, the patient's temperature remained normal and pressure on the ovaries or electric shock stopped the seizure.[112] Even the more ordinary type of hysteria showed similar patterns, although in attenuated form, Richer and Charcot believed. Thus hysteria always looked like epilepsy, but "real" epilepsy played no part in hysteria itself.[113] Voisin also stressed the differences, arguing that epileptics lost mental acuity over time, whereas hysterics did not.[114] The way the Salpêtrière group traced the borders between the two diseases did not win universal consensus, but it proved influential among contemporaries.

Some doctors complained that despite these distinctions, epilepsy had become a meaningless repository for wildly disparate physical and mental abnormalities. A profusion of possible signs, including what once passed as ill temper and eccentricity, identified the disease. It did not always involve the motor system; it might even exist in the absence of sudden attacks, loss of consciousness, or amnesia. Symptoms identified with neurasthenia also multiplied, so that no set of indicators guaranteed its presence and little eliminated it. Neuroses, noted Pierre Janet, served as a catchall for what doctors could not explain, elevating medical ignorance to a diagnostic standard.[115] The result, he insisted, lumped together a range of symptoms and diseases with little in common. Neurasthenics said they couldn't sleep, move, or digest properly, but a physical examination and tests indicated nothing amiss. To what extent was neurasthenia a figment of the patient's imagination? In the case of epilepsy, the patient's amnesia and the absence or unreliability of witnesses encouraged doctors to rely on behavioral characteristics. Did what they called the epileptic temperament stem from a nervous disorder or from a difficult upbringing or a nasty personality? The possibility that patients imagined or fabricated the symptoms threatened doctors' credibility, especially since neurasthenia figured prominently in damage suits and epilepsy played a role in criminal cases. Féré spoke for others, however, in insisting that no one could simulate all the signs of these neuroses; only "feckless beggars and vagabonds, or avowed criminals" managed to do that.[116]

Despite the loose use of the category, Janet applied the term "neuroses" to functional disorders. This definition, he claimed, challenged a century-long preoccupation with pathological anatomy, one which emphasized the physical over the physiological. He urged scientists to shift the focus from organs to functions, especially when dealing with neuroses, because they always involved operation rather than structure.[117] In his view, the nervous system developed and refined its role in stages, with the earliest acquisitions more solidly entrenched than the latest. Neuroses affected the recent and still developing functions, what he termed the "superior" functions or, as Janet specified, they disturbed the dinner party not digestion, not sex but the honeymoon. Until they became automatic, the superior functions still required thought, so that neuroses affected the psyche as well as the nervous system. Especially at moments of transition in individual development and at points of change in societies, neuroses flourished, he concluded.[118] Unlike psychoses which affected established processes, neuroses involved the higher phenomena, including the will. As a result, psychoses came with deterioration and neuroses with disrupted development. Clearly real and clearly pathological, Janet contended, neuroses thrived when heredity and the effects of infections, bad diet, emotional strain, and overwork prepared the ground.[119]

Like Janet, most doctors convinced themselves and others that neurasthenia and epilepsy existed in one or several variants and as a disease or as a syndrome.[120] With epilepsy as with neurasthenia, how they understood the nervous system and its ability to process stimuli helped explain the diffuse nature of the symptoms and the absence of identifiable anatomical defects. Including epilepsy and neurasthenia in the family of degenerative disorders also helped prove their existence. If doctors could not pin down their organic roots, they understood that they belonged to a group of pathologies produced by a common abnormality. This put the diagnosis of epilepsy and neurasthenia on a more reliable footing. Doctors thought they could conclude with reasonable confidence that if gout, diabetes, mania, or imbecility appeared somewhere in the patient's family, then what looked like neurasthenia or epilepsy actually likely was. French doctors, in particular, saw neurasthenia as a progenitor of *dégénérescence*, while epilepsy—especially in the view of Italian doctors—came toward the end of the line either in terms of its seriousness or in terms of Morel's downward spiral toward sterility. In that vein, Silvio Tonnino identified idiots, and after them epileptics as the quintessential degenerates.[121]

Implications

Neuroses ruined the lives of individuals and their families and undermined the health of future generations. Lucien Angelvin, a French doctor who explicitly addressed the social dimension of neurasthenia, detailed its impact. A successful businessman invests in another branch of industry, fails, and the anxiety reduces him to a bedridden shadow of his former self. Moody and irritable, he makes life miserable for the people around him. If neurasthenia strikes the wife, she neglects the house and the children and "the husband, disgusted by home life, takes to drinking."[122] Such disruptions of family life helped explain the alarming increase in suicide and crimes of passion, he asserted. A social evil and a social danger, neurasthenia required vigorous personal and public action. To this end, Angelvin urged adults to put health over ambition, and he called on lawmakers to take measures to reduce infectious disease and improve diet, limit the flow of peasants into the city, mandate weekly rest, and establish annual two-week vacations.[123] Carito saw the dangers even more starkly. In a clinical and social study of neurasthenia directed at doctors, teachers, and political leaders, he incited them to fight a disease which "assails humanity, and threatens to transform the places where Culture is the most intense and the Psyche works the hardest, that is, the great population centers, into vast and gigantic insane asylums."[124] It all began, he warned, at school. Worn down by the work, children became harried adults whose marriages ended up in mutual conflict and hatred. Their offspring showed the signs of mental weakness that opened the way to illness, especially neurasthenia. In ever-widening circles, neurasthenia "touched everything, leaving its corrupting trace" on individuals and society as the current state of painting amply indicated. "So-called Impressionism is striking evidence, is it not?"[125] "The neurasthenic constitutes a *bankrupt existence*. Where are we going? Into the abyss, because the neurasthenic is a negative element."[126]

Epileptics frightened observers even more. Driven by their disease to depraved behavior, they could end up in asylums, only to be released to strike again. Or, they remained at home, and they and their families never knew when the next attack might come or what its psychic aftermath might entail. Silvio Tonnino leant medical authority to these disturbing possibilities. An epileptic, he observed, "can be harmless for many years, [but] with the accumulation of the lesions...one day becomes a ferocious killer."[127] Sufferers often could not work, causing them to depend on others to live, a troubling destiny in a culture which placed such value on jobs and independence. Concluded Voisin, it "poisoned their existence, because it makes it impossible for them to enjoy life."[128]

What appeared at the turn of the century to be a fact of modern life, indiscriminate in its victims and staggering in its social consequences, practically disappeared from the diagnostic lexicon after the First World War. During the war, traumatic neurasthenia and hysteria provided a rubric for understanding what front line soldiers experienced. When it was over, traumatic neurosis and post traumatic stress syndrome wound that thread of neurasthenia into a new skein of words and symptoms. Other forms, hereditary neurasthenia and "classic" or "true" neurasthenia among them, also dissolved as their symptoms got reassigned to other diseases, primarily to modern stress disorders and depression. Now the word "neurasthenia" evokes shell-shocked soldiers, Victorian ladies suffering undefined and incapacitating ailments, and delicate, anxious artists. But in its heyday, neurasthenia extended far beyond these groups. At the end of the century, it affected the most energetic and successful sectors of the population. Doctors saw the symptoms as genuine; they testified to neurasthenia's remarkable reach, and they warned of its menace to society. Neurasthenia no longer inspires similar urgency, but by medical standards and the scientific understanding of the body prevailing at the turn of the century, it was real.

Neurasthenia appeared, then, to decline almost as rapidly as it rose, and what explained its escalation might well explain its exodus. Beard extracted neurasthenia from patterns he observed, identified a set of related symptoms, determined its causes and its course, and called it a disease. He saw it as a new disorder, while others claimed something like it had always existed but with a different name and in reduced proportions. Particular concerns and understandings, Ian Hacking's vectors, made neurasthenia plausible, even necessary as a phenomenon. It responded to the realization that managing the pressures of life in modern society depended on willpower. Situating the will as a late and therefore less resilient addition to the body, helped scientists explain why people faltered. But even a fully developed will flagged if the nervous system's supply of energy ran low, they observed. To clarify what made people run, they invoked electricity as explanation and metaphor. People experienced sparks, surges, and blackouts, and they relied on something like batteries to keep going.[129] Economics also influenced how they presented the body's operation. Investigators reminded their audience of the importance of reserves, expenditures, and deficits. They pointed to the advantages of thrift, the costs of risky behaviors, and the negative impact of sudden crises. A faulty balance sheet led, they stressed, to the bankruptcy of the nervous system.[130]

These concepts came together to assign apathy and passivity to invasive fatigue, and fatigue to energy deficits and weak will. It disassociated indolence from savagery and made it instead a predictable consequence of too much civilization. Like a contemporary English variant, the nervous breakdown, neurasthenia named and pathologized what people experienced and doctors recognized as persistent anomalies. Possibly it disappeared because, as Beard predicted, the body adapted to the pressures of modern life and developed adequate resources of energy. Perhaps it lost momentum because individuals took to heart doctors' warnings and slowed down, refrained from excess, or avoided marriage and children when affected by nervous disorders. More likely the frame that defined neurasthenia fell apart and its pieces reappeared in other configurations.

Medical science and ordinary people continued to believe that trauma and overwork adversely affected the body, but not in the form of neurasthenia. How scientists understood the nervous system, the brain, and energy changed, and in ways less compatible with the concept of nervous fatigue. Medical specialties also congealed, and doctors' professional interests and priorities may have shifted. Or, as historians such as Janet Oppenheim argue, doctors had developed neurasthenia as a diagnosis of convenience. It reassured their patients, and it gave them work and credibility as specialists. When it lost its utility, they presumably turned to other more profitable constructions. However, it took more than new theories and professional advantage to dislodge neurasthenia. The First World War played a major role in interrupting the epidemic. In that context, traumatic neurasthenia became sharply relevant as doctors faced cases of what they called shell shock or its equivalent. Initially British doctors attributed the symptoms to concussion, but then, as they had with traumatic neurasthenia, they recognized emotional shock as the prime mover. The collapsing of neurasthenia into traumatic neurasthenia and that into shell shock helps explain why neurasthenia faded away after the war.[131] The effects of the war on the home front also likely encouraged discipline and sacrifice and provided people with a different perspective on their nervous ailments.

If neurasthenia largely evaporated and the word lost its descriptive power, its elements lived on in different configurations and with other labels, including "clinical depression," "posttraumatic stress disorder," "chronic fatigue syndrome," and "stress-related disorders." Major depression, in particular, resembles neurasthenia in key ways.[132] In twenty-first-century society, it is apparently on the rise, and it affects widely different groups. The grind of modern life, emotional shocks, the secondary effects of other illnesses promote it, and a hereditary predisposition appears to make it more severe. Its effects include insomnia, stomach problems, reduced libido, lethargy, sadness, and anxiety.[133] Turning this diagnosis around and looking backwards, neurasthenics did look like candidates for antidepressants. The parallels invite the assimilation of the two diseases and the use of depression as a synonym for neurasthenia. As a device to help the modern reader understand the nature and the seriousness of neurasthenia, that reversal has some merit.

Applying modern labels to old diseases requires caution, however. In the case of neurasthenia, it obscures differences in the nature of the two conditions and in the use of the word "depression." When turn-of-the-century doctors used depression in connection with neurasthenia, and they did, they used it to describe the decrease in mental energy and sharpness. It meant a slowdown, a trough, a stifling. Paralyzing sadness of the kind associated with clinical depression now, they assigned to melancholy as Esquirol had described it decades before. They did recognize that neurasthenics could become sad as a result of their condition, but it constituted a secondary rather than a primary symptom. "The patients," specified Émile Laurent in a text on neurasthenia written for doctors, "are dejected, desperate, seized by a profound sadness.... They get irritated, morose, [are] always worried and agitated, irascible."[134] These changes, along with listlessness, inability to concentrate, and forgetfulness, he and others saw as the effects of the functional decline, or depression, of the nervous system. Resumed Laurent: "the collapse of mental energy, the loss of will, the reduction of all types of mental activity, these are the main signs of the mental depression of the neurasthenic."[135]

Hysteria also waned as a viable diagnostic category. Mark Micale provides a detailed description of its demise and a useful postmortem on its life as an illness. In his view, the disappearance of hysteria depended on two factors: the diagnosis changed and its place in the overall scheme of medical classification changed. These two shifts, in turn, came from new diagnostic techniques and assessments of the roots of disease and from sociological factors that influenced how doctors constructed diagnoses.[136] Micale argues that Emil Kraepelin, a leading German psychiatrist of the day, drew from hysteria his identification of manic depression and precocious dementia, so that some of what once announced hysteria now belonged to these other two disorders. The identification of schizophrenia and multiple personality disorders also absorbed elements of hysteria.[137]

Epilepsy did not disappear, but it retracted into its original and more restricted dimensions. Some later nineteenth-century research on sensory-motor epilepsy remains pertinent, but the additional types identified then now indicate other defects or pathologies, or belong to the realm of the normal. The idea of an epileptic temperament and of psychic epilepsy seems these days to affirm the shaky nature of turn-of-the-century science. Most of the time irascibility and irritability count as passing reactions to annoying situations or to stress. In persistent or marked form, they may indicate multiple personality disorder or the effects of other illnesses. The association of epilepsy with genius no longer seems as plausible as it once did, and born criminality, moral insanity, and fugue have disappeared into other categories. Degeneration which held the key neuroses together and joined them to different mental and physical abnormalities continued to unravel as a concept after the turn of the century. Without its reinforcement, its components lost some of the substance those interconnections gave them.

Part II

Social Misfits

5

Vagabonds

*The true vagrant, the one who constitutes a real danger
to public security… is the tramp, the hobo… in revolt
against society, game for any crime, true wild beast lost
in a civilized country: it is the sluggard, the idler.*

Alexandre Bérard[1]

*Vagrancy exists as a psychological fact; but it is a fact
of extreme complexity joined by
economic necessities.*

Auguste Marie and Raymond Meunier[2]

Idleness is the enemy of the soul.

St. Benedict[3]

Vagrancy drew a lot of attention at the end of the century. Said French expert on crime Henri Joly in 1889: "People certainly decry the murderer and the thief; but they especially complain about the tramp [*rouleur*] and the vagabond, because that group of criminals is growing faster than the others."[4] The French in particular felt surrounded by drifters and menaced by the homeless, jobless, and destitute. "A single voice rises from the city and the countryside," asserted physician Armand Pagnier, "to demand that the country be purged of these social aliens."[5] A matter of public "indifference" in the 1860s, vagrancy produced "panic" in the 1880s, historian Gordon Wright asserts. "Why," he says, "is not easy to discover."[6] The alarm came, commented a contemporary, from the "instinctual hatred" sedentary French peasants felt for rootless people.[7] It also reflected the popular suspicion that vagrants spurned social norms and that they survived by crime. Everywhere in the countryside, the French deputy Alexandre Bérard insisted, peasants complained about vagrants roaming around alone or in families pillaging crops, begging, and stealing.[8] Rumors and local reports of theft and arson fed the sense of insecurity in the countryside, while the numbers of people living by expedients made it hard to ignore the problem in the cities. The occasional highly publicized crimes of a vagrant such as Joseph Vacher only magnified public fears.

The problem

Statistics circulated at the time fed public alarm about vagabonds.[9] The Société Agricole calculated that 400,000 vagrants roamed the roads in France in the 1880s; estimates based on reports of the number of vagrants housed in rural shelters cut that number by half, a number still sufficient to disturb settled citizens.[10] Statistics published by the minister of the interior indicated that police arrested an average of 18,000 vagrants a year at the turn of the century[11] compared to an average of 2,940 for the period from 1826 to 1830.[12] The numbers of vagrants brought to trial also rose steadily, from 2,500 in 1830 to 7,000 in 1850, to 13,000 in 1880, and to 20,000 in 1890.[13] According to judicial records, the rate of increase for vagrancy and illegal begging between 1838 and 1888 surpassed population growth and significantly exceeded the increase in violent crimes, theft, suicide, and offenses to public morals.[14] As telling, the numbers confirmed the popular belief that tramps survived by crime. According to informed observers, vagrants convicted of every sort of crime filled the prisons, while those without criminal records populated mental asylums.[15]

Responding to public concern, local authorities in France pressed the government to take more effective action, and lawmakers answered by organizing investigations and producing anti-vagrancy bills. The public discussion also drew on the amply documented studies of experts—jurists, criminologists, sociologists, and doctors—who claimed that controlling vagrancy required knowing what caused it. These reports, combined with attention to the problem in the press, gave weight to public fears, as did evidence that more Frenchmen and foreigners seeking work took to the roads hoping to find it.

Vagrancy did not just worry the French at the end of the century. Italian social theorists and lawmakers also tried to understand and to control vagabondage, and their conclusions both drew from and influenced French thinking. But whereas the French responded to what they perceived as an acute and intensifying crisis, official statistics in Italy recorded a sharp decline in vagrancy. Between 1872 and 1891 the number of idlers and vagrants monitored by the police fell from 25.4 to 1.5 per 100,000, whereas in France in roughly the same period, the number of people accused of vagrancy increased from 27.4 to 44.8 per 100,000. As in France, however, the experts asserted that the official statistics underestimated the real numbers. Alexandre Bérard, for example, observed that the "immense crowds" of homeless people in Italy made the French problem look mild in comparison. Looking from inside, the authors of a major study of vagrancy, Eugenio Florian and Guido Cavaglieri, thought the figures accurate for vagrancy in Italy but far too low for those who lived by begging.[16] Adding the statistics for begging to vagrancy numbers showed rates comparable to France: an average of 13,040 judicial cases a year, or 42.1 per 100,000.[17]

The numbers attracted attention, and so did the efforts of lawmakers, the courts, and the police to control what they saw as a problem. Whether laws criminalized vagrancy or governments left it to the police to monitor it depended on the country. The Napoleonic Code, applied in France, established the most commonly used legal approach to vagrancy. It identified vagrants or *gens sans aveu* as those without a stable residence and without means of subsistence who did not regularly exercise either a trade or a profession.[18] The terms excluded the idle rich, people in itinerant trades, or those temporarily out of work. The code punished vagrancy with prison sentences of three to six months followed by five to ten years of police surveillance. More severe penalties applied if caught wearing a disguise, carrying weapons or instruments useful in theft or other criminal acts, or in possession of unexplained sums of money or valuables. Punishment also increased in cases of violence or attempted violence.[19]

The criminal code adopted in 1889 for united Italy distinguished between vagrants and idlers (*oziosi*), those who had a stable residence but no profession, trade, or job and no other source of income.[20] Following the French example, vagrancy counted as a crime punishable with three to six months in prison. In contrast, idleness did not in itself constitute a crime, but failing to meet an official order to find a stable job carried a prison term of three to six months followed by police surveillance.[21] Special legislation passed soon after Unification allowed prefects to prohibit idlers and vagrants from living in certain areas, increased prison sentences from five to six months, and authorized the minister of the interior to send repeat offenders to penal colonies for up to five years.[22]

No matter how precise the language, the legal definitions of vagrancy required interpretation, because they did not fit apparent realities or popular perceptions of the problem. Plenty of people moved around; plenty of people did not work in one place; some worked periodically, others not at all. Increasingly, people lost their jobs and moved to the cities or to other countries to find work. Harmless roamers and malevolent tramps, beggars and vagrants, itinerant workers and the unemployed, *rentiers* and shirkers looked a lot alike. In order to reduce vagrancy, lawmakers, judges, and the police needed to know more about it. Convinced that they could and should influence policy, doctors, criminologists, jurists, and sociologists set about studying the phenomenon and its causes.

Explaining vagrancy

These experts addressed vagrancy in much the same way that they did other social issues such as criminality, prostitution, and abnormal sexual practices. They intended to examine the problem scientifically, and that meant discarding metaphysical assumptions and going straight to the facts. Italians Eugenio Florian (1869–1945) and Guido Cavaglieri (1871–1917), well-known authorities on the subject, aimed for a broad comparative examination of when, where, and how often vagabondage occurred. They and others used statistics to try to correlate vagrancy rates with topography and climate, levels of economic development and performance, and social factors such as wealth and gender. Generally, Florian and Cavaglieri concluded that climate and topography weighed more heavily in primitive societies and demographics, social structures, and the state of the economy more in contemporary society.

Committed classifiers, those who investigated vagrancy took pains to define various types based on causes or characteristics, or both. Just what they thought qualified as vagrancy varied, however. Some authorities took a sweeping view, including gypsies and runaways, mystics, eccentrics, and anarchists; others narrowed the field to strictly legal definitions—to healthy people regularly without work, residence, or means of subsistence. Within the limits that they selected, they sought to understand why people became vagabonds, and that required them to take a closer look at individual examples. Observers found them in prisons, asylums, hospitals, local refuges for beggars and vagabonds, and in the streets. Using this population, doctors, in particular, developed case studies that gave investigators common points of reference for categorizing other examples. Whether they drew from statistics or from case studies, the experts proclaimed the novelty and validity of their scientific methods and conclusions, and with some reason, since what they reported differed markedly from assessments typical earlier in the century. At the same time, they studied vagabonds and idlers from a definite perspective, notwithstanding their earnest professions of objectivity. Like ordinary citizens, experts worried about vagrancy, and they made it clear that vagabonds violated civilized norms of work and family. That attitude, and the seriousness of their studies, reinforced public concern about drifters and their potential for crime.

The laws in both countries explicitly recognized that those too young, too old, or too infirm to work, or those engaged in itinerant or seasonal labor did not count as vagrants. Studies acknowledged these exceptions and focused, as the law did, on the able-bodied who did not work regularly and who lacked the wherewithal to support themselves. As they organized their data, it became clearer to physicians and to sociologists that unemployment contributed to the problem. As a result, they increasingly stressed the importance of distinguishing between those who wanted jobs and those who did not or could not seek work. The first group required help and support, the second an explanation.

Biological factors gained favor as the source of what the experts labeled as professional or habitual vagrancy. According to one theory, vagrants regressed to a more primitive, nomadic state; according to another, pathologies related to inherited degenerative disorders or to illnesses affected their capacity to work. Each approach had defenders on both sides of the border, but the French took the lead in relating vagabondage to mental illness and the Italians in making the case for primitivism. French doctors looked back to Jean-Etienne Dominique Esquirol and James Cowles Prichard, who noted that vagabondage frequently accompanied lucid folly and moral insanity.[23] Achille Foville, Jr. (1831–1887), doctor at the Asylum Quatre-Mares near Le Havre, reignited interest in insane travelers in 1875 when he published a study of patients who left unexpectedly and covered great distances. All of them showed symptoms of deep melancholy accompanied by hallucinations that drove them to leave either to escape their persecutors or to fulfill a grandiose dream.[24] Taking up where Foville left off, other doctors added evidence that mental disorders could provoke an uncontrollable impulse to flee. In 1888, Jean-Martin Charcot opened an intriguing new angle when he presented what became an iconic case in one of his Tuesday lessons. The following year, he returned to the case to update his diagnosis on the basis of new facts.

Charcot introduced a delivery man (later identified as Men ... s) who was married with two children and employed for eighteen years at a company that produced artistic bronzes. Until the odd "adventures" began, Men … s enjoyed sound health, as did his children, his parents, and his other close relatives. Mild-mannered and responsible, the patient did not abuse alcohol or engage in any other excesses, Charcot specified.[25] Prompted by Charcot, Men … s explained to the audience what happened to him. He recalled completing a delivery and then waking up fourteen hours later in the Place de la Concorde not knowing how or why he got there. Other than the sense that he had passed by St. Cloud and Mont Valerian, he had no memory of the episode. His worn shoes and dusty clothing showed that he had done a lot of walking, but nothing indicated incontinence or that he had passed out. He must, Charcot observed, have walked normally with his eyes open, since passersby noticed nothing unusual.

Three and a half months later, Men … s decided to check on the Eiffel Tower construction site on his way back from delivering a set of candelabra. He woke up two days later in the Seine River and realized that he had jumped from the Bercy bridge and swum to shore. After resting for a couple of hours, he felt fine and returned home. During this fugue, he had presence of mind enough to buy some tobacco and a railway ticket to Bercy and to wind his watch. As far as he knew, he had not eaten or taken a hotel room to sleep, since he did not have enough money with him to cover those expenses. A similar event occurred three weeks later when a fisherman found him sleeping under the bridge at Asnières. That time, in a span of thirty-six hours, he had traveled a considerable distance without any memory of what prompted him to leave or of where he had been. He recalled having a headache before each of the flights and feeling very thirsty and tired after them.

After three attacks, coming at shorter intervals and lasting for longer periods, he sought treatment. Charcot presented his diagnosis: epileptic-like ambulatory automatism.[26] He reminded the audience that epileptics often started talking or walking mechanically after seizures, sometimes committing indecent or violent acts. When they woke up, they remembered nothing. Men … s, in contrast, showed none of the intense emotions typical of such episodes, and he walked normally, apparently with a destination in mind.[27] His fugues looked a lot like sleepwalking, Charcot admitted. But sleepwalking occurred mainly at night and to children or adolescents. What happened to Men … s seemed closer to epilepsy, although his calm demeanor and modest behavior clearly made it a distinctive variant. In any case, Charcot said he favored that diagnosis, because it allowed him to prescribe a treatment: an escalating dose of bromide of potassium mixed with bromides of sodium and aluminum. A month after he began the cure, Men … s fell asleep in the coach on the way to a delivery. When he woke up, he continued to conduct his business but with no awareness of what he was doing. Feeling an overwhelming thirst, he went home, drank water, and reported feeling as if he'd been beaten with a stick. The coachman and his employer recalled that he seemed unusually pale that day, but other than that they noticed nothing unusual in his behavior. The attack lasted about three hours, shortened, Charcot concluded, by the potassium bromide.

Over a year later (February 12, 1889), Charcot featured Men … s again in a Tuesday lesson. He reported having reduced the dosage the previous spring after the patient passed some months with no attack. In the fall, Men … s took it upon himself to discontinue the treatment entirely. Several months went by with no ill effects. Then in January, he spent the day making deliveries, collected several payments, and early in the evening went blank. He returned to his senses nine days later on a bridge in a town he did not recognize but later learned was Brest.[28] This time his shoes and clothing showed no signs of wear, and checking his funds, he realized that he must have paid for food and hotels. As in the previous attacks, he retained a few vague and fragmentary memories.

Charcot reviewed all the previous episodes and reiterated the diagnosis of a variant of epilepsy characterized by the compulsion to walk, almost total amnesia, and the absence of violent emotions or repugnant behavior.[29] Based on reports of other cases, blows to the head or epilepsy could produce similar patterns of automatism and amnesia. The fact that Men…s responded to potassium bromide reinforced the diagnosis of epilepsy or something close to it. Charcot reported reinstating the treatment regimen and promised to supply Men…s with an affidavit signed by the Public Assistance Office of Paris, certifying the nature of his illness so that if he came to the attention of the authorities during another fugue, they would not arrest him but see that he got help.

The concept of impulsive walking accompanied by amnesia caught hold, and it generally took the label Charcot gave it: "ambulatory automatism" or fugue. A number of doctors confirmed the connection to epilepsy and extended it to the companion neuroses, namely hysteria and neurasthenia.[30] Hysterics, explained doctors such as Armand Pagnier, also took off unexpectedly, driven by some fixed idea. They behaved normally enough not to be noticed, but when they woke up, they, like epileptics, could not remember what prompted their departure or what they did along the way. However, under hypnosis, they could recall every detail of the episode. How much they remembered indicated that they were fully aware during the fugue. Perhaps, doctors theorized, they had a double personality, with the second one gradually gaining control over the first one, an idea which won substantial support.[31]

In his 1887 study of mental illness and wandering, Philippe Tissié (1852–1935) described a case that became a prototype of ambulatory automatism in hysterics. According to Ian Hacking, Tissié's account launched an epidemic of medical fugue sightings.[32] Tissié met Albert D…, later identified as Albert Dadas, when he ended up in the hospital at Bordeaux. He found the patient tired from a long trip on foot and crying because he could not resist the "imperious desire" to wander.[33] When the impulse seized him, he walked fast (seventy kilometers a day) and far. At Tissié's invitation, Albert D… recounted an itinerary that alternated periods of work and flight and took him as far as Moscow, where he woke up in prison and discovered that the courts had tried and convicted him as a nihilist. Before his flights, he reported that he had headaches, sweated profusely, masturbated frequently, trembled, felt dizzy, twitched, and became taciturn and morose. Once he left, he said he was unaware of where he went or what he did, unsure whether or how he ate or drank. During the episodes, he kept himself and his clothing clean. When he woke up, he felt disoriented and done in, but once he recovered, he found work and stayed in the area until he felt the need to travel again, or he returned to Bordeaux. Other times, the police picked him up and, finding he had no papers, put him in jail or ordered him to return home by a specific route. If he ended up outside France, the authorities escorted him to the border with orders to leave the country.

When in Bordeaux, he got a job at the gas company and performed well. Early on he decided to join the army but immediately experienced severe headaches and bed-wetting. Hospitalized and sent home on medical leave, he returned to his unit, but when the desire to move seized him, he deserted, leaving France in order to avoid arrest. A general amnesty allowed Albert D… to rejoin his regiment, but when a friend urged him to leave, he deserted again. This escapade got him three years of forced labor in Africa. Pardoned for good conduct, he returned to work at the gas company, fell in love, and planned to marry. But then he disappeared for three months, only to find when he came back that his intended had met someone else. After being hospitalized and then escaping, he ended up back at the hospital, under observation and in Doctor Tissié's care.

Rather thin but fairly strong, Albert D… had an elongated head, some color blindness, and a normal appetite, Tissié wrote. He could appear lively or dull-witted, intelligent or stupid, forgetful or with extremely precise recall. He showed affection for people, especially for his mother. Albert D… neither drank nor smoked, but he masturbated regularly and sometimes excessively, Tissié reported.[34] His siblings were healthy, he noted, but the fact that Albert D…'s father grew senile and his mother died at fifty from lung problems indicated hereditary weaknesses, Tissié concluded.[35] Albert D… recalled being healthy as a child until he fell from a tree and lost consciousness at age eight. After that he experienced frequent migraine headaches and vomiting for a time, and then persistent and intense headaches.

Responding to Albert D…'s desire to correct the problem so that he could settle down and marry, Tissié offered hypnosis as a possible solution. Under hypnosis, the patient recalled what happened during his fugues with remarkable detail, and then forgot everything when he woke up. More important, he responded to instructions to perform specific tasks, such as to stop masturbating and to stay in Bordeaux. When he relapsed into former habits, another session of hypnosis brought him back in line, Tissié reported. The treatment turned out to offer a reprieve rather than a cure, however. In a postscript to the case, Henri-Barthélemy Géhin, who saw Albert D… between 1889 and 1892, said that as before, the "escapades" alternated with periods of work and hospital stays.[36] In 1887 Dadas married and moved to Paris with his wife and daughter. When his wife died of tuberculosis, a local couple took his daughter in, an indication that the fugues persisted.[37]

In Tissié's view, Albert D… got a random idea about visiting a place and it gradually took over, conquering his hesitations. Although he managed the logistics of travel during his fugues, he could recall his motives and his itinerary only under hypnosis. In fact, Tissié observed, Albert D… behaved the whole time as if he were in a hypnotic trance, responding to a suggestion he planted in his own head. Noting that his conscious desires overpowered his will, Tissié classified him as obsessed.[38] Other doctors diagnosed hysteria and used the case as a standard for identifying this variant of ambulatory automatism.[39] Unlike the abrupt and often violent and unrestrained episodes typical of epileptics during seizures, hysterics identified a goal beforehand, and despite their lack of awareness, they performed complicated tasks when away. For example, they navigated around obstacles, while the epileptic in the midst of a seizure tended to crash through them.[40] In their calm demeanor and in their appearance of control, they resembled M … s and his epileptic-like fugues. Like either the violent or the passive variants of epileptic fugue, victims experienced amnesia after the episode, but hypnosis allowed hysterics to remember everything temporarily, while it had no effect on epileptics. These patterns caused doctors to agree that hysterics possessed a second, subconscious personality that periodically gained control over the dominant self. According to Géhin, patients showed "a perfect coordination of their acts, and even logic in carrying out the perceptions of their second personality."[41] The presence of hysteria's characteristic physical signs and the ineffectiveness of potassium bromide sealed the diagnosis.

Neurasthenia, the third major neurosis of the day, also promoted a distinctive type of fugue, according to doctors. Neurasthenics knew where they were going and why, they did not lose consciousness or perform disreputable acts, and they did not experience amnesia. The idea of leaving developed slowly, and no unusual physical signs announced the impulse to depart.[42] When examined afterward, trembling hands and tongue and headaches sometimes confirmed the diagnosis of neurasthenia. Asked why they left, they could only say that they were sleeping poorly, began to think about traveling, and just wanted to leave.[43] Once they departed, they reported a sensation of liberation or relief. They understood that leaving compromised their jobs and troubled their loved ones but, like epileptics and hysterics, their will faltered and they could not stand up to their impulses.[44] They were, reflected Alix Joffroy and Roger Dupouy, doctors at the Sainte-Anne asylum outside Paris, "tired, overwhelmed, exhausted, listless, more or less hypochondriacal."[45]

A student of Charcot, Henri Meige (1866–1940), applied the diagnosis to the legendary wandering Jew in a thesis that drew considerable attention at the time and later. Victor-Charles Dubourdieu, who studied vagrancy and degeneration, referred to the work as "very curious … really very original and very new." He invoked the study in describing "real vagabonds," a pathological group continually driven by the need to move.[46] Meige collected versions of the story of the wandering Jew as well as printed images from the past, and then compared the mythic profile to Jewish patients he observed at Salpêtrière between 1880 and 1890. He found that the two groups matched. Partly because of their race and partly because a "profound neurosis" compelled them to travel, they moved around frequently.[47] The Jews of Salpêtrière also resembled traditional images of the wandering Jew in their appearance, clothing, and mannerisms. Based on their similarities, Meige concluded that the legendary and the real figures both suffered from neurasthenia, sometimes in conjunction with hysteria.[48] In fact, he added, not just these patients but "almost all Jews are neurasthenics."[49]

Meige described the group of patients as "poor, miserably dressed devils. Their thin faces, with deep and sad wrinkles disappear behind their huge and uncombed beards. With a lamenting tone they recount a story full of painful happenings."[50] Most of them came from Poland or eastern Germany, driven by illness and poverty, dissatisfied with all treatments, and incapable of working, Meige reported. To support his diagnosis of neurasthenia, he detailed their symptoms: weak digestion, insomnia, headaches, aches and pains, and the desire to travel to find new remedies. Meige did admit that not every Jew experienced neuroses or wandered and that other neuroses and mental illnesses also caused habitual vagabondage.[51]

All three neuroses—epilepsy, hysteria, and neurasthenia—produced impulsive wandering. The drive to flee overpowered the will, and people set off mechanically. At the moment of departure, their centers of inhibition shut down, because "cerebral anemia" or degeneration weakened their nervous system, Henri Barthélemy Géhin argued in his often-cited thesis on impulsive vagabondage and ambulatory automatism.[52] Depending on which neurosis provoked their flight, they registered complete, some, or no awareness of their actions. How often epilepsy, hysteria, and neurasthenia provoked vagrancy remained an open question. Vagrants often showed signs of these pathologies, but the condition did not always produce their wandering, concluded doctors; sometimes they feigned the symptoms to obtain temporary shelter. Overall, experts hypothesized, nervous disorders accounted for a minority of pathologically driven vagrancy.

More vagrants wandered as a result of mental illness, as the number of accused and convicted vagrants in asylums and hospitals showed.[53] Doctors published numerous studies that explored the connections between insanity and flight, offering examples they expected to be useful to fellow physicians and to judges. Tissié's list of the psychoses likely to cause fugue included delirium, hallucinations and dementia, obsessions, in addition to impulsions, including epilepsy. Among the delirious, he specified, alcoholics fled to escape an impending crisis, claustrophobics to avoid getting closed in, and erotomaniacs to satisfy their drives.[54] When affected by delirium, the normal balance between instincts, desires, and ideas disappeared, and judgment faltered.[55] In a broader and more detailed analysis of the link between mental illness and vagrancy published in 1909, Joffroy and Dupouy noted that not all vagrants were insane or all those who impulsively left home qualified as vagrants. To clarify the differences, they stressed that some mentally unbalanced adults, especially those suffering from obsessions, could not muster the will and attention necessary to persevere in the workplace.[56] In addition to imbalance, dromomania, paranoia, delirium, dementia, mania, depression, and confusion produced recognizable variants of the flight syndrome. In contrast to the ambulatory automatism unleashed in epileptics and hysterics, these subjects decided to move for reasons that they understood; they retained awareness; and with the exception of some alcoholics, they remembered what they did, and why. Succinctly put, "epilepsy brings the death of memory, hysteria the apparent death of memory, in pure insanity, it is the normal life of memory."[57]

Behind these fugue-promoting disorders lurked degeneration, some experts argued. Case studies routinely began by reviewing the health of family members to check for inherited abnormalities. Measurements and tests also identified defects associated with degeneration. Understood in the broadest sense, *dégénérescence* predisposed people to the neuroses and mental illnesses thought to produce fugue. A connection this general did not arouse much dissent. In a more focused and contested approach, Armand Pagnier saw the "flight syndrome" as a form of degeneration rather than a secondary effect of it. Whether the flight was conscious or unconscious, sporadic or continuous, depended on the type of degeneration. Thus idiots and imbeciles, the inferior degenerates, acted on reflex, while superior degenerates, including obsessives and neurotics, knew and remembered what they did.[58] Doctors, such as Charles Féré, who identified a related set of degenerative illnesses, typically included vagrancy among them. Victor-Charles Dubourdieu, a student of Albert Pitres and Emmanuel Régis at the medical faculty at Bordeaux, added dromomania, a special degenerative form of ambulatory automatism, to that group.[59] Dromomaniacs, like normal people, loved their country and their families; they were "honest, good, courageous, [and] disciplined." But they experienced real and conscious impulsive crises.[60] Usually an insignificant idea about a place took hold, and headaches, insomnia, and nervousness announced their imminent departure.[61] Convinced by the diagnosis, Joffroy and Dupouy devoted a chapter to dromomania, joining other doctors in recognizing an illness that still denotes a mania for travel.[62]

As they analyzed the pathologies that fed vagabondage, French doctors stressed the uncontrollable impulse to move whether to pursue an idea, to escape demons, or to respond to the urging of a second self. Italian experts generally favored a different biological approach, one that emphasized the vagrants' inability to work. They built the theory on a view of primitive societies common at the time. In the study of vagrancy they published in two volumes in 1897 and 1900, Florian and Cavaglieri reviewed the argument. Driven by the survival instinct, primitive people naturally adopted a nomadic lifestyle as they moved from place to place to forage for food. Scarcity did not suffice to explain their penchant to roam, however. Even if they had wanted to settle down, they could not have, because they had not yet evolved sufficiently to engage in agriculture. Until the brain developed the functions of reason and self-control, people lived a catch-as-catch-can existence, one defined by their natural indolence and impetuosity even more than by the ready availability of food. According to this theory, once evolution gave them the capacity for disciplined work, primitives stopped roaming and turned to farming and later to manufacturing.

Because citizens of modern societies used their highly developed brains to manage long work hours and settled domestic routines, vagrants must lack these faculties, according to the theory. If, as some investigators argued, everyone retained residues of the primitive, atavism or a sudden reversion offered a plausible explanation for vagrancy. Or, scientists turned to current theories of gestation to explain why evolved modern citizens showed signs of primitive behavior. According to the view popularized by the German zoologist and professor of comparative anatomy Ernst Haeckel, each person played out the history of the species as they grew from infancy to adulthood. Vagrants appeared to be locked into an earlier stage of development, lacking the discipline and self-control to operate in modern society.[63] According to some studies, noted Florian and Cavaglieri, these vagrants exhibited primitive physical characteristics such as protruding foreheads and prominent jaws, just as born criminals did.

For their part, Florian and Cavaglieri did not see convincing evidence that vagrants fit a specific physical profile, even though their appearance sometimes showed primitive traits. However, vagrants did possess distinctive psychological features including, Florian specified, "repugnance for work, an organic incapacity to perform continual and methodical jobs, deficient will power."[64] These "psychophysical" weaknesses made vagabonds apathetic and lazy and, as a result, inattentive and undisciplined. A good deal of conclusive data indicated that "psychic atavism" characterized vagabonds, they argued, including public opinion, laws, and high rates of recidivism.[65] Like primitives, their natures made them yearn for leisure and avoid work, and like primitives, they exhibited impulsiveness and excitability.[66] Either regression or arrested development explained these patterns, they concluded. But Florian and Cavaglieri also acknowledged that neuroses, especially neurasthenia, and psychoses could turn people into idlers by sapping the body's will and energy.[67]

French investigators Auguste Marie and Raymond Meunier, in their well-regarded analysis of vagrancy, took issue with Florian and Cavaglieri. The assertion that primitive people lacked drive left them unconvinced, and in any case, they did not see evidence that vagrants regressed to a primitive state, whatever that state might be.[68] However, even though they and most other French doctors did not attribute vagrancy to atavism or arrested development, they did find merit in the diagnosis of a general psycho-physical weakness. Noting the number of vagrants with multiple criminal convictions, René Beck (1877?–1952) argued that even those without clear pathologies suffered from inadequacies that qualified them as borderline insane. Too restless or too passive to hold a job, they rotated in and out of prisons or asylums, never quite up to the discipline required for modern life.[69] Whether they returned to their ancestral state or adapted poorly to their environment, or owed their ineffectiveness to degeneration, their actions proved their inferiority. They fit somewhere between the unbalanced person who occasionally succumbed to vagrancy and the imbecile who never stopped wandering, Beck argued.[70] Pagnier also acknowledged their social deficiencies. "True" or "real" vagrants, he asserted, displayed the maladjustment typical of degenerates, in addition to their other degeneration-related malformations and asymmetries. As the medical literature noted, these misfits appeared frequently in prisons and reformatories and in hospitals.[71]

Whether they favored atavism or arrested development as an explanation or they emphasized nervous and mental disorders, or they recognized a set of distinctive psychological traits, experts agreed on the fundamental problem. All these conditions affected the will, and an underdeveloped, weakened, or defective will diminished self-control and opened the way to impulse. Had the vagrant's will functioned, Pagnier insisted, he would have been able to "master his desire to wander and adopt the sedentary ways customary in modern societies."[72] The "instinctual" or "physiological" vagrant was, as he put it, "a weak person, or a degenerate, an individual who, in terms of intellect or mental capacity, is in a state of least resistance. The imbalance in emotions, will, and intelligence is often clear..."[73]

The idea that vagrants did not think straight or will efficiently commanded considerable attention and support among doctors and sociologists alike. So did the theories that these problems resulted from illnesses or from developmental flaws. Making sense of what they saw as the flagrantly antisocial and self-defeating renunciation of the foundations of civilized life—family and work—pointed to mental disturbance, and they found evidence to confirm the connection. The accumulation of research, Pagnier asserted, indicated that the vagrant "is often ill."[74] Marie and Meunier shared that conclusion: "The real and the genuinely effective causes [of habitual vagrancy] must be sought in the vagrants' own mental life."[75] But illness did not entirely account for vagrancy. As the only explanation, it failed in two ways according to investigators. It looked at individual vagrants rather than at the phenomenon of vagrancy, and it did not include social, economic, ethnic, or personal reasons for flight.

By the end of the century, physicians and social thinkers settled on some basic distinctions among vagrants: those physically unable to work, the able-bodied and temporarily out of work, and physically able habitual vagrants.[76] They understood that circumstances produced a shifting group of occasional or accidental vagrants in search of a job or better opportunities. Florian and Cavaglieri devoted much of their study to a systematic analysis of vagrancy as a social phenomenon. Their backgrounds and political views likely drew them toward this approach. Cavaglieri obtained a law degree at the University of Padua in 1892 and established a law practice in Rome. There he joined others to establish the *Rivista Italiana di Sociologia* (Italian Journal of Sociology) in 1897. In addition, he taught administrative law and administration at the University of Padua and Rome.[77] Also a lawyer, Eugenio Florian held a number of different university positions in law and criminal procedure. In their view, vagrancy rates varied according to population density, national wealth, and levels of economic development. Industrialized England, according to Florian's analysis, had a high and stable rate of vagrancy, while less economically advanced Italy registered a significantly lower rate. In part, the higher incidence in large, rich, and more developed countries reflected the volatility of the industrial workforce and, in part, "imported vagrancy," or the movement across borders of people in search of work. With the help of statistics, they also tried to correlate vagrancy to fluctuations in the economy and to unemployment rates. Although several factors influenced short-term shifts in vagrancy, they stressed that bad times forced more people to the roads especially in prosperous and developed countries.[78]

In his analysis of vagrancy, French legislator Alexandre Bérard (1859–1923) emphasized both contingent and structural factors, arguing that the depression in prices closed factories just as phylloxera increased rural unemployment. These shorter-term conditions exacerbated the constriction of jobs produced by mechanization.[79] Others noted that industrialization produced an unstable workforce, as unskilled workers took jobs out of necessity and were the first to lose them when demand declined.[80] According to critics of capitalism, the system itself relied on this large, mobile population of unskilled workers. Thus, unemployed workers, the Italian social critic Carlo Manes observed, did not endanger society; they made it work.[81] Florian and Cavaglieri agreed, arguing that because the economy required a reserve of available workers, vagrancy filled a social function in the modern period just as it had in primitive societies. More important, in their view, "modern social organization ineluctably produced an indigent class," and poverty more than anything else influenced local vagrancy rates.[82]

Still other commentators attributed vagabondage less to economic conditions than to social values. In a well-received treatise on idlers, Dino Carina (1836–1872) stressed the effects of Italy's subjugation to foreign powers. No matter what their social position, Italians lacked a work ethic and a sense of civic responsibility as a result of long periods of domination by outsiders, he argued. By securing independence, unification allowed Italians to develop the will and fortitude to embrace work as a value.[83] If they did not, he warned, they would achieve neither freedom nor economic prosperity. Writing in 1870, Carina saw indolence as the predilection of a people new to modern freedoms. That argument recurred in analyses of why the South seemed to lag behind the North after unification.

Twenty years later, observers assumed that ordinary citizens worked hard, and they tried to explain the outliers. In some cases, they invoked the backwardness of the region or the character of the race to explain an inability or a reluctance to accept modern work regimens. But they also speculated that modern life itself caused the public's fortitude and moral rigor to flag. For example, Paul Collin, a former police commissioner in France, thought that weak social organization and ineffective education contributed to vagrancy.[84] The problem began in childhood, particularly when poverty forced mothers to work or when parents turned to alcohol or crime. Children ended up in the streets or in factories where boredom and unhealthy influences drove them off course. Like adults, they might start out looking for work, but they soon gave in to the allure of indolence. Henri Joly (1839–1925) agreed, but he also attributed vagrancy to a decline in public morality characterized by greed and egotism.[85] "Depravity and slacking, love of easy pleasure, absence of conscience, that is, a dearth of reflection and refusal to make an effort … [are] found just about everywhere."[86] He fretted that the love of gain and the attraction of leisure corroded self-discipline and elevated individual desire over social duty.

Investigators agreed, then, that pathologies or circumstances forced most vagrants into vagrancy. But a few vagrants voluntarily accepted the lifestyle, according to most studies of vagabondage. Unlike occasional vagrants or those too old, infirm, or sick to work, they chose not to hold a job or settle down. Among them, observers generally distinguished between eccentrics and social parasites. Drawn by adventure and spontaneity, free spirits abandoned routine and delighted in flouting social expectations. Marie identified them as independent dreamers, "more or less aware, more or less impulsive who have a taste for the itinerant trades or, simply, for the day by day life of the wanderer."[87] Other sane people, noted Marie, found themselves driven to the vagrant life to escape their worries or out of wanderlust, as in the case of poets and artists such as Rousseau, Wagner, Musset, and Verlaine.[88] Vagabonds of the kind celebrated in literature could be, he pointed out, "perfectly normal" but they could also be "insane … eccentrics, malingerers, neurotics and even sometimes geniuses: Francis of Assisi, for example."[89] Usually these social truants had a steady means of support, if not a regular residence, and much of the time, they returned to normal life after a bout on the road. Because they had money, they seemed harmless enough. Not all those who chose the nomadic life fit the stereotype of the footloose eccentric, however. Some people, observers specified, opted for the road because they did not like to work. Committed to "inertia, idleness, or vice," these professional vagrants violated the rights of others by refusing to do their part.[90] Other commentators also condemned "voluntary idlers as extra social or antisocial parasites."[91] These, insisted Pagnier, were corrupt repeaters.[92] Unwilling to submit to the discipline of office or factory, they lived by their wits or from their family's fortune. This group fit the traditional view that vagrants chose that lifestyle, an assumption basic to anti-vagrancy laws.

At least some analysts doubted the sanity of this category of voluntary idlers. Florian and Cavaglieri saw them as mildly deranged, and Joffroy and Dupouy diagnosed paranoia or persecution complexes. This variant of deliberate vagrancy, they specified, included "the morally insane, tramps, beggars who refuse to work, violent impulsives who recoil from no criminal act in order to express their contempt and satisfy their hatred of humanity." These egotistical misanthropes, they asserted, blamed the government and society for all their ills. As an example, they offered the case of Mo…, whom they examined at the Sainte-Anne hospital in April and May 1908. An alcoholic, thief, and murderer, he had twenty-eight convictions for vagrancy and had served three prison sentences by age twenty-eight. He took pride in being a vagrant and made no effort to find work in the intervals between prison and the asylum. People of this type, they emphasized, "resist laws, have a twisted mind and selfish, self-congratulatory tendencies." Often they suffered from delusions of grandeur or an unreasonable passion for reform; always they resented society for impinging on their freedom.[93]

Which of these causes of vagrancy predominated occasioned considerable debate. Florian and Cavaglieri argued that pathology accounted for a small percentage of vagrants; more, but still a minority, exhibited the physical and psychological traits typical of vagrants.[94] Most, however, resorted to vagabondage under the pressure of poverty or unemployment. Marie and Meunier disagreed. Those who would settle down if they could constituted a "very small number of the total contingent of vagrants." Even members of that small group often owed their situation to their "nervous and mental problems."[95] Statistics left scarcely any doubt, they argued, that most adult vagrants were physically and psychologically deficient or were neuropaths or psychopaths.[96] Like Marie and Meunier, Joffroy and Dupouy believed that even occasional vagrants presented at the very least "incontestable psychological flaws or defects."[97]

Distinctions and affinities

Studies of vagrancy insisted on classifying variants, because it made it easier to understand and to control a complicated, amorphous, and worrisome phenomenon. They agreed on the existence of two main categories of vagrants: the accidental (also called occasional or functional) and the intrinsic (habitual, born, or professional). The temporarily unemployed dominated the category of "accidental" or "occasional" vagrants. These people did not, the studies generally agreed, choose to leave home or to live without working. Rather, they formed part of a collective phenomenon produced by capitalism or according to others by occasional economic downturns. Able-bodied and often unskilled workers, they qualified as vagrants under current laws, but not for long periods and only sporadically. Motives and the little social danger they posed separated accidental from chronic, pathological vagrants. Neither group controlled its actions, but changeable external conditions explained the first type, and intractable internal weaknesses, the second. While the first category at the worst experienced periods without work, the second at best enjoyed periods of normalcy, either because they recovered from the condition or because illnesses such as hysteria or epilepsy allowed reprieve. For most biologically determined vagrants, however, the pathologies responsible resisted treatment. Those seen as healthy and willful shirkers also fit in this category of habitual vagrants. Whether ill or ill-willed, vagrants of this type caused alarm, because it seemed likely that without legitimate means of support, they lived by crime.

The range of categories extended the causes of vagrancy beyond eccentricity, age, and physical disability to include illness, psychological predisposition, and job loss. All of these subgroups stressed determinism, while underscoring the difference between biological and social drivers. The people caught by hard times or unemployment were ordinary people down on their luck. They would return to their normal routines when the situation changed. Congenital defects or illnesses that adversely affected the capacity to work, in contrast, took people out of the mainstream, often permanently. Depending on their perspective, the experts saw either the social or the biological variant as dominant, but whichever they chose, they still acknowledged that the other determinant played a role in promoting vagabondage.

Even though occasional and habitual vagrants occupied different orbits, the one laid down from the outside, the other from within the person, commentators such as Marie and Meunier recognized some connections between them. They saw evidence that nervous conditions kept accidental vagrants from finding work or stable residence.[98] Healthy, resilient people, they suggested, kept their jobs even in tough times. They, and others, also worried that repeated periods of unemployment fostered bad habits and risked turning accidental into habitual vagrants, especially if they discovered lucrative alternatives to honest work.[99] The same pattern held true for the children of unemployed workers; a lifestyle imposed by circumstances too easily became one supported by character, the experts warned. While mental imbalance crept into explanations of socially induced vagrancy, circumstances also played a role in pathological vagrancy, primarily by causing the illnesses which weakened the will or triggered a reflex to wander. Neurasthenia offered a prime example since it developed when the stresses of modern life exhausted the nervous system.

As they analyzed the phenomenon of vagabondage with an eye to medical and environmental factors, doctors, sociologists, and jurists discovered striking parallels with other socially aberrant behavior, and they drew on these affinities to reinforce their understanding of vagabonds. Florian summarized the insight: "Vagrancy is a secondary and accidental manifestation of an interior condition which in turn is the fulcrum of other socially abnormal behaviors."[100] The connection between criminality and vagrancy seemed obvious to the public. If they did not work and lacked a means of support, then vagrants must beg or steal. They might ask for food or a spot in the barn for the night, but if rebuffed, people worried that they would take what they wanted, and possibly burn the place down for good measure. The laws punishing vagrancy also assumed the risk of crime, as did the police rules that singled out vagrants for surveillance, because they threatened society. Statistics supported the correlation between crime and vagrancy rates, especially in the case of theft, Florian and Cavaglieri showed. The numbers also indicated that people who moved away from their native province committed more crimes and that a relatively high proportion of criminals did not live where they were born.[101] Not surprisingly, prison records also confirmed the link between vagrancy and crime. Bérard reported that in 1890, 78 percent of repeat criminals in France had been previously convicted for vagrancy.[102] Whether or not they had vagrancy charges on their records, active and former criminals often did not have jobs or a stable residence.

What bound vagrants and criminals went much deeper than their circumstances, however. Experts emphasized that crime and vagrancy stemmed from a similar source: defects that reduced self-control and willpower. A vagrant took to the road for the same reason a hardened criminal resorted to crime, they argued. "We find," reported Florian and Cavaglieri, "a strong resemblance, almost an identity," between the psychological profiles of habitual vagrants and those of hardened criminals, a connection supported by statistical studies indicating criminals' distaste for work.[103] In both cases, some illness, trauma, or flaw corroded the brain, diminishing the capacity to work and to govern impulses. Whether these characteristics led to vagrancy or to theft depended on chance and the immediate circumstances, according to Pagnier.[104] Prostitutes shared the psychological profile of vagrants, according to Florian and Cavaglieri. All studies, they asserted, concluded that prostitutes hated work and exhibited "the most absolute apathy."[105] They moved from place to place, because they lacked the discipline to stay with their families or with one man. That behavior indicated organic deficiencies of the will and inhibition, anomalies that also showed their defiance of social convention.[106] They exhibited, Florian and Cavaglieri contended, attributes common to all women, but in exaggerated form.[107] In their short attention spans and aversion to work, normal women resembled primitives and children. Any developmental delays could lead to the female form of vagrancy, prostitution, they specified.

Observers, then, emphasized the common pathological roots of habitual criminality and vagrancy and, according to some of them, of prostitution as well. Individual cases bore out these connections, and none dramatized the symbiosis more effectively than Joseph Vacher, who in "his sinister grandeur, was a perfect example of [the] vagrant murderer," proclaimed Pagnier.[108] A vagrant-assassin-pervert-anarchist-madman, experts believed he wrapped up all the "socially abnormal behaviors" in a single devastating package. Vacher admitted to murdering and mutilating the corpses of eleven people, and he likely committed another fifteen or sixteen horrifying murders between 1894 and 1897 as he crisscrossed France. He looked like a French version of Jack the Ripper, although he outdid his counterpart in the number if not the villainy of his crimes. The vagrant played the assassin, the assassin the pervert, and that troubling trinity exposed in turn the lucid insanity of the morally demented.

The apparent interchangeability of his antisocial selves indicated, according to the experts who flocked to analyze him, some deep malfunction that contained the potential for the whole gamut of dangerous behaviors. His array of extreme actions came, they contended, from a single source. At bottom, an organic impulsiveness explained the episodes of violence that marked his life, just as the companion to this lack of restraint, his indolence, indicated a mind short on self-discipline and willpower. By Vacher's own account, one endorsed by some of the experts, waves of uncontrollable rage surged over the fragile structures of reason and drove him to acts of mayhem. More skeptical diagnoses insisted that his apparent premeditation and the careful way he did the killing and covered his tracks indicated that he exercised some reason and self-restraint.

The Vacher case drew the attention of Cesare Lombroso, and he, along with three other experts, received slices of Vacher's brain for analysis.[109] According to Lombroso, even the most cursory psychological assessment revealed signs of "moral insanity" or of psychic epilepsy, both conditions associated with born criminality. The episodes of rage and flight, Lombroso argued, pointed to the "irascibility of the epileptic" and to "propulsive epilepsy."[110] The fact that Vacher suffered seizures when he was in the army reinforced the diagnosis, as did evidence that the attacks intensified after he shot himself in the head, he noted. Either moral insanity or psychic epilepsy accounted for why he killed random people, but they did not explain why he mutilated and violated the corpses of his victims. In Lombroso's view, those acts indicated "bloody sadism," the form of criminality closest to epilepsy and the expression of a primitive association of love with blood and violence.[111] He based his diagnosis on Vacher's actions, but the illnesses also left clear anatomical signs. His examination of Vacher's brain sample revealed the same anomalies in the right and left hemispheres that other experts found in "moral lunatics, epileptics, and many inferior animals."[112] His physical features and the results of physiological tests indicated other abnormalities linked to his crimes, and Lombroso criticized the judges for not paying attention to them.[113] Moreover, looking to the crime rather than the criminal and intent on ignoring "the illuminating light of science," the judges dismissed as feigned important evidence of his behavior in prison, Lombroso complained.[114]

Vacher's behavior invited observers to consider the connections between vagrancy and sexual perversion. Vacher insisted that he did the deeds in a fit of rage, a version that coincided with symptoms of propulsive epilepsy. But Vacher seemed aware of what he did, a pattern that aligned more with what observers knew about necrophiliacs, although they did not kill their victims. Either way, Vacher's was clearly an extreme case. Studies of other vagabonds suggested less dramatic sexual abnormalities. Tissié, for example, added Albert D...'s ardent onanism to other clinical signs of a coming attack, and when he used hypnotism to cure Dadas, he suggested that he stop masturbating, a therapy Tissié considered effective.

It was harder to marshal concrete evidence for vagrancy's links to intellectual deficits or to "the highest and most noble anomaly, the sublime anomaly, that of genius."[115] Most studies included idiocy, imbecility, and feeblemindedness among the conditions that led to vagabondage. Underdeveloped mental capacity left the impulses in control, increasing the likelihood of fugue and making it impossible for victims to work. Fewer experts suggested that what produced genius also inspired vagabondage, and then they relied primarily on coincidence to make the case. It sufficed, observed Florian, to examine the itinerant lives of Rousseau, Cervantes, Wagner, and Musset, to be convinced of the connection.[116] Pagnier also thought that geniuses, along with anarchists, prostitutes, and men of action, had psychological proclivities for vagabondage.[117]

When Florian observed that habitual vagrants possessed the "characteristics of thieves, idiots, epileptics, alcoholics and so forth," he summarized a common assumption.[118] Evidence that some vagrants committed crimes and some accused criminals lacked an address or a job, and that alcoholics and epileptics blacked out and took off indicated that aberrant behaviors came in packages. Along with other experts, Florian believed that the coincidence indicated deeper psychological affinities among the transgressive behaviors. Whether congenital or acquired, temporary or lasting, atavistic or pathological, vagabonds operated with impaired will and consequently could not meet the basic requirements of life in modern society.

Managing vagrancy

A look at the past revealed cyclical patterns of toleration and punishment as vagrancy benefitted or threatened societies, Florian argued. The earliest peoples by necessity and by their natures lived a nomadic existence, one their leaders fully accepted. Once they settled down and developed agriculture, the need and the opportunities to move declined. In this phase, the authorities punished mobility, because it weakened the community. Later on, Florian and Cavaglieri explained, when landowners and manufacturers wanted a stable workforce, governments treated vagrancy as an economic threat and punished it even more vigorously than before. As modern governments recognized the utility of mobile reserve workers, they anticipated a return to greater leniency. But they also acknowledged the countervailing pressure to calm public fears of wandering strangers by imposing restrictions.[119]

Legislation in the mid- to the late 1880s brought some changes. In 1885, the French passed a law designed to meet popular demands for stiffer penalties. Focused on repeat offenders, it provided for perpetual internment in the colonies after more than four convictions for aggravated vagrancy.[120] The law lifted police surveillance for other vagrants, but it authorized the government to declare certain areas off-limits to them after their release.[121] In addition lawmakers extended the category of *gens sans aveu* to include those whose livelihood depended on illicit gaming or promoting prostitution on the public streets whether or not they had a stable address.[122] A modification approved in 1903 removed pimping from the list.[123] While the revisions reinforced controls over vagrants, they did not change the basic prescriptions of the Criminal Code.

Italy's new Criminal Code (1889) maintained the distinction between vagrants and idlers and continued to treat beggars differently, just as the Napoleonic Code did. In a break from prevailing practice, it did not outlaw idleness and vagrancy, although it continued to criminalize certain types of begging. Instead, lawmakers shifted responsibility for controlling vagrancy from the courts to the police. Under the public order laws approved in 1889, judges, on the recommendation of the police, could subject vagrants and idlers to a series of conditions and to police supervision. They had to find work and a place to live, stay home at night, avoid suspicious people, stay away from taverns and brothels, not bear arms, and inform police when they left town. Failure to meet any of these demands was a crime that carried a sentence of up to one year in prison followed by special surveillance. Violating the conditions more than twice could result in one to five years of internment, usually in an isolated region.[124] The Italians took care to specify that only "habitual, healthy" idlers "without means of subsistence" required police attention.[125] That standard eliminated the idle rich, the temporarily unemployed, and those physically incapable of working.

This sharper juridical definition spoke to economic development, just as the move to decriminalize vagrancy reflected liberal theories of the law. Liberals acknowledged that people had the right to move about, change houses, and choose whether or not to work. But they believed that those without a stable address or job and without other sources of support lived by crime. That suspicion warranted taking preventive action to protect citizens, and it moved responsibility from the courts to the administration. By imposing restrictions and criminalizing the failure to meet them, Italians believed that they preserved basic freedoms while managing what they perceived as their disadvantages. Nervous governments also used the system, called *ammonizione*, for other alarming groups, including anyone widely believed to have committed criminal acts, to belong to the Camorra or Mafia, or to deal with stolen or smuggled goods. Anyone tried for murder or assault or anyone who threatened, attacked, or resisted public authorities, whether convicted or not, also qualified for surveillance, putting vagrants and idlers in frightening company.[126]

Toward the end of the century, the measures designed to control vagabondage came under increasing attack in France and Italy for reasons of both utility and principle. Despite the differences in their approaches, French and Italian laws presumed that the homeless, the habitually unemployed, and some types of beggars chose their lifestyles and that punishing them or mandating that they get a job and an address or face jail would pull them back into the mainstream. That assumption appeared increasingly at odds with what all the studies reported about vagrancy. Only a minority of vagrants fit the profile assumed by French anti-vagrancy laws and Italian police rules. Most did not want to leave home or be idle. They lost their jobs and went looking for work, or poverty drove them to more prosperous areas. Other able-bodied vagabonds lacked the gumption and concentration to manage methodical, sustained work. Whether driven by economic circumstances or by their psychic makeup, neither group commanded its situation and consequently neither benefitted from mandates or penalties.

Those who worried about rising vagrancy rates in France blamed the laws and their inconsistent enforcement. Far from being deterred by punishment, vagrants welcomed brief jail terms to gain respite from life on the road, according to some critics.[127] Critics also felt that the 1885 law produced mixed results. Declaring certain areas off-limits to vagrants after their release aggravated problems in the countryside, since urban authorities forced vagrants to move to another city or to find agricultural work.[128] The provision to rid France of the most dangerous repeat offenders proved more effective. Between 1885 and 1900, the government deported 9,978 habitual vagrants. But according to Joly, too many of them were listless, worn-out men rather than the "ferocious and determined" evildoer targeted by the law. The more experienced and wily vagrants, he said, contrived ways to spend time in jail without getting deported.[129] Other critics looked at the increasing vagrancy rates and concluded that the prospect of relegation did not deter offenders.

The effectiveness of the laws, however flawed, also depended on applying them, and governments urged the local authorities to intensify their zeal. A circular from the French minister of the interior informed prefects that recent investigations attributed insecurity in the countryside to "the inertia or the negligence of the agents with policing power, especially mayors and the rural police." The fact that some communes decided to dispense with a rural police force aggravated the problem, but in any case, the minister enjoined prefects to remind mayors of their responsibility for the security of citizens and their property.[130] The perceived laxness came in part from inadequate staffing, but it also reflected judges' hesitation to apply maximum penalties or to deport the repeat offenders singled out in the 1885 law.[131]

In Italy, critics of *ammonizione* such as Carlo Gatteschi pointed out the obvious. Identifying people as suspicious and requiring that they inform the police when they left town did not make it easy for them to get a job or settle down. It was, said Gatteschi, like "breaking someone's legs and telling him to rise and walk."[132] Unless they managed to appeal the judge's *ammonizione* order, vagrants and idlers faced mandates that were almost impossible to meet. Their invasive nature virtually assured violations and the criminal convictions, escalating punishments and social isolation that necessarily followed. Not only did *ammonizione* put its targets in a cruel catch-22, it violated liberal principles, critics charged. All systems of prevention, argued some, unjustly limited the freedom of innocent people. Others accepted the existence of laws that preemptively controlled suspects, provided that the police and not the courts administered them. These measures, liberals insisted, crossed the line between prevention and punishment. Only the courts had the authority to punish, and then only when citizens actually broke the laws.

Anti-vagrancy laws also fell short because they addressed such a small part of the problem. In its nature and proportions, modern vagrancy outgrew Napoleonic prescriptions, critics pointed out. If judges focused on the act itself as the law intended, they condemned inadvertent victims, but if they also weighed intention, then the law applied to only a small subset of vagrants: those who chose not to work. Marie and Meunier berated judges whose ignorance of the constraints that forced people into vagabondage led to "cruelty, injustice, or the abuse of power."[133] Relying on the existing codes to control vagrancy, then, applied a blunt and antiquated instrument to a complicated, disruptive phenomenon. Because the Italians substituted public order measures for criminal laws and the police for the courts, they enjoyed greater flexibility. However, by focusing on public order and targeting only the dangerous, they, too, addressed only a piece of the problem. In both countries doctors, criminologists, jurists, and social thinkers called for a more comprehensive and realistic approach to vagrancy.

They sought above all to address the difference between unintentional and intentional vagrants. Only willing, habitual vagrants deserved punishment, and only the truly dangerous, if any at all, required preventive surveillance. The others did not fall under the purview of the courts or the police, these students of the matter argued. They urged judges to learn to recognize the differences and, if in doubt, to seek their expert advice. If intentional vagrants merited punishment, those who could not help their condition deserved help, and reformers called for policies and institutions designed to meet their needs. To justify repressing one group and supporting the others, they invoked the same principle: social responsibility. "Yes, it is necessary to take rigorous and severe measures against habitual vagrants," observed the deputy Alexandre Bérard, "...but for the unfortunate, the old people, the ill, the orphans among them it is the duty of the nation to develop programs of social solidarity."[134] Or, as Pagnier succinctly put it: "punish or care for, eliminate the creatures or remake men."[135]

The experts expected to influence the development of these more effective and just solutions. Their entire study, said Florian and Cavaglieri, existed to convince lawmakers and judges to adopt better strategies for dealing with vagrancy. While theirs was an especially long, meticulous, systematic, and authoritative examination of the problem, other works also assessed current policies and offered recommendations. Louis Rivière (1845–1922), for example, devoted his book to policy, whereas others such as Pagnier and Marie and Meunier limited their advice to a section of their analyses. Even doctors primarily interested in the pathology and psychology of vagrancy addressed the legal implications of their findings.

Classical jurisprudence equated legal responsibility with knowing the difference between right and wrong, and arguing that impaired willpower exempted people from standing trial strained that principle. Even if judges accepted the argument, they faced the dilemma of deciding which vagrants fell in this category. That required them to examine the accused's medical record, past actions, and motives for evidence of a relevant pathology or psychological profile. To interpret the data, doctors urged, judges needed to consult the abundant literature or get some advice from medical experts. Judges' reluctance to entertain the idea of pathological vagrancy or to inform themselves about its symptoms frustrated doctors. Reacting to Men...s's experience in Brest, Charcot complained about the injustices perpetrated by tin-eared judges. Concerned that he might experience another attack and spend more of his employer's money, Men...s asked the police to watch over him until he could get back to Paris. Instead, they arrested him, and the judge refused to believe his story or the documentation about his illness that he carried with him. Only after his employer certified that he was ill did the judge release Men...s. If there was ever a case when judges should pay attention to doctors, Charcot insisted, this was it. To ensure that judges took the accused's mental state into consideration, he and other doctors tried to make consulting medical experts routine.

In France, the options available to judges also raised questions about sentencing. Being judged incapable of standing trial established the accused's insanity, while a conviction with extenuating circumstances lightened responsibility without erasing the illegal act. Either way, judges needed to determine whether to send the accused to prison, the asylum, or back home. Temporary or longer-term confinement in asylums or in workhouses where they might stiffen their will through regimented labor seemed the most appropriate strategies to the experts.[136] But when habitual vagrants appeared dangerous, prison seemed more sensible than hospitals or asylums. The borderline cases presented particular challenges. Incapable of holding down jobs but still not completely dysfunctional, these types seemed too disturbed for prisons and too sane for asylums. René Beck proposed confining them in special institutions where a corrective regimen of work might equip them to return to society. If they proved incapable of adapting, he recommended that they be kept there and provided with the minimum necessary to survive.[137] Italian judges, whose role was to decide whether or not to impose *ammonizione*, faced the same pressures their French counterparts did to exempt pathological or psychological vagrants from surveillance. However, they had another option: the criminal insane asylum.

Supporting unemployed workers presented different issues. Because they sought work, they did not belong in court or under police surveillance, experts argued. If they did commit crimes, then the courts needed to prosecute them as thieves, or arsonists, or disturbers of the peace, not as vagrants. The French anti-vagrancy laws left some latitude to judges to determine whether the accused had a trade or regular work, and Italian police and judges also had discretion in deciding whether or not the idle and homeless threatened public order. Much depended on an appraisal of the suspect's intent. Because wanting to work did not get accidental vagrants jobs, reformers called for programs to reduce unemployment. They sought to meet two goals: to get the unemployed off the roads and to prevent them from lapsing into habitual vagrancy. Joblessness, experts reiterated, could become an acquired taste or, as indolence broke the will, an inescapable condition. Energetic intervention to assist the unemployed might rescue individuals on the brink and secure society against the spread of "antisocial parasitism."

With this in mind, reformers pushed for local governments and private organizations to provide more refuges for unemployed workers on the move. The more important issue—jobs—elicited a range of proposals, including creating employment bureaus sponsored by employers or by local authorities. As a stop gap, a number of experts called for the establishment of workhouses which would provide jobs and a wage and would allow workers to come and go.[138] A more repressive option proposed by French reformers required the unemployed to remain in the workhouses until they secured a job. Any proposal that implied the right to work, however, met stiff resistance, so activists such as Rivière emphasized the curative and restorative function of workhouses. More ambitious and more controversial, the call for unemployment insurance acknowledged the reality and the utility of a mobile workforce.

Commentators generally agreed that if anything required legal attention, it was not roaming around itself but refusing to work. In their view, it made no sense to prosecute the idle rich since they did not endanger others, but they were of two minds about those without means who nonetheless intended to avoid working. The more sympathetic saw these "real" vagrants as unbalanced and deficient if only because they resisted employment. Marie and Meunier described them as social innocents treated "cruelly, unjustly, and arbitrarily" by judges ignorant of the conditions that turned a man into a vagabond.[139] Closer scrutiny would reveal deranged people, incapable of functioning in society and not legally responsible for their actions. If sick, they deserved treatment; if insane, they required attention either inside or outside asylums.[140] "You have to think," Marie and Meunier observed, "that they less than anyone else have a responsibility to society, since they most often have been rejected by the society to which they owe very little. The individual background of most vagrants leaves no doubt in this respect."[141]

Most other observers did not see every person who refused to work as mentally unbalanced or as a victim of society. According to them, the class of "guilty" vagrants, those with no excuse to abstain from labor, merited prosecution, because this type of vagrancy violated basic social norms. Societies, like living organisms, depended on the active contributions of every able member; the shiftless drew from the community without returning anything to it.[142] The idler, Pagnier complained, "does not furnish the daily sum of work that each man owes to justify his existence."[143] Worse, by violating something as basic as the duty to work, "social parasites" threatened the social order itself. Seen as either an assault on rights or as stealing from other citizens, vagrancy qualified as a crime according to both classical and positivist juridical standards. These arguments for criminalizing vagrancy further justified anti-vagrancy laws in France, and in Italy they supported calls for reinstating deliberate, habitual vagrancy as a felony.[144] These willing vagrants required a special regimen, experts believed. They did not benefit from prison; in fact, they appeared to seek convictions and time them for the colder months.[145] For self-professed empiricists such as Florian, the Italian system of surveillance made no sense as a source of control either. It assumed that ordering people to work sufficed, but like prison, *ammonizione* did little to discourage inveterate and deliberate vagrants. What they needed was the discipline of forced labor in prison work camps or agricultural colonies. There, Pagnier reasoned, the shirker could be "employed, directed, given discipline to replace the will which he lacks and to make him useful to society."[146] However, he despaired of actually curing this type, arguing that "socially the adult cannot be changed; the prison or work establishment is, therefore, a pis-aller, a necessary pis-aller."[147]

Each type of vagrant required a different response. Pagnier resumed the range: for the aged, the old people's home; for the sick, the insane asylum or hospital; for the unemployed, assistance to find work; for the foreign vagrant, expulsion; for the professional vagrant, supervised work; "for the unemployable residue of the cities, and for him only: jail."[148] Knowing when to use which strategy required understanding which vagrant fit what profile. Anyone without work looked a lot alike to the public and the authorities. It was easy to peg cultural or ethnic types such as the gypsies, and to identify intellectuals, well-heeled and restless eccentrics, and young people from good families in search of a direction. But distinguishing between "occasional" and "habitual" vagabonds and between deliberate shirkers and the ill proved more difficult. Sociologists and doctors went to great lengths to highlight the differences between safe and dangerous vagrants and between socially induced and pathological vagrancy. To develop reliable criteria, they used clinical tests and measurements, case studies, and statistical tools, as they did with other misfits. The results produced detailed classifications of causes and types supported by real-life examples, tables, and numbers.

The director of a criminal insane asylum in Tuscany, Vittorio Codeluppi, provides an example of the assessment process. He published the "spontaneous" autobiography of a patient who described a succession of jobs, moves, and run-ins with the police. Usually the authorities sent him back to his hometown, but when his drinking caused excessive behavior, he reported, they sent him to a mental institution. He never stayed long, because the doctors judged him sane and released him. In a medical review of the case that he appended to the autobiography, Codeluppi described his patient as "a tall young man, fairly attractive and with a strong physique" but with certain signs of degeneration: "a small head, enlarged face, crooked ears, uneven eye sockets, and an absolute lack of moustache or beard." The patient proved "lucid" but showed "a not minimal degree of weakness of ethical feeling," although "he never exhibited any dangerous tendencies." Codeluppi labeled him a "born vagrant" and recommended, evidently successfully, that he be confined in a criminal insane asylum since he was too sane for an ordinary asylum yet not well-enough behaved to remain in society.[149]

This case showed the limits of such evaluations, particularly those based on the anthropometric approach used by criminal anthropologists and some doctors. Categorizing Vacher presented a far more difficult dilemma. The three court-appointed medical experts who advised the judges on his fitness to stand trial included the prominent professor of legal medicine Alexandre Lacassagne.[150] Based on his actions, it seemed that Vacher closely fit the categories of the "habitual" vagrant and the innate killer. The heinous nature of his behavior and his insistence that uncontrollable anger overcame him pointed to insanity, but how he chose and killed his victims, and how he covered his tracks demonstrated lucidity. His constant wandering also supported two contrasting assessments: either he couldn't or he wouldn't work. Especially in such contested cases, criminologists urged attention to the criminal, and by seeking the advice of forensic experts, in Vacher's case the judge showed that he agreed.

The forensic doctors based their evaluation on an examination of the autopsy reports of Vacher's victims, a detailed investigation of Vacher's life, and observations of his behavior in prison. They interviewed Vacher several times, spoke with his family, tracked down people who knew him as a schoolboy and a soldier. They scrutinized his school and army records for clues about his character and health and looked at family members for signs of degenerative illnesses, such as epilepsy. The search provided plenty of evidence of mental imbalance. Repeated episodes of anger and violence brought him to the attention of the police when he was young and led to his discharge from the army, with a certificate of good conduct and a diagnosis of mental problems. After he shot his fiancée and tried to kill himself, the judge ordered him confined to an asylum, and after several months of treatment, the director pronounced him cured and released him. Within months, he began the series of murders that eventually led to his arrest.

Like the actions themselves, the information about the man permitted a number of conclusions. It confirmed, in the view of some experts, that Vacher was too deranged to stand trial. Either an illness or the bullet in his brain caused the "moral insanity" which explained his wandering as well as the grisly denouement to his disturbed life. But the official forensic report drafted by Lacassagne concluded that Vacher planned and carried out his actions, fully aware of what he was doing. The report concluded that Vacher feigned insanity in order to escape prison, just as he had after he shot his fiancée. In a separate report, Lacassagne provided a more exact diagnosis. Vacher suffered from a disorder in which the "destructive instinct" overpowered the normal sex drive and produced sadistic and grossly antisocial behavior. This illness did not affect its victims' ability to plan and execute the ruthless murders that fed their sick desires, as Vacher and, argued Lacassagne, Jack the Ripper proved. The jury accepted that logic, and Vacher died under the guillotine.

Reformers such as Pagnier and Collin understood that reducing vagrancy also required preventive measures. These efforts focused attention on juveniles. Too many minors either spent time in jail for vagrancy or, too young to be charged, led lives on the streets. Pagnier estimated that 60 percent of prison inmates were young and about three-quarters of them were first-time offenders.[151] Most of those lived with their families but lacked appropriate guidance, because mothers worked or unemployed fathers drifted into lethargy or crime. Orphans, abandoned children, and runaways also ended up in jail. According to some commentators, the children who drifted about also suffered developmental delays, weak intelligence, and inherited or acquired pathologies that took them outside the mainstream.[152]

In response, both countries took steps to protect children from the worst abuses. Lawmakers imposed controls on the use of children in ambulatory trades, and after intense debate, they passed child labor laws. In 1873, the Italians eliminated the practice of buying children and reselling them to street vendors, as part of the law controlling the itinerant sector, and the French passed a law in 1874 that punished parents who let their children work for acrobats or street performers or beg in the streets.[153] After 1882, compulsory schooling occupied children from age seven to thirteen in France, but a dearth of schools and weak enforcement delayed full implementation. Rivière estimated that in 1894 across France, 600,000 school-aged children did not go to school.[154] After several abortive tries, Italian legislators approved watered-down restrictions on child labor in 1886. They set the minimum working age at nine, except in mines where they made it ten, and managed to impose an eight hour work day. Since compulsory primary education affected children through age eight, the laws allowed them to move directly into the workforce, a benefit, argued some, to their moral development.

Those most concerned about preventing vagabondage called for bolder and more extensive measures. The more optimistic among them urged sustained intervention to salvage children, or, if incorrigible, they encouraged supervised care. Either way, given the number of children on the loose, strategies aimed at the young promised to reduce both the prison and vagrant populations. In a minimal response to the problem, the Church and private benefactors ran orphanages and boarding schools, and some local authorities provided support in foster homes or schools. In 1889, French lawmakers reinforced these haphazard initiatives by requiring the courts to end parental rights in certain conditions and to assign children to a guardian or to Public Assistance, a law extended in 1898 to children convicted of crimes. At the end of 1900, in the Department of the Seine alone, the director of Public Assistance supervised 48,063 children aged from day one to twenty-one who lived in foster homes, or if difficult or delinquent in boarding schools or reformatories.[155] When the Italian police identified children under eighteen as idlers or vagrants, the court ordered a parent or guardian to supervise their conduct and to provide training. If they did not, they risked losing their parental rights. Children in this situation or with no parent or guardian lived with foster families or in reformatories until they learned a trade or reached majority.[156] Reformers in both countries also campaigned to change the conditions that put minors on the streets in the first place: poverty and weak families.

Their logic

Public worry about vagrants at the end of the nineteenth century verged on panic, provoking lawmakers and medical and social scientists to take a new look at the problem. The old explanations and the laws and policies that they inspired did not make sense for any but a minority of the wanderers, studies contended. The idea that vagrants chose their lot and should bear the consequences no longer conformed to the evidence. Either physical defects that impaired self-discipline explained the incapacity to work or social factors prevented people from obeying norms, or, more rarely, pernicious types chose to flout expectations. Biology explained inveterate vagrants, and society explained the "occasional" types, but deliberate vagrants fit uneasily in either category. In the first case, people lacked the mental equipment needed for the disciplined life, and in the second economic conditions prevented them from leading the lives they desired. Either way, they did not reject the settled, civilized lifestyle; factors beyond their control denied it to them. The same did not hold for healthy people who decided to live without working. If it looked like a phase or benign eccentricity, they got a pass; if wealth let them be idle, they might get condemned as parasites; if they lived by their wits, they likely got pegged as dangerous parasites.

Their new understanding of vagabondage contained sharp ambivalence. On the one hand, occasional and pathological vagrants merited compassion, since neither type chose their condition. They needed social support in the form of jobs, charity to tide them over, medical treatment, or care in a hospital or asylum. As science updated and "rationalized" long-standing fears of vagabonds, sympathy for their plight coexisted with a remarkable animus. Studies reinforced the common idea that vagrants committed crimes by making lawlessness not just a matter of expediency but the response to deeper drives. Understanding that both criminals and vagrants lacked the will and self-control to obey social norms dramatized their distance from ordinary people. Even if they wished it otherwise, they failed to perform as evolved humans and effective citizens did, because inherited defects or illness set them apart. Or according to a different explanation, they operated with the mental equipment of primitives and children, because they did not mature fully.

Voluntary vagrants, in contrast, did more than exhibit bad judgment; they attacked society. Former police commissioner Collin expressed the view starkly: vagrancy "eats away at the social body … it must be combated."[157] Because vagrants refused the basic obligation to support themselves and contribute to the whole, they sapped society's foundations, contended Florian.[158] Anyone who willfully failed to conform to the commandment—support yourself—had to be anti- or extra-social, a dangerous misfit as prone to embracing crime as vagrancy. From imagining that vagrants undermined society, it was an easy step to believe that they infected it. Pagnier and others coolly labeled vagrants as sources of contagion, arguing that they threatened public health by causing epidemics and spreading infectious diseases. Because gypsies and tramps ignored basic hygiene, they put ordinary citizens at risk. "Individuals carrying around contagion, filth, pillage," noted Pagnier, "sow germs of infection everywhere and in spite of everything."[159] Less literally, they also infected others by example, luring them into lives of indolence and irresponsibility. Inveterate and especially willing vagrants drew the most negative reactions, but the idea that unemployment might infect the victim and his children with permanent indolence gave "legitimate" vagrancy a terrifying twist as well.

These stark warnings showed that vagrancy aroused fears even in aloof students of the phenomenon. As investigators gave scientific weight to arguments once made primarily on moral grounds, the tramp emerged as a very dangerous outsider and an intolerable affront to social norms. Science did not see most vagrants as rational but misguided people who chose the vagrant life any more. These voluntary vagrants-for-life existed on the margins, and the contempt they engendered made accidental and innate vagrancy seem more appealing by comparison. At the same time, the idea that biology prevented some and the economy others from living a civilized life underscored their abnormality. Seen as a social and medical problem, vagabondage properly involved politicians and doctors rather than the courts, the experts argued. It fell to them to find ways to avoid the worst consequences of endemic unemployment and to institutionalize those biologically incapable of living according to modern norms and standards.

Their insistence on distinguishing the unemployed from the shiftless indicated the extreme importance put on work as a foundation of society and a standard of normality. Investigators would not have taken such pains to exonerate those who looked for but could not find jobs if they did not assign such significance to working. But here, too, the analyses of vagrancy exposed a certain ambivalence. Studies stressed how much will and self-discipline it took to function in modern society. Only the most developed brain allowed individuals to tame their passions and channel their emotions enough to submit to long hours in factories and offices and to stick with the routines of family life. Primitive people could not muster such discipline, but the descriptions of their lives sometimes carried unmistakable whiffs of envy. The soberest studies also left a space for those whose youth, oddness, or genius gave them reason to wander and whose wealth permitted them to do so without alarming or harming others. They admitted that mostly sane people with social standing might free themselves from conventional restraints, though usually just for a time.

Their concern about the "contagion" of example and about the unemployed making vagrancy a habit suggests that observers saw the allure of indolence. Just a taste of it, they worried, made it more difficult to muster the determination to return to a more regimented life. If they were out of work for too long, French doctors in particular believed that lethargy would become an acquired characteristic likely to pass on to the next generation. Others carried the germ of vagabondage inside themselves from the start. When sorrows, nervous disorders, and certain kinds of mental illness triggered the impulse to run, a buried and more natural and authentic self resurfaced as willpower wavered. This second self played the role of a freer, more spontaneous double. For those who believed in ontogenesis, even healthy adults carried traces of the indolence and impulsiveness that they experienced growing up. These qualities lay beneath the surface, barely contained, but contained nonetheless due to the hold of the civilized mind.

Looking from individuals to the phenomenon of vagrancy also produced some double vision. Studying vagrancy in the past showed that it waxed and waned and that the public and governments responded with repression or tolerance according to conditions. Experts understood, and shared, public distress about rootless people, and they presented themselves as addressing a pressing social problem. At the same time, studying vagrancy brought a clearer understanding of socially driven mobility and with it greater appreciation for "legitimate" vagrants. The experts began to pay attention to the dynamics of work in industrializing and urbanizing societies. They showed that modern economies relied on unskilled workers and on a mobile workforce so that what passed as vagrancy by the old definitions was reasonably benign and possibly even useful. Seen from that perspective, unemployed workers responded to grand and constructive forces. In addition to the bursts of mobility provoked by economic crises, observers recognized steadier and longer-term movement across borders and from rural to urban areas. Rapidly growing cities registered the influx in more poverty, dislocation, vagrancy, crime, and violence. But these migrations also added to the vitality of society, Florian and Cavaglieri claimed. They pointed to reputable sociologists who argued that mobility favored change in the most advanced societies. It produced "a healthy and beneficial energy, symptom of a broad and intense life." That some governments moved to decriminalize vagrancy indicated that they wanted to foster the free circulation of people, even if abiding public worries about its dangers prompted them to maintain some restrictions.[160]

Criminals

[B]ecoming a criminal is not a matter of choice, just as no one decides to go crazy or to get tuberculosis or leprosy.

Gaspare Virgilio[1]

Habitual criminals and vagrants led lives that made them misfits. According to contemporary students of social behavior, they could not do otherwise since some defect in the brain or nervous system prevented them from living by civilized society's rules. Organic abnormalities also accounted for people with excessive, inadequate, or misdirected sexual desires. Those who could not stay put, obey the laws, and manage heterosexual marriage appeared to lack the self-control and moral sensibility that normal people possessed. Their numbers and their antisocial behavior alarmed the public and sent experts and lawmakers looking for the source of their problem.

What counts as criminal behavior differs according to time and place. Observes French historian Dominique Kalifa: "Except for murder … the existence of crime and delinquency is relative, highly 'constructed' by society, and it fluctuates according to the evolution of custom, norms or forms of social control."[2] In an earlier study of crime, Michelle Perrot argued that "there are no 'facts of crime' as such, only a judgmental process that institutes crimes by designating as criminal both certain acts and their perpetrators. In other words, there is a discourse of crime that reveals the obsessions of a society."[3] In fin-de-siècle Italy and France, an apparent increase in crime unsettled, when it did not panic, citizens. "Acute anxiety" about crime between 1870 and 1890 spurred the birth of criminal anthropology, according to Mary Gibson in her study of Cesare Lombroso.[4] Kalifa describes the French as obsessed with crime throughout the nineteenth century, but especially so in the early 1900s, during what he refers to as a security emergency.[5] Public pressure prompted French lawmakers to consider strategies of crime deterrence and ways to rehabilitate criminals. Medical and social scientists also weighed in, promising to use science to help policymakers find the most effective ways to address the crisis. As they broadcast their new theories about delinquency, they both substantiated and alleviated popular alarm.[6]

The problem

Official crime statistics provided an incentive for policy initiatives and grist for public concern. Commenting on the reports, experts cautioned that changes in the criminal codes, the competencies of courts, and policing techniques might account for the fluctuations in numbers. Decriminalizing some acts and criminalizing others could produce spikes in the data, as could variations in record-keeping and in levels of enforcement. Moreover, they acknowledged that interpreting the figures themselves demanded care. A comforting dip in the conviction rate meant little if the number of crimes dismissed for insufficient evidence or the lack of a suspect shot up.[7] Within these limits, however, analysts believed that the official statistics revealed patterns worthy of their attention. If anything, many observed, the numbers underestimated the severity of the problem since a good deal of crime likely went undetected and unreported.

Records for united Italy indicated a steady although not dramatic increase in the overall crime rate, with serious crime numbers remaining stable or declining and minor violations growing.[8] A virtual doubling of cases heard by the lower courts and a decline in those considered by the higher courts confirmed the trend. Looking at the ten-year period from 1883 to 1892, Enrico Ferri, the prominent lawyer and deputy, counted 3,352,910 Italians convicted for felonies and misdemeanors, the equivalent of one tenth of the population. Most of them (2,734,452) appeared in the courts of first instance on misdemeanor charges, he reported. The Criminal Code passed in 1889 partly explained these numbers. It shifted jurisdiction over several crimes from the higher to the lower courts and criminalized certain misdemeanors.[9] While legal reforms accounted for some of the reduction in felonies, statistics also indicated real changes in the type of crimes committed. Per capita figures for the most serious crimes, including murder, fell, although Italy still led Europe with almost twenty times the murder rate in England and six times that of France.[10] At the same time, violence against public officials, crimes against public order, thefts, and illicit economic activities including fraud, forgery, and embezzlement rose.[11] Similar changes in the nature of illegal activity occurred in England, Germany, and France, as courts dealt with more crimes, particularly against property.

Looking across the border, Ferri concluded that the situation was significantly worse in France, even considering its larger population.[12] French commentators agreed on the gravity of the problem. Because governments began to keep crime statistics in 1825, they could and did take a longer view than the Italians. In 1889, Henri Joly, whose publications on crime and comparative psychology attracted attention, estimated that crime had increased by 133 percent over the last fifty years.[13] Reporting fifteen years later, Gabriel Tarde (1843–1904), a well-known sociologist and criminologist and head of the Office of Judicial Statistics of the Ministry of Justice, estimated that between 1825 and 1882 felonies and misdemeanors tripled, while the population only increased by a tenth. Such a striking progression of criminality led to "pessimistic" and even "alarmist" conclusions, he observed.[14] And yet the statistics indicated, as they did in Italy, a relative decline in serious crimes. Joly refused to credit improved public morality for the change, arguing instead that reassigning crimes once dealt with by the Assizes to the lower courts accounted for it.[15] His closer examination of conviction records showed variations generally parallel to those evident in Italy.[16] Experts agreed that armed robbery declined, and embezzlement and fraud rose, although they differed about the relative increase of crimes against property and people.[17] The number of murders receded in France, but rape and indecent assault soared, particularly the sexual abuse of children.[18] But of all the categories of crime, vagrancy and illegal begging multiplied the most in the 1880s, a spike that contributed to public alarm.[19]

Focusing on just the 1880s and 1890s and on convictions, Tarde reported a dip in violent crime and a surge in offenses driven by cupidity and lust.[20] Relative to prior decades, first-degree murder and manslaughter trials continued to decline, and sentences for assaults on children dropped.[21] Convictions for property crimes also diminished, even though armed robbery and murders driven by greed figured more prominently than they had before 1880. But, Tarde argued, looking at the cases dismissed for lack of evidence and at acquittals told a different story. In 1900 compared to 1880, examining magistrates dismissed cases at higher rates, and when they did come to trial, the record showed more indulgence on the part of juries and judges. Tarde also noted a decline in arrests in the Paris area and blamed the police for looking the other way.[22]

Analysts also examined the statistics with an eye to regional, class, age, and gender differences. French reports noted exceptionally high crime rates in Corsica, while Italians pointed to significant and endemic criminality in the South. "Naples and Sicily are for judiciary statistics in Italy what Corsica is for judicial statistics in France, a disrupting element, commented one."[23] These areas also saw more blood crimes compared to central and northern Italy and mainland France. In contrast, regions that registered fewer murders saw increases in crimes related to economic development and identified more with the upper than the lower classes.[24] Investigators' analyses revealed higher per capita crime rates in cities than in rural areas and more male than female offenders. Toward the end of the century, correlations to age provoked an eruption of concern about juvenile crime, especially in France.

What really drew attention was the increase in recidivism. Between 1875 and 1880, close to half of all convicted criminals in France already had records compared to a third twenty-five years earlier.[25] Of the most serious cases, those heard by the Assize Courts, almost two thirds involved repeat offenders in 1905, forensic doctor and criminologist Alexandre Lacassagne (1843–1924) pointed out.[26] In Italy, the percentage of prisoners with prior records almost tripled between 1870 and the early 1890s.[27] Such high recidivism rates pointed to the existence of a group of habitual, even professional offenders, apparently undeterred by punishment. Their stubborn criminality challenged the idea that rational but misguided people broke laws and that punishments calibrated to the gravity of the offense and delivered swiftly and inexorably reformed them and deterred others. Habitual criminals did not follow that calculus; they took the punishment and returned for more, making them both a mystery to resolve and a danger to thwart.

The numbers worried the public, but levels of concern knew their seasons. In France, a wave of alarm rose in the early 1880s in response to the sharp increases in recidivism.[28] Another swell occurred between 1900 and 1914, as the popular press publicized crime and as experts and government officials publically fretted about moral and social decline and its expression in juvenile delinquency.[29] In Italy, unification drew attention to political dissent, endemic violence in the South, and to crime rates as a measure of national backwardness. Deep concern about public order caused early governments to debate whether to preempt crime or wait for it to happen and in 1889 to approve police surveillance for potentially dangerous individuals. That system singled out groups that inspired the greatest fears, including vagrants, bandits, smugglers, mafiosi, arsonists, thieves, blackmailers, and political dissidents.

Understanding crime

Brandishing the weapons of science, physicians, criminal anthropologists, and sociologists took on the problem of crime in treatises, articles, interviews, and at international meetings. They exchanged information with each other, and they made an effort to inform policymakers and the public about their findings. They sought to understand criminals, more than crimes, basing their analyses on statistics, on studies of prison and asylum populations, and on investigations of the "criminal class." Using this data, experts worked out elaborate taxonomies of criminal types and carefully assessed the impact of "cosmic," social, and biological conditions on delinquency. Their empirical approach promised, they asserted, to dispel fictions and to promote more rational and effective approaches to deviance. It would, proclaimed Cesare Lombroso, enhance justice and reinforce "the very shaky destiny of the social order."[30]

Their work followed different paths of inquiry. One effort involved using the statistical data to correlate criminal behavior to a range of possible causes. Most of these investigators started by rejecting the idea that misguided individuals chose crime for largely idiosyncratic reasons. Whereas jurists of the Classical school believed that anyone could make a poor choice, these analysts looked for connections between particular conditions and crime rates. They examined the effects of factors such as the weather, geography, and race on crime; they checked the impact of economic ups and downs and of income levels and occupation. Studies also looked at the population of accused and convicted criminals, trying to relate types and rates of crime to age, gender, and family background. Ettore Fornasari di Verce, for example, explored the connection between income and crime. He contended that in 1889 of every one hundred prisoners in Italy, fifty-six were indigent, thirty-two just barely got by, ten were reasonably well-off, and just under two (1.72) qualified as wealthy or comfortable.[31] While the figures could indicate the immorality of the lower classes, Fornasari rejected such an assessment. Rather, most people living at a subsistence level followed the law, proof of their stoic resignation to misery or their heroic resistance to crime's temptations. Luigi Roncoroni looked at gender and crime, observing that of every one hundred convictions, eighty-four were men and sixteen women. The more serious the crime, the greater the gap, he pointed out. Looking deeper, he evaluated female criminality in terms of region, age, civil status, and type of crime and concluded that the simpler organization of women's brains limited the number of possible crime-inducing anomalies and moderated the effects of immorality.[32]

Using numbers to identify connections and patterns provided one perspective, the examination of individual lawbreakers and their lives another. Doctors, criminologists, and sociologists evaluated criminals' physical features, mental and physical health, personal and family medical histories, their emotional development, as well as their behavior in and out of prison. Their region, town, and upbringing, and the values and customs characteristic of their social milieu all figured in analyses of what caused them to break the law. Typically these investigators took a wide view, with physicians and criminologists attending to social factors and sociologists gathering and using medical data. Their reports focused on notorious individuals, or they offered more general assessments of a prison population, type of criminal, or notable neighborhood hotbed of crime. Case studies, statistics, tables, and sometimes photographs buttressed their arguments with what they, as committed Positivists, touted as hard evidence.

Whatever their method or focus, the research staked out some common ground. A scientific approach, investigators asserted, looked less at criminal acts and more at what drove criminals to commit them. As they learned more about criminals, they made key distinctions based primarily on the etiology of their crimes. They took a comprehensive view of causes, looking at relevant anatomical aberrations, physiological disorders, mental problems, ethnicity, and social factors. Although experts disagreed on specifics, they generally stressed the difference between occasional and habitual criminals, just as they distinguished between accidental and inveterate vagrants, partial and full insanity, talent and genius. The first group chose to break the law, yes, but circumstances forced their hands. Like the unemployed who left home to look for work, temporary deviants responded to economic emergencies or personal misfortunes. Habitual or grand criminals, a distinct and dangerous minority, attracted more interest and aroused more debate. So did the growing number of repeat offenders. In these cases, traditional explanations of malevolent character or faulty logic no longer made sense to these experts. Repeat criminals might appear mean-spirited or dense, but criminologists took these attributes as signs of deeper problems. As with a fever, better not to conflate the symptoms and the disease, they asserted. Figuring out, then, who did what and why and therefore who merited which treatment dominated the new field of criminology in the last decades of the nineteenth and the opening years of the twentieth century.

Statistics confirmed that the murder rate put Italy first among "civilized" nations. This damning laurel raised questions about the new nation's stability and its legitimacy. It challenged its claim to stand with its counterparts in western Europe, a title greatly valued by Italy's leaders. Those concerns and high recidivism rates focused attention on the causes of what experts called "true" crime. The high stakes associated with finding answers help explain why Italians took the lead in explaining inveterate criminality. The most debated and influential theory attributed both repeated lawlessness and one-time brutal deeds to organic abnormalities. The best-known advocate of the biological approach, Cesare Lombroso, proclaimed the novelty of "legal medicine" in 1876.[33] Understanding the criminal from the inside out, he contended, clarified the (limited) role free will and rational choice played in crime and allowed judges to assess legal responsibility more accurately. It also promoted more enlightened treatment of convicted criminals, by encouraging graduated punishments, the use of reformatories, and the creation of criminal asylums for those deemed too sick to stand trial and too dangerous to live in society.

Considered the founder of criminal anthropology by contemporaries, Lombroso gained international attention for his work. One of his earliest studies, *Criminal Man*, published in 1876, outlined a theory of criminality so controversial that for years it crystallized debates among specialists and inspired studies designed to demonstrate its merits, demolish it, or further refine it.[34] In five successive editions of *Criminal Man*, Lombroso extended his theory to incorporate new research and to meet the objections of his critics. The updated versions continued to stimulate investigation and debate in Italy in particular, but also in France and Germany. In addition to *Criminal Man*, Lombroso turned out a prodigious number of books, treatises, and articles on a range of subjects including pellagra, genius, cretinism, anarchism, and sexual deviance.

Lombroso also acted as something of an impresario, organizing and promoting forensic medicine and criminal anthropology. He convened the first International Congress of Criminal Anthropology in Rome in 1885, and his theories largely set the agenda. Subsequent meetings allowed participants to present research and to reinforce collaborations. The meetings also concluded with resolutions designed to publicize the new discipline and to influence policymakers. The journal Lombroso and others founded in 1880, *Archivio de Psichiatria, Antropologia Criminale e Scienze Penali per Servire allo Studio dell'Uomo Alienato e Delinquente* (Archives of Psychiatry, Criminal Anthropology and Penal Studies to Support the Study of the Insane and of Criminals), brought together the widely disparate fields that dealt with social and mental deviance and kept readers informed of current publications in an extensive and international book review section. As his compatriot Cesare Beccaria had done a century before, Lombroso played a key role in reshaping the debate about crime and jurisprudence.

Both Beccaria and Lombroso sought to rationalize systems that they found arbitrary and irrational. Other than that goal, however, the two shared little common ground. Lombroso took aim at Beccaria's belief that because criminals chose crime, well-designed punishments deterred them. Most criminals did not act freely, Lombroso contended. Because they could not control their actions, they could not reasonably be held legally or morally accountable for what they did or be expected to respond to punishment. If it did not reform criminals, punishment served only as a measure of retaliation against them, he proclaimed. While Lombroso rejected vengeance as unworthy of civilized societies, he insisted that they had the right to protect themselves against dangerous misfits. With social defense in mind, then, he urged judges to gear penalties to the criminals' threat to society rather than to the gravity of their offense. To make that assessment required them to evaluate the individual criminal rather than the crime.

In the first edition of *Criminal Man*, published in 1876, Lombroso identified a criminal type to whom crime came naturally. These criminals, he argued, had organic anomalies that predisposed them to crime, and these anomalies left identifiable anatomical marks. Smaller and more irregular skulls and in "nearly all" cases "jug ears, thick hair, thin beards, pronounced sinuses, protruding chins, and broad cheekbones" distinguished criminals from non-criminals.[35] In addition to these physical signs, the criminal type showed an insensitivity to pain, "precipitous passions," moral indifference, and noticeably large doses of pride and vanity.[36] Moreover, observations of prisoners revealed distinctive practices, especially tattooing, and characteristic ways of speaking and writing. These and other attributes bore a striking resemblance, Lombroso argued, to those of primitive peoples.[37] Based on the similarities in appearance, character, and demeanor, Lombroso concluded that primitive instincts drove modern criminals. Biological throwbacks, their savage drives surfaced in certain conditions and led to serious crime. The precipitating factors included "illness, the weather, bad examples, and a sort of spermatic inebriation induced by excessive continence" that explained crime during puberty and among groups forced into celibacy by circumstances.[38]

Lombroso set out to understand what, if anything, distinguished those criminals from non-criminals and from the insane. He theorized that irregular features, "something strange" about their countenance, discordant emotions and values, and distinctive imaginations separated the criminal type from ordinary citizens.[39] It was harder, he asserted, to distinguish between criminals and madmen, because many criminals were insane, and many mental patients were criminals. These patterns confirmed that crime "often" resulted from defects in the brain and sometimes from mental illness.[40] For example, the passionate intensity characteristic of some criminals looked a lot like "impulsive mania."[41] The similarities went further, Lombroso believed. "Many" insane patients exhibited the anatomical, physiological, and emotional marks of the criminal type, suggesting that but for their madness, they would be criminals.[42] The connections struck still deeper. The same conditions, Lombroso discovered, promoted both criminality and insanity: "trauma, anomalies of the head, and alcohol" as well as "civilization, celibacy, a hot climate, being male, living in an urban area, and working at certain jobs."[43] The underlying causes differed, however. Insanity was an illness, while instinctive criminality was an inborn condition, a distinction significant enough, in Lombroso's view, to make the insane and criminals two separate groups.[44]

The 1876 edition of *Criminal Man* offered a stark and single-minded version of what Lombroso later called the "born criminal."[45] It gave primacy to anatomical characteristics and described born criminals as a separate race, distinguished by atavistic features and behaviors. As he learned more and as he responded to critics, Lombroso revised his theory. He produced four more editions of *Criminal Man*, and his daughter, Gina Lombroso, published a shortened version in 1911, after his death.[46] His revisions came at regular intervals over a period of twenty years, with the second in 1878, the third in 1884, the fourth in 1889, and the last in 1896, each one longer and broader in scope as he progressively expanded and complicated his theory.[47] Mary Gibson and Nicole Hahn Rafter's English translation of *Criminal Man* draws from all five editions and offers an exceptional resource for understanding the development of Lombroso's ideas. In successive versions, Lombroso identified different categories of criminals, extended the range of causes beyond atavism, and laid out recommendations for dealing with crime. In each edition, he enriched the profile of the born criminal's anatomy and physiology, reporting the results of a growing battery of tests and an ever-expanding sample of criminals. Direct observation added information on their personality, behavior, and habits. For example, in the second edition he called on a handwriting expert to analyze signatures, and in the fourth, he reported on inmates' gestures and on their penchant for pictographs and hieroglyphics. Lombroso added statistics, case studies, photographs, and illustrations to reinforce his arguments. For the fifth and final version, he attached an atlas containing tables and extensive sets of photographs of different types of criminals to the text.

The single criminal type gave way to a more complicated set of categories and subcategories. The second edition added criminals of passion to born criminals. They acted on impulse, driven by overwhelming "rage, love, or offended honor," and they typically regretted their acts. Their remorse and the intensity and relative nobility of their intentions distinguished them from atavistic criminals.[48] In the next version, in 1884, Lombroso mentioned the madman, the occasional criminal, and the alcoholic as still different types of criminals, but he left it to the fourth edition to describe them in detail. New evidence about the number of prisoners who were mentally ill, most often before their convictions, encouraged Lombroso to assign them their own category.[49] Among the insane, he identified three distinct subtypes: the alcoholic, the hysteric, and the mattoid, this last including those, usually males, who resorted to crime to fulfill their grandiose ideas.[50] Unlike insane and born criminals, occasional criminals reacted to external circumstances. With this group, too, Lombroso made distinctions. Pseudocriminals committed crimes by mistake (they accidentally pulled the trigger), or acted under pressure, or did something ordinary that happened to be labeled a crime by society. They did not exhibit any sort of degenerative anomaly.[51] Criminaloids carried a hidden predisposition to crime that certain conditions activated. With good moral training, propitious circumstances, or legal outlets for their immoral tendencies, they never got in trouble. If they did turn to crime, it easily became a habit, and then criminality became "an organic phenomenon, flesh of their own flesh."[52]

Lombroso also extended the range of biological factors that produced habitual criminals. By the third edition, he added disease to atavism, arguing that autopsies showed illness-induced anomalies in the brain and nervous system that produced an innate criminal drive.[53] The effects of epilepsy proved especially potent, he discovered. Initially unsure about the links between moral insanity and born criminality, he believed he discovered the key in epilepsy. It brought the two "together in one great natural family."[54] Epilepsy resulted when trauma, degeneration, or alcohol abuse irritated the cortical centers, producing motor or psychological reactions, or both.[55] Understanding that epilepsy appeared in a less-recognized larval or psychic form explained its similarities with born criminality and moral insanity. While seizures characterized the better-known motor-sensory variant, larval epilepsy manifested itself in a set of distinctive and abnormal physiological and psychological traits. The same anomalies also occurred in born criminals and the morally insane, especially impulsiveness, high emotivity, and a penchant for evil.[56] Other similarities, Lombroso contended, eluded statistics but did not escape observation. Like vagabonds, epileptics took flight; they could commit obscene or destructive acts; they had "frequent" suicidal tendencies.[57] In his view, then, epilepsy constituted a substratum for different sorts of pathological behavior, beginning with occasional crime and, in combination with other conditions such as atavism, moral insanity, and born criminality, extending to true crime.[58]

From the first edition, Lombroso observed that multiple factors influenced crimes, and he gave increasing attention to social conditions. In 1878, he considered the effects of weather and ethnicity; of civilization, heredity, and alcohol; and of grain prices on the types and rates of crime. Correlations indicated, for example, that more civilized societies experienced a decline in blood crimes but an increase in property crimes and offenses against morals and, with the growth of cities, more crimes involving stimulants.[59] He built on the social causes of crime in the last edition published in 1896–1897. By this time, several studies had evaluated the impact on crime rates of such factors as immigration into the cities, population density, alcohol consumption, wealth, and faith.[60] He also added analyses of the effects of heredity, sex, and the form of government on the incidence and nature of crime. In the main, Lombroso argued that these factors determined the what, when, where, and how often, and they influenced certain categories of delinquents. Thus, circumstances provided the context for the illegal actions of born criminals and the morally insane; they activated a propensity for crime in criminaloids, and with pseudocriminals, they caused the act. Social conditions could also produce the biological defects responsible for habitual criminality, he contended. For example, poor diet or alcoholism could irritate the cortex and weaken the normal restraints on impulsive behavior.[61]

As he both complicated and refined his ideas, Lombroso rethought but did not abandon his original emphasis on atavism. In the third edition (1884), he noted the parallels between children and born criminals. Both, he argued, were inherently criminal, but with a sound moral education, children left their immorality behind, whereas real criminals did not. To support the argument, he observed that children behaved badly and displayed "large numbers of physical anomalies."[62] Adults who suffered from moral insanity showed a similar impetuosity and indifference to rules. The idea that normal adults passed through a criminal phase drew on Ernst Haeckel's theories of ontogeny, the idea that humans replayed the stages of evolution from birth to adulthood. While inherited defects sometimes slowed or interrupted the maturation process, illness and trauma could also cause primitive tendencies to appear later on. Others attributed crime-inducing anomalies to *dégénérescence*, a term Lombroso dismissed as too broad to be useful unless it referred to arrested development.[63]

As his work evolved, Lombroso classified criminals based on degrees of physical impairment, ranging from no to a few defects in the pseudocriminal, to some in the criminaloid and borderline-insane, to significant anomalies in born, epileptic, and morally insane criminals. In contrast, occasional criminals and criminals of passion responded to circumstances, rather than to organic conditions. They had options, while the others reacted to innate criminal impulses difficult to control or eradicate. It followed that the causes of crime lined up on a spectrum with external, social factors on one end and internal physiological and psychological conditions on the other. Within this range of factors, Lombroso continued to emphasize biological determinism, using tests, measurements, and observations of prison inmates to give scientific heft to his views. His use of experimental methods to study criminals opened a new field of study. Initially Lombroso called it criminal anthropology to underscore the focus on man, according to Mary Gibson, but an important proponent of positivist approaches to crime, Raffaele Garofalo, called it "criminology" and that term gained acceptance after 1885.[64]

In promoting criminology, Lombroso found two prominent allies: Garofalo (1851–1934) and Enrico Ferri. Together they constituted what a contemporary called the "uncontested masters of the Italian school."[65] Although they promoted Lombroso's theories, each took an independent approach. Garofalo addressed the definition, causes, and the appropriate response to crime in *Criminologia* (Criminology), first published in 1885. Definitions of crime depended on the time and place, he argued. No act counted as criminal everywhere, but those that offended the moral values prevailing in that place and time always did, and since societies accepted different values, what they condemned as offensive or disruptive varied.[66] Modern societies, he argued, punished violations of altruism, piety, and probity, and to these "natural crimes" governments added acts they judged deleterious, including threats to public order.[67] According to Garofalo, normal citizens innately understood, valued, and conformed to prevailing moral standards, although they might still run afoul of the more arbitrary laws inspired primarily by power politics.

When defects impaired a person's center of moral sensibility, crime resulted, Garofalo argued. Deficiencies in altruism produced premeditated murder, low levels of piety led to violent crimes, and a limited sense of probity explained theft.[68] Illnesses could weaken the mechanism responsible for moral feeling, or it proved defective from the start as a result of congenital or inherited anomalies.[69] In his view, criminals generally exhibited more than their fair share of pathologies, including degenerative and chronic diseases, mental illness, epilepsy, nervous disorders, and alcoholism.[70] These illnesses, often hereditary, affected the body's operation and through it a person's character. Even though criminals resembled children and possibly primitives in their limited morality, Garofalo did not attribute their deficiencies to atavism or arrested development. Rather, the flaws affected the body from the beginning, causing it to adapt poorly to the environment, or they resulted from a later illness.[71]

Whether the product of an inborn anomaly or an acquired change in their character, the source of criminality resided in individuals and not on outside conditions. Here Garofalo took issue with many other experts who distinguished between occasional and born criminals. "I believe this idea [of occasional criminals] is entirely wrong," he stated.[72] Since not everyone responded to difficult circumstances with crime, the vitality of the moral centers must make the difference, Garofalo reasoned. The immediate situation did influence when, where, and how criminals broke the law, but it did not explain why they committed the crime in the first place. Social conditions could also affect criminality indirectly by causing the illnesses or defects that damaged moral sensibility, he contended.[73] Poverty, for example, made the organism vulnerable to degenerative disorders and flaws, and these likely passed to the next generation.[74]

The third Italian architect of criminal anthropology Ferri commanded considerable attention. An accomplished lawyer and advocate of positivist jurisprudence, he tirelessly elaborated a more scientific approach to crime and defended it in the courtroom, parliament, international conferences, articles, and books. His work *Sociologia criminale* (Criminal Sociology), first published in 1881, proposed that the individual's inherited biological and psychological make-up as well as social conditions such as poverty, alcoholism, and unemployment contributed to crime. They joined "cosmic" factors such as geography and climate in "an indissolvable network" to explain criminals.[75] Taking a stand against unilateral explanations, such as Garofalo's, Ferri argued that each element contributed, though in different proportions depending on the category of criminal.[76] Those variants Ferri identified as occasional, passionate, habitual, insane and born. Social determinants weighed more heavily on the first three and internal, biological factors on the other two.

As followers of Lombroso, Ferri and Garofalo called themselves criminologists, because they used empirical methods to study criminals. Dismissing free will, they looked for the internal and external determinants of crime. Ferri argued that the conditions worked together, while Garofalo stressed biological factors. In his successive editions of *Criminal Man*, Lombroso drew closer to Ferri's multicausal approach, although he did not set aside his early theory that atavism, identifiable by anatomical stigmata, explained some crime. Objections to the positivist approach came from advocates of the Classical school of jurisprudence and from the Catholic Church. Both defended free will and stressed the personal and legal responsibility that resulted from choice. Holding to Classical principles, jurists and judges resisted pressure to base their rulings on an evaluation of the criminal rather than the crime and to calibrate punishment to the risk criminals posed. But, in Italy, they faced growing acceptance of positivist propositions from criminologists, lawmakers, and from fellow judges.

If criminal anthropologists, sociologists, and doctors for the most part challenged free will and Classical jurisprudence, they agreed on little else. They launched theories, presented new information, and responded to each others' work at meetings and in their publications. The sharpest debates, and those with the greatest symbolic heft, occurred at the quadrennial International Congress of Criminal Anthropology. After the first Congress met in Rome in 1885, a second met in Paris in 1889. The program featured reports, social occasions, and plenary sessions devoted to the discussion of common resolutions, and the president's summary of the proceedings and of the state of the discipline.[77] Reports of the meetings published in journals such as the *Archives de l'anthropologie criminelle* (Archives of Criminal Anthropology) distilled the debates, but not always accurately as the French historian Marc Renneville points out.[78] Drawing from discussions at the meetings and exchanges in print, French criminologists came to describe a clash between the Italian bio-anthropological school and their own social school, and historians followed suit, a divide that minimizes the complexity of views in both countries, as Renneville and Laurent Mucchielli effectively argue in recent work.

Lombroso's propositions, and his vigorous and prolific defense of them, clearly shaped the emerging field of criminology. Although he significantly revised his position, Lombroso remained identified with the idea that criminals conformed to a single, recognizable type characterized by atavism. Each element of that theory drew both detractors and supporters. Some critics took aim at the underlying premise that biology influenced moral behavior. Linking such things as prominent foreheads, flat noses, or the absence of facial hair to particular actions required, at the least, more data, some asserted.[79] Others challenged Lombroso's evidence. It was hard, skeptics such as Charles Féré contended, to find any criminal who conformed completely to the prescribed type.[80] Moreover, the same features assumed to characterize criminals appeared in the non-criminal population as well. Unless a certain minimum number of traits or an essential subset of them sufficed to distinguish a criminal, the anatomical signs occurred too indiscriminately to define a type, they argued. Others questioned his methods. Using prisoners as the sample left out considerable numbers of criminals who were never arrested or convicted, and unless accompanied by a control group of normal people, conclusions lacked credibility.[81] Gabriel Tarde, one of his most outspoken French critics, outlined his objections in a response to the third edition of *Criminal Man*. He complained that Lombroso and his followers described the criminal type too precisely. Taken as a general profile, whose characteristics might or might not be present, the idea had some merit since nationalities and professional groups shared some physical traits, in his view.[82] But as an anthropological type considered criminal in every context, no.[83]

Associating anatomy, atavism, and crime drew even sharper criticisms from Tarde. He questioned Lombroso's assessment of the criminal as primitive and his conclusion that atavism drove crime. Available information did not warrant Lombroso's conclusions about the physiques, practices, character, or morality of primitive peoples, Tarde asserted. For example, Lombroso mistakenly took prisoners' tattoos as evidence of atavism. In primitive societies, tattoos expressed religious feelings; they had meaning, while convicts marked their bodies out of boredom or to publicize a personal message.[84] Even if atavism and regression occurred, and Tarde believed they did, they did not necessarily explain crime. To make the point, he noted what he took as an obvious inconsistency in the theory. Because of their less-evolved state, women exhibited the characteristics Lombroso assigned to born criminals, but they committed four times fewer crimes. This being so, Tarde concluded that primitivism did not influence crime. In fact, he suggested, women's attachment to family, religion, and social norms likely offered a more accurate image of primitives than Lombroso's vision of the impulsive, violent savage.[85]

What resisted criticism was Lombroso's emphasis on biological determinism. If not the result of atavism or of atavism alone, organic anomalies nonetheless contributed to crime, experts agreed. Responding to proponents of a broader biological approach, Lombroso along with others theorized that in addition to inborn defects disease disrupted developmental processes or damaged healthy adults.[86] Especially in France, doctors and sociologists explored the link between degeneration and the deficiencies responsible for criminality. Charles Féré, a doctor whose work made him a central figure in discussions of deviance, spelled out this approach in *Dégénérescence et criminalité: essai physiologique* (Degeneration and Criminality: Physiological Test), published in 1888. Referring to the literature and to his own observations, Féré connected morality to physiology and moral lapses to a permanent or transitory physiological anomaly or organic change. While strong, sharp emotions sometimes exploded into lawless behavior, as in the case of epileptics, Féré contended that usually, "a certain physiological deficiency" more slowly prepared the body for crime.[87]

Such impoverishment of the organism indicated *dégénérescence*, a physical and psychological phenomenon often evident in criminals.[88] Usually inherited, degeneration took distinct and interchangeable forms, according to Féré, so that it manifested itself differently within and across generations. More often than other types of degeneration, criminality appeared repeatedly in families, although not often enough to create a "fatal disposition to crime" generation to generation.[89] When the families of criminals exhibited no pathological heredity, as occurred in a "good number" of cases, Féré proposed that arrested development explained the abnormalities. Judging from the number of mental cases in prisons, insanity also affected crime, he emphasized.[90] Féré blamed both criminality and insanity in large part on the strains of modern life. Trying to adjust to its demands exhausted the body and left some people vulnerable to degenerative disorders and illnesses that could affect their children as well.[91] The effects showed in their inability to work and to concentrate on anything that required sustained attention. Unable to muster the energy to support their families or to get ahead, they fell behind and turned to crime. Their weaknesses risked to transfer as congenital anomalies to the next generation, reinforcing the progressive weakening of society, as Morel had suggested.

Writing thirty years later, Émile Laurent (1861–1904), a doctor with experience in prisons and asylums, advanced similar theories in a study on criminals.[92] By that time, the link between degeneration and crime was among the most solidly established hypotheses, according to Jules Dallemagne, the respected Belgian doctor and criminologist. Although the term cloaked a range of assertions and eclectic applications, most authorities equated "degeneration" with developmental anomalies, and in this form found that it offered a plausible explanation of criminality.[93] Although he did not believe criminals bore any distinctive anatomical or psychological marks, Laurent argued that degeneration, usually in concert with heredity, made the criminal.[94] The degenerate "carries in himself, at birth, a special terrain, an abnormal state that marks him indelibly so that the least thing turns him into a criminal or a madman."[95] Specifically, degeneration disrupted the operation of the nervous system, and the resulting imbalance caused the anomalies that predisposed the victim to crime. Prisoners provided strong evidence for his conclusions, Laurent asserted. They displayed physical malformations "infinitely more" than people in the streets. "They squint, stammer, shake… they have pointed or flat skulls, flattened noses or elongated jaws."[96] Degeneration also explained why they suffered more frequently from physiological and psychological disorders, including epilepsy and hysteria, he added.

Heredity played an obvious, although usually indirect role, Laurent clarified. An insane person had children: the result was "neurotics, weaklings, lunatics, and criminals." He offered B … as an example. His father had tuberculosis and his mother was an hysteric who died insane. By age twenty-one, B … already had three convictions for drunkenness and disorderly conduct.[97] This case confirmed, he asserted, that a group of interconnected inherited defects caused criminality. "You can't believe how many criminals are the sons of hysterics," Laurent observed. "Epilepsy also occurs very often in their antecedents. But of all the hereditary defects, without doubt the most frequent, the one that one sees operating alone or in concert with the others, is alcoholism." If a criminal's relatives were not madmen, or epileptics, or hysterics, Laurent advised, then "nine times out of ten" alcoholism "is the source of the evil."[98] The association of criminality with degeneration described by Féré, Laurent, and many others won broad acceptance among experts.

Although they assigned deviance to an individual's organic makeup, Garofalo, Féré, and Laurent all gave social conditions a role as well. For Garofalo, they determined time and place; for Laurent, they acted as a catalyst for a criminal act; and according to Féré, they exposed the body to defects that promoted criminality. Other commentators focused their research on the interconnections between biology and society. Giuseppe Sergi, distinguished Italian anthropologist and professor, focused on evolution's effects on society. He described a world in which some people emerged from the struggle for life unscathed while others bore the scars of the fight. Like Féré, he saw the defeated and the victors or, in his terms, "the *degenerates* and the *normal*" on two sides of a divide, one that set races, groups, and individuals apart.[99] Those with physical and psychological deficiencies began at a disadvantage, and the fight to survive, especially when intensified by economic hardship, further "weakened and mutilated" them.[100] Sergi recognized three sources of vulnerability: regressive flaws, inherited or congenital defects, and organic abnormalities resulting from harsh conditions and from over or under using vital bodily functions. Character, an organ like any other in Sergi's view, exhibited the degenerative anomalies, and it also registered the secondary effects of problems elsewhere in the body, especially in the brain and nervous system.[101] Because the damaged ones lacked the willpower to act on their own, they lapsed into begging, prostitution, theft, and vagrancy, or they killed themselves.

Another explanation of criminality also stressed the interplay of evolution and social conditions. Michel Angelo Vaccaro (1854–1937) in *Genesi e funzioni delle leggi penali* (The Origins and Purposes of Criminal Laws), an often-cited work published in 1889, examined the way natural selection functioned in human communities. In the proper circumstances, the struggle for existence could produce progress; more often it resulted in what he called "regressive selection."[102] The underclass, in particular, waged a desperate struggle to survive, and only the toughest avoided death, suicide, or vagabondage. The battle produced "evident signs of degeneration, either because of arrested development, the harshness of their life, or illnesses that resulted from problems during gestation or after birth."[103] These "organic flaws and more or less serious infirmities" passed from parents to children, creating over time "unhappy classes of degenerates."[104] The weak turned into criminals, because they violated laws invented by the powerful to secure their domination, Vaccaro contended. In all societies, in all periods, subordinate groups either adjusted to the elites' demands or suffered punishment.[105] Vaccaro argued, then, that the mechanisms of struggle and adaptation evident in the natural world also applied to society. But in human communities, those in charge exacerbated the effects by setting the standards of civilized behavior and marginalizing as criminals those unable to accept them.[106]

A starker version of Vaccaro's argument took biology largely out of the equation, making all crimes circumstantial and all criminals social constructions. Achille Loria (1857–1943), a well-known and iconoclastic Italian Socialist, took aim at capitalism, arguing that it reduced people to a level of misery that invited law breaking. But he also admitted that because not all poor people broke the law, some anthropological factors also came into play. These "anomalies... [which] must fatally lead to criminality" themselves developed as a result of economic conditions, and they adversely affected the rich as well as the poor.[107] Loria explained that unhealthy living conditions, working too hard during pregnancy, bad food, abuse of alcohol, poverty, as well as the corrosive effects of wealth and ease led to a "profound degradation" progressively worsening with each generation.[108] In his view, Lombroso pinpointed the organic factors that determined who turned to crime, but he failed to understand the economic conditions that underlay them. Therefore, when economic equality reigned, crime would disappear, Loria contended.

Loria's claims framed the social explanation of crime in economic terms. Napoleone Colajanni (1847–1921) took a broader and more exhaustive view, one that influenced thinking in and beyond Italy. A deputy from 1890 until his death in 1921, he sat with the Extreme Left, but increasingly took his distance from the Socialists as they shifted more into the Marxist mainstream. Although he took a degree in medicine, his long career as a republican militant (initiated at age fifteen) prompted him to write about social issues. In *La sociologia criminale* (Criminal Sociology), first published in 1889, Colajanni made room for his own theory of criminality by first sweeping away criminal anthropology. It operated on a set of assumptions that science refuted or at best left open to question, he contended. To imagine a criminal type recognizable by looks and actions and propelled to crime by organically based character defects presumed a view of the mind and body that he found dubious. He doubted that anatomy influenced ethical behavior, and he questioned that an anomaly in one organ affected the operation of others. For all its pretensions to scientific accuracy, Colajanni insisted that criminal anthropology based its conclusions on speculation rather than fact.

Colajanni himself, however, proclaimed to stick to the facts, nothing but the facts. Observation indicated that normal people shared every characteristic attributed by criminal anthropologists to the criminal type. Nothing, then, separated the two except for special conditions in their lives that caused one group to obey laws and the other to break them. If the idea of the born criminal made no sense, neither did the effect of what Ferri called "cosmic" conditions. For example, statistics did not bear out the notion that cold climates deterred crime or that summer weather increased it. But a harsh climate might indirectly influence crime by increasing poverty, and summer weather could favor the crowds that facilitated theft. The purported impact of race on crime did not stand up to scrutiny either. In the first place, Colajanni observed, races intermingled too much to draw conclusions about any one of them. They all developed moral values and habits, although at different rates so that what looked like inferiority came from timing rather than anything intrinsic or permanent.[109] Variables such as gender, age, and marital status correlated better with criminality, but not in constant or predictable ways. Nothing intrinsic to their sex, for example, explained why women usually committed fewer crimes than men. Rather, their detachment from public life protected them from the circumstances that caused males to break laws. The more women got involved in society, Colajanni worried, the more likely they were to commit crimes and to lose their positive influence on public morality.

Of all the possible factors, the social environment provided the simplest and most reliable, although not the exclusive, explanation. "[C]rime is above all," proclaimed Colajanni, "a social or historical phenomenon."[110] Although he took his distance from Achille Loria and Marx, who, he said, wrongly attributed every social activity directly and only to economics, Colajanni emphasized the impact of the structure and the performance of the economy on morality. Statistics convincingly correlated crime to poverty levels and to fluctuations in the economy, he reported. The economy influenced other important sources of crime, including "war, the current organization of industry, the family, marriage, political institutions, revolutions, unemployment and vagrancy, prostitution, education, etc."[111] Vagrancy, for example, resulted from overproduction, mechanization, the enclosure movement, and poverty more than from an organic indisposition to work, he argued. Living on the road too long could, he admitted, lead to physical and moral degeneration, but the original cause was social and not biological.[112]

Social factors also accounted for the recidivism that others took as evidence of an innate predisposition to crime. Because ordinary citizens found crime increasingly abhorrent, they shunned former prisoners out of fear and vindictiveness, denying them the work and support they needed to reintegrate into society. Referring to numerous studies of prisoners who left jail as more accomplished and confident criminals, Colajanni argued that prison also pushed offenders to crime as a way of life. Worse, in his view, the prison system's efforts to impose uniformity and obedience caused inmates to lose their ability to think and act as individuals. "Everything ends up mechanizing the prisoner whom they want to turn into a kind of unconscious automaton."[113] To the extent that prison officials succeeded, the prisoner left without the energy to find work or the willpower to resist the considerable pressure to break the law again.

Colajanni concluded, then, that social conditions explained fluctuations in criminality and the phenomenon of recidivism better than the body did. On the level of the individual, however, social conditions acted together with heredity and education to determine the response to a given situation, Colajanni argued. After all, not everyone responded to misery or unemployment by committing theft, fraud, or murder. Different psychological traits, perhaps inherited, perhaps part of the general makeup of their immediate group influenced their decisions. Parents, he said, passed not only physical characteristics but also "bad tendencies and mean spiritedness" to their offspring.[114] Upbringing also determined how people identified and evaluated their options in given situations so that the level of social responsibility learned at home either restrained or invited crime as a response to dire straits.[115]

After 1,400 pages of insistent analysis based on an impressive command of the literature in Italy and other countries and in fields such as sociology, medicine, and criminal anthropology, Colajanni demolished, or so he hoped, the bio-anthropological theory of criminality. He did recognize that criminologists also gave weight to social factors, just as he himself let biology back into the picture with his hesitant salute to the role of heredity in pushing individuals toward crime. He derived and defended these conclusions using the same scientific standards his adversaries said that they adopted. The difference involved less their proclaimed allegiance to empiricism than the nature of the data they used. Very generally, the bio-anthropological approach extrapolated patterns from case studies of criminals, while the sociological lens used criminal statistics to identify critical variables. Neither side relied exclusively on one source or the other, and both made claims beyond what the evidence allowed. Critics challenged biological theories, arguing that too little information on the inner workings of the body existed to link crime to organic defects. To argue that atavism played a central role, as Lombroso did, accepted a questionable portrait of savages and an unproven pattern of reversion in criminals. Skeptics about social explanations also identified holes and contradictions. For example, dire circumstances pushed people to crime, but not always, so that something other than the situation must explain why some people resisted the pressure to break the law and others did not.

A key figure in French criminology, Tarde also emphasized the social nature of crime. Like Colajanni, he insisted that "its origin is above all historical; its explanation is above all social."[116] Unlike love that always existed and always affected society, the propensity for crime and the forms crime took changed. For example, theft became embezzlement, and what drove criminals to certain offenses in one period turned them in different directions in another. He, too, argued that social determinants outweighed climate and topography and factors such as race and gender. What others described as racial propensities for crime actually represented social practices entrenched over time, in Tarde's view. As to gender, the evidence that females committed fewer infractions at school and fewer crimes as adults than males could show their innate moral superiority, or more likely, Tarde insisted, the nature of their upbringing and the effects of their relative seclusion. It was also statistically true, he wryly observed, that lightening struck men more often than women, but no one claimed as a result that women enjoyed an innate immunity.[117]

Tarde's distinctive contribution to the social determinants of crime centered on imitation. In all periods, the natural human inclination to follow others' example spread crime, particularly from the top to the bottom of society, he noted. Alcohol abuse, once the province of the rich, drifted to the poor; poaching derived from the feudal privilege of hunting; and vagrancy plausibly took inspiration from noble pilgrimages in the Middle Ages.[118] Especially in cities, criminals also copied each other, as the high recidivism rates indicated. Their example resonated beyond the underworld, giving "a place to the *déclassés*, an occupation to the indolent, the prospects of a new more emotionally rich self to all sorts of bankrupt types."[119] Rapid change and unstable government multiplied the number of these social losers and potential criminals. When they considered crime, they found that greater general prosperity increased its rewards just as the clemency of juries reduced its risks.

Inspired by example and self-interest, crime became, in Tarde's terse judgment, among the "least dangerous and the most profitable professions an indolent person can choose."[120]

Like Colajanni, Tarde emphasized the importance of social factors, but he did not completely get rid of biology. "It is in the bosom of the race, aided by the climate," Tarde argued, "where the candidates for genius rest, as well as those for madness and crime. But it is society," he continued, "that chooses the candidates and consecrates them, and since we see that it pushes some toward the academies and others toward insane asylums, we should not be surprised that it determines that others end up in prisons."[121] Social conditions led to crime, but when one illegal act inspired another, antisocial penchants became entrenched, eventually settling into the marrow and turning the one-time into the inveterate criminal. When others took up the example, a criminal class formed, Tarde believed.

Colajanni presented a position commonly associated mainly with French criminologists who made the social milieu either the first cause among others or the exclusive driver of crime. The French, and in particular Alexandre Lacassagne and his followers, stressed their opposition to the Italian school's bio-anthropological theory and touted their own more realistic emphasis on social factors. They took credit for developing social theories of crime and pointed out that earlier French thinkers such as Morel, Broca, and Gall, not Italians, inspired biological anthropology.[122] Representing early criminology as a duel between French and Italian experts injected some drama into an emerging discipline. At the time, the French identified an Italian school of criminology. They associated it with Lombroso, Lombroso with the theory of the born criminal, and that theory with atavism. Others referred to the French School and its rivalry with Lombroso and his followers. Dallemagne, for one, labeled the School of Lyons advocates of a strictly social explanation in his summary of the criminological theories in play at the end of the century.[123] For their part, historians have featured the conflict in studies of criminology, "vulgarizing it to the point of caricature" in some cases, according to Laurent Mucchielli.[124]

In her substantial study of early French criminology, Martine Kaluszynski accepts the national divide. She credits Lombroso with stimulating the French to develop alternative theories to his own biological determinism.[125] Although initially in the thrall of the "lombrosian temptation," Lacassagne and his followers soon took issue with atavism and the idea of a criminal type, she argues.[126] She describes Lacassagne as firing the first official salvo when he challenged Lombroso over the role of social conditions at the 1885 meeting of the International Society of Criminal Anthropology and the second when he created the *Archives of Criminal Anthropology* to match Lombroso's review. That journal, she argues, created the Lyons or French School by giving it a forum and a leader, and it "fed a controversy lasting over twenty-eight years (1886–1914) with its counterpart across the Alps."[127] In this period, the primacy of the social milieu over biological determinism gained consensus in France, and although alternative theories appeared, she observes, they did not win acceptance.[128]

Portraying criminology as a duel between French and Italian schools and between social and biological determinism minimizes the complexity and dynamism of the emerging field. The split, such as it was, did not follow national lines. Nor did the idea of a grand theoretical divide accurately capture the substance of the debate, since the boundaries between the theories blurred considerably as criminologists refined them. Advocates of social explanations such as Colajanni and Tarde believed that organic propensities explained why similar conditions led some but not all to crime. On the other side, those who traced crime to organic defects recognized that some criminals responded primarily to circumstances and that social conditions affected even true or born criminals. Most noticeably, by incorporating social, psychological, and pathological conditions into his theories of criminality, Lombroso crossed the lines assigned him. The same can be said for Lacassagne.

Lacassagne promoted criminology primarily through his advocacy of forensic science. A doctor and professor of medicine at the University of Lyons, he cracked some notorious cases using innovative autopsy techniques. His success facilitated his campaign to get the police to adopt standard protocols for collecting information at crime scenes and to develop more sophisticated, exacting procedures for autopsies. To this applied aspect of criminology, he added publications and talks on the nature of crime and criminals. Lacassagne liked aphorisms, and he used them to frame his positions. An article summarizing developments in legal medicine between 1810 and 1912 encapsulated the Lyon School in a list of lapidary statements: "Anything that harms the existence of a collectivity is a crime. Every crime obstructs progress. The social milieu is the medium in which criminality grows; the germ is the criminal, an element that gains importance only when it comes in contact with a medium that activates it. Societies have the criminals that they deserve."[129] Society, then, played a direct and essential role in producing crime. In an earlier public lecture, Lacassagne showed that crime rates followed the seasons as well as fluctuations in the economy and in the quality of the grape harvest. They also registered the effects of events such as revolutions, political crises, wars, and elections, he contended.[130]

However, Lacassagne proposed that factors such as temperature, cheap wine, and political instability affected those already predisposed to crime. He explained that society contained three main groups of people distinguished by their levels of brain development: the frontals, the parietals, and the occipitals. When the back of the brain dominated, feelings took the lead; when the sides commanded, action resulted; strong frontal regions put intelligence in charge. In most people, the occipital regions still ruled, and they lived more by their instincts and emotions. Intelligent people had the most highly developed brains and the strongest sense of morality, while the parietals responded to both instincts and intelligence.[131] Each group produced its own sort of criminal, Lacassagne proposed. Inveterate criminals came from the group that operated according to feelings or instincts, and defective heredity or organic changes caused by habitually practicing crime landed them in that category. Most criminals, though, lived between thought and instinct, and they acted out of passion or in response to circumstances. Intelligent people fell into crime when heredity or illness caused insanity. This last group, according to Lacassagne, included a large number of homicidal epileptics who "make rivers of blood flow."[132]

Although he said he challenged Lombroso's theory of the atavistic criminal type, Lacassagne shared the view that organic anomalies returned some criminals to the primitive state. In his lecture, he told the audience the stories of two famous criminals and showed them molds of their skulls. Martin Dumollard, he said, "is a monster … he is one of the types of primitive man." He had a pointed skull, large jaws, prominent cheek bones, enormous ears, long arms, lots of hair, a thick and malformed upper lip. Like savages, he was "cunning, violent, envious, greedy, lustful," and like them, he appeared indifferent to death. These characteristics corresponded, he said, to those Lombroso identified in criminals and primitives and to travelers' accounts of savage societies.[133] Lacassagne's thinking remained remarkably consistent, observes Laurent Mucchielli in his analysis of the heredity versus social milieu controversy.[134] He responded enthusiastically to Lombroso's ideas early on, Mucchielli argues, and remained attached to the importance of heredity throughout his career.[135] For the most part, his journal, the *Archives of Criminal Anthropology*, spoke to doctors and psychiatrists more than to sociologists, while his own work and that of his followers did not emphasize social explanations or advance sociological methodology.[136] Why, then, did Lacassagne insist on drawing a line between French proponents of the social milieu and Italian defenders of biology?[137] He and others in France knew better, according to French historian Marc Renneville. They realized that Lombroso attributed criminality to more than atavism and that he alone did not define Italian criminology. According to Mucchielli and Renneville, Lacassagne deliberately created the divide between the Italian and French schools to distinguish and to legitimize French criminology. He and others probably calculated, Renneville suggests, that taking aim at Lombroso and claiming that they owned the social milieu theory would bring recognition and prestige.[138] The strategy of "differentiation" and even "rupture," made the idea of a French School one of "combat, justification, and demands," in Mucchielli's view.[139] He also speculates that professional jealousy might have spurred Lacassagne's efforts to set himself apart from Lombroso.[140]

Though not the ones trumpeted by Lacassagne, some substantive differences in approach did exist. The French uniformly rejected atavism and favored degeneration, a position that showed Lamarck's continuing influence and an abiding suspicion of Darwin's theory, in particular his emphasis on the struggle for life. The French understood reversion as a phenomenon but saw it as occurring slowly over successive generations. They credited Morel with the idea that social conditions could produce organic anomalies and that these acquired lesions passed to the next generation. They also attributed backsliding to the vulnerability of the most recently evolved elements of the body to damage and decline. Thus the French argued that organic anomalies influenced criminality, pointing not to atavism but to degeneration as the source of the defects.[141]

The theories applied

Italian and French students of crime, whether doctors or criminologists, wanted lawmakers, judges, juries, and the public to understand the latest theories and their implications for change. To that end, they broadcast their discoveries and spelled out their practical applications. They also offered their services to the courts as forensic experts. When judges did ask them to evaluate the accused's mental state, their reports added to the literature on criminals, and in high-profile trials of notorious criminals, they attracted the attention of the press and the public. The most striking crimes inspired other experts to offer their secondhand assessments, creating a broad and public debate about the latest theories. The case of Giuseppe Musolino displays, in spades, this side of criminology. It also illustrates the growing influence as well as the inexact nature of the new science.

The Assize Court of Reggio Calabria sentenced Giuseppe Musolino, a native of Santo Stefano d'Aspromonte, to a stiff twenty-one-year prison term for attempted murder in September 1898. An argument in a bar between Vincenzo Zoccoli and Antonio Romeo turned physical and Musolino, according to some accounts, intervened to stop it.[142] Once outside the bar, Zoccoli jumped on Musolino with a knife, wounding him in the right hand. A few days later someone took a shot at Zoccoli, and the authorities charged Musolino. At the trial, witnesses testified against him, and his lawyer, Deputy Biagio Camagna, decided to argue for a reduced sentence based on extenuating circumstances, even though Musolino proclaimed his innocence from the beginning.[143] Camagna described the fight, and he explained how Musolino defended his innocence: the wounds on his hand prevented him from firing a gun, and the hat found near the scene he had lost the night before, allowing his accusers to plant the evidence against him.[144] Some of the locals suspected another villager, Pietro Travia, and in 1933 he confirmed to a friend that he was the one who shot at Zoccoli.[145]

On January 19, 1899, Musolino escaped from the prison of Gerace. Over the next three years, he killed seven people and wounded another eight, targeting those he held responsible for his conviction or suspected of collaborating with the authorities to capture him. He also shot his way out of a trap set by the police and the carabinieri. As the assaults and killings multiplied, local and then national authorities intensified their efforts to seize him, using subterfuge, bribery, and force. At one point, the government committed 20,000 lire to the hunt and detailed as many as a thousand soldiers and carabinieri to scour the mountainous region around his village.[146]

Musolino's defiance won him increasing public sympathy, particularly in the South. Songs, newspaper articles, cards with his image turned him into a hero and his odyssey into legend. Local support, perhaps from fellow members of the recently formed *picciotteria*, a mafia-like secret organization, and certainly from sympathizers and friends, complicated the authorities' efforts to track him down and turned the manhunt into a campaign in hostile territory. In October 1901, almost three years after his escape, the police gave chase to a suspicious person in Acqualagno in Urbino, hundreds of miles from Santo Stefano d'Aspromonte. As he slipped away, his foot caught in a rabbit trap, and the police seized him. Although he gave them a false identity, they later recognized him as Musolino.

His case showed the influence of contemporary debates over criminality. The judge called on medicolegal experts to assess Musolino's ability to stand trial. They ran tests and conducted observations according to protocols accepted by criminologists, psychiatrists, and forensic doctors. Other experts, not directly connected with the trial, also analyzed Musolino and his crimes based on what they read, and they reacted to the forensic reports and to the court's verdict. Still others who lacked expert credentials described the case and the trial for popular audiences, using categories and terms that indicated familiarity with the emerging field of criminology. No one labeled Musolino a run-of-the-mill occasional criminal. The fact that he killed so many people, with such unwavering purpose, and that he vaunted his deed as just and necessary excluded such an assessment. The same facts, however, pointed either to the weight of his upbringing and cultural milieu or to pathological mental or physical problems. Depending on their perspective, observers claimed he was a son of Calabria, that remote, primitive, murderous region or, equally possible, the son of a family of degenerates, or some combination of both.

The nature of Musolino's crimes and his extraordinary popularity—the "Musolino phenomenon"—as well as his behavior in court "gave the outcome of the trial an exceptional importance," particularly for criminology. The trial attracted unprecedented public interest and publicity, as crowds of journalists flocked to Lucca to report on the proceedings.[147] Two teams of forensic experts drawn from all over Italy examined Musolino. The defense team included Leonardo Bianchi, director of the clinic of psychiatry and neuropathology at the Insane Asylum of Naples, and physiologist Mariano Luigi Patrizi (1866–1935), professor at the University of Modena. For the prosecution, Enrico Morselli (1852–1929), a doctor, and Sante De Sanctis, a psychiatrist specializing in dreams, collaborated.[148] Bianchi and Patrizi claimed to apply "the most stringent methods of clinical and psychological observation" to their study of the accused.[149] Their counterparts, Morselli and De Sanctis, promised similar diligence. Although they ended up differing over Musolino, the experts likely agreed on the importance of their own role and of the place of science in the modern courtroom. They felt entitled to offer testimony, in the name of justice, and they understood its importance in increasing public awareness of the new positivist approach to crime and criminals. To broadcast their conclusions, both teams published studies of the case and the trial when it was over.

Musolino's case put the experts and the court to the test. He admitted most of the charges against him and provided detailed, lucid explanations of his motives. According to Classical principles of justice he deserved to stand trial and suffer punishment, because he planned to hurt or to kill his victims. His upbringing and his earlier and unjust conviction for attempted murder did not, by this optic, change the fact that he killed seven and injured eight people. But positivist criminology complicated the issue of legal responsibility by showing that premeditation and lucidity no longer reliably indicated free choice. Some madmen carefully planned their crimes, and some entirely rational people fell prey to passions and obsessions. Moreover, in assessing legal responsibility, the judges who applied Classical principles focused on the acts themselves and neglected other relevant factors. Using scientific methods, the experts aimed to fill the gaps. They attempted to evaluate Musolino's state of mind and his general health to determine whether he fully controlled his actions. In the view of the experts, the answer should determine whether he stood trial, and if he did, it should influence the verdict and the sentence.

The medicolegal teams based their findings on identical tests and interviews and reported their conclusions toward the end of the trial, May 30, 1902. Those representing the defense advised the court not to hold Musolino fully responsible.

His father suffered from epilepsy, and they found enough other instances of epilepsy, premature death, tuberculosis, and alcoholism in his family to seriously compromise his heredity. Musolino himself seemed to have no degenerative physical defects or sensory abnormalities, other than unusually acute vision. They judged his intelligence "sufficiently normal," describing him as "alert, agile, rapid, sure, and lucid" as well as credulous, restricted in ideas, and easily distracted.[150] However, a lesion on the brain provoked by a blow to the head caused left-handedness and the dominance of his left side. More critically, the damage and other defects produced full and partial epileptic seizures along with intense headaches. The lesion also affected his psyche, they reported, causing emotivity, impulsiveness, destructive urges, and a diminished capacity for moral feeling.[151]

Musolino, the defense team argued, conformed to an established type: "The family background, the anthropological profile of the accused, the blow to the head, the partial and general physical epilepsy, the clearly epileptic psychological profile, constitute a harmonious, integrated whole, a noted syndrome, an always recognizable pathological type, that is affirmed in all the treatises and in all the monographs, in whichever country they're published."[152] They asserted, "without fear of contradiction," that epilepsy determined his moral character. It weakened his will and moral sensibility, allowing his violent impulses and chaotic passions to take over. His intelligence remained largely unaffected, so Musolino knew what he did and why. But because epilepsy damaged his will, it allowed his emotions and impulses to take over. For that reason, he could not be held fully responsible for his actions. Much more than ethnic or regional factors, unhealthy personal and family conditions explained his crime spree. These made Musolino "a psycho-anthropological inferior type," possibly a degenerate or a primitive. Of those two options, they concluded that his religiosity and credulity and his defense of vendetta as a right pointed to the primitive.[153]

Morselli and de Sanctis, for the prosecution, concurred that the tests revealed no noticeable deformities or aberrations in stature or physiognomy or serious physiological abnormalities other than partial epilepsy caused by a blow to his head as a child. Neither epilepsy nor any other mental disease damaged Musolino's lively intelligence. The signs of degeneration that the defense experts detected in his family they dismissed as insignificant or nonexistent. Musolino was, they concluded, "the full example of the intelligent and willful criminal" entirely responsible for his multiple crimes.[154] He did, though, manifest in exaggerated form attitudes and behavior natural to his region, in particular his arrogance, desire for vengeance, and his "complete absence of faith in [the system of] justice." Like his fellow Calabresi, Musolino believed in the right of individuals to take justice into their own hands, while rejecting "the most sacred of all rights and that is the right to life." Morselli and de Sanctis blamed his indifference to the people he killed and injured on local values and on his vanity. Influenced by the "ethnic social factor" and egged on by public support, his troublemaking bent caused him to embrace the role of bandit and play it until the end.

Musolino, they told the court, fit none of the recognized categories of criminal types. He did not qualify as a born criminal or a criminal madman, nor as the victim of overpowering passion. Because his "criminal temperament" completed the work of social circumstances, he did not fit the model of the occasional criminal either. That left him a lombrosian criminaloid, a little bit of everything, or a primitive criminal.[155] In the study published just after the trial, they applied more popular labels. His carefully calibrated actions distinguished him from the ferocious, bloodthirsty brigand, while his high sense of honor and pride made him "a true blue bandit" with some signs of the "pseudo-brigand."[156]

After the closing statements of the prosecution and the defense and an uncharacteristically rambling intervention by Musolino, the jury deliberated and ruled him guilty with extenuating circumstances on one charge and guilty on all the others. They ruled that he acted with premeditation and without mental impairment of any kind.[157] The sentence condemned him to life in prison, with ten years of solitary confinement. After an unsuccessful appeal, the authorities moved Musolino to a prison on the island of Elba, where he slowly went mad. In 1916, they transferred him to a criminal insane asylum in Reggio Emilia, and he remained there until pardoned August 18, 1946. Judged incapable of living outside an institution, he stayed in a civilian asylum in Reggio Calabria until he died in 1956 at age 81. Thousands attended his funeral.

The trial and the verdict precipitated a number of commentaries. Lombroso assessed Musolino from a distance and reported his findings in a study published in a widely diffused periodical, the *Nuova antologia* (New Anthology), and later in a special collection of his articles.[158] He examined photographs of Musolino and drew on Patrizi's report. From these sources and an assessment of Musolino's actions, Lombroso classified him according to his own well-known typology. Musolino did not show the physical signs of the born criminal, although the more intelligent among them sometimes did not, Lombroso established.[159] In his actions he did not fully match the born criminal type either. He showed affection for his family, and he killed not for evil ends but for vengeance, in keeping with the values of a region that made vendetta a duty. At the same time, like born criminals, he showed no remorse for his deeds. Judging from his behavior, Musolino showed some signs of degeneration, Lombroso concluded: a distaste for work, a propensity for delinquent behavior, and a weak sense of the moral implications of his actions. Not a "pure born criminal" then, nor even a perfect criminaloid, Lombroso located him somewhere in between, although closer to the second category than the first.[160]

Lombroso's examination of Musolino's family history revealed criminality, alcoholism, and nervous disorders, strong evidence that he inherited degenerative traits. His father suffered from dizzy spells that Lombroso diagnosed as embryonic epilepsy, and two of Musolino's three sisters suffered from epilepsy, he observed.[161] Lombroso noted Musolino's record of epileptic seizures, as well as the extreme agility and the mood swings he considered characteristic of the epileptic. In his opinion, the public adulation Musolino received during his escape turned the "delirium" born of his "epileptic-like illness" into a strong sense of mission.[162] At the same time, Musolino's unhealthy psyche operated in the context of the ethnic and social structures of Calabria, and these promoted the local ethic of vendetta. The narrow elite's abuse of power and neglect of the land produced the poverty and despair that made brigandage and criminality endemic in the area, Lombroso contended. Settlement patterns and isolation also shaped the prevailing culture. The wild, remote region where Musolino grew up remained "at the primitive stage," its mixed race settlements characterized by a naturally "low level of conscience."[163] Out of touch with civilization and kept out of school by the rich and powerful, the Calabresi continued to make revenge a duty in the way of savages, a situation not likely to change, insisted Lombroso, until the government stopped throwing money away chasing down bandits and invested it in modernization.[164]

Musolino's actions and the public acclaim that sustained him depended to an important degree on social conditions, in Lombroso's view. The low-level morality of the region made crime a virtue, but Musolino's and his family's degenerative pathologies guaranteed that he would make vendetta his mission. In another assessment of the case, Vincenzo Nisticò challenged Lombroso and supported the position developed by the attorneys for the defense. Small wonder Lombroso arrived at "mistaken conclusions" when he based them on facts produced by "the popular imagination or the nervousness of some journalist."[165] Lombroso twisted even this "vague, largely false information" to fit his view of criminals, Nisticò accused. The resulting profile made Musolino a "little bit of everything"—partly criminaloid, partly born criminal, somewhat paranoid, and an epileptic.[166] Nisticò himself tried to produce a clinical profile using medical and psychological reports and many letters and poems written by Musolino, and his investigation led him to reject out of hand most of Lombroso's diagnosis. The medical examination conducted after his capture indicated that Musolino showed none of the physical features of the born criminal and none of the physical abnormalities that Lombroso identified. His character did not resemble that of the congenital criminal either. He worked hard; though like all woodcutters, he worked sporadically. Unlike either the born criminal or the criminaloid, Musolino demonstrated intelligence as well as kindness and consideration. More important for Nisticò, Musolino lacked the attachment to the group common to criminals and especially to brigands, and he clearly showed his capacity to suffer. Because he did not look, think, or feel like a born or a semi-born criminal, he was not one, Nisticò concluded.[167]

Musolino did, however, suffer from psychic epilepsy, Nisticò confidently asserted. Like Lombroso, Nisticò stressed the tarnished heredity passed to Musolino by a family afflicted by alcoholism, strokes, epilepsy, and various nervous disorders. "And degeneration took solid roots in the poor Musolino. His brain was affected by one of the worst illnesses that can devastate the organism: epilepsy."[168] He exhibited the signs of sensory epilepsy about age ten, but later the psychic variant prevailed. Confinement in prison added to the problem, provoking in an already defective nervous system latent tendencies toward mental illness, in particular paranoia with delusions of grandeur. As these tendencies became more pronounced, Nisticò insisted, Musolino's old self gradually gave way, and a new personality "took charge ... without the true, normal Self noticing this transformation." Musolino did not lose the battle against an obsession he recognized and resisted, nor did his regular personality change; rather, a second self snuck up and overpowered him.[169] Thus, whereas normal people submitted to injustice knowing they could do nothing about it, epileptics and paranoids magnified the affront, and believing themselves more powerful than the authorities, they embraced vendetta as an obligation. Because he exhibited symptoms of paranoia and epilepsy, Musolino qualified as an insane criminal. The paranoid in him exacted revenge carefully, deliberately, sparingly, while the epileptic occasionally took over and produced impulsive and ferocious acts. In Nisticò's judgment, the diagnosis jumped out from the record: afflicted by epilepsy compounded by paranoia unleashed by the unjust sentence and the experience of imprisonment, a new Musolino, a criminal madman, took charge. Nisticò closed his treatise, written before the conclusion of the trial, with a prediction that future developments confirmed: "Madness will close the frame of this ever so adventurous life."[170]

Judging from Musolino's trial, by the early twentieth century criminologists shared a vocabulary, a set of procedures, and recognized categories for evaluating criminals. They usually favored one of the contending nosologies and etiologies over the others, and the resulting range of possible conclusions fueled debate, as Musolino's case amply indicated. Such confusion among the experts did not speak well for the authority of science, Morselli lamented.[171] Seeking to soft-pedal their differences, the two teams refrained from directly challenging the other side's arguments in their reports. At the same time, even had they agreed on approaches, Musolino's temperament, his upbringing, and happenstance supported contrasting assessments. He could be mentally imbalanced or a typical Calabrian, or a combination of the two. Or in light of the evidence of repeated cold-blooded murders, he could be a vulgar criminal. Representing the prosecution, Morselli and de Sanctis predictably concluded that Musolino controlled his actions. But they paid close attention to the medical and social factors that prepared the way for premeditated murder. Their condemnation of the severity of the sentence suggests that they saw the weight of extenuating circumstances. The jury accepted the prosecution team's report, but by a seven-to-five vote. Later Morselli insisted that by exposing the legendary Musolino as a common criminal, the verdict did Italy a great service.[172]

Implications

Musolino's trial, and others like it, brought criminal science and jurisprudence face to face. Criminal law in both countries followed juridical principles articulated in the Enlightenment by thinkers such as Cesare Beccaria and defended by liberals as guarantors of individual rights and public order. According to Classical theories, laws expressed the more fundamental and changeless organic Law that held society together so that breaking a law also attacked the substance of the social order. According to the Classical school, criminals made a choice, reasoning mistakenly that crime paid. Reducing crime depended, then, on clear, swift, predictable, and convincing punishments. In addition to deterring real and would-be criminals by making crime unattractive, punishment also reasserted the supremacy of the Law. Whether justified as a means of deterrence or as a measure of retribution, every crime had an established and limited punishment. The convicted criminal paid the price and returned to society, presumably understanding the high costs of "dishonesty" well enough to avoid crime in the future.

Challenges to Classical views of law became more pointed and strident after mid century. The procedures that liberals defended as just and effective fell under attack primarily from medical scientists and from experts in the new fields of criminal anthropology and sociology. By adjusting current practices to established facts about the body and society, Classical jurisprudence would gain the authority of scientific truth or disappear. Observed one of the most prominent advocates of liberal jurisprudence, Enrico Pessina (1828–1916): the demands provoked "a terrible crisis in the theory and practice of criminal law."[173] The same held true for France, but there Positivists maintained stronger connections with jurists than they did in Italy.

Not surprisingly, critics dismissed as baseless metaphysics the argument that a fundamental, unchanging Law stood at the core of legal systems. Laws did not express invisible Law; they performed the concrete social task of defending citizens from deviants. On this more practical level, the current approach clearly failed, the critics claimed. Little change in overall crime rates and high recidivism indicated that prison terms did not discourage crime or change convicted criminals into law-abiding citizens. In fact, it seemed that jail sentences contributed to the increase in recidivism by turning inmates into professional criminals.

The system failed in part because it punished the crime not the criminal, critics contended. According to current practice, judges assessed the criminal's state of mind at the time of the crime in order to establish legal responsibility, nothing more. Reformers called on judges to broaden the criteria for mental incompetence to include defective will and impaired moral sensibility. They also insisted that duress forced rational people to commit crimes, and when that happened, they were not responsible for their actions. In practice, courts treated crimes of passion differently, because they recognized that circumstances could drive actions. But reformers insisted that the same logic applied to perfectly lucid people faced with impossible situations. For judges to assess responsibility accurately, they needed to evaluate the context and the accused's background, reformers argued.

When it came to sentencing, criminal laws in both countries established minimum and maximum penalties, giving the judge some latitude. But that approach did not serve justice or the public interest, according to criminologists. Lombroso, who paid more and more attention to policy in successive editions of *Criminal Man*, opposed the existing system of punishment and advocated calibrating penalties to the level of threat the criminal posed. This idea that punishments served primarily to defend society against dangerous lawbreakers gained ground in the last decades of the century. Basing sentencing on social defense required judges to assess the criminal, proponents of the principle urged. Occasional criminals required alternative penalties, while those affected by organic anomalies needed special regimens since rehabilitating them did not work.

The most extreme cases, in the view of some criminologists, warranted capital punishment, an option the French had but the Italians did not. While some French reformers called for its end, or at least for ending it as a public spectacle, the objections to capital punishment diminished after the turn of the nineteenth century. Italians established criminal insane asylums for those judged too mad for prisons and too dangerous for regular hospitals, and Lacassagne and others in France recognized the merits of this approach. In both countries, still other ways of marginalizing dangerous misfits added to these options. The 1885 French law on recidivism relegated hardened criminals to penal colonies, while Italians allowed the police to recommend internal exile in isolated areas for certain types of offenders. For occasional criminals, criminals of passion, and those whose defects posed limited threats, prison, especially the cellular system to reduce the contagion of example, remained the preferred response.

These measures gave governments an array of weapons to protect society against criminals. The emphasis on innate and inherited criminality and on its identifying marks also drew attention to strategies of prevention. Lombroso clarified that even if they could recognize a born criminal from external signs, authorities should not take preemptive action. Nonetheless, the idea of innate criminality helped to justify the practice of *ammonizione* in Italy by reinforcing suspicions that certain people harbored the potential for crime. The theory that degenerates could transmit criminality-inducing anomalies to the next generation led to prevention of another sort, as a number of experts urged them not to reproduce. Some, including Lacassagne, took the next step and supported sterilization to prevent the decline of the race.

Applying the logic of social defense, criminologists also called for a different approach to the criminals who did not endanger society. The same year that they approved stiff penalties for repeat offenders, the French Chamber established parole, and in 1891 the Bérenger Law allowed judges to suspend prison sentences or fines for first offenses.[174] Subsequent measures subtracted time served before trials from the sentence and extended from sixteen to eighteen the age for trial as an adult. At the same time, reformers called for initiatives to remove the conditions that promoted crime. The idea of "substitute punishments" laid out by Ferri attracted attention and considerable support. He targeted, in particular, poverty, excessive wealth, and indolence by proposing measures including public housing, social insurance, child labor laws, electoral reform, free trade, the end of monopolies, the reduction of tariffs, popular credit, divorce, and the control of alcohol production and consumption.[175] For occasional offenders, he encouraged the substitution of fiscal penalties for detention, adjusting the fines to the crime and the criminal's capacity to pay.[176] Some convicted criminals did require punishment, but he urged that the penalties reflect the individual's potential to readapt to society.[177]

These strategies aimed to reduce the reasons for occasional crime and to discourage repeat offenses by awarding good behavior. In both countries, the initiatives focused on juvenile crime sought the same results. A 1904 measure in Italy, for example, suspended the sentences of children under eighteen in the case of minor offenses and for serious infractions if a charitable organization agreed to supervise them.[178] The French also eased penalties on underage offenders and created reformatories to get children out of the prison system. In addition, they made provisions for taking care of abandoned children and providing foster care for neglected children, a move that limited paternal rights.

Shifting the focus of justice to social defense, then, supported contrasting initiatives. Gibson stresses two sorts of applications of criminology: sympathetic and harsh, while Kalifa notes that an initial humanistic and prophylactic emphasis gave way to more repressive and exclusionary policies.[179] French critics denounced what they saw as a trend toward coddling criminals, and their accusations that judges and juries treated dangerous criminals too lightly contributed to the "security crisis" in France in 1900.[180] Lacassagne, among others, complained that too few cases came to trial, and when they did, parole and suspended sentences allowed the guilty to escape punishment. Amnesties let recidivists count their next crime as a first conviction, a practice that amounted to an incentive for the worst criminals, in Lacassagne's view. His complaints joined those of other prominent criminologists and jurists and added to the frenzy fed by the press. The call for repression countered initiatives to end the death penalty and caused the government to investigate sentencing practices and to remind judges to apply the law.[181]

In Italy, a different sort of security crisis developed at the end of the century as significant unrest in the South provoked the government of Luigi Pelloux to impose martial law and try to sideline the legislature. Liberals and socialists joined to defeat these efforts and to produce the "liberal turn" associated with Prime Minister Giovanni Giolitti. The public-order crisis reinforced concerns that under the guise of defending society against threats, political leaders intended only to secure their own power. Writing for the fourth edition of *Sociologia criminale*, Ferri admitted that events in the 1890s and reading Marx caused him to rethink the idea of social defense.[182] Like other Positivists, he originally saw that society legitimately took measures against antihuman criminals who acted for themselves and against the community. These included atavistic, habitual, and passionate criminals who struck at the foundations of society. But when governments began to repress challenges to their power, and even to act against "heterodox political and social thoughts," things changed. By singling out altruistic "evolved criminals" for punishment, they practiced "class defense" under the guise of "social defense."[183] Ferri understood that they did what came naturally; they defended their power. But their actions exposed the conflict between invoking social defense to protect the collectivity and exploiting the principle to secure the interests of a minority. He made the point as a Socialist.

In their efforts to look at crime scientifically, doctors, criminologists, and sociologists focused attention on the individual rather than the act, on defects not decisions, and on factors beyond the criminal's control rather than on free will. Their discoveries set aside universal human weakness as an explanation for crime and left little space for evil people. Abnormalities, they asserted, marked the most dangerous criminals. The anomalies took them out of time by turning them into savages or out of biological step by obstructing their development. Or the flaws registered the unfortunate effects of illness or trauma. These criminals, recognizable by some combination of behavior, personality, physiology, physical features, and family background, required control and confinement. Duress drove another category to crime, and they deserved support and access to education. Whether compelled primarily by innate anomalies or by circumstances, crime could be contagious. Not only did it encourage repetition, it could inspire imitation, and, worse, when it affected the body, it could contaminate the next generation. This framework drew from and influenced the analyses of other disturbing and mysterious social behaviors.

Sexual Deviants

All you see before you is a kaleidoscope, a museum full of strange facts, bizarre cases, strewn about without order or connection, something which resembles a collection of sexual oddities.

Julien Chevalier[1]

According to French and Italian experts writing in the closing decades of the nineteenth century, few people freely chose lives of crime or vagrancy. If they lived in civilized society and if their bodies operated properly, then they settled down to routines of work and moderate pleasure. They managed to control any impulse to break the law or leave home unless poverty drove them to steal or take to the road in order to survive. When people with jobs and apparent good health committed crimes or abandoned their families, investigators theorized that they suffered from a hidden defect which surfaced by itself or as a result of trauma, illness, or harsh circumstances. A rather different domain, that of love, also caused concern, occasioned study, and prompted analysis by Positivists. Romance mostly occurred in private, but people still claimed to know enough to generalize about the matter. They understood what forms of love society sanctioned and which it prohibited, but they also knew from what they heard or read or did themselves that people transgressed these norms.

A spate of sensational crimes and highly publicized trials as well as stories in the press and popular literature drew attention to what stood out as aberrant sexual behavior. As with vagrancy, suicide, madness, and neurosis, crimes of passion and illicit and unnatural sex acts appeared to flourish in contemporary society. Perhaps more people actually did violate sexual taboos, but maybe, commented some observers, the attention given sexual practices by journalists, writers, and scientists only made it seem that way. The fact that doctors, psychologists, and sociologists detailed abnormal practices in textbooks and treatises and testified as expert witnesses at trials added weight to the public's interest. "Never has the psychology and the psychopathology of sexual life drawn greater attention than today," remarked Julien Chevalier (1860–1943), an authority on same-sex love. "If [my work] has no other merits," he modestly observed, "it is at least timely."[2]

An abundant literature addresses sexuality in this period from several different disciplinary perspectives. Attitudes toward same-sex love command special attention, particularly following Michel Foucault's claim that homosexuality changed from an activity to an identity after 1870. Subsequent studies examine the extent and the nature of the break, some supporting the idea of a rupture, others stressing continuities. They also confront definitions of homosexuality, exploring the mix of identity, desire, and acts. Assessed from the vantage points of widely diverse disciplines and from current debates about sexuality, the profusion of analyses enriches and complicates Foucault's original assessment.

Concentrating on homosexuality illuminates one aspect of the discussion of sexuality in the fin de siècle and puts others in the shadows. Applying their usual methods for examining misfits, contemporary investigators set out to identify and to classify the full range of abnormal sexual behaviors. They set expansive limits, considering everything from rape and prostitution to same-sex love. As they tried to uncover the roots of abnormal sexual practices, they used familiar formulas: biological and social, inborn and acquired, real and occasional. Did departures from the norm stem from free choice, circumstances, or some identifiable mental or physical defect? Did defects affect structure or function? Did victims inherit or develop them? Investigators did not examine same-sex love in isolation, but in the context of other sexual behaviors and other types of social and mental difference. That broader framework helps explain why they discovered a new type of same-sex love, inversion, without setting aside the old type, pederasty.

Laws, religion, and convention defined the territories of licit and illicit sexual behavior. The borders between the two changed during the nineteenth century, and so did those who defined and patrolled the lines, as the state extended its claims to social control and science asserted its authority to dissect, explain, and deal with abnormalities of all types. The Napoleonic Code regulated sexual behavior in ways that granted males a latitude denied to women. In the interest of defending the family and within it the role of the father, laws reinforced the religious dictums that tied sex to marriage and procreation. Male adultery went unpunished unless the husband installed his mistress at home, and then he paid a fine. Wives, on the other hand, faced imprisonment for violating the marriage contract.[3] The criminal code adopted for united Italy in 1889 outlawed acts judged threatening to the family. It specifically excluded morality from the state's purview unless the acts involved violence, damage, fraud, or scandal.[4] It criminalized adultery (women) and concubinage (men), when the man kept his mistress in the family home or publically maintained her elsewhere. The courts, however, only acted at the victim's request. If convicted, the same penalties applied to the guilty wife and husband.[5]

What the law did not mention says as much about definitions of unacceptable behavior as what it forbade. French law, following the Napoleonic example, allowed consenting adults the broadest variety of sexual practice, outlawing only the use of violence, the involvement of children, and public offenses to morals. The same held true for Italy. The criminal code did not outlaw "unnatural sexual acts" unless accompanied by violence, involving minors, or done publically.[6] In licensing all sorts of behavior behind closed doors, the law followed the distinction common in classical jurisprudence between the private and the public realms. Disgruntled citizens, for example, might complain and even conspire against the government in private without risking punishment. Only when they passed to overt action did the law impose sanctions. Similarly, as long as adults did not use violence or abuse children, and as long as they exercised discretion, the law left them considerable latitude in their sexual activities.

In areas where the law kept silent, the Church and social convention regulated behavior. Religious doctrine associated legitimate sex with reproduction in the context of marriage and condemned departures from the protocol as sinful disobedience to God's will. Everyone knew, however, the power of temptation and the difficulty of mastering the commands of the flesh. As the influence of the Church declined, its constraints on individual behavior weakened, leaving people without firm moral direction. Those who welcomed the retreat of the Church did not necessarily applaud the relaxation of its hold on sexual behavior.[7] Middle-class worries about the spread of vice caused secular governments to take up the Church's role in regulating sexual behavior. As Michel Foucault argues, the press, schools, and learned authorities identified the prohibitions and advertised the penalties of ignoring them, while the prison and the clinic confined and corrected those who would not or who could not conform to social expectations.

Science also reinforced traditional norms, as it replaced the Church as the arbiter of sexual mores. Georges Lantéri-Laura, a French psychiatrist, contends that some scientists proved willing to "envelop with their scientific prestige prohibitions required by the culture," all the while professing their objectivity.[8] Medical authorities, in particular, claimed to understand sex, and their discoveries exposed as physical defects what the Church described as moral failings resulting from original sin. Moreover, they said they could tell when illness rather than ill will caused the behavior, and they could consequently assess degrees of legal responsibility and danger to society. These claims gained credibility, and governments increasingly relied on physicians to analyze sexual deviance and to evaluate deviants.

For the same reasons that they studied murderers, vagabonds, geniuses, neurotics, and maniacs, doctors, along with anthropologists and social theorists, put sexual practice in their sights in the nineteenth century. In fact, a torrent of publications addressed issues once surrounded by silence, particularly in France.[9] The attention these researchers focused on the subject troubled some publishers. Would describing sexual abnormalities in print inspire imitation, they wondered? No need to worry, Charles Féré clarified at the outset of his study on sexual impulses. Reading about perversion did not cause people to become perverted, since only people from weak stock or afflicted by certain illnesses developed those problems.[10] Others lacked Féré's confidence and asserted that detailing abnormal sexual practices could affect impressionable people. Julien Chevalier reported that he took care to make his work difficult to read, because he judged the subject inappropriate for the general public and for women.[11] Other writers showed less restraint and deliberately targeted a wider audience, hoping to inspire healthy practices (or attract more readers) by using vivid details to dramatize the negative consequences of illicit behaviors.

Sexual behavior, then, drew the same sort of attention that criminality, insanity, and nervous disorders did, and from some of the same experts. The exceptionally prolific Lombroso wrote on prostitution, lesbianism, and on crimes of the libido, for example, just as Charles Féré added the study of the sexual instinct to his work on epilepsy and criminality. Other observers concentrated on sexual behavior, identifying and categorizing abnormal types and offering explanations of the causes. Just as they did with other medical and social issues, the French and Italian experts drew from and contributed to an international exchange on the nature of abnormal sex. A few key texts, especially those of Karl Heinrich Ulrichs (1825–1895), Carl Friedrich Otto Westphal (1833–1890), Richard von Krafft-Ebing (1840–1902), Albert Moll (1862–1939), and Havelock Ellis (1859–1939), framed and fed the discussion. Their work, and in particular the case studies they presented, informed other investigators, whose findings appeared in medical textbooks and popular manuals, in press accounts of expert testimony, and indirectly in popular literature. The information raised public awareness about sexual practices and added to the alarm about what looked like a general disintegration of moral restraint.

As investigators examined sexual behavior, they began with some givens. Everyone already knew, for example, that love could drive people crazy. Normal men and women could display uncharacteristic excesses when they fell in love, pursued a love, or lost a lover. Possessed by passion, people got distracted, suffered insomnia, took risks, made unusual sacrifices, contrived to get noticed, challenged social convention, and sometimes broke the law. Understanding that love could overpower reason, public opinion and juries tended to soften their verdicts when jilted lovers exacted revenge, when pure-hearted but socially mismatched lovers sought happiness, or when a person defended a lover's honor or life. This sympathy applied mainly to conventional relationships; when people chose inappropriate partners, their actions caused bewilderment and discomfort, particularly as people became more aware of the possible deviations.

The issue of sex proved more problematic than love since the two did not depend on each other. Neither sex nor a good marriage required love, according to thinking at the time. Nor did genuine love automatically involve sex. Chaste love and loveless sex joined the union of love and sex in and outside marriage as possible, although not equally desirable or respectable behaviors. What fell outside this catalogue of recognized patterns occasioned more comment. Shocking excess or unnatural objects of affection indicated, according to accepted wisdom, the work of original sin or venal character, and perhaps in a very limited number of cases the effects of insanity.[12]

In the first half of the nineteenth century, doctors such as Philippe Pinel, Jean-Etienne Dominique Esquirol, and Etienne-Jean Georget expanded the conception of mental illness to include lucid folly. People could be rational, they pointed out, and still qualify as mad if their behavior violated social norms. They based their conclusions on the observation of people who acted immorally despite the fact that they understood the difference between right and wrong. However, these early alienists clarified that this explanation did not apply to abnormal sexual behaviors such as "pederasty, sapphism, masochism, or sadism."[13] These practices resulted from intentional defiance of accepted moral codes, and those who indulged in them publically belonged in the courts, not in clinics, they insisted. They did acknowledge some exceptions to this rule, however. Insanity played a role, they theorized, when familiar forms of mental illness, such as obsessions or hallucinations, took a sexual turn. Or in extreme cases, such as that of sergeant Bertrand, who was accused in 1847 of bestiality and of violating graves, doctors thought some unidentified defect of the sexual impulse might be responsible.[14] These early students of mental disorders, then, assigned eccentric sexual behavior to corrupt character, or when accompanied by clear signs of insanity, they took it as a manifestation of a recognizable mental disorder. The most egregious and inexplicable cases they attributed to some problem with the sexual instinct. What early observers thought explained exceptional cases, their successors identified as the principal cause of most aberrant sexual behavior.

Contemporaries credited the German doctor Carl Westphal's work on sexual inversion published in 1870 with shifting the causal paradigm from vice to perversion. By divorcing illicit sex from malign choice and assigning it instead to a biological anomaly, he changed the emphasis from sin to sickness and identified normality with sound physiology and fortunate heredity. Westphal demonstrated, Féré observed in his 1899 treatise on sexuality, "the existence of an instinctive perversion stronger than the will pushing certain individuals to achieve sexual pleasure with other individuals of the same sex."[15] Other experts followed, and although they did not entirely dismiss the impact of evil character or social conditions, they looked primarily inside the body and the mind to locate and account for sexual abnormality. "Today," Féré intoned, "one tends to attribute all corrupt practices to a pathological state."[16]

As they classified sexual practices, doctors and social thinkers labored to establish what counted as natural and unnatural, healthy and morbid, normal and abnormal. The perversions which they identified involved either performance—excessive or deficient sexual desire—or the object of desire—one's self, one's own sex, or things and body parts standing in for the whole person. But with phenomena as universal yet individualistic as love and sex, they found it difficult to draw the line between normality and abnormality. For example, at what point did a woman's moral probity or a man's disinterest in his wife qualify as frigidity? When did fascination with a lover's eyes or hair turn from normal to perverted? If pederasty was normal in some cultures or situations, could it ever be labeled as unnatural? Did circumstances always explain why women and men engaged in prostitution, or were some people born promiscuous? In view of the circumspection surrounding sex, discovering who did what with whom how often and for what reasons made it even more difficult to delineate the abnormal.

The problem

In order to study sexual behavior, physicians, criminologists, and social thinkers tried to develop a common vocabulary and a shared set of criteria for what passed as natural and as normal and what did not, but their efforts did not enjoy much success. The experts identified anomalies, but there were as many as there were writers, Chevalier complained. "Each one takes pains to create a new form," and lacking a method for categorizing them, the aberrations appeared in order of their monstrosity.[17] In some measure, experts based their lists on what public opinion considered odd. Like everyone else, doctors just "knew" that certain forms of sexual behavior such as necrophilia or nymphomania qualified as aberrant. What else fell in that realm generated much more debate. Generally, excessive manifestations of accepted behavior and examples of respectable citizens who practiced unusual sex caught their attention. But when they moved from extreme and widely recognized perversions, they faced the problem of finding the line between ordinary and aberrant and between fleeting and ingrained practices.

Getting those distinctions straight mattered to doctors and to the courts. When did infatuation turn into obsession? And when did an obsession turn from benign to dangerous? Knowing which aberrations could not be helped and which resulted from choice determined whether a man's persistent and unwelcome advances showed inexperience or poor judgment or whether they invited legal or medical attention. It also influenced how the police treated pederasts and prostitutes. The first step according to students of sex involved developing an agreed-upon lexicon of sexual disorders along with a set of signs to recognize them. As with mental illness and criminality, a few classification systems gained currency but none commanded general support. In the absence of widespread agreement about general types of perversion, work on sexual behavior often focused on the case studies of individuals. These provided a growing number of standard profiles which served as reference points for other investigators as they tried to identify and categorize sexual deviance.

These working definitions showed the influence of traditional views of normalcy. Religious doctrine defined correct sex by its purpose—procreation—and polite society formally endorsed the equation. That view recognized the couple as male and female, valued consummation, endorsed moderation, and preached monogamy. While the Church's view minimized pleasure as an objective, it acknowledged it as a fact and took resisting desire as a test of an individual's will, a trial confronted by the faithful with self-discipline and prayer. Although those who came to be called sexologists typically announced their distance from religious and social dictums, what they actually classified as aberrant showed that they held on to those values more than they admitted. As they defined deviance, they focused on the object and on the intensity of a person's affections.

Experts qualified as abnormal either excessive passivity or exceeding ardor. Impotence drew more scrutiny than frigidity, since what passed as normal for women included a sizable dose of disinterest and restraint. Doctors traced impotence to psychological difficulties or to physical problems associated with age, illness, or unhealthy practices, especially masturbation. In the case of the Italian newly wed Y..., the court-appointed doctors, including Leonardo Bianchi who reported on the case, proceeded by a process of elimination. Married for eight months, Miss X...left Y...and sought an annulment, reporting that her husband was incapable of consummating their union. The judge asked the medical experts to determine whether Miss X...was, as she claimed, a virgin, and whether Y...performed adequately before he married her. After examining Miss X...the doctors confirmed her virginity and found her normal physically.[18] They concluded that she was not a neurotic or an hysteric and that neither she nor her partner had characteristics that the other might find repugnant.[19] Miss X... professed her passionate love for Y... and reported that she had chosen him over other suitors and had herself won out over a number of other candidates for his affection.[20] She insisted that she had not criticized her husband for his repeated failures and that she had helped him as best she could. The investigators, Bianchi reported, found her straightforward and measured account of their sex life convincing.

The problem lay, then, with Y.... He insisted that he had performed regularly and normally (except for once) before he married, citing his use of prostitutes every eight to ten days from age sixteen on, sometimes four to five times a visit. He blamed stress, pressure from his mother-in-law, and his wife's lack of help for his unexpected conjugal difficulties.[21] With time and patience, these problems would pass, Y...'s lawyers argued. The court-appointed doctors agreed that anxiety and distraction might disrupt relations temporarily, but not for eight months. They ruled out psychological factors and found Y... physically normal, although unresponsive to electrical stimulation. Like other forensic doctors, they rejected as "immoral and deceptive" using manipulation or a woman to test Y...'s potency.[22] According to their report, everything pointed to a "functional anomaly having to do with the nervous system" and specifically to sexual neurasthenia, a condition which was not uncommon among vigorous young men, Bianchi claimed.[23] Y...'s lawyers rejected the medical verdict, suggesting that what the doctors called neurasthenia was a transitory emotional condition and not an organic disorder.[24]

Bianchi's team called the existence of such a thing as sexual neurasthenia an "incontestable fact."[25] Like general neurasthenia, it came from a congenitally underdeveloped or flawed nervous system, or it stemmed from some weakness in the sexual organs. Men could also develop the condition later in life "as a result of having drained the cup of pleasure, consuming in this way the capital and interest of what mother nature had supplied them."[26] Intense sexual activity, especially of the lonely sort, sapped reserves of energy and led to unwelcome lapses, but working too hard also brought on neurasthenia, and with it, in some cases, impotence. In his comments on the case, another doctor and professor of psychiatry and criminal anthropology at the University of Naples, Pasquale Penta, agreed that psychological or emotional problems could not explain such prolonged and unsuccessful efforts to consummate Y...'s marriage. He concluded that Y... suffered from a congenital weakness of the "cerebral-spinal axis" that prevented him from acting on sexual stimuli.[27] In Penta's view, overuse did not exhaust Y...'s supply of energy; he lacked the capacity for sustained activity in the first place. Although he disagreed with Penta about the causes, Bianchi was equally pessimistic about Y...'s prospects. In his view, the duration of the problem and its resistance to treatment indicated damage at the cellular level and made a cure unlikely. Based on their evaluation, the medical experts confirmed that the conditions for an annulment existed, and the judge, Bianchi reported, granted it.

Normal performance for males depended, then, on the woman's physical and emotional health, on her attractiveness, and on her non-judgmental support. With those factors in order, men might still experience impotence due to anxiety and distraction or to depression caused by poor sexual performance itself. Specific physical flaws also hampered sexual activity, and nervous exhaustion whether produced by the frenzy of modern life or by excessive devotion to Venus, as they delicately put it, could also sap energy and lead to impotence. The men who deliberately overindulged in sexual pleasure paid for it later, and those who defied the ample warnings and masturbated too much also risked losing their sexual vigor.

Particularly when it came to young men, inordinate levels of sexual activity showed bad judgment and could exhaust reserves of sexual energy, producing problems later. However, in some cases, the excess resulted not from youthful ardor but from an uncontrollable sexual appetite, and contemporaries classified the condition itself rather than its likely effects as abnormal. Studies referred to idiots and imbeciles who automatically gave in to their instinctual drives as victims of unbridled lust. Old men, too, could lose the restraint imposed by reason and convention and succumb to shocking lechery. In women, menopause could provoke overwhelming desire, according to Emile Laurent, just as hysteria and epilepsy sometimes unleashed uncontrollable sexual urges in both sexes by weakening the centers of moral restraint.[28] A hypersexual drive led to indiscriminate sex or to a form of insanity characterized by obscene thoughts and dirty talk. Or it could cause a person to act "so without good sense [and] intelligent reflection, that one cannot explain these patients in any other way [than mental illness]," observed Benjamin Ball, the first holder of the chair of mental illness and the brain at Sainte-Anne Hospital in Paris.[29]

In the most serious forms of excess, nymphomania and satyriasis, victims exhibited unrestrained sexual activity. It proved difficult to diagnose satyriasis since some promiscuity passed as normal in males, married or not. Falling for someone from a different social milieu or failing to stay with a well-born husband or wife raised suspicions that uncontrollable urges had erased good sense. Especially when women sought inappropriate partners, pathological levels of desire appeared to be the problem. These women, according to the literature, took up with the first comer and moved from partner to partner, disturbingly heedless of propriety and self-interest. In a case first presented by Ulysse Trélat (1795–1879) in *Folie lucide* (Lucid Folly) and used by Benjamin Ball in 1888 to illustrate this type of excessive sex drive, Mme. V … appeared reserved, but she threw herself at any man she encountered even after she got married. Dispatched to a clinic, she enjoyed impeccable health and showed no signs of mental illness, but when released, the behavior surfaced again, a sure sign of a pathological condition, Ball concluded.[30] The diagnosis indicated that women whose appetites and indiscretions drew attention risked the label nymphomaniac, no matter how modest their external demeanor. Except for their high octane urges and indiscriminate choice of partners, nymphomaniacs usually led respectable lives, and that fact contributed to the definition of their behavior as aberrant. People did not expect proper middle- and upper-class women to consort with any available male, especially not with social inferiors, and transgressing those limits called their self-control and even their sanity into question. One type of sexual aberration, then, involved degree. Indifference to sex or the inability to perform on the one hand and inappropriate excess or indiscriminate relationships on the other warranted professional advice or treatment. Still, it wasn't easy to distinguish between proper and pathological female reserve, between a virile man's desires and uncontrolled urges, or between the unbridled passion of young lovers and more troubling excesses.

The difficulty of drawing reliable lines between normal and aberrant behavior also applied to what aroused desire. Usually people found contemporaries and social equals of the opposite sex attractive. But it also happened that they pursued unacceptable partners with singleminded devotion and chaste intention. Esquirol identified this condition and labeled it "erotomania," and authorities at the end of the century took pains to describe its elements and to identify its causes. Ball described "erotomania" or "chaste love" in *La folie erotique* (Erotic Insanity), first published in 1888. He specified that the victims fixed amorous attention on an imaginary person or an object. As children they behaved strangely, and during puberty they developed romantic fantasies which could take concrete form when by chance they met or read about someone who corresponded to their inventions. When that happened, they began to lose sleep and concentration, then slipped into delusions, and finally surrendered to hallucinations. If they persisted in pursuing the object of their fantasies and met rejection, "they became completely intolerable and ridiculous, [and] they got themselves arrested" and confined in asylums. No treatment rid them of their obsession and, Ball observed, they usually sank into an "absolutely incurable" delirium.[31]

The case of a 34-year-old Latin teacher, whose father came from healthy stock but whose mother showed signs of neurosis, demonstrated the pattern. At age twenty he was drafted, joined the infantry, and fought bravely in the Franco-Prussian War. Other than a penchant for getting drunk with his fellow soldiers, he "was not only honorable but heroic," although still "absolutely crazy" during the entire period of his military service, Ball explained.[32] When he returned to civilian life, he daydreamed about an ideal woman until one day, on an outing with his students, he saw her on the street and fell passionately in love. He discovered where she lived and asked her mother for permission to marry her. Rebuffed, he returned a second and third time, prompting the family to report him. He ended up in Sainte-Anne Hospital, where he proved to be a model patient. He accepted confinement as a test of his love, but Ball took his forbearance as evidence of his insanity, a diagnosis confirmed by the fact that he suffered convulsions as a child and had a neurotic mother. Chaste fixations of the sort that the Latin teacher suffered met the test for erotic insanity, Ball concluded.

In a related form of obsessive yet chaste love, the person fixed on a part of the body or an object connected to the target of desire. Alfred Binet (1857–1911) laid out the fundamentals of this disorder in two articles published in the *Revue philosophique* (Philosophical Review) in 1887.[33] He labeled the phenomenon "*fétichisme*," a term which became standard for this behavior. Binet noted that worship of objects played a central role in religion, especially its primitive forms, and the same tendency to focus on a particular attribute or possession often accompanied love. "It's important to add that everyone is more or less fetishistic when it comes to love; there is a constant quantity of fetishism in the most ordinary love. In other words, there is major and minor fetishism."[34] Binet catalogued various forms of the practice, accompanying his list with detailed descriptions of relevant cases. People could fix on any part of the body, or on a personality characteristic. He noted the lover of eyes, hands, or hair, and attachment to a person's scent or voice. Binet provided the example of Jean-Jacques Rousseau, who reported being attracted to arrogant, proud women and taking pleasure in their hitting him.[35] Objects such as boots and even the buttons on boots could become targets of obsession, Binet explained. Finding particular attributes or objects associated with one's partners attractive was quite normal, he emphasized, but when those substituted for the person, the attraction turned aberrant. In serious forms of fetishism, the object drew all of the person's attention, and it alone provoked desire, sometimes irresistible desire. Fetishism, he summarized, "consists of the exaggerated sexual importance attached to a secondary and insignificant detail."[36]

To illustrate fetishism run amok, Binet referred to what became a signature case, one also reported by Jean-Martin Charcot and Valentin Magnan (1835–1916) in two articles they published in 1882. They described a 34-year-old male who grew up around highly nervous and emotional parents and who reported suffering convulsions as a child. "X…" remembered first becoming attached to the nails in women's shoes when he was about six years old. He liked to imagine looking at the nails and torturing young girls as he masturbated. Although he tried to stifle the images, they kept surfacing until he married. After a brief respite, the obsession reemerged when he saw or heard about nails, accompanied this time by a feeling of pressure at the top of the head followed by violent headaches and spasms. The closer the contact, or the larger and more numerous the nails on a woman's shoes, the more devastating his physical reaction, Charcot and Magnan reported.[37]

An intelligent, hardworking person, with important responsibilities, X… despaired at the persistent appearance in himself of what he felt was a different person. The episodes tired him out, but still he could not sleep at night. His neck hurt after the spasms; he had headaches; his legs swelled so much that he struggled to walk uphill; and he constantly felt thirsty. No matter how hard he tried, he could not escape the fixation or resist the impulse to indulge it. When police caught him masturbating in front of a shoemaker's shop, they arrested him for acts of public indecency, but the judge dismissed the case, concluding that X… could not be held responsible for his actions. In different and equally influential patient profiles, Charcot and Magnan described M. L…'s erotic attachments to night caps and C…'s obsession with white aprons. All of these aberrations, M. X…'s included, were "episodes of the same illness; in every one of these patients," they observed, "heredity played a role."[38]

Amorous fixation on parts of the body and on objects or abnormal levels of sexual desire, whether too much or too little, involved the opposite sex and recognizable emotions. Ball, among others, reserved a separate category of sexual perversion for unnatural feelings and partners. It included sadists, necrophiliacs, pederasts, and the inverted. Their acts, he argued, "directly contradicted nature," whereas erotic insanity at least involved natural feelings.[39] Even among these anomalies, important distinctions held. Necrophiliacs shunned the living for the dead, and sadists expressed their attachment to their lovers with cruelty, but they both reserved their attentions for the opposite sex. Pederasts and the inverted, in contrast, went for the wrong sex, and that perversion of nature deserved special attention and explanation.

Of all the so-called perverted forms of sexual activity, same-sex love generated the greatest consternation and the most debate. The instinct to preserve the species, most believed, meant that sex existed for the purposes of reproduction. Nature (and God) favored heterosexual relationships, even though not all relationships fell in that category. Unlike in Germany, Austria, and England, French and Italian law did not directly prohibit homosexuality. How, then, to categorize a practice taken as normal in some situations and in some societies and as legal in their own? Until the 1870s it passed as a sin or a vice, a deliberate act produced by weak or corrupt character. Normal people obeyed the dictates of the Lord or of social convention, and at least in Paris, the police took public signs of pederasty as punishable offenses to public morality. The equivalent of the vice squad kept close watch and careful records, and when their quarry made public contact, they arrested them.[40]

In 1858, Ambroise Tardieu (1818–1879), professor of legal medicine at the University of Paris, published a forensic analysis of crimes against public morals which crystallized attitudes at the time.[41] As a doctor and forensic expert, he offered testimony at trials about what likely caused the accused's behavior in order to help judges and juries establish grounds for criminal charges. In his *Étude médico-légale sur les attentats aux moeurs* (Medical-Legal Study of Offenses against Public Decency), Tardieu supplied information to potential expert witnesses on exhibitionism, rape, child molestation, pederasty, and sodomy. More and more cases of pederasty involved doctors' testimony, he argued, because public outcry demanded more surveillance by authorities, because pederasts got involved in crime, and because they were forming groups.[42] He based his analysis on a study of trials involving both pederasty and murder or blackmail and on information he drew from ninety trials involving three hundred accused pederasts in which he served as an expert witness.

Because modern language had no word for "the shameful vice," people used the term "pederasty," he said, but he preferred the term "sodomy."[43] The equation of the two reflected the understanding of pederasty current at the time. "Marital sodomy" occurred, he noted, but such incidents rarely reached the courts. For the most part courts dealt with attempts on young boys and with male prostitution which, he observed, involved individuals hustling customers with the intention of blackmailing them later or working out of brothels to sell pleasure to interested buyers. When charged with the act, most pederasts denied it, Tardieu noted, but "very numerous and eloquent" physical signs confirmed the practice, particularly when the subject took the passive role.[44] Dress and mannerisms also gave pederasts away, and they looked unwell since such unnatural acts "must inevitably affect general health, in more or less serious ways." In some cases, the practice produced "physical and mental exhaustion which led to respiratory failure, paralysis, insanity."[45]

Tardieu condemned the "shameful habits of pederasts," particularly when not explained by the need for money or by an interest in blackmail. "I ask myself, as physiologist and physician, what unknown causes can help us understand the aberration of pederasts." When asked for an explanation, they invoked "the ardent transports of true love," he noted with undisguised skepticism.[46] In his view, same-sex love could result from certain disorders such as epilepsy, but in general, "moral perversion" or in the case of married men consorting with children, excessively strong libido had to be the cause.[47] Nothing, though, mitigated the shocking nature of the behavior. No matter how "incomprehensible, no matter how unnatural and irrational pederastic acts seem to be, they [pederasts] cannot escape either moral responsibility or the just severity of the law, nor, especially, the contempt of honest people."[48] However much he shrouded his analysis in science, Tardieu held on to the view that same-sex love was a vice. But that assessment began to change in the last third of the century as doctors in particular traced it to physical or psychological sources. In some cases, a defect or illness disrupted normal sexual function and explained same-sex love, they theorized.

These experts acknowledged the influence of Carl Westphal's 1870 study of what he called the "contrary sexual sense."[49] Specifically, Westphal proposed that some anatomically normal males possessed a female mind. Since sexual attraction depended on ideas and emotions rather than sensations, the female in them found other men more attractive. The same disjunction between the psychological and physical held true for women who preferred their own sex. The notion of an inversion of the sexual instinct, as Arrigo Tamassia labeled it, or inversion of the reproductive sense in Charcot's and Magnan's lexicon gained credence in the late 1870s and the 1880s.[50] Tamassia (1848–1917), professor of legal medicine at the University of Pavia, addressed the issue in an article he published in 1878. Taking note of the work of Westphal and of Krafft-Ebing, he described a case of his own, that of P … a 33-year-old peasant employed as a domestic who preferred female tasks and liked to dress as a woman.[51] P … reported that he enjoyed women's company but never experienced any physical attraction to them. Caught wearing a ring he stole from his mistress, Tamassia interviewed him when he was in prison. He considered the possibility that P … invented the persona, but concluded that he was too dull witted for such subterfuge. Rather, P … showed the signs of having an inverted sexual identity: normal sexual organs, indifference or hostility to the opposite sex, precocious attraction to the same sex fulfilled platonically or at most with mutual touching or masturbation.[52] Unlike Westphal, who labeled it a nervous disorder, Tamassia classified it as mainly psychological because it affected the personality and sense of self, and because it limited mental acuity.

Charcot and Magnan drew considerable attention to inversion in the articles on aberrant sexual practices that they published in 1882. The example they presented, labeled "X" (like the fetishist they profiled), became a standard reference for detecting inversion. As he described his condition to the doctors, this M. X … remembered watching a soldier masturbating and imitating him when he was six years old, a practice he continued as he imagined naked males.[53] At age twenty, he stopped masturbating, but reported that it sufficed to imagine a young man in the buff or to see a statue of a naked male to become aroused.[54] Although he said he liked to talk with women about fashion and try on women's clothing, he found men more attractive. He specified, however, that he did not want to have sexual relations with them, and although tempted, he did not even dare to court them. At the most, he found himself seized by the desire to see their genitalia, an impulse he tried unsuccessfully to cast out of his mind.[55]

In their evaluation of the case, Charcot and Magnan detailed the main characteristics of inversion. M. X … was a 31-year-old professor who got along well with others and who showed no signs of physical abnormality. Elements of his past, however, suggested deeper problems, they observed. An investigation of his family revealed that his maternal grandfather abandoned his practice as a notary to follow his artistic friends and that his devout mother liked to party. The patient himself admitted to stealing from his schoolmates and teachers when he was younger.[56] He began to experience seizures when he was fifteen, sporadically at first and then at least every three months. The symptoms looked like epilepsy, but because he could return to work when they passed, Charcot and Magnan diagnosed hysteria. The hysteria along with the peculiar behavior of family members and his early moral lapses indicated inherited organic flaws, which also explained his erotic fantasies and behavior, they contended. Women could exhibit similar symptoms. They referred to the cases of two females who liked to wear boys clothing and who only played with girls. They became infatuated with other women, and when spurned, they threatened suicide. Examination revealed enough evidence of physical abnormalities and mental stability to conclude that like M. X… they suffered from an underlying illness which manifested itself in same-sex attraction.[57] "You can see it, the instinctive perversion that interests us is a strong manifestation of a much deeper psychopathological state."[58]

Pursuing the diagnosis, doctors and other investigators publicized more and more cases, broadening the compass of the term "inversion" and refining its meaning. Almost a quarter of a century after Westphal described the contrary sexual sense, Chevalier proposed to synthesize the approaches sociologists, moralists, anthropologists, psychiatrists, and specialists in forensic medicine took to the pressing matter of same-sex relations.[59] He described inversion as a durable and deep attraction to the same sex accompanied by a real antipathy to the other sex.[60] That definition, he admitted, extended the sweep of inversion beyond its accepted meaning to include several variants of same-sex love. The narrower profile of inversion, the one traced by Westphal, he called "true" inversion. It stood at one end of the spectrum, and pederasty and sapphism occupied the other.

He confirmed the established view of "true" inversion as a condition produced by a degenerative flaw in the sexual impulse that mismatched sexual identity and anatomy. The case literature showed that true inverts were often successful and respected members of the community. They experienced strong attraction to their own sex but never or very rarely engaged in sodomy. "[P]ederasty repels him as a grotesque act; if he succumbs, it is in an impulsive, accidental way, leaving a feeling of disgust," Chevalier reported.[61] Typically, inverts tried to lead normal lives despite their abnormal urges. But beneath the surface, they suffered from "the disarray and the unspeakable sadness" produced by the appeal of their own sex as well as from a host of other health problems. Because it derived from inherited or congenital defects, the condition resisted treatment. In contrast, what Chevalier called "acquired inversion" or "real pederasty and sapphism" responded to outside factors and "smacked of vice and perversity." Pederasts and sapphists unhesitatingly consummated their relationships. They responded to situations, or passing fancies, or to corrupt influences, and provided they didn't make it a habit, they returned easily to normal relations, Chevalier contended.[62] Other investigators confirmed the distinction between pederasty and inversion, making the first a matter of taste, gain, or opportunism and the second the result of an inherited or congenital disturbance or the offshoot of another illness. Pederasty involved consummation; inversion occupied the imagination and led to, at most, limited physical contact.

Several practices considered aberrant made the list of sexual perversions without much debate. They deviated from standard expectations of who, how, and how often.

In addition to departing from convention, investigators grouped them together because they all resulted from a malfunction or organic deficiency, innate or acquired or both. In Penta's view, they also shared common characteristics. The perverted act was "acute, irresistible, almost blind like an impulsive, spasmodic, violent act, seeming sometimes even to be an impulsive fixation." Always, he asserted, the perversion simplified the sex act, eliminating its human qualities, and returning it to "the old and perhaps buried animalistic characteristics."[63] Whether inversion belonged in this group raised some questions. Investigators typically included it with other biologically based abnormal sexual behaviors, but while it resembled fetishism according to Charcot and Magnan, it did not look like other conditions such as necromancy or sadism. Because they believed that pederasty, in contrast to inversion, usually resulted from choice, they did not count it as a perversion, no matter how twisted they said it was.

How to treat prostitution and rape caused even more hesitation. Experts recognized that poverty played a major role in forcing women into prostitution, and some of them left it at that, suggesting that any reasonable woman caught in similar circumstances would do the same thing. According to this view, prostitution did not qualify as pathological or deviant. But the fact that not all desperate woman took to the streets convinced other observers to look further. Some saw that prostitution, like theft and other crimes or like vagabondage, became a habit and from there an organic proclivity. These women started out normal, but then they lost the ability to abandon the trade. Another theory suggested that an inherited organic defect pushed women to prostitution. Potential prostitutes from early childhood, these women acted as a result of aberrant sexual instincts.[64] The studies that mentioned male prostitution stressed the role of money and warned that if they made sodomy a regular practice, it would permanently alter their bodies and their minds.

Rape also commanded the attention of criminologists and doctors, because statistics showed pronounced increases in France and Italy, as well as in other European countries. The rise in attacks on children, in particular, provoked comment. Unlike many other practices identified as perversions, the law prohibited both rape and the corruption of minors, whether they occurred in public or in private. Drawing from official statistics, Tardieu reported 4,360 cases of rape or attempted rape involving adults between 1851 and 1875, and 17,657 involving children.[65] He examined 632 cases involving minors and counted 435 under thirteen years old.[66] Lombroso recorded that child rape rose from 136 reported cases in 1826 to 791 in 1885 in Italy, a pattern of escalation apparent in England as well. Because social conditions played a primary role, Lombroso labeled these attacks "occasional rape."[67] If they addressed it at all, other studies of sexual perversion also usually recognized rape as circumstantial. But some experts stressed its organic roots in certain, or in all, cases. One recurring explanation linked child abuse to senility, suggesting that the older the man, the younger the amorous target. Another approach described rapists as primitives. In a chapter he devoted to them, Penta insisted that rapists differed from the sexually perverted, because their drives appeared later and consumed them less. "In most cases," they came from the lower classes, poverty, or a bad milieu, and from families with criminality, alcoholism, and mental and nervous disorders.[68] His study of sixty rapists confirmed his conclusion that they were primitives, always "a step backward, nothing more, nothing less" and "always," like other delinquents, they lacked moral sensibility.[69] Silvio Venturi added some detail to that profile. He described rape as a sexual expression of atavism or arrested development and for that reason a practice natural to born criminals.

Explaining the problem

Sin and vice originated in the mind. People with weak characters gave in to passion, and evil people willingly ignored the strictures of religion and the contempt of society and indulged in prohibited sexual behavior. They could, with the help of the Lord or extra effort on their parts, decide to dominate the flesh, but they did not. Fin-de-siècle medical authorities, criminologists, and other social commentators regarded these explanations with skepticism. Fortunately, claimed Pasquale Penta, sexual perversions are no longer considered the result of a "simple release of evil or foul instincts."[70] With the exception of pederasty, where such moral explanations persisted, they looked to the physical rather than the spiritual and to the reproductive organs, nerves, and brain rather than character for the sources of errant behavior. As they did with other abnormal social behaviors and with disruptions of the mind, they looked at anatomy and physiology, at the body's structure and its operation for the site of problems. They examined patients for visible biological abnormalities and tested them to evaluate their basic health, and when possible, they did autopsies to detect anomalies, particularly in the brain.

For the most part, though, they relied on case studies in order to identify patterns. Chevalier called on his colleagues to apply clinical methods to the study of sexuality in humans and in animals and "to keep," as he did, "to the facts and only the facts, and to ask of them only what they could yield." As with other experiments, Chevalier admonished, scientists needed to observe and interpret with care, understanding that when it came to sexual psychopathology, their preconceived ideas might cause them to see something that wasn't there.[71] The cases came from doctors' practices, from hospitals and asylums, or from the courts when judges sought medical appraisals. Because of the nature of their subjects, experts primarily learned about what they considered as abnormalities. In order to locate the organic causes of perversions, investigators needed to know more about sexual structures and processes, and they found themselves in the familiar position of using the abnormal to infer the normal. As they developed the case studies, they applied common protocols to uncover family histories and the patient's own health record. What they sought from these and what they found reflected, as Chevalier warned, what they already theorized to be true about the body. In healthy people, anatomy and physiology operated in concert, animated and directed by undamaged sexual impulses.

Those who analyzed sexual behavior typically saw it, as they did other forms of activity, in the context of interdependent physiological processes developed over time or corrupted over time. The optimal operation of the body depended on the health of the organs and on a steady supply of energy to power their operation. Structural damage to any of the key pieces or disturbances elsewhere in the body that affected them determined how a person expressed affection. This mechanistic view stressed the dynamic interaction of the elements of a system. Those who accepted Westphal's theories also stressed that the system's pieces needed to match. They pointed out that healthy components did not ensure normality if a woman's mind ended up in a man's body, or the reverse. Understanding how sexual activity operated did not, however, explain desire itself. Some more basic impulse, what many called the sexual or reproductive instinct, seemed to underlie both sexual activity and identity.

When Benjamin Ball classified sexual pathologies and their organic causes in *La folie érotique* in 1888, he adopted Esquirol's categories of "insane chaste love" and of excessive sex drives, including nymphomania or hypersexuality. Ball added a third category, "sexual perversion"; it included sadism, necrophilia, pederasty, and inversion. These aberrations resulted from defects in the sexual instinct, and they often "lead the ill to these squalid excesses which the courts are called upon to repress."[72] Autopsies performed on sadists exposed damage to the brain, evidence that they were "really sick, true madmen," and not willful criminals.[73] When sadists exhibited only minor mental impairment, further investigation revealed that they came from unhealthy families. Whatever the cause, the defects affected the impulse responsible for directing and calibrating desire. Necrophiliacs, like sadists, suffered from a defective sexual instinct, according to Ball's scheme. He referred to the notorious case of Sargent Bertrand, the well-regarded soldier garrisoned in Paris who turned out to be responsible for desecrating graves in the Montparnasse cemetery. His morbid activities followed regular attacks triggered by intensely painful headaches. Despite the evidence of an organic problem, the court martial bowed to an outraged public and sentenced Bertrand to a year's imprisonment before pronouncing him insane.[74] Like sadists and necrophiliacs, inverts responded to inborn impulses; they exhibited their sexuality in the only way that they could, Ball contended.[75] Although Ball put pederasty along with inversion in this third group of sexual perversions, he explained that the two differed, even though the law often confused them. Pederasty did not stem from an organic anomaly, Ball insisted. Rather, he saw it as "a vice that results from a conscious, determined decision, and public decency properly revolts against it and the law punishes it."[76] Pederasty, most commentators agreed, was a matter of choice, the activity of perverse and sinful types or of common criminals.[77]

Féré's more pointed analysis of sexuality, *L'instinct sexuel: évolution et dissolution* (The Sexual Instinct: Evolution and Dissolution), appeared in 1899. He drew on the work of others, including Théodule Ribot. Ribot postulated that initially their biological makeup allowed humans just to seek their own survival. Later, evolution enabled them to value the survival of the race and to think of beauty, morality, religion, and science. Adopting a similar developmental framework, Féré specified that the sexual impulse emerged after the instinct for self-preservation and until recently took second place to it.[78] When it first appeared, the impulse favored promiscuity, but as humans evolved, it promoted polygamy and in the latest stages the monogamy that Féré considered vital to civilized society. Under its sway, women practiced continence to secure civilization and the race, and men did well to follow them in order to avoid the inconveniences of adultery, illegitimate children, and disease.[79] Deviations from behavior normal at a particular evolutionary stage resulted, he argued, from an inherited or pathological disturbance of the sexual instinct.

Like Ribot, Féré argued that just as the species passed through these phases, so did individuals as they grew from infants to adults.[80] In modern society, according to Féré, adolescents practiced the promiscuity and "unregulated polygamy" of primitives, while adults managed the self-control permitted by a more fully developed sexual instinct.[81] However, at any point the developmental process could slow down, stall, slip backward, or abruptly revert to an earlier stage. As Féré explained the process, old age and insanity could dissolve the later and most fragile advances, exposing the person's more primitive self. Or an illness or shock could reverse the process and return a person to an earlier stage. In still another scenario, a person might stop developing psychologically, while continuing to mature physically.[82]

Other investigators focused on identifying how sexual differentiation occurred. Two competing theories influenced the debate: one proposed that people lacked sexual identity at birth and the other that they initially contained both sexes in equal measure. Leonardo Bianchi, for example, assumed that during gestation and early childhood, people identified with both sexes, and only in adolescence did one of the two win out.[83] According to the other approach, infants were asexual, but they gradually left that state behind as they grew comfortable with their own sex and attracted to the other. Whichever model of differentiation they accepted, experts acknowledged that the complexity of the process left plenty of opportunities for anomalies. Usually, compromised heredity did the damage, giving people the divided identities that made them members of what contemporaries sometimes called a "third sex."

These theories of the origins of sexual desire and identity emphasized a dynamic developmental process, one prone to error. Doctors also traced sexual behavior to anatomical and physiological sources. Valentin Magnan described the mechanics of sexual desire as early as 1885. Normal behavior involved the proper coordination of ideas, appetites, and reflexes, and each of these in turn depended on the health of the brain, spine, and genital organs. Disrupt one and specific "sexual anomalies, aberrations, and perversions" appeared, Magnan contended.[84] According to his theory, troubles in the spinal-genital zone produced either complete frigidity or frequent and spontaneous orgasm. If the brain malfunctioned and could not check desire, then the entirely reflexive carnal urges characteristic of idiots emerged. When, however, the brain imposed excessive restraints, ideas overwhelmed sexual impulses and produced the erotic yet chaste manias identified by Esquirol earlier in the century. Still different aberrations resulted from physical and mental defects in either the posterior or frontal parts of the spinal-cerebral area, Magnan argued. The back of the brain housed perception, and when reflexes moved directly from this region along the spine, an image sufficed to provoke uncontrollable sexual desire. He offered as examples two women, both of them imbeciles who threw themselves at any man they saw.[85] If, on the other hand, the front of the brain and spine coordinated poorly, the problem affected the object of love more than the intensity of desire, according to Magnan's scheme. In these cases, a distorted idea commanded physical responses, leading to completely inappropriate obsessions—with an object, or a child, or men with men and women with women.[86]

Magnan classified all these abnormalities, whatever the original site of the problem, as forms of insanity, noting that they often accompanied other "obsessions, impulsions, and various diseases." Except in cases where the brain shut down and the physical reigned, these people appeared to be in full possession of their faculties. Despite their lucidity, those afflicted by overpowering desire or misplaced love suffered from mental illness and could not be held legally responsible for their actions. "They are not then just eccentric," Magnan argued, "but they are psychopaths, genuinely insane, [people] who in every way require the help and the attention of the doctor."[87]

Ball took a similar approach when he explained chaste fixations and excessive desires. The first, erotomania, which included what Binet called fetishism, resulted from malfunctions of the brain and therefore qualified as mental illness. Some variants of the irresistible sexual urges included in his second group also stemmed from abnormalities in the brain, Ball argued. Like exhibitionism and erotic hallucinations, hopeless infatuations with inappropriate partners indicated defective mental equipment.[88] Madame V ... displayed signs of this type of mental derangement. Other types of hypersexuality, as well as nymphomania and satyriasis, in contrast, resulted from lesions on the sexual organs or nervous centers, not the brain. In Ball's view, "a permanent irritation, which results from an anatomical flaw," produced these insatiable and overpowering sexual drives.[89] These aberrations did not qualify as a mental illness because they originated outside the brain. In serious cases, they came on fast and led to death.

Writing for laymen, Annunziato La Cara provides a later example of the link between abnormal sexual practice and "anomalies in the external genital equipment, or in the nervous pathways between it and the cerebral cortex."[90] Desire, he argued, originated in the sexual organs and communicated itself to the brain via a web of connecting nerves. The cerebral cortex received the impulse and directed the organs to act. If something disturbed the vibrations in the cerebral cortex, it could cause the organs to fulfill unusual functions or not to act at all.[91] Defects in the nerves of the sexual organs, in contrast, could produce "abnormal sexual impulses and ideas," or they could twist the directives they received back from the brain. For example, insensitive or misdirected nerve endings and malformed (male) genitals led to masochism and prolonged onanism and in some cases to inversion and pederasty, La Cara argued.[92] As he explained it, normal sexual behavior depended on the health of each element of the interdependent system of nerves, cerebral cortex, and sexual organs.

Doctors and other observers worked, then, from a set of general assumptions about the body and the mind and from some particular ones about the mechanics of sexual activity. They concluded that the brain, nervous system, and reproductive organs worked in concert to stimulate, modulate, and express sexual desire. Any defect in the elements themselves or in the levels of energy required to maintain their harmonious interaction produced abnormal behavior. Evidence of the unbridled sexuality of idiots or of chaste fixations on inappropriate love objects demonstrated the role the brain played in directing the sexual urges that emanated from the reproductive organs, they believed. Conversely, they surmised that excessive or abnormally low levels of desire in mentally healthy adults likely stemmed from malfunctions of the sexual organs. Or, as neurasthenics showed, a flagging nervous system could affect the transmission of stimuli and result in impotence in psychologically and physically sound men and women.

Unusual sexual behavior also responded to social conditions, according to some investigators. Depending on the type of act and on the observer's perspective, society played a direct or an indirect role, it determined or it contributed, or it watched (and judged). As observers described them, prostitution and rape offered the clearest examples of society's influence. Like occasional theft and temporary vagabondage, prostitution was a last resort in desperate conditions. Other less dramatic factors such as "poor upbringing, the contagion of example, getting caught up in [prostitution], lack of work, laziness, the desire for luxuries" also tempted women to engage in what Laurent called a "monstrous and incomprehensible" activity.[93] Male prostitution also drew attention, especially in France. As Michael L. Wilson points out, the police, judges, journalists, and doctors came to identify pederasty with male prostitution.[94] At the time, the more scientific analyses of pederasty recognized that some younger men sold their favors in an emergency or with the idea of blackmailing reputation-conscious citizens. In the first case, like female prostitutes, they acted opportunistically, choosing sex rather than theft to support themselves in a pinch. However, when they engaged in prostitution rings or extortion, these pederasts joined or flirted with a criminal world, a connection the Paris police accepted as a given.[95] They took on a particular role, becoming predators in their own way, a choice that indicated their dubious character rather than expedience, according to commentators.[96]

Social factors also appeared to influence the increase in rape, particularly when directed at children. Lombroso, for example, explained that civilization and education stimulated the nervous system and the brain and intensified desires, first among them sexual desire.[97] Because modern children went to school and worked in factories, they made easier targets than they once did, he observed. Improved diet and higher alcohol consumption also contributed to the problem by intensifying libido, as did loveless marriages with no escape route. Scientists also acknowledged the weight of the popular legend that sexual contact with a small child or a virgin cured venereal disease.[98] The laws contributed to the incidence of rape by giving rapists an out, historians such as Domenico Rizzo add. For example, Italian criminal procedure required that individuals bring charges against those who corrupted or engaged in carnal violence against minors. At any time in the proceedings, they could withdraw the complaint. This arrangement allowed child molesters and rapists to avoid punishment by paying off the family while keeping public officials from taking the initiative and pressing charges.[99]

Studies also argued that circumstances could cause people to seek out same-sex partners. Chevalier, for example, observed that fear of syphilis could prompt "weaker types" to avoid relationships with women and slake their desire with men. More often, men living together without access to women resorted to pederasty, faute de mieux. As Chevalier described it, deprivation "pushes these individuals to relationships against nature, the endemic-epidemic perversion of the masses."[100] It happened in prisons, hospitals, the military, in religious houses, schools, and workshops, but the participants never considered it anything more than an expedient, observers noted. Eugenio Tanzi, addressing sexual perversions in his textbook on mental illness in

1905, labeled such occasional, opportunistic episodes as "pseudo homosexuality," abnormal but not unnatural.[101] Whatever the circumstances which drove them, opportunists acted in deliberate and knowing response to their situations. Unlike inversion or the rare cases of pathologically driven pederasty and sapphism, these practices developed slowly and in the context of normal sexual relations. Usually the activity proved temporary, and it did not accompany or produce any other mental or physical problems, at least not immediately. "To sum up," said Chevalier, "[there is] nothing pathological about it."[102]

Sapphism could work the same way, Chevalier argued. Women resorted to it when confined in female communities or when their fear of maternity turned them away from men.[103] But beneath these evident and widely acknowledged factors, Chevalier saw other social forces at work. Either as a result of their upbringing or out of economic necessity, women were gaining greater independence and freedom and were "little by little ... [becoming] more like men." The modern female grew up, he observed, "with not much innocence, almost no modesty, no ingenuousness at all, and of freshness and reserve, only the words."[104] How could one not connect changes in women's social position to the explosion of lesbianism particularly in Paris and other large urban areas, he asked. These women entered the marketplace; they claimed political rights; they played sports and engaged in other manly activities. Some of them no longer depended on men financially, and soon they would dispense with their love as well. As evidence, he noted that lesbianism attained "worrisome proportions" especially in the worlds of the boulevard, the theater, the popular arts, in the bas-fonds of society, and the brothels.[105]

If increased autonomy unsexed women, literacy could also turn them to lesbianism, Chevalier believed. The contemporary novel "is the most active of the agents of contamination and propagation of evil."[106] Few novelists addressed pederasty; it was too revolting, he contended. But sapphism retained the quality of surprise, and it formed a titillating subject for serious writers such as Diderot, Balzac, and Flaubert and for popular writers whose tastes bordered on the pornographic. According to Chevalier, hucksters also described the practice in pseudoscientific treatises often addressed to "Illustre Maître" to give the works a learned air. Advertising sapphism in these ways augmented the practice, he insisted.[107]

A more general erosion of inhibitions added to the list of conditions promoting aberrant sex, experts argued. Some commentators blamed the decline of religion and others continual political instability for cutting the moorings which anchored society. Urban life also seemed to breed license, especially among the popular classes whose living conditions forced them into unhealthy propinquity. More broadly, civilization refined sensations, they theorized, causing moderns to search for sharper and more varied satisfactions. Either that occurred or society lost vitality with age, and people sought new and stronger sources of stimulation. Similar patterns affected individuals who faded as life's hectic pace depleted their energy and dulled their senses. Tumbling all these elements together, La Cara observed: "One must conclude that the feverish life, the expenditure of energy, the violent desires that civilization brings along with it, the refinement of the senses, idleness and the legitimization of libido among the well to do, predisposes people to perversions."[108]

The norms of respectable society also encouraged abnormal practices, a number of critics argued. Silvio Venturi, for one, insisted that society's stringent moral codes interrupted the natural development of sexuality and led to "prolonged and creative onanism, to pederasty, and to bestiality."[109] Locked into loveless marriages, women aged prematurely, losing their "sweetness, good humor, expansiveness, and affection."[110] Men caught up in the drive to succeed felt the consequences as illnesses such as neurasthenia stifled their libidos. Chevalier specified: "the struggle for life, intellectual exhaustion, and nervous disturbances which result from it, the fever of currency transactions, market speculations, gambling, artificial stimulants, alcohol, tobacco, morphine"[111]—these assaults weakened the body, bringing internal propensities to the fore and exposing it to destructive pathologies.

Circumstances contributed the most directly to male and female prostitution and to pederasty and sapphism, according to investigators. But their critics pointed to the numbers. Most indigents found a legal survival strategy or resorted to begging or stealing, and most men and women in conditions of enforced chastity did not seek same-sex partners. Those observers who saw prostitution as opportunistic and pederasty and sapphism as venal dismissed situational pressures as irrelevant. But others postulated that rough circumstances activated an inherited proclivity toward prostitution or pederasty just as they did with occasional crime and vagrancy. Men looking for sexual adventure or release in pederastic encounters had abnormally strong libidos or weak self-control, they speculated. As specified by La Cara, the initiator lacked normal powers of inhibition as a result of a defect in the brain.[112] Thus even though they emphasized the role of circumstances, some investigators backtracked to theorize that, after all, an unrecognized biological penchant influenced the person's decisions.[113]

Whatever caused them to break taboos the first time, if they made it a practice, pederasts and sapphists risked irreversible damage, most experts contended. Repeated acts altered a person's biological makeup in ways likely to affect their progeny. In Chevalier's view, they took on the attributes of the opposite sex, and the more they engaged in the practice, the deeper and more pervasive the alteration of their personalities became. Habitual pederasts, Chevalier warned, turned into "*neo-women* in morality, manners, in feelings, intelligence, and character."[114] Unwilling and in some cases now unable to engage in sexual relations with women, they could only form intense attachments with men. What began as an occasional act affected a person's organic makeup, a conclusion which drew force from Lamarckian theories of acquired characteristics.

The literature, then, recognized a rich array of conditions and situations likely to promote perverse practices. Experts also stressed that personal habits could lead to trouble by disrupting normal operations or triggering inner propensities. Frenzied sexual activity, many agreed, drained energy and could produce temporary or ongoing impotence. Masturbation, in particular, posed these dangers in the view of most experts. Toward the end of the century, however, more of them moderated their judgment about its nefarious effects. La Cara, for one, observed that if onanism led to sexual perversions, there would be more of them, given the commonality of the practice among children and adults. Too much masturbation could, he acknowledged, lead to neurasthenia or other problems, but not always and then only when the person was "congenitally predisposed" to the conditions.[115] Referring to the sexologist Albert Moll, he suggested masturbation might prevent or temper rather than promote perversions by providing a sexual outlet.[116] That sharp departure from the conventional wisdom about masturbation mirrored distinctions between the occasional and habitual that scientists made for other misfits. The first practice appeared benign, especially in contrast to the drastic risks and dangers of the second.

In addition to medical and social causes, commentators left a space for what once counted as the standard explanation: the deliberate flaunting of social convention by vile people. Emile Laurent noted that there were prostitutes whose persistence in the trade could only be explained by inescapable congenital defects or, failing these, by a corrupt character.[117] The association of pederasty or sodomy with vice proved more convincing and tenacious than the circumstantial explanations. After taking out the weak-willed and oversexed, observers typically concluded that vice accounted for most pederasty. In the "great majority" of cases, Ball argued, pederasts are "in no way insane, but they are profoundly corrupt and often [they are] ordinary criminals."[118] Investigators were usually not as hard on sapphists, proposing that women's more emotional makeup and suggestibility led them astray. The same distinctions held for prostitutes. Descriptions of male prostitutes stressed their interest in blackmail and their criminal associations. The idea advanced by Lombroso that female criminality took the form of prostitution won some support, but it represented an extreme position. More commentators characterized prostitutes as amoral rather than venal, but unlike their male counterparts, they shared with all women underdeveloped moral sensibility. They could not, then, be so easily accused of vice when they lacked the capacity to make moral choices.

Assigning abnormal sexuality to organic defects, to circumstances, or to perverse character did not exhaust the question. Investigators wanted to know what caused the defects or illnesses that led to abnormal sexual behavior. Even when the situation or bad character appeared responsible, they looked deeper. The predominant explanation attributed most sexual abnormalities to heredity, and as they sought its source French and Italian experts alike suspected degeneration. Observed Penta in 1896: "all the authors, the most diverse and the most far apart" agree that sexual perversions, "at least the most serious" among them, stem from degeneration.[119] Its victims inherited anatomical or functional defects or the predisposition to develop them. Or their inherently weak constitutions left them vulnerable to the effects of overexertion, contagion, or trauma. The inborn anomalies adversely affected levels of sexual energy and the targets of desire. In explaining inversion, for example, Charcot and Magnan claimed that inverts and what Binet called fetishists exhibited signs of one of the illnesses described by Morel as degenerative.[120] Inevitably, examination revealed "on the part of the patient or his family … a nervous or psychological condition of the most serious sort."[121]

Writing a decade later, Chevalier argued that heredity, and in particular degeneration, almost always accounted for what he called true inversion. He referred to a case described by Krafft-Ebing to make the point. "[T]he father was bizarre, extravagant, a drunkard, an epileptic." As a result, his son showed aberrant sexual instincts. "Thus, just as with pyromania or kleptomania, inversion constitutes a psychic stigmata, a symptom of degeneration."[122] Chevalier believed that other doctors, whatever terminology they used, also saw inversion as "not willed, [but] congenital and undergone, innate and imposed by heredity, without change in the genital organs; for all of them, it is a symptom of an abnormal and rare psychopathic or neuropathic state, which only appears in this category of the ill that one calls *dégénérés*."[123]

Evidence from case studies reinforced inversion's connection to *dégénéréscence*. Although inversion itself rarely appeared in family medical histories, related conditions such as alcoholism, epilepsy, and erratic behavior did. The invert M. X...'s unconventional mother and grandfather and his own early proclivity for theft sealed the diagnosis of degeneration for Charcot and Magnan, for example. The fact that inverts displayed other symptoms of degeneration also confirmed that inversion belonged to the group of characteristic problems that it caused. According to Chevalier, "true" inversion always occurred along with any of a number of manias, phobias, paranoia, and, "in several cases," a yen for vagrancy.[124] By the time they reached adulthood, inverts suffered from "spasms, trembling, tics, contractions in various parts of their body, but especially their face," and they almost invariably developed neurasthenia.[125]

In the 1905 edition of his textbook on mental illness, Eugenio Tanzi specified that "true" inversion involved "definitive and irreversible" tendencies that resulted from degeneration.[126] In the "monstrous and rare" cases when women sought out other women and felt no interest in men, and when men disliked women and "gave themselves to tough guys or to semi-inverts," Tanzi saw the effects of "degenerative anomalies." The man who felt like a woman and yielded to other men "from a spontaneous impulse and with joy is often an *imbecile* or a *paranoic*," while the woman who takes a comparable role "is almost always a violent *immorale* who demonstrates her profound lack of ethics with indelicacies, frauds, and crimes."[127] Even chaste attraction to one's own sex combined with aversion for the opposite sex indicated "organic perversions."[128] A chance event or random experience caused degeneration to congeal into inversion, he argued; a different trigger and it would have taken a different form—perhaps alcoholism, epilepsy, or neurasthenia. Ribot was not so sure. He accepted the possibility that heredity explained how the mind of a woman got in the body of a man and vice versa, but he could not explain why degeneration took that form rather than another.[129]

Degeneracy also explained why some women could not escape prostitution, according to some analyses. Émile Laurent, for example, drew from his experience in the hospital at the Santé prison and at Sainte-Anne Hospital in Paris to demonstrate that some prostitutes refused to lead an honest life when offered the chance. "Is it possible," he asked, "that there are girls destined for prostitution? Couldn't the prostitute sometimes be an abnormal, a person marked by heredity, a victim of degeneration, a deranged person?" Some women, "and this is close to proven," Laurent said, "get into prostitution instinctively, fatally, like the morally insane fall into evil and vice," no matter what the situation. "Prostitution could perhaps be just a type of criminality, and certain prostitutes are undoubtedly just unfortunates suffering from *moral insanity*, madwomen, and degenerates. Such are the facts."[130] He referred to a study of 150 prostitutes conducted by the prominent Russian criminologist Pauline Tarnowsky (1848–1910) to back up his hypothesis. She reported that of that sample, 124 came from families of alcoholics. Growing up in troubled circumstances contributed to their fall, Laurent acknowledged, but more likely alcoholism in the parents passed to the daughter in the form of a propensity to prostitution.[131] The incidence of tuberculosis, nervous disorders, and mental illness in prostitutes' families and of epilepsy in their parents confirmed prostitution's link with degeneration.

Seen as a defined set of interchangeable inherited conditions, *dégénéréscence* lost authority as an explanation toward the end of the century. That approach no longer served as effectively as an analytical framework, diagnostic tool, or as an accepted shorthand for certain patterns of abnormality. Investigators continued, however, to use the term to refer to inherited defects and weaknesses, and more specifically to developmental abnormalities. Tanzi, in the second edition of his textbook, confirmed the validity of Morel's basic insight: inherited weaknesses created the terrain for many abnormalities. While scientists continued to emphasize heredity, they increasingly stressed that external circumstances activated an inborn and unhealthy predisposition to problems.[132] These deficiencies affected how degenerates developed physically and psychologically and exposed them to illnesses, making them ill-adapted to life in society.

The association of degeneration with developmental anomalies reinforced theories common in Italy, where Darwin and Herbert Spencer influenced thinking. Drawing on theories of criminality pushed by Lombroso, writers such as Penta and Venturi discovered atavism or arrested development at the root of some sexual perversions. Like Féré and Ribot, they believed that the sexual instinct developed in stages, and they argued that the more evolved the society, the sharper the sexual differentiation. Lombroso and others also emphasized that behavior evolved from promiscuous and violent to more measured and constant. More generally, they argued, and French experts agreed, that evolution increased complexity and distinctions and that these patterns affected sexuality along with everything else. It followed, then, that some aberrations involved a return to the primitive. Any anomaly that did not favor reproduction, however, characterized primitive sexuality no more than it did the modern.

In the second edition of his textbook, Tanzi, now joined by Ernesto Lugaro, updated his analysis. They emphasized that developments in biochemistry and pathology had changed how doctors viewed the body. Research revealed more about the role of the cerebral cortex in mental processes and more about the structure of the nervous system, especially at the cellular level. Moreover, blood tests gave information about the organic sources of psychological problems once available only through autopsies.[133] They also pointed to the use of psychoanalysis as a method of understanding the brain's operation, but registered their skepticism about its effectiveness. They held to the view that "bad chemistry or bad structure" produced "bad psychology" so that psychotherapy changed little.[134] The revised edition provided more details about the sexual instinct and what forms its aberrations took and omitted references to psychopathic pederasts and immoral lesbians. Tanzi and Lugaro rejected the idea that a random event in childhood produced the same-sex attachment that later turned into inversion or homosexuality, as they now labeled it. Rather, it started with early or acute sexual feelings prompted by degenerative nervous or psychological disorders, including mental retardation, organic immorality, hysteria, bipolar disorder, neurasthenia, obsessive psychoses, and paranoia.[135]

Not only inherited defects but also disease, often degenerative in nature or origin, could produce sexual abnormalities. Epilepsy affected sexual impulses, in particularly striking ways. Féré noted: "Among degenerates, epileptics are those who present ... the most numerous and the crudest defective signs."[136] Even pederasty, which Ball attributed mainly to corrupt character, could appear as a secondary effect of other conditions, including epilepsy.[137] When linked to epilepsy, it erupted suddenly in the form of an uncontrollable impulse, Chevalier contended, describing a fifteen-year-old patient he observed at Bicêtre. "[W]ell developed ... ordinarily calm, gay, intelligent, a good worker," he periodically fell into "a pederastic rage of unbelievable violence." When the "homosexual ictus" seized him, he took after the first fellow patient he saw with "indescribable fury." The unexpected bouts compelled the staff to keep him under continual surveillance to "prevent a sodomic rape or a murder."[138] In addition to epilepsy, mental deficiency or mental illness, including manias, depression, or chronic delirium, could also encourage same-sex attraction, Chevalier argued.

As with criminality and vagrancy, the likelihood of correcting abnormal sexual behaviors depended on what caused them. When they resulted directly from defects in the genital organs, the nervous system, or the brain, cures seemed unlikely. Then, as with other forms of biologically induced deviance, the experts recommended confinement, especially if the problem posed a danger to the individual and to others or risked public scandal. Pasquale Penta recommended asylums for the perverted, because they provided a "stupendous resource for cures." Rapists, however, belonged in criminal insane asylums or labor camps, he insisted.[139] In some cases, experts advocated training aimed at compensating for the defects. For example, some doctors urged inverts to focus their thoughts on the opposite sex or find a willing partner to help activate their more normal carnal desires. Others doubted the efficacy of such initiatives. Experimenting with various regimens to relieve the symptoms of inversion or fetishism, Charcot and Magnan reported some success with potassium bromide, cold baths, and zinc lactate in the case of M. X.... In addition to those treatments, X ... pushed himself to daydream about women, and eventually he began to feel physically attracted to them. Lombroso reported using potassium bromide, belladonna, and camphor to combat an epidemic of "tribadismo" (lesbianism) in the asylum at Pavia. Seeing no improvement, he resorted to cauterizing offenders' clitorises, but the positive effects proved temporary.[140] That left, he concluded, the more radical option of expelling them. The nature of his response indicates deep concerns about controlling female sexuality and about the possible contagion of practices considered abnormal.

In addition to cures, doctors thought about strategies for prevention. Authorities such as La Cara worried that sexual "infirmities" might spread, pointing out that they usually involved two people. For the same reason that they took measures to contain the spread of infectious diseases, La Cara insisted that governments needed to control sexual perversions. The idea that people had hidden abnormalities waiting to be activated also put a premium on prevention. La Cara urged special training to alert the healthy and to help those prone to deviate find other outlets for their sexual energies. To keep the young on track, he and others recommended parental education and close supervision.[141] In addition to the contagion of example and concern about latent abnormalities, the role of heredity encouraged preventive strategies. Commentators routinely reminded readers of the importance of choosing healthy partners. Reminding his fellow doctors to think about the species, Féré urged them to encourage their patients to practice continence and to avoid having children.[142]

Those who believed that modern society contributed to sexual perversion urged reform as a solution. Lombroso followed early sexologist Iwan Bloch (1872–1922) in calling for the legalization of divorce and for facilitating separation. Providing a way out of unhappy marriages promised to limit pederasty and sexual violence as well as to reduce the number of crimes of passion. La Cara called for greater social equality, and in particular for putting the idle rich to work to discourage them from seeking perverted pleasures. Individuals could also insulate themselves against the ravages of society by avoiding stress, masturbation, reading novels (women), marrying into families with evident neuroses, and situations of enforced celibacy.

Implications

Often cited by his contemporaries, Féré's treatise apparently struck responsive chords at the end of the century. In the opening pages, Féré specified that perversions of sexual desire occurred only as a result of hereditary predisposition or pathological conditions. Healthy people with solid bloodlines need not worry, then, about deviating from sexual norms. They might read about or witness perversion without falling under its spell, unless, of course, a latent deficiency or flaw pushed them toward promiscuity or other aberrant habits. Fortunately for moderns, the evolution of the sexual impulse banished or subdued that constant companion of sinners: temptation. Normal members of advanced societies could, he argued, depend on their bodies to enforce the sexual restraint that defined civilization. Féré presented with unusual and unself-conscious clarity a defense of dominant values. He made reproduction an instinct and monogamy part of the biological equipment of evolved human beings. By his scheme, women displayed more developed sexual feelings, because they cherished their children and because they proved more continent than men.

At the same time, Féré recognized the fragility of the body's most recent acquisitions. Because the latest and the most complex developments were the most vulnerable, attachment to spouse and family foundered first, reducing sex to the act itself. In this context, rape resulted from the dissolution of the evolved sexual instinct rather than from a throwback to the primitive.[143] When reversion of sexual feelings did occur, it disturbed individuals' lives and tore at the fabric of civilized society, he warned. In particular, it undermined what people accepted as the "condition of civilization": female modesty and restraint.[144] When the erosion affected the instinct to reproduce, the distinctions between the sexes diminished, and more men seemed effeminate and more women remained virgins. The seriousness of the threats to civilization required concerted efforts to reinforce the impulse to reproduce, and Féré urged people to assume personal responsibility and combat degeneration and illness. Properly mobilized, he argued, the willpower and self-discipline permitted by evolution supported the effort.[145]

What investigators discovered about abnormal sexual practices exposed their affinities with criminality and vagabondage. Investigating similar populations, those in asylums, clinics, prisons, hospitals, and doctors' private practices, they found little evidence for vice and strong evidence for the destabilizing effects of organic defects and disorders. Attributing sexual perversions to degeneration put subjects in the company of—among others—born criminals, inveterate vagrants, neurotics, alcoholics, and epileptics. All of them shared deficiencies which affected anatomy, physiology, and the psyche in some measure and combination. Prostitutes served as an example. In Laurent's view, they bore the physical and physiological signs typical of degenerates. They were lazy and naive, weak-willed and lacking in moral sense, with "minds that were distracted and vagabonding here and there"[146]—that profile explained why Lombroso argued that prostitution expressed born criminality in women, and Florian and Cavaglieri equated female vagrancy with prostitution.

Exposing the biological roots of deviance provided a measure of reassurance for ordinary people. In the absence of tainted relatives and with good health, most joined the ranks of the normal, and so did their children. But if they did find themselves drawn to crime, vagrancy, or unconventional sexual practices, they could usually blame their unfortunate heredity. According to the latest science, people had achieved the highest evolutionary state when their feelings matched their physiques and when they remained faithful to their spouses and attended to their children. Sound health rather than divine grace and individual effort enabled their virtue; their bodies allowed them to care about and to enact the good. But if they paid attention to the experts, people understood their vulnerability to unexpected damage and ruin. Illness, accident, or trauma could undermine their strength and activate deeply buried anomalies. Unemployment and poverty also triggered hidden propensities and pushed well-meaning citizens to crime, vagabondage, and prostitution. More, latent weaknesses responded to random events. For example, a childhood fancy could determine later patterns of affection. Binet explained: "An external circumstance, an accidental event, undoubtedly forgotten, caused the patient to pursue people of his own sex; another circumstance, another event would have changed the direction of his obsession, and such a man, who today only loves men, could in a different context have loved only night caps or the nails of a woman's boot."[147]

Hedged around with such cautions, staying to the straight and narrow must have been daunting, were it not that studies of abnormalities made normalcy so unusual. First, behavior fit a continuum where degree, intention, and conventions of the moment distinguished between what passed and what did not. The ends looked different, the middle area less so. Some level of fetishism usually accompanied love, Ball emphasized, and it was common knowledge that infatuations had an obsessive quality. Everyone, according to one theory of sexual differentiation, expressed some characteristics of the other sex, making a degree of inversion natural. In normal sexual relations, science confirmed, men naturally assumed the active and women the passive role. Accepting a measure of aggression as normal for males influenced the outcome of sexual violence cases in their favor in Italy, according to Bruno Wanrooij in *La storia del pudore* (The History of Modesty).[148] Moreover, it appeared that declining morals, the thirst for sensation, and the effect of overwork affected sexuality. If aberrant sex came with modern life, it looked less exceptional and more routine.

The exploration of sexual habits suggests the ambiguous position of science as it turned its attention to a realm monopolized by arbiters of morality and keepers of the law. Scientists exposed what appeared to be a mysterious, sidelined world to the rigors of empirical study, illuminating well-known yet unmentionable practices and establishing limits of normality for familiar attributes of love. As they broadened the scope of their examining lens and as they simultaneously refined its focus, observers gained new perspectives which they transmitted to the public in books and articles, popular manuals, fiction, and trial testimony. As they collected and processed the evidence, they applied to sexual practice the same framework of understanding that they used for other types of abnormality. They considered the effects of biology, society, and character and found disruptions of the sexual instinct a convincing source for most perversions. The roots of these aberrations generated debate, with some emphasizing the congenital, others the acquired bases of abnormalities, some anatomical defects, others mental disorders. Which causes prevailed depended a great deal on the type of aberration, with same-sex love generating the greatest controversy. More than they did with satyriasis, nymphomania, or fetishism, in homosexuality they recognized choice as a factor, with rotten character or the constraints of circumstances more often the drivers than love.

Singular Analogies

The dégéneré *from the physical point of view is the same as from the mental point of view, as we'll see; he is an imbalanced, irregular, asymmetrical person.*

Valentin Magnan and Paul-Maurice Legrain[1]

Beginning in the interwar years and gaining momentum in the 1960s, historians turned more attention to the lives of ordinary people, including those seen by contemporaries as operating outside conventional social boundaries. Historians used the torrent of studies of criminals, vagabonds, and other outliers produced by nineteenth-century medical and social scientists, and they took advantage of little-explored sources, including government records and statistics. These materials allowed them to explore class and gender as well as the broader phenomenon of social separation. Seeking terms applicable to different periods and contexts, they came up with a varying and contested lexicon to describe the social "other." Three of the labels appear particularly relevant to the fin de siècle: "deviant," "marginal," and "excluded."

In the 1930s, a group of American sociologists gave "deviance" a distinct meaning. The Chicago School associated the term not with particular actions or actors but with mainstream society's reactions to different behaviors. When transgressions against norms shocked decision makers and even ordinary citizens, they qualified as deviant. According to these sociologists, actions recognized as deviant depended on what people, especially the rule makers, condemned. Because what one group found objectionable others did not, definitions of deviance varied considerably. However, some actions provoked widespread hostility, and these brought demands for control through laws, the courts, or special measures. Building on these theories, Symbolic Interactionists subsequently argued that deviant groups developed their own identities and rules and that their solidarity in turn affected how the public reacted to them.

Influenced by American sociologists' work on deviance, the idea of marginality took shape in the 1960s.[2] After 1968, the current became a trend, and French historians and the press began to use the term "marginals," according to medievalist Jean-Claude Schmitt. It referred to individuals and groups which, seen from an insider's perspective, challenged social values. Some marginals, such as hippies and beatniks, put themselves on the margins; others got put there by established society.[3] Either way, they occupied the liminal space between insiders and outsiders, poised to move back into or further away from society. The "conscious and contestatory" marginals largely controlled their status, while the others depended on society or on their own efforts to change it. Although historians adopted the idea of marginality, they disagreed about which groups belonged in the boundary zone and about how societies drew them back in or pushed them further away.

Looking beyond the transitional zone to that occupied by the excluded also engaged historians. A conference on exclusion organized in Paris in 1998 concluded with a roundtable exchange on the meaning and utility of the term. Initially a narrow and workable concept, exclusion had become more expansive and amorphous, asserted Robert Castel.[4] Among the identifying criteria offered by participants, some won general consensus. Unlike marginality, exclusion happened to people; they rarely sought it. And in contrast to marginals, the excluded stayed on the outside, because society resisted efforts to reintegrate them. The relevance of the category in modern French history also stirred discussion. "I am very critical of the use of the concept of the excluded," historian Madeleine Rebérioux flatly stated.[5] Others cautioned against using a term for outsiders that contemporaries did not use. To avoid anachronism and inaccuracy, they urged historians to adopt labels current at the time.[6]

The three concepts—deviance, marginality, and exclusion—describe a space somewhere outside power structures, social norms, and cultural dictums. Deviance and exclusion identify robust barriers which separate outsiders from insiders. What, if anything, distinguishes deviants from the excluded continues to interest historians. Depending on how they apply the terms, these two types overlap entirely, partially, or not at all. Marginality, in contrast, imagines a boundary area porous enough to let some groups cross the line in both directions. "In society as in books," comments Schmitt, "the margin is empty and the unexpected figure of the marginal who arrives there is most of the time fugitive, ready to melt in or to fall to the wayside, because the marginal defies the preestablished categories that social 'logic' established."[7] Although historians generally accept a topography of dissonance, they continue to discuss how to define the different areas and assign their occupants.

Used singly, none of the concepts fits the situation in turn-of-the-century France and Italy. Applied collectively, they come closer. However, employing any of these terms follows the common practice of applying categories and language meaningful in the present in order to clarify patterns in the past. Their effectiveness depends on how closely they represent the thinking and policies evident at the time. Understood as a label assigned by the elites or the public to acts they deplore, "deviance" arguably applies to two broad types of misfits: degenerates and deliberate iconoclasts. Those born to crime or to vagrancy aroused fear because of what the experts described as their intractable antisocial instincts. Lawmakers in both countries responded by curtailing their liberties, putting them under surveillance, and in cases considered particularly dangerous confining them to isolated areas, prisons, or asylums. Taking fear and loathing as the distancing mechanism, not all degenerates would qualify as deviants, however. For example, people with degenerative disorders such as tuberculosis, rickets, and pellagra did not provoke the same level of distaste. At the same time, Morel's alarmist predictions made all degenerates the carriers of still more loathsome conditions, and that stigma set them apart.

The willfully perverse also provoked the negative reaction that scholars connect to the phenomenon of deviance. Experts such as Lombroso and Pagnier excoriated those who deliberately flaunted social norms. Not compelled by biology or circumstances, they chose to defy convention, and they deserved uncompromising punishment. Of all the antisocial behaviors, investigators most often put pederasty in this category. Seen as a vice rather than a condition, they associated the practice (sodomy) with corrupt predators and scheming opportunists. More than for their actions, the willfully perverse provoked anger because they chose to defy norms. The label "deviant" fits them because of the intensity of the reaction they provoked. But the idea that marginals can decide to cast themselves out of society makes "marginality" an appropriate term for intentional misfits as well.

Understood as a classification imposed by insiders on those who do not conform to social expectations, exclusion applies broadly. Unlike deviance, it includes those who did not contribute to society but who inspired empathy rather than hostility. Contemporaries singled out indigent children and people too old, sick, or mentally incompetent to work or care for themselves as a category apart, one deserving support, including possible confinement in hospitals or poor houses. Exclusion also applies to those who inspired a more ambiguous response. For example, because able bodied people without jobs or a conventional family life looked like malingerers and vagabonds, they provoked discomfort and diffidence. The victims often saw themselves this way as well. Knowing what society expected, neurasthenics and inverts also experienced a sense of estrangement and isolation, according to the literature. Extended to describe the poor or those who lacked the means for self-fulfillment, exclusion includes even larger portions of the population, so large it loses meaning as a category of analysis.[8]

Because "marginality" includes people temporarily outside society, the term fits a subset of those viewed as outsiders at the time. It includes people put outside norms by illness or trauma but considered curable. With successful therapies, they would regain their place as ordinary, functioning adults. If marginals could return to society, they could also move definitively away from it. When therapies proved useless, victims became outsiders. For occasional criminals and vagrants, the concept of marginality conforms less easily to contemporary views. Seen as likely to return to normal when the situation permitted, they looked more like ordinary people than marginals. However, when experts described occasional offenders as harboring inborn tendencies activated by circumstances, they saw their potential for moving away from society or turning back to it. By this reading, these offenders fit the category of marginals. Finally, when experts warned that making occasional deviance a habit caused irreversible biological changes, they put them in the zone of no return.

Marginality, exclusion, and deviance illuminate subcategories but used singly or in combination they do not capture the complexities of contemporary thinking about counter-social behavior. Experts at the time broke the problem down in different ways and used other terminology to name its elements. They concentrated on creating typologies and categorizing causes and then on defending and refining these systems of classification. Judging from the importance they assigned to the taxonomies of difference, they made ordering the tumult of types a priority. Naming also mattered in pinning down the distinctions they saw as important, and the dynamic and far-reaching efforts to achieve consensus on variants and labels dominated scholarly exchange.

They attacked a moving target, since the more cases they reported, the more nuances they identified. The appearance of new professional specialties added to the permutations and combinations. No wonder, then, that modern terminology does not correspond exactly to the thinking at the time. Categories developed in the later twentieth century match some of the boxes earlier experts created, and used together they cover more of the grid. Of the three terms, the diffuse meanings of "exclusion" make it the most expansive and flexible rubric. However, Christian Topalov suggests a fundamental inconsistency in applying the concept of exclusion to contemporary understandings of difference. Rather than leave anyone unclassified, he points out, physicians and social theorists extended the categories to create space for new variants. Their effort indicates, he observes, that they thought in terms of inclusion rather than exclusion.[9]

The experts laid out a broad, encompassing grid, and they agreed on what determined the divisions within it. Evolution provided one important guide, and it explained why they expanded their scope beyond individuals and groups to include the human species. Because they applied the process of change evident in nature to society, history also influenced their systems of classification. The two converged, investigators believed, because biological change enabled humans to create more complicated societies and to gain greater control over nature. Accepting this pattern encouraged observers to situate groups and societies in a progressive sequence of biological and social changes. Primitive people occupied one end of the line, civilized men the other, with women trailing along behind males in each phase. The continuum also applied to individuals, as they grew from embryo to adult. Depending on their evolutionary stage, they followed a short and simple or a long and complicated developmental path. Unless defects or damage derailed the process, people at any stage moved naturally toward achieving their full biological and social potential. If they stopped short, jumped ahead, or slipped backwards, or if they took a wrong turn, they ended up in, for them, an unnatural place on the evolutionary and historical scales.

Investigators often described these exceptions as "anomalies" and "abnormalities," terms whose logic the classification system helps to explain.[10] Among the terms that encompass abnormality, "misfits" serves as a reasonable synonym. It suggests that people saw society as a structure into which people more or less easily fit. That is, they filled a place on the species grid, but not the expected one. Misfit also depends on the idea of the fit, just as abnormal presumes the normal. If fit allowed the notion of misfit, the equation worked the other way as well, as thinkers argued that abnormal clarified normal and what did not fit showed what did. The term "misfit" also incorporates different states and multiple variants without becoming shapeless. It accepts dualities common in thinking about difference: incurable and curable, involuntary and voluntary, shocking and benign. It also evokes the labels "maladjusted" and "ill-adapted," other terms regularly used by contemporaries to describe the other. Finally it accommodates the emphasis on defect and deficiency central to descriptions of biologically based abnormalities.

Broader than terms such as "deviant," "excluded," or "marginal" and narrower and more accurate than "outsider" or "outlier," "misfit" describes how specialists and the public saw the dissonance around them. But experts also adopted a more specialized vocabulary to mark narrower categories of behaviors and pathologies. In some cases, they gave different meaning to accepted labels, such as "epilepsy," and in others they adopted new labels—the "American disease," "moral insanity," and "sexual inversion," for example. Qualifying adjectives also permitted them to distinguish among variants and intensities. They referred to motor, sensory, and psychic epilepsy and used real (or true), occasional, partial, and complete to make critical etiological distinctions. Hybrid words such as "hystero-epilepsy" registered connections, just as they revealed uncertainties about diagnoses. New names such as fetishism caught on and lasted, while others made sense for a time, and then got sidelined as classifications shifted. Especially when the terms they favored fell out of use or took on other meanings, it is tempting to provide modern equivalents. While the practice helps clarify their theories for modern readers, something can go missing in the translation. For example, depression and posttraumatic stress disorder now stand in for neurasthenia, but they only approximate what contemporaries understood by the term.

Analogies and distinctions

Most studies of deviance single out a type of social dissonance, an emerging field of study, or prominent theorists, usually in one country. For example, they look at crime, criminology, or Lombroso, or at neuroses, neurology, or Charcot. Individually the analyses suggest and considered collectively they demonstrate a significant confluence of perceptions about deviance. Studies of particular thinkers show the breadth of their competencies and interests. Physician and criminal anthropologist Lombroso, for example, claimed an extensive territory for inquiry, one including crime, genius, madness, pellagra, and race. Charles Féré ranged almost as widely. Works focusing on new fields of study indicate the fluidity of their boundaries. Jan Goldstein's study of French psychiatry describes its proximity to psychology and the still more recent invention, neurology. Other nascent disciplines operated in an equally dynamic context. Finally, analyses of one type of deviance refer to theories and thinkers featured in studies of different kinds of aberrant behavior. Degeneration, to take an obvious example, appears in monographs on criminality, genius, mental illness, and neuroses.

Another approach, the one favored here, is to look at how experts in different fields in two countries understood several types of contemporary misfits. It highlights what the recent literature indicates when read with the search for connections in mind: experts on deviance thought a lot alike. Fin-de-siècle investigators recognized affinities among misfits, beginning with their exceptional and, geniuses aside, alarming behaviors. That's hardly surprising, considering the importance they assigned to separating the abnormal from the normal. More striking, whatever form of deviance they examined, they traced the source to biology and to society. Born or made, the distinction applied with some telling yes-buts to any misfit. When they got down to the roots of the problem, their theories reveal still deeper complicities. They came to conflate different types of misfits into one prototype with several distinct but recognizable guises. Thus, whether criminal anthropologist or neurologist, Italian or French, expert on vagrancy or abulia, they employed similar methods and proceeded from common assumptions. As they worked on one type of difference, they recognized and built on its fundamental similarities with other types, particularly in the area of biologically induced abnormalities.

Investigators theorized that organic anomalies accounted for very disparate conditions. On the most general level, they potentially affected anyone seen as incapable of operating normally in advanced society. That collection included born criminals and vagrants, as well as inverts, and for many experts, geniuses. People who suffered from nervous and mental disorders caused by innate or acquired defects also fell in the category. The list broadened, in the view of some investigators, to include people with conditions such as tuberculosis, rickets, binge drinking, and pellagra. As they pressed their analyses, they discovered that the offending anomalies had a similar effect. They prevented full adaptation to the milieu. Whether the misfits went beyond, as happened with geniuses, or fell short, as the others did, the defects made them abnormals, understanding normality as adjustment to the group's current stage of biological and social development. In modern societies, normal meant leaving behind the nomadic, lawless, indolent, and volatile lives believed to characterize primitive people or children and displaying the self-control and compliance to social norms achieved by fully developed adults. Those biologically incapable of meeting these standards fell outside the civilized space enabled by nature and laid out by society.

Not only did the anomalies obstruct adaptation, they discovered, they did it in the same way. Whether they focused on born criminals or geniuses, they conjectured that the organic flaws produced imbalance. Normal bodies hoved to the middle, possessing neither deficit nor surplus, each element appropriately calibrated. With everything in proper proportion, each piece performed its function, enabling the body to operate efficiently. But when lacunae or excesses produced ruptures or surges, the elements fell out of sync. Like the rest of the body, the mind operated best with every faculty present and in its place. In studies of insanity, nervous conditions, confused sexual identity, uncontrollable immoral impulses, and wanderlust, experts concluded that pieces of the brain and nervous system had fallen out of alignment and no longer interacted normally. Whatever the reasons, the internal imbalance left telltale marks, a number of physicians and anthropologists contended. Asymmetrical facial features, overly long or short limbs, and bulges in the skull indicated disorders, while harmonious proportions registered internal equilibrium.

People did not fit in, therefore, because imbalances impeded their adjustment to society. Whether they examined vagrants or neurasthenics, as criminologist or neurologist, they found that they could narrow what made a misfit even further. The key imbalances, they observed, affected the capacities distinctive to fully developed civilized adults—intellect, willpower, and moral sensibility. The will proved especially important to mental health and social adjustment. As Leonardo Bianchi explained in his handbook on psychiatry, the will controlled everything from individual instincts to the higher social self.[11] It coordinated the body's responses to an intensifying barrage of stimuli, and its effectiveness depended on the instincts, emotions, and intellect operating in concert. When the will developed poorly, got damaged or weakened, as typically occurred with misfits, internal restraints faltered, and the resulting imbalances disrupted behavior. Experts detected wavering willpower in vagabonds and criminals, and diseased will in victims of abulia, epilepsy, and neurasthenia. In contrast, towering will even more than superior intellect defined genius according to commentators such as Nordau.

When scientists explained how the anomalies responsible for the imbalances occurred, they agreed that heredity played a role. Analyses of genius as well as idiocy saw evidence of congenital anatomical irregularities in the brain. But their research also indicated that old age and illness damaged mental capacity and produced imbecility or dementia. Psychiatrists and neurologists reached similar conclusions about psychoses and neuroses. Inherited anomalies disrupted the operation of the nervous system and brain or, more typically, produced incipient weaknesses. Similar conclusions held for nervous diseases such as epilepsy, hysteria, and neurasthenia. More often than not, specialists asserted, compromised heredity caused the nervous system to operate at too high or too low a pitch, although stress, accidents, and other illnesses could produce similar effects.

Discoveries about antisocial behaviors fit the same template. When they addressed the conundrum of lucid criminals, experts concluded that the mechanism of moral sensibility lost its potency or did not develop fully. They applied similar reasoning to habitual vagabonds. In a society that equated work with worth, home with comfort, and both with civilization, a life of wandering in penury seemed incomprehensible. The rare person might choose that lifestyle, observers contended, but most inveterate tramps could not concentrate enough to work or could not control an impulse to wander. Capricious, impetuous, and easily distracted, they acted like children, leading scientists to speculate that, in fact, inherited or acquired defects kept them at that stage. In the same vein, observers from Charcot to Lombroso traced odd sexual behaviors to inborn or acquired flaws. Atypical fixations or levels of desire appeared to result from organic problems, likely disruptions in the process of sexual differentiation and attraction. Despite some reservations, investigators extended that diagnosis to same-sex eroticism. Inversion, like moral insanity and habitual vagrancy, indicated faulty maturation. Because they did not complete the process of sexual differentiation, inverts hovered between female and male, creating an intermediate or third sex. Most commentators did not, however, attribute pederasty (sodomy) to biology but to the lifestyle choice of misguided individuals. There, as they did for other social misfits, they left room for perversity. The play of theories across specialties and types of misfits also weighed heavily on assessments of prostitution. While most investigators saw it as a matter of survival for women caught in extreme circumstances, many argued that these emergency prostitutes harbored a proclivity for it. Observers such as Emile Laurent took a more extreme position, arguing that an inborn error made promiscuity irresistible to some women.[12]

A common refrain echoes through analyses of diverse sorts of misfits. In a subset among them biology was to blame, because organic anomalies impeded their full adaptation to society. These defects disrupted the usual balance by damaging a piece of the body's structure or disturbing one of its functions. In misfits, the anomaly most often affected their will, moral sensibility, or intellect. Looking beyond the similar pattern to its possible roots, they discovered that the defects grew from the same ground, and because they did, they produced a set of interchangeable disorders. Pasquale Penta, for example, argued that "a great affinity, a real connection exists among nervous disorders, diathesis, and insanity, in the sense that they can come together and substitute for each other in the same person and in the offspring of the same person and in successive generations."[13] Generally, scientists concurred in labeling these unhealthy changes as degenerative. How they defined *dégénérescence* varied a great deal, a fact that they readily admitted.[14] Although many physicians and social thinkers acknowledged Morel's influence, his theory looked very different by the end of the century.[15] Especially early on, scientists tried to narrow the symptoms, but the set became progressively broader.[16] Charles Féré, for example, extended degeneration to include any failure to adapt successfully to the environment.[17] The category got so large, Georges Genil-Perrin (1882–1964) commented, that it "looked like it was going to die of plethora."[18]

Degeneration, then, became a convenient rubric for explaining numerous abnormalities. By disrupting adaptation or maturation, degeneration left people poorly adjusted or deficient. It made them, Agostini contended, "inferior beings" unable to live normally in society.[19] The "ordinary types of degenerate," included, he specified, "the criminal, the insane, the suicide, the prostitute, the sexually aberrant, the social parasite."[20] Degenerates, Charles Féré explained, passed any of the set of related disorders to their children in no apparent order. The list of degeneration's "neuropathic family" grew as investigators studied its effects. In the nervous branch of the degenerative clan, Albert Mathieu included neurasthenia, hysteria, epilepsy, migraines, chorea, neurosyphilis, and general paralysis. The insane, criminals, suicides, geniuses, and imbeciles occupied the mental branch, and those who suffered from gout, diabetes, and rheumatism belonged to the arthritic group of degenerative disorders, he added.[21] Other scientists varied the list of disorders to some extent, but they usually included an equally broad range of abnormalities. Of this collection of interchangeable organic problems, experts tended to focus on criminality, vagrancy, sexual perversions, neuroses, and psychoses. They understood, however, that evidence of gout or rickets or tuberculosis in a family increased the chances that what they saw as the more serious anomalies would appear.

When neurologists, psychiatrists, and social theorists looked for signs of degeneration, they singled out epilepsy with remarkable frequency. It was, according to many experts, the quintessential degenerative disorder, one tightly linked to other degenerative conditions.[22] They found it in bad crimes, fugue, imbecility, some mental illnesses, and genius. Except for the seizures, epileptics closely resembled born criminals, Bianchi pointed out. They adjusted poorly to the milieu, and they gave in to their instincts and to "cruelty, idleness, vagabondage, organized crime, sexual precocity and excesses, irascibility and impulsiveness."[23] Epilepsy also shared characteristics with moral insanity, a connection Lombroso emphasized. By no means everyone agreed on its ubiquity, particularly when it came to explaining genius, but they nonetheless considered its role and rarely completely excluded its influence.

The concept of the born misfit constituted a dominant motif in the literature. As it gained clarity and force, it provoked a counter-punctual theme. Convinced as they were of the effects of organic anomalies, investigators saw that not every misfit followed a twisted biological blueprint. When it came to antisocial actions—crime and vagrancy, in particular—criminologists, sociologists, and doctors uniformly identified "occasional" or "accidental" offenders. They drew uncertain lines, and they debated which misfits fell where, but they saw a divide and defended it with increasing insistence. Hard times, not inner anomalies, generated a class of involuntary vagabonds and idlers, studies of vagrancy asserted. Criminologists also identified most criminals as "occasional"; they defied the law in order to live. They specified that poverty pushed children to petty crime, women into prostitution, and exasperated men into theft or worse. Unless they succumbed to the appeals of crime and made it a habit, they turned "honest" again when their situations improved. Experts and the public also recognized the power of emotions; they knew that some people, in some situations succumbed to passion, or they held their ideals so strongly that commitment to them overpowered their respect for the law. They stood out, because they usually recovered their reason, realized the implications of their actions, and experienced regret. It also happened that passion overpowered reason and then the law codes and public opinion dissolved them of legal responsibility.

Experts also applied the distinction between innate and accidental to same-sex relations. They recognized that in conditions of enforced celibacy, some men and women resorted to encounters with their own sex. Once the situation changed, these pseudo-homosexuals returned to conventional practices. When pederasty occurred outside such constrained conditions, opportunism also appeared to play a role. Observers typically concluded that pederasts fell into two categories: those in it for money or adventure and those who embraced it as a lifestyle. Circumstances explained the first group's choices, perverted values the second group's actions. Understood this way, pederasty illuminated the distinctive features of inversion. Pederasty involved practice, whereas inversion affected identity. Unlike pederasts, scientists concluded, inverts responded to their dissonant organic makeup, and even if they suppressed or reoriented their desires, they could not erase the nature of their sexuality.

When they described mental misfits, the experts also differentiated between temporary and lasting and between occasional and inveterate variants. Psychiatrists recognized that physical illness, emotional shock, or some unfortunate combination of circumstances could provoke insanity. It subsided by itself or it responded to treatment, and the victim returned to normal. Experts on genius believed that external factors also explained the difference between talent and genius. Hard work and determination could produce the first, but not the second. Neurasthenics also fell into two groups, according to physicians. In the first, the nervous system was weak from the beginning or damaged by other illnesses, overexertion, or serious trauma. In the second, outside factors temporarily affected the nerves, and the condition went away with some combination of time, rest, and changes in lifestyle.[24] Studies of insanity made less categoric distinctions. They recognized that inborn defects and inherited weaknesses of the brain left some people vulnerable to mental disarray. Moral insanity, for example, resulted from inherited, congenital, or acquired flaws. More often, however, they attributed mental disorders to environmental factors such as illness, shock, and stress.

While medical and social scientists emphasized that society made some of the misfits and nature others, they also identified links between the two groups. Casual observation showed that a minority turned to prostitution and theft in adversity. Similarly, work on neurasthenia showed that overexertion and trauma left most people unscathed. They concluded that those who did develop neurasthenia must harbor an undetected weakness activated by shock and stress. The same explanation appeared in studies of crime. To opt for theft when in dire straits suggested some internal proclivity for crime. Whether they responded to a hidden drive or not, experts warned that repeatedly engaging in theft, vagrancy, or homosexuality produced unhealthy changes in the body, and these transmitted to the next generation as innate defects.

The empirical eye saw through their apparent differences and fit mental and social misfits into one large category: not normal. Their actions set them apart from those whose organic makeup and situations allowed them to live ordinary lives. The normal on one side and the abnormal on the other, who belonged where mattered to the public and politicians, and because it did, specialists in the volatile mix of new fields helped with the sorting. Assigning cases and even types to categories depended on an accepted definition of abnormality. Two logical possibilities emerged. Abnormality could be more or less than normal, a perspective which meant that at some point quantitative differences added up to abnormality. Or, abnormality constituted a departure, something distinctly different from normality, so that the two occupied different planes on a scale or rows on a grid. According to French physician and philosopher Georges Canguilhem, the first model prevailed among mid-nineteenth-century French scientists, such as Claude Bernard. They accepted as "a kind of scientifically guaranteed dogma" that while they appeared to differ, the normal and the pathological were basically the same.[25]

A good deal of evidence indicates that the view persisted through the end of the century. Scientists and social theorists associated normality with a predetermined step-by-step process of development and anomalies with falling short of or exceeding the usual end point. Understood as not achieving the goal or as slipping backward, abnormality meant being less than normal. It did not mean being nonhuman, since what counted as aberrant at one stage passed as natural at another. According to this idea, healthy individuals encountered the other as part of themselves. As they grew from infant to adult, they did not transcend or dissolve the primitive. It remained within, since maturation proceeded by accretion, depositing one layer over another. Ribot's sequence of reflex, feelings, and intellect spelled out the process. From instincts, to emotions, and then to ideas and from reflex, to impulse, and finally to deliberation, one element added to another, making the fully evolved adult both more capable and more complex.[26] Time and experience entrenched the earliest acquisitions, so that reflex and feelings dominated normal activity much more than people thought. As a result, not only did ordinary adults pass through a primitive stage, its characteristics continued to direct routine actions.

This understanding of the modern self led scientists to admit the mix of abnormalities in healthy people. In his study of the physiology of the will, Jules Dallemagne affirmed that balance defined normality and imbalance characterized abnormality.[27] But since nobody operated in perfect balance, the will never operated undisturbed by anomalies. For that reason, he put abnormality and normality on a continuum and saw individuals as slipping and sliding along it according to the effects of pressures from inside and outside the body.[28] "Our existence," he observed, "is most often nothing more than a succession of passing into and out of the realms of normality and abnormality."[29] Ribot offered an equivalent verdict on abnormality's normality. Everyone, he argued, contended with the chaos of their beings and with the delicacy of the mechanisms, mainly the will, that managed them. Congenital defects left some people with no self-restraint; in others, such as hysterics, disease suppressed it.[30] Most people, though, felt divided between at least two selves, each going its own way, and only some of them managed to impose direction sporadically by deliberately exerting their will. For Ribot, as for Dallemagne, no one escaped disequilibrium, and when they did achieve some balance, it did not go deep or last for very long. It could not when good health depended on constantly synchronizing the contributions of every stage of development.

Responses

Investigators routinely added recommendations for action to their analyses. As with their diagnoses of the problem, despite differences over specifics, they delivered a similar message. When society made misfits, they urged reforms; when born, not made, they cataloged the risks and called for defensive action. Judging from the earnestness with which they pushed their agendas, they expected to influence policy, and to some extent they did. The authority enjoyed by science at the time worked in their favor, as did Positivism's influence on standards of truth. Pointing to the rigor of their methods, medical and social scientists promoted their credibility as specialists. However convincing their claims, if they wanted to make a difference they needed an audience, especially one in decision-making positions. Very few investigators influenced policy directly as deputies or high-level administrators, but they had colleagues in their fields who served in local government, parliament, and the administration.[31] Lawyers, for example, formed an increasingly large contingent in the Italian Chamber of Deputies after Unification. They accounted for between 36.61 percent (in the 8th legislature) and 57.55 percent (in the 24th legislature) of the deputies.[32] Jurists also outnumbered other professionals in the French parliament. In the 1881–1885 legislature, deputies holding law degrees held almost 41 percent of the seats and in the 1906–1910 Chamber, a little over 37 percent, Jack Ellis reports in his study of physician-legislators in the early Third Republic.[33] Doctors represented the second largest contingent of liberal professionals. A total of 358 doctors served in both the French Chamber and the Senate from 1870 to the Great War, and thirteen held cabinet posts, Ellis reports.[34] Italian doctors played a smaller role, with an average of twenty-six deputies in legislatures from 1861 until the Giolittian period when their numbers increased.[35] Although most doctors in Italy sat with the center left, more of them aligned with left-wing liberals or the Socialist Party than other professionals did.[36]

Their personal connections and publications broadened the influence of doctors and social thinkers. Politicians, prominent physicians, and professors moved in the same social circles, especially in Paris, and these informal connections likely promoted an exchange of ideas. Professors such as Charcot, Lacassagne, and Lombroso also built networks of students who populated universities and held administrative posts. Mary Gibson offers an example in her study of Lombroso, identifying the advocates of criminal anthropology who applied Lombroso's ideas as professionals in the courts, police departments, and prisons.[37] The experts' impact on policymakers also owed something to their role as public intellectuals. Because they addressed issues of public concern, their work appealed to a wider audience than more recondite studies did. In some cases, they publicized their theories in accessible treatises, or they contributed to reviews such as the *Nuova antologia* and the *Revue philosophique de France et de l'étranger* that cultivated an educated readership. In their role as expert witnesses, the forensic doctors got plenty of attention from journalists and a crime-obsessed public. Their theories also cropped up in the abundant popular literature about crime.[38]

The policies they urged for treating misfits and for reducing their numbers reflected their theories of the main causes of dissonance: biological abnormalities, social conditions, and perverse character. The experts who focused on willful misfits believed that the justice system covered those who deliberately violated laws, provided that judges and juries actually held them accountable. In these cases, strategies for dealing with individuals and with the general problem of consciously antisocial behavior coincided. How to deal with born and accidental misfits provoked more thought and debate. Occasional thieves and vagrants ran afoul of the law and the police and courts took charge. If they acted discretely, opportunistic pederasts violated no laws, although the Paris police apparently kept them under tight surveillance.[39] When doctors diagnosed a bout of neurasthenia or mental disturbance, they recommended bromides, tonics, hydrotherapy, and rest, with some hope for success. When the same disorders stemmed from inherited or acquired defects and damage, doctors typically applied similar treatments, hoping to alleviate the symptoms. Some experimented with behavior modification in the cases of inverts, born criminals, and vagabonds. Encouraging inverts to awaken their normal urges by practicing with the opposite sex or using hard work to instill impulse control in criminals and vagabonds illustrate this strategy. Increasingly, however, they recognized that these conditions resisted treatment and pronounced them incurable. Agostini, for example, explained the unlikelihood of stopping or avoiding mental illness when a "congenitally compromised constitution" accompanied the "serious physical and psychological signs of degeneration."[40] To deal with this population, doctors pushed for measures requiring their care in hospitals and asylums.

Directed to an audience of fellow physicians, criminologists, and sociologists, much of the literature includes treatment strategies and their results. The medicines and regimens aimed to return misfits to their regular routines or, if that proved impossible, to control the worst effects of their conditions. Because individual misfits contributed to what contemporaries saw as a larger social problem, experts often discussed ways of treating its underlying causes and containing their effects. Social determinants required social solutions, and a number of investigators urged immediate, corrective intervention. For example, experts on vagrancy called for refuges, work houses, and labor exchanges for the unemployed and joined criminologists in urging foster families for orphans and troubled children and special reformatories for juvenile offenders. The more radical among the investigators pressed lawmakers to get beyond palliatives and address what they saw as the fundamental problems. Their calls for unemployment insurance, child labor laws, and extended primary education encountered stiff resistance from politicians committed to limited government and local power. A few, such as Pasquale Penta, insisted that any serious effort to reduce deviance meant nothing less than establishing social equality.[41]

Addressing the roots and manifestations of biologically induced counter-social behavior proved far more complicated. Securing the future by trying to break the chain of inherited disorders received a good deal of attention. In light of Morel's dire predictions about collective decline, nations as well as families needed to do everything possible to escape their fates. Efforts to overcome heredity varied from innocuous campaigns for personal hygiene to more questionable initiatives to control reproduction. The advice depended on the audience. Some experts targeted groups considered vulnerable to degeneration, while others focused on the known carriers of hereditary defects. To the first group, they advised taking strong prophylactic measures and then hoping for the best. Even if they felt healthy, physicians warned, these individuals probably harbored congenital weaknesses, and that made it essential to avoid illnesses and trauma and follow healthy regimens. Pasquale Penta urged individuals with a degenerate parent to train their will in order to curb their impulses. He also cautioned them against taxing the body with too much work, alcohol, sex, or "the vice of onanism which exhausts the nervous system."[42] "Moral traumas, strong and premature passions, the violent disappointments that can result from them, wavering desires and weak character" all magnified the risks of caving in to degeneration, Penta intoned.[43] He, along with others, made it clear that potential degenerates should avoid marriage. In the case of obvious degenerates, medical and social scientists worried still more about prevention. When addressing the issue, most said that they used moral suasion to convince patients not to reproduce, or they admitted that confinement helped to ensure that outcome. A few, notably Lacassagne, considered forced sterilization for a subset of the most socially dangerous.

Because it looked as if incipient weaknesses put some people and modern life put all people at risk for illnesses and accidents, specialists of all sorts urged normal people to take preventive measures. Among the many tactics they touted, the most common targeted energy levels and willpower. Pointing out that everyone enjoyed a fixed supply of energy, experts urged people to conserve it carefully in order to ward off nervous collapse. Children, in particular, needed to avoid the draining effects of masturbation and overwork. Experts counseled close supervision, plenty of outdoor exercise, and tonics to keep the young healthy, and they warned adults not to overdo work or pleasures. Pointing out the biological penalties of illicit activities, they promised that, barring accident or trauma, moderation and balance maintained good health. Whether people heard them, and if they did, whether they followed instructions is difficult to discern. If multiple editions indicate demand, there seemed to be a market for popular manuals on risks and remedies and even for more technical but accessible studies such as Ribot's works on psychology.

Careful management of their energy levels kept the average person going, but it did not keep them on track. To control the primitive impulses raging in children and embedded in every civilized adult took more than tonics. For children and adults alike, it required stiffening the will, and nothing worked better than work. Performing "regular, methodical labor," Guglielmo Ferrero pointed out, had produced revolutionary changes "in the psychology of millions of men."[44] This premise put a premium on discipline and education for the young. If properly trained, children reaped the benefits in self-control as adults, although investigators such as Ribot insisted on the fragility of these gains. Once it developed, keeping the will in fighting trim required personal vigilance. Because regular work demanded attention and discipline, it, more than anything else, helped the will retain its edge. Efforts to keep intellect and emotion vital enough to restrain the instincts also reinforced the will's power. But, according to Ribot among others, the body's complexity exposed even the most diligent defender of the nervous system to failure.

Inciting citizens to defend their health and urging the government to support efforts to extend care to everyone fell naturally to doctors. They joined social scientists who sought to protect citizens against dangerous degenerates and against a cycle of decline thought likely to imperil society itself. But the experts also hoped to affect other policies, and they appeared to have the greatest influence over public order, especially the legislation aimed at habitual lawbreakers. In this domain, their discoveries about born criminals and vagrants matched the public's alarm over what it saw as persistent social scourges. Their theory that repeat offenders responded to uncontrollable inner drives gave scientific sanction to widespread suspicions and fears. At the same time, it fed the sense of danger and helped make the case for preventive measures. The possibility that inner drives produced hardened criminals and vagrants also meant that those pressed by circumstances posed less threat than previously imagined. Observers continued to believe that the deliberate scoff-laws responded to deterrents, and if those failed, to well-chosen correctives. Among these, however, prison proved less effective than the experts and policymakers hoped, and they sought different ways to rehabilitate perverse offenders while safeguarding citizens.

According to medical and social scientists, those born to crime and vagabondage posed the greatest threat, because punishment offered little hope of reintegrating them into society. Judging from the initiatives adopted to deal with repeat offenders, the experts got the policymakers' ear. The Italians chose to reinforce existing measures of prevention, those centered on public denunciation, surveillance, and confinement. Claiming to reinforce public security, they tightened the system of *ammonizione* and extended its reach to include political dissenters. Confined in full public view, the *ammoniti* struggled to conform to the regimens imposed on them. If they failed to meet the conditions, they broke the law and that led to their forced relegation to an isolated area. Officials defended this regime of supervision and sequestration as a means of protecting society from potentially dangerous types, a category which included those thought to harbor internal propensities to crime. For convicted criminals diagnosed as sick or defective, criminal insane asylums served as an alternative to prison. By providing long-term confinement and medical supervision, experts argued, these institutions protected society while treating the abnormalities and their effects to the extent possible.

The French anti-recidivism law of 1885 also drew from the growing literature in forensic medicine and criminal anthropology. To begin with, it recognized the problem of repeat offenders and connected it to rising crime rates. Lawmakers concluded that prison sentences did not rehabilitate these criminals and that releasing them posed a serious threat to society. The alternative, confinement in far-away penal colonies, took disruptive misfits out of circulation, with the added advantage of enabling triage. According to their reasoning, the stark conditions might convince the pernicious types to decide to change their ways. For those too prone to give in to their impulses or to imitate other delinquents, a regimen of work might stiffen their self-restraint and allow them to return to society. And finally, making release contingent on evidence of rehabilitation kept those whose pathologies explained their crimes out of the way.[45] Here, as in Italy, the scientific literature on misfits influenced the debate. Already convinced of the disruptive effects of rising criminality and vagrancy, biological theories confirmed the intractability of serious recidivism. At the same time, experts caused lawmakers to rethink strategies based on the assumption that criminality resulted from bad choices.

Accidental misfits made decisions, but they responded to situations that radically limited their options. Propelled to crime and vagrancy by necessity, they easily became repeat offenders, investigators argued. When they got caught and did time, prison drew them further into lives of crime. Pointing to these facts, social scientists, in particular, championed substitute punishments for these offenders and urged politicians to address the conditions that drove them to crime. Shortly after they approved the anti-recidivism law, French legislators liberalized judicial procedures for petty crimes and first offenders. Decriminalizing some acts, substituting fines for prison sentences in others, and establishing parole responded to what reform-minded jurists and medical experts urged.[46] In Italy, too, the Criminal Code of 1889 set out a range of punishments, allowing judges to evaluate the criminal's risk to society and calibrate penalties accordingly.

When experts called for social reforms to eliminate occasional crime and vagabondage, they received a more mixed response. For one thing, advocates of reform spoke with multiple and for the most part muted voices. Not all of them made social correctives a priority, but those who did fixed on the conditions that temporarily pushed people off course or that undermined their health, or both. Thus appeals for reform legislation came from physicians as well as social scientists; their goals and preferred tactics coincided with their political inclinations. Those who identified with left-wing parties targeted inequality and poverty, called for structural changes, and favored government intervention; conservatives sought help for narrow, well-defined groups, leaned toward palliative measures, and supported private, charitable initiatives. Politicians divided along similar lines, and their differences slowed action. Nonetheless, parliaments in both countries approved several reform initiatives between 1860 and 1919, including child labor laws, protection for new mothers, and social insurance.[47]

Historians emphasize the pragmatic political motives behind these measures. The record in Italy, Enzo Bartocci argues, confirms that pressure from the working class and their representatives drove reform.[48] In the first decades after Unification, governments concentrated on building infrastructure, creating national law codes, and modernizing the economy. With most liberals committed to laissez-faire doctrine, they moved slowly when reform involved extending the scope of government. But when Italy experienced a rapid industrial takeoff toward the end of the century, and a surge of popular unrest in 1898 caused an institutional crisis, Prime Minister Giovanni Giolitti promoted a "liberal turn around."[49] He encouraged lawmakers to cut working hours for women and children, create a state-supported maternity fund, and give the vote to most adult males. According to historians, including Bartocci, he and his supporters wanted above all to take the bite out of class conflict by reaching out to reform-minded Socialists and to the workers.[50] Similar motives explain why post–First World War governments rapidly issued royal decrees which made old age and accident insurance mandatory (April 21, 1919) and established compulsory unemployment insurance (October 19, 1919). In France, pressure from Socialists and syndicalists, in addition to denatalism, inspired a similar sense of urgency and a suite of concessions designed to promote maternity and defend the Republic.[51]

According to this assessment, politicians adopted reforms to address pressing crises and reinforce their power. Historians make a convincing case for these motivations. It is also clear that political expediency drew substance and legitimizing cover from scientific studies of social issues and marginal groups. Mandating unemployment insurance earned support from socialists, but it also won over some liberals who believed that it addressed vagabondage more effectively than *ammonizione* or criminalization did. Similarly, while reducing work hours and providing maternity support served immediate political goals, politicians in both countries echoed expert opinion about society's duty to protect the vulnerable and about the benefits to the nation of a healthy population. Alexandre Bérard, deputy from l'Ain, for example, insisted that "for the unfortunate, the old people, the infirm, the abandoned children, it is the duty of the nation to develop works of social solidarity." He went further, calling for a more equitable distribution of taxes in order "to break the large fortunes and bring down the financial powers," a far less palatable summons to change things.[52]

Their reasoning

The fear that disruptive change made progress a distant and even spurious possibility helps explain interest in misfits at the end of the century. The desire to understand them created a space where new specialties and aspiring experts flourished and where their calls for social reforms as well as for social defense met receptive ears. The experts themselves likely shared the public's concerns, and if they did not, their colleagues' interest made investigating misfits hard to escape. As the evidence in this study indicates, the answers that they and power brokers in both countries found convincing conformed to their faith in science and their identification of modernity with progress. These convictions help to explain why thinkers saw habitual misfits as deficient and unbalanced, and why that idea won support. Although they doubtless thought about their own professional status and that of their disciplines when they publicized their discoveries or sought to affect policy, careerism did not dictate the substance of their theories. Their hypotheses and lines of argument developed in a context of recognized but still contested givens about the operation of the natural world and of society. In the case of the natural world, they accepted some variant of the theory that species changed and adapted and that energy existed in matter. Regarding society, they drew on liberalism and its promise of progress and individual fulfillment. These starting points confined their thinking, showing them where to look and limiting what they might plausibly conclude. At the same time, their attachment to empiricism made researchers particularly attentive to evidence, whether it confirmed or contradicted their assumptions.

Scientists generally accepted the premise that the human species changed according to mechanisms governed by natural laws. In lectures to medical students published in 1890, Benjamin Ball offered his assessment of the thinking in France. You did not have to accept all of Darwin, he said, to acknowledge that heredity improved the human race just as breeding improved horses. At the same time, drawing on Lamarck, Ball clarified that every repeated act and every sensation left marks on the body that heredity could preserve. Without setting aside that theory, most Italian scientists accepted Darwin's argument that variation and natural selection worked through heredity to alter the species. In both versions, heredity acted as the agent of cumulative changes. "Civilization," Ball specified, "is a particular attribute of the nervous system, acquired as a result of long and laborious efforts, and whose effects are preserved by hereditary transmission."[53]

How medical and social scientists understood the impact of evolution on the human species affected what they saw as aberrant. They concluded that evolution changed the body in three main ways: it complicated, connected, and integrated. Its structures and operations moved from simple to complex and from autonomous to interdependent. Ribot clarified the accepted sequence: reflexes first, then instincts followed by feelings, and finally intellect and moral sensibility. Because these capacities responded differently to external stimuli, they competed for control, and the will developed to manage the conflicts and to authorize action. History demonstrated, Ribot and others theorized, that as the species changed, people constructed increasingly complex economies and polities. As Paolo Mantegazza put it, a European child had the intelligence and feelings of an Australian aborigine, but whereas the European continued to fulfill the stages of evolution, the aborigine did not.[54] The laws of nature, then, both enabled and sustained progress and its civilizing achievements. What most observers saw as primitive societies confirmed the process while their own societies appeared more and more to challenge it.

Worries that modern life obstructed progress reinforced theories of decline. Morel imagined both a positive and a decidedly negative sequence of changes. His description of the downward spiral proved tenacious, particularly as evidence indicated that civilization either moved backwards or that it had not yet won out. Pasquale Penta, the expert on sexual perversions, found it natural that heredity took a backward turn: "an imbalance first, a disintegration and then a descent that goes in the opposite direction of this evolution, that is from the complex to the simple."[55] How exactly such forward-backward movement might work perplexed scientists. While Morel identified opposing processes of progress and decline, developments in biology, medicine, and anthropology toward the end of the century produced more complicated theories. Some of the later thinkers saw progress and regression as linked parts of a single process. Because the latest and most complex achievements of the species were the most likely to give way, advance contained within it the risk of retreat, some argued. A more intriguing and paradoxical position saw regression as the condition of progress. In other words, advance depended on retreat. Both perspectives coincided with the much-discussed phenomenon of degeneration and both influenced explanations of deviance based on regression.

Another response to the apparent disconnect between civilization and progress looked to the evolutionary process itself for some answers. In society, as with the species, each change overlaid the last, creating a complex and dynamic whole, as every layer added capacities along with the need for greater integration.[56] More a multidimensional accumulation than points on a line, evolution built a volatile mix with later and more sophisticated elements vying with the earlier and more elemental ones. This picture put conflict inside the evolved body and the modern societies it permitted, making instability a condition and a consequence of change. Shifting the analysis of evolution's effects from the species to the individual also helped account for uneven progress. Ernst Haeckel's theory of ontogenesis laid out an appealing possibility. Ordinary people followed the path determined by nature as they acquired the biological mechanisms that equipped them to act as responsible citizens. To account for abnormality, observers reversed the equation. Those who did not act normally must not *be* normal. They must suffer from defects and deficiencies that obstructed their maturation, especially in its final stages—precisely those essential for managing modern life. Applying this theory, regression and arrested development made misfits, especially those affected by moral blindness and deficient willpower. The idea that ontogenesis worked in reverse as people aged proved equally convincing. Studies, especially those of imbecility, born criminality, and excessive libido acknowledged that self-restraint and intellectual acuity dissolved first, then feelings, followed by instincts, until reflexes alone commanded.

The notion that individual maturation followed an established script also informed changing definitions of *dégénérescence*. Investigators came to associate the cluster of degenerative defects with developmental abnormalities. While others evolved fully, misfits fell short. Those who stressed that degeneration prevented or interrupted the process of development accepted that abnormality meant not achieving full biological potential. The theory favored by Lombroso and his followers that degeneration took the form of reversion or atavism also equated normalcy with regular development.

Other experts stressed Darwin's theory of adaptation to explain modern society's rougher edges. Adjusting to the milieu involved struggle, and the resulting strain damaged the body, they contended. Italian anthropologist Giuseppe Sergi made the case. Those "wounded and mutilated" by the struggle for life, he argued, developed distinctive and "inferior forms of adaptation."[57] Unlike normal people who "had overcome every difficulty without bearing a trace of the struggle ..." those who started out weak displayed the marks of the fight.[58] Some showed the signs of regression, others of congenital or inherited defects, and still others registered the negative effects of harsh exterior conditions or the "abuse or ill use" of their vital functions.[59] The strains of living in modern society compounded the problem for those who, "born weak," could not resist the "continual excessive stimulation of the brain, and exhausted themselves."[60] Degeneration, he asserted, resulted from this effort to adapt. It caused suicide, criminality, prostitution, vagrancy, begging, insanity, servitude, and social parasitism. Any reasonably adept observer found evidence of the deleterious effects of adaptation everywhere, he argued. Often criminals suffered from mental illness and from pathologies such as "epilepsy, hysteria, scrofula, neuroses, paralyses, malaria, cachexia."[61] Sergi also pointed out that atavistic responses to the fight explained prostitution as well as begging and vagrancy.[62] Bruised by the fight to adapt, misfits stopped too soon, fell backward, or surged ahead of the developmental curve.

Investigators mobilized the idea of phases in the development of the species and of societies not only to explain mental and social dissonance but also to temper its gravity. If abnormality meant not fulfilling their biological potential, then modern misfits behaved as people normally did at an earlier stage. What benefited humans at one time in the species' past, they contended, could not be intrinsically anti-biological or antisocial. Regression or arrested development, then, produced not monsters but primitives. Except for behaviors such as sexual inversion that did not serve the organism, normality and abnormality depended, then, on the context.[63] Although skeptics challenged prevailing descriptions of the earliest human communities, for the most part scientists accepted the idea that primitive societies in their time repeated the initial stages of human development. This perspective worked a strange alchemy: while it served to deprecate criminality, vagrancy, prostitution, and hysteria in the present, it legitimized these behaviors in earlier societies.

Investigators, whatever the type of misfit they studied, incorporated still another element of the evolutionary process into their conclusions: heredity. Whether they favored the Lamarckian theory of acquired characteristics or leaned to Darwin's idea of natural selection, they accepted that heredity incorporated anomalies into the destiny of the species. Because the body replicated itself, bad habits and random defects mattered in the longer run. Although animal breeding offered some information, the mechanics of heredity remained uncertain. From Morel, they drew the idea that defects magnified in gravity from generation to generation until they extinguished the race. That proposition lost ground, but the idea that a set of anomalies moved through families gained support. Based on the evidence that seemingly disparate conditions such as "neuroses, crime, artistic tendencies, lesions of the brain or the spine, diseases of development" so often recurred in extended families, Féré found the idea of indirect heredity plausible.[64] Henry Maudsley shared that view: "In families where there is a strong disposition to insanity … one perhaps has epilepsy, another is afflicted with a severe neuralgia or with hysteria, a third may commit suicide, a fourth become maniacal or melancholic. And it might happen sometimes that a fifth evinced remarkable artistic talent."[65] Indirect heredity came, then, to confirm that the same basic matrix generated degenerative abnormalities. That insight invited investigators to examine any disorder on the list. In fact, heredity offered compelling evidence that their expertise in criminality, for example, enabled them to understand hysteria. Recognizing that born deviants marched to the same organic drummer also encouraged exchange and collaboration, as data about one type of misfit informed the analysis of another.

Evolution supplied one of the frames thinkers used to fathom abnormality. It prompted them to focus on how the body developed and to see that it matured according to an entrenched and predictable process. How the body worked gave them a second frame, and this one featured volatility and tension. Two main features of the body's operation struck them as pertinent to explaining misfits: energy use and the brain's architecture. These properties drew attention across fields of study, and they shaped the prevailing theories of abnormality. The experts referred to in this study assumed that energy acted through the nervous system to animate life processes from digestion to higher thinking. Accepting the theory that energy inhered in matter, they pictured a set supply available from birth. If they understood the laws of thermodynamics developed at mid-century, they realized that the body contained sufficient energy in itself, but that its activity caused energy to degenerate and collapse.[66] Normal people, they reasoned, kept going with what energy they had for their lifetimes. Heredity favored them with a large enough reservoir, and their moderate lifestyles helped them deploy it wisely. If those conditions did not pertain—if they began with too little energy or dissipated their stock with excessive work and play, then they could not function normally, scientists theorized. Applying that idea to misfits, they discovered a host of problems traceable to diminishing energy: fatigue, indigestion, impotence, and indolence, among others. In geniuses and epileptics, in contrast, some thought they detected sudden energy surges.

Interest in energy and its uses explains the attention given to the nervous system and to the field of neurology. Neurologists wanted to know how the nervous system operated, and their theories directed discussions of both mental and social misfits. How the nerves processed sensations from the outside and how they connected to the brain seemed especially relevant. They and investigators from other fields speculated that too much noise, speed, and bright colors put healthy citizens on edge and overwhelmed those with weak nerves. Seeing the nervous system as vulnerable, they detected signs of nervous collapse in city dwellers and in victims of shock and trauma. How much weak or damaged nerves affected the brain generated considerable discussion, especially among scientists interested in accounting for mental illness, genius, and lucid criminality. The anatomy of the brain itself affected thinking about misfits even more directly. Reacting against the idea that from the beginning the brain reasoned and only reasoned, thinkers theorized that the brain developed distinct and multiple functions. This view invited investigators to hypothesize that anomalies in the development of one part of the brain produced certain behaviors.

They applied that idea, in turn, to their explanations of born criminals, vagrants, and inverts. Their accounts of certain mental disorders also relied on this model of the brain, as did the theory that genius happened when one area of the brain made a freakish forward leap.

When medical and social scientists looked for what caused biologically based abnormalities, generally accepted theories about the body and additional research in multiple fields directed their search. Journals, books, international professional meetings, and smaller research communities such as the ones gathered around Charcot and Lombroso diffused new data and hypotheses. This information helped them correct deficits in their knowledge about the defects that produced abnormality. Their reading of evolution and body mechanics gave observers an alternative to sacred views of odd and antisocial behaviors. If sin did not convince, biology did. It kept the source of transgressive behaviors internal and personal, determined, and not contingent. Natural laws, divinely ordained or not, regulated the development of the species, just as discernible processes managed the body's systems. Substituting organic anomalies for original sin, they saw that corrupted bodies led misfits astray. While the evolved body's complexity made everyone vulnerable to defects and damage, heredity and lifestyle protected most and exposed others. Experts readily acknowledged that much remained unknown, but their continual efforts to observe, classify, and explain indicated their conviction that what appeared inexplicable was not.

Biology clearly offered a compelling explanation of difference at the end of the century. Heredity, developmental glitches, illness, and trauma put bodies gone awry into the picture and sidelined individual choice as the determinant of dissonance. The biological, and more specifically medical, perspective defines the epoch, according to many historians. It does, but medical and social scientists alike put misfits into a third frame. This one consisted of ideas about how society did and should work. Applying this perspective, observers picked out misfits from the social landscape, singled out the most dangerous among them, and identified the others as occasional outliers. Current issues and anxieties, the premises of liberalism, and personal experiences defined this frame, and these elements in turn centered on rapid change and its dislocations and promises. Like politicians and ordinary citizens, experts on deviance experienced the effects of industrialization, global economic fluctuations, and political revolution. They were not isolated from liberal debates about the social question or from socialist critiques of capitalism. Uncertainties about the effects of modern society made it an object of examination and, they discovered, a major source of deviance. The rivalry between the Italian and French schools notwithstanding, most experts acknowledged both biological and social determinants whatever their specialty or research interest.

Aware that the milieu influenced behavior, investigators weighed multiple variables: topography and climate, economic structures, social organization, and the form of government. Their interest in the seasons and the weather and in fluctuations in markets and in the impact of trauma, toxins, hardship, and lifestyle on the body belonged to this effort. To assess these variables, they relied mainly on statistics and on case studies built on interviews and tests. Judging from how they used statistics, quantitative data supported comparative analyses of different types of deviance as well as cross-country comparisons. Featuring social as well as medical data, case reports routinely included vital statistics and individual and family medical histories. Along with test results and measurements, investigators recorded information about lifestyles, jobs, loves, and losses, believing such personal details were relevant to their diagnosis. Cases filled the literature as investigators presented their own and summarized others to buttress their theories. Some cases, such as Binet's lover of women's boot nails and Musolino, achieved special prominence, serving as standard reference points for other researchers at home and abroad. Exchanging cases fed the mania for classification, just as it fueled discussion of what counted as esoteric and what permitted valid generalizations.

Confronting the details of these lives gone awry, investigators filtered the data through their understanding of current political and social realities. Like pebbles hitting a pond, the circles of relevance moved outward as they looked from the individual, to the type, to the phenomenon, or from Musolino, to killers, to criminality, to deviance. As they applied current issues to the data before them, they moved from the outside in, beginning with factors shaping their attitudes about deviance. In the last decades of the nineteenth century, the Italians and French shared a sense of departure accompanied by an awareness of the past that they carried behind them. As Pick argues for Italy and Kaluszynski for France, neophyte liberal governments sought to secure control and legitimacy. Liberals believed that unified Italy and the Third French Republic initiated new eras characterized by freedom and the promise of prosperity and progress. Especially in Italy, leaders valued unification as a step toward the modern, while France saw itself among the vanguard of nations but worried about losing its place in that company. In addition to coveting the label "advanced," new liberal governments put a high value on political harmony. Not only did dissent threaten public order, it disrupted the consensus considered basic to the exercise of freedom. In both countries, change fueled strident opposition and popular unrest, and those pressures contributed to parliamentary factionalism. Alongside these overt threats, the disturbing signs of individual lawlessness and mental breakdown suggested a pervasive and perplexing malaise, one that challenged their expectations that liberal government favored the rule of law and the reign of reason. In this context of uncertainty and disappointment, the outliers became a social problem, one that required explanation. Social and medical scientists took on the project, often explicitly justifying their research in terms of its practical outcomes.

These perspectives on contemporary society affected both what investigators wanted to know and what they found out. The common description of habitual lawbreakers as poorly adjusted and deficient paralleled concerns about their countries and liberal governments coming up short. Normal citizens naturally developed the equipment for success in the modern world, just as they hoped the nation would. Misfits, in contrast, did not fit in, because they could not fit in. Applied to every outlier, the diagnosis of innate problems delivered a mixed and unconvincing verdict. On the one hand, it deflected responsibility from leaders and institutions. On the other hand, it precluded effective action, an unpleasant prospect for lawmakers determined to reduce or eliminate social dissonance, and for specialists anxious to identify solutions. As an all-encompassing explanation, innate deficiency did not make sense, the experts concluded, because it did not acknowledge the critical role that society played in determining behavior. Circumstances, they insisted, made some, and even most, misfits occasional misfits. They resorted to crime to get out of a tight spot, or they left home to look for work, or they engaged in same-sex relations, *faute de mieux*. They experienced a patch of madness or a bout of hysteria; they achieved creative breakthroughs through hard work, not genius. What investigators knew about poverty, markets, unemployment, overwork, and emotional shocks supplied ample evidence for circumstantial misbehavior. When misfits appeared normal in every way but their actions, experts saw society at work.

That social and medical scientists noticed occasional misfits registers their keen awareness of the insistent and intrusive signs of contemporary life. What they saw around them, what they read in the press, and what they knew about policy discussions informed the assessment of deviance at every level, from occasional thieves and prostitutes to traumatized survivors of railway accidents, to neurasthenics laid low by failing energy supplies. More generally, investigators recognized the struggle and the strain generated by trying to get by or get ahead, and they alerted citizens to the risks of excess work, pleasure, and stimuli. These pressures, investigators warned, could push anyone off course. Their concerns about the dangers of modern life reflected their ideas about its satisfactions. They accepted that civilized people could and should work regularly, settle down, practice monogamy, and like it. Anything else indicated that something serious was amiss. With few exceptions, investigators deplored anyone who chose to defy the norms and felt compassion for anyone whose circumstances conspired against their best efforts. That modern life itself prevented some people from enjoying its benefits sharpened their interest in reform.

The social frame, then, left its mark on thinking about misfits born and misfits made. In less obvious ways, it permeated discussions of abnormality by influencing perceptions and supplying analogies. The healthy body, investigators agreed, functioned best when it integrated impulse, emotion, and intellect. An internal imbalance of these forces meant trouble as did asymmetrical facial features and a disjunction between the right and left sides of the body. That assessment matched ideas about the body politic. Effective government depended on balancing competing interests and on orchestrating agreements. When those efforts failed, the discordant voices seemed to sound from outside the system, tempting politicians to silence them, even at the expense of the basic rights they said they valued. To control the extremes required restraining them, just as scientists said containing individual impulses did. The will served as the agent of constraint. It collected conflicting responses to outside stimuli and determined which harmed or benefited the organism. Liberals assigned governments a similar role as managers of competing interests with an eye to the common good. Their functions matched, and so did descriptions of the deleterious effects of weakness and failure. When they described the body and the body politic in similar terms, investigators intended to communicate facts rather than to generate convenient analogies.

The will's role paralleled the government's in managing discordant pressures and enabling citizens to live their lives. It developed, scientists decided, for two reasons. First, the body's growing complexity required an adjudicator. Second, modern society's surfeit of stimuli had to be channeled. If not controlled, constant and instantaneous fluctuations led to collapse. The modern body and modern society operated at a feverish pitch, investigators believed, and the frenetic pace put both at risk. As the epidemic of neurasthenia proved, too much stimulation could overburden the body, causing it to fall into torpor and impotence. Neurasthenia usually followed a period of accumulating stress generated by too much work, too much pleasure, too much noise and motion. But railway accidents also taught doctors that intense, abrupt shocks could shatter or shut down the nervous system. Just as the hurly-burly of modern life intensified the volatility of the modern body, so misfits exacerbated the sense of social disorder. How they explained misfits seemed to encapsulate the sharp and discombobulating changes brought on by neophyte regimes, industrialization, and new ideas.

No grand chasm separated the biological and social frames; rather they intersected in important ways. Unpredictable change constituted one cross-cutting vector and determinism another. Together, the points of meeting predicted both sequential change for the better and continual and intensifying volatility. At the junction of these contradictory elements, the frames created spaces for misfits and traced their origins to the body and society. Internal anomalies, external conditions, or a convergence of the two pushed misfits out of the mainstream. The lot assigned to choice diminished dramatically as religious ideas of free will and original sin and the secular idea that mistaken or twisted judgment caused people to flaunt the rules lost credit. In light of what they knew about biology and society, it made more sense to conclude that misfits did not control their destinies. A third vector sliced across the two frames and reinforced their conception of abnormality: individualism. The idea that emancipated moderns made decisions served as a tenacious counterpoint to determinism and to contingency. Because of it, the category of deliberate transgression by no means disappeared completely. It continued to prevail in the courtroom where judges remained attached to the liberal premise that misguided citizens broke laws. Even among the experts on innate and accidental troublemakers, character came into play by default. When they could not establish the role of the body or the situation, they invoked evil and vice. Except for pederasty (sodomy), that diagnosis typically applied to individuals rather than to a type of deviance. Because they abused their autonomy, these misfits cast themselves out of society. Other misfits effectively lost their power to choose to social pressures and organic defects. Unlike them, normal people retained some autonomy, autonomy recognized as self-control.

Authorities on deviance at the end of the century looked for the sources of abnormal behaviors in nature's laws, the evolved body, and advanced society. In each of these contexts, they assigned a central role to change: the evolution of the species, the body's maturation, and human history. Their sensation that the self and the world were in continual motion corresponded to their experience. They believed that change followed laws and prescribed patterns, but what actually happened too frequently defied their predictions. Misfits took their place among other signs of undisciplined, disruptive change. Pushed off course and out of step, outliers appeared as canaries in a coal mine. If experts could understand what their presence announced, they believed that they could better channel change. Based on the evidence, they concluded that in their defects, imbalances, and vulnerabilities, misfits displayed the complexity and the fragility of both the evolved body and of the modern citizen-body. Tied to deviance, disruptive change got normalized, but largely within the confines of the exceptional, just as autonomy gained in value, but as a mechanism for adapting or fitting in.

Ambiguous verdicts

Understood as the end result of the laws of nature and the course of history, modernity appeared not only natural but inherently superior. If, as the informed believed, the highest stages of evolution brought reason, rights, and freedom, it changed lives for the better. At the same time, grounding these changes in the body, rather than the soul or mind, created complications, primary among them a different understanding of the self. Scientists made the modern self multifaceted, dynamic, and vulnerable. It developed over time and in layers, they asserted, adding components and the capacity to manage them in a prescribed sequence. Like the body, the mind changed from simple to complex and from single to multiple functions. Personality did not arrive from the outside, all of a piece, but it slowly gained specialized components in response to the milieu. Over their life spans, individuals repeated the long, evolutionary trajectory of the species. But at every instant, the organism also changed under the pressure of internal and external stimuli. As Ribot explained it, sensations initially triggered automatic responses, but when emotion and then intellect appeared, they added more receptors to the mix, intensifying the internal tumult.

Scientists planted the self in these organic processes. They constituted the "I", Ribot contended. "It is the body and its highest manifestation the brain, that is the real personality, containing what remains of all that we have been and all that we will be."[67] All the impulses, emotions, and thoughts, along with the constellations of cells that produced them, combined to constitute the personality at a particular moment. Purely physiological, the self continually changed as it matured and as it reacted to internal and external sensations, psychologists such as Ribot believed. For the most part, the formation of the self operated beneath the level of consciousness. People usually acted according to reflex or instinct, and when feelings and intellect directed their actions, they rarely noticed. The behind-the-scenes activity surfaced in disorders such as hysteria and epilepsy, concluded the psychologists, psychiatrists, and neurologists. Normal people operated in exactly the same way; they just possessed more robust wills.

Accepting the organic basis of character seemed to cut down reason and disgrace morality, and this change raised fundamental questions about the properties and possibilities of humans. Functions identified with the soul passed to the brain, and the province of free will contracted as the psycho-physiological work of willpower expanded. Such theories provoked serious debates over the boundaries between the physical and the moral. As scientists clarified the implications of their discoveries, they held on to the idea of morality but gave it a different and rather ambiguous look. Like reflexes and instincts, morality operated in the cells of the nervous system and brain and responded to stimuli and sensations. "According to the basic evidence produced by the facts, we must conclude," said Lorenzo Ellero (1856–1923), assistant at the psychiatric clinic of the University of Padova, "that if man is moral, he is moral not because his free will twitches, but because the fortunate organization of his ethical sense requires it … ."[68] Despite its contingency, experts nonetheless argued that moral feeling occupied a superior place in the body. Not present in animals or in primitives and children according to many experts, the moral faculties developed later, along with the intellect and the will. Or, by another theory, the moral sense resulted from choices originally driven by survival, made into habit by repetition, ingrained then as an inherited instinct, but a "higher" instinct. When seen as the result of generations of development, morality regained the supremacy that an association with the soul had given it. At the same time, however, arriving late in the sequence, the will, intellect, and moral feeling proved vulnerable to defects and diseases and disarmed against the better-entrenched basic instincts.

Experts had more trouble salvaging the dignity of moral choice. According to traditional views, choice involved reason, and reason implied consciousness. By locating the process of choosing in the brain and nervous system, the new theories sharply reduced the degree of control once associated with a moral life. Evidence now indicated that even when people consciously weighed their options, their reason played a far less important part than they thought. What actually "chose" to incite or inhibit action, the will, followed physical dictates, and it operated somewhere beyond consciousness. When people experienced choice and even consciousness itself, they registered the sensory effects of physical processes. Ellero specified, "What we experience as free will, is in fact, the struggle between appetites, feelings, and ideas."[69]

This reconsideration of reason's role diminished its authority. Once the mirror of the divine and the main site of moral choice, it now relinquished part of that power to other faculties. In fact, few authorities used the word "reason," avoiding it as they did spirit and free will because of its metaphysical connotations. Instead they tended to divide up its essential properties and refer to intellect and will. Knowing the difference between right and wrong remained in the province of the intellect, the result of a work of individual education. But lucid madmen, primitives, and children proved the limits of moral understanding. They did good to please others, or not at all. When sane and civilized adults acted morally, they did so mainly because they could put a value on moral action. Whether they actually carried through on what they considered important depended on the health of the cells responsible for will and self-restraint. Their ability to make ethical distinctions and to appreciate the good constituted a late acquisition of the human species. Along with willpower, moral sensibility allowed people to master their impulses and to lead civilized lives.

The evolved body, experts generally believed, enabled modern society, but many also blamed modernity for disabling its benefactor. Medical and social scientists interested in pathologies, whether organic or social, began to add their voices to critics on the radical left and right and describe the downsides of modern life. Not only did the struggle to adapt leave people behind, as some argued, society took a toll on those who arrived. The cellular complexity and the exquisite sensibility of the evolved body exaggerated the impact of every stimulus, taxing the nervous system. As they diagnosed the problem, investigators showed that what bourgeois liberals valued the most wrecked the body. Obvious material signs of progress—the railroad, telegraph, and the industrial city—increased the cacophony and confusion ordinary people experienced daily. The modern economy, with its boom and bust cycles and its competition for wealth, ground down both the poor and the rich, and the uncertainties of freedom, especially in the form of changing governments, caused generalized confusion and disorientation, they observed. When people responded to the call to find individual happiness, investigators added, they risked falling into a frenetic and debilitating search for pleasure. Or, ambitious strivers for money and acclaim found that the effort exceeded their forces, while the ticket to rise, public education, overburdened generations of children.

If modernity took on a double face, so did normality, and in both cases scientists exposed a darker side. As abnormality became the operative explanation for dissonance, it supplied the terms for its opposite, normality. The early use of the adjective "real" or "true" to distinguish inborn from temporary deviations established a basic definition of deviance.[70] It gained specificity as investigators refined the term "degeneration" and recognized the role of heredity, especially transformative heredity. Described as incorrigible and dangerous, degenerates provoked fear and insecurity, along with some compassion for their unfortunate destiny. Spared defects and damage, ordinary citizens operated in sync with society, except when circumstances pushed them out of step. The idea of accidental and temporary misfits caused citizens to feel an "in the same situation, I too would ..." connection. The divide, then, rested between the irreversible and reversible, the innate and situational, and the abnormal and normal. One side inspired a sense of separation and anxiety, the other admitted greater comfort and identification.

Toward the end of the century, leading investigators reversed course and called attention to the virtues of abnormality and the limits of normality. In his study of psycho-sexual degeneration in 1892, Silvio Venturi encouraged others to look at innate misfits differently. "What seems defective ... dangerous, extravagant in an individual" can "have a high interest for society as a whole" when anomalies serve "important social needs and become instruments of biological functions."[71] Enrico Ferri took a similar position eight years later in an article published in *La Scuola Positiva*. He asserted that when Morel and Lombroso identified abnormals with "delinquents, degenerates, the unbalanced, geniuses, madmen, fanatics, the perverted, the immoral, with suicides, incorrigibles, rebels, etc.," the public began to distinguish between "the normal man" and "the abnormal man."[72] They were right to separate the two, Ferri argued, but they wrongly lumped all the abnormals together and sought to "exterminate" geniuses along with delinquents and crazies.[73] Fortunately, though, people came to see that degeneration sometimes improved and perfected society. In fact, Ferri contended, abnormal people accounted for all human and social progress, although only the "more or less *altruistic*" among them had such a positive effect. To capture this critical distinction, he proposed to call these more constructive misfits the "anormali *evolutivi* [evolved abnormals]" and the "egotists" who undermined positive change the "*involujtivi* [regressives]."[74]

Geniuses made Ferri's point. But he and others argued that other types of misfits could also change the world for the better. "The abnormal, from conquerors to criminals, from saints to geniuses" move history, he asserted.[75] Criminals, he specified, could be either "involuted" or "evolved," and Ferri invoked French sociologist Emile Durkheim's argument that criminality contributed to the health of societies to support his point. He agreed, especially when ideas about bettering the world so obsessed men that they stopped at nothing to enact them. Marie and Meunier accepted Ferri's distinction and called attention to vagabond mystics and apostles who could be "pioneers of progress."[76] All vagabonds, they argued, "have been unable to adapt to the social milieu. They are part of that fraction of humanity who are either below or outside or above the normal and daily collectivity; some serve human progress; others return it sometimes to its lowest state; without these extreme types there would be neither crime nor genius."[77]

Abnormalities could, then, stop or reverse development, or they could cause disruptions and mutations that pushed societies and the species forward. Max Nordau explained, "The best today are clearly more advanced, but tomorrow the masses will have moved just as far, and in order to have the right to call them backward... the geniuses of tomorrow must be as superior to those of today as these are to the present population."[78] According to this perspective, the machinery of evolution and of history required misfits; they made it run. It followed that well-adjusted, normal people threw sticks in the wheels of progress. "The majority," Nordau insisted, "is made up of average or mediocre or normal men, who vegetate from the sunrise to the sunset of their existence."[79] Ferri underscored the paralyzing effects of evolution. "Individual and social selection" produce a "mediocre" result: the normal man. Well adapted to the current historical moment and context, normal men transmitted "from generation to generation the life and the habits and the traditional incrustation of prejudices which pass as basic truths." Like department store clothes, he continued, they cover the body but lack the personal touch.[80]

While the public prized normality, experts should know better, Ferri implied. Evolution enabled humans to create more and more complex societies, and the mechanisms of adaptation kept them operating. But even more forcefully, biology embedded the status quo; it favored stalemate and blocked change. Without the "evolutionary energy of human degeneration," Ferri insisted, "sterility and exhaustion fatally strike society."[81] Once thought to push races inexorably to extinction, degeneration now appeared to ensure vitality and continued growth. Commenting on Lombroso's work in 1906, Paolo Orano clarified the implications of his views of genius. If today's abnormality becomes tomorrow's normality, then misfits push society forward. Better, then, not to fight abnormality, and "if the choicest part of humanity results from it," better still, Orano concluded, to encourage it.[82]

Putting degenerates, including criminals, vagrants, and madmen, in the forefront of evolutionary change, showed a striking reversal in perspective. When Lombroso attributed genius to degeneration, he raised a chorus of objections. Now, for at least some experts, his assertion served as a paradigm for deviance. Although it could disrupt society in regrettable ways, biological difference also held the key to progress. That result made it senseless to resist abnormality and socially costly to try to eliminate it, they asserted. Normality, in contrast, showed its negative side, since well-adjusted citizens brought society to a standstill. By equating order with lamentable stasis and disorder with revivifying novelty, they justified a measure of chaos. The same perspective appeared in assessments of how the body worked. The will developed in order to manage impulses and to reinforce the intellect, Frédéric Paulhan confirmed. To do its work, it required "a certain disorganization of the mind and a certain independence of its elements." Will, he continued,

> constitutes one of those so frequent expedients in human nature where a certain disorder is the condition for a superior order, it is one of the applications of this great law of systematic association, of internal goals, according to which the mind uses in one way or another, as long as it lives, everything which is in it, even the flaws which damage it or which risk to damage it, and that it sometimes turns to the good.[83]

If a measure of disorder enabled individuals to develop successfully, the same held true for the species itself. Early on, Morel's predictions of progressive decline influenced thinking about biological destiny. They shaped Lombroso's association of abnormality with atavism and regression, and they reinforced the widely accepted idea that defects passed to the next generation, and in more serious form. Evolution, however, countered Morel's scenario, because it moved humans forward. As scientists saw that evolution on balance ensured positive change, they became less concerned about the negative effects of biological anomalies. For example, Eugenio Tanzi, in the 1905 edition of his textbook, minimized degenerative heredity. He argued that environmental conditions rather than heredity explained the persistence of conditions such as pellagra, goiter, and cretinism in families. When degenerative variations did occur, they did not pass on to progeny nearly as frequently as scientists thought, he argued. In fact, because the body worked against anomalies, the next generation more often inherited a resistance to defects.[84] While he acknowledged that conditions such as paranoia and youthful dementia did transmit, they did not, he concluded, intensify in the next generation.[85]

Taking the laws of evolution as a whole, some investigators also found less reason for pessimism. The body's adaptive mechanisms enabled it to adjust to environmental toxins and stress. For those influenced by Darwin's theories, natural selection reinforced the more positive reading of evolution's long-term effects. They pointed out that nature favored variations which benefited rather than damaged the species. Working together, then, natural selection and adaptation discarded disadvantageous anomalies. This understanding of evolution coincided with the idea that beneficial abnormalities produced social progress. Whether they focused on the body or on society, these experts effectively tamed dissonance and disorder by making it a necessary part of evolution, history, and individual health.

Projecting this more positive reading of abnormality forward, investigators such as Ribot found reason for optimism. He pointed out that time would embed the intellect and will, just as it had instincts and feelings. A select few, clearly in the advance guard of the species, showed the outer limits of the possible, he asserted.[86] As with other adaptations, evolution would make the will more automatic and the brain more capable of coordinating the elements of the self. That scenario promised to reinforce society by decreasing the number of misfits. For the time being, though, the shaky state of the psyche and the self hampered progress, he warned.

When they attributed progress to misfits, observers associated normality with mediocrity and stagnation. That negative image provoked some criticism. Padovan acknowledged that to describe geniuses as abnormal implied an unfavorable vision of normality. But no one, he commented, conformed to that or any other standard of normality. "The normal man, is not a living, flesh and blood being, but an unnatural, imagined and imaginary prototype."[87] No real person could be completely normal, if abnormality meant what some experts said it did. Lacking it turned a man into "an automaton, with no weaknesses and no energy, without kindness or meanness, neither prodigal, generous, egotistical, or altruistic, neither passionate nor apathetic, gray as fog; a neuter like a hermaphrodite, as insubstantial as a myth."[88] Everyone, then, incorporated something of the abnormal and the degenerate, Padovan insisted. By this optic, abnormality constituted not a perversion but a property of normality.

For reasons best understood by examining contemporary conditions and values, the spotlight fell on misfits, scientists got to wield it, and its filters exposed the biological anomalies and social pressures at the root of difference. Their methods and their mind-set convinced investigators that they diagnosed real conditions and uncovered their plausible causes. Directed by their worries and expectations and constrained by what they took as given and by what they did not yet know, they scrutinized cases, discovered patterns, and refined nosologies and etiologies. They subjected their investigations and conclusions to rigorous empiricism and scorned sloppy, impressionistic research. Later techniques and procedures make theirs look elementary, and new discoveries—genes, among them—make their breakthroughs seem archaic, and sometimes arcane. Looking back, some theories (degeneration, for example) invite skepticism or derision; some disorders (hysteria, sexual inversion) charges of bias; certain policies (eugenics) condemnation.

Events also got in the way of their hypotheses as well as of their certainties; they dislodged values and hopes, and they took contemporary insights in unexpected, and sometimes unwelcome, directions. The First World War blasted their hard-thought amalgamation of chaos and progress and of disruptive and productive change. In its aftermath, the equation of personal happiness with work and of joy with self-abnegation lost its allure and legitimacy. So did reliance on the will to pull the self together. Jules Payot's confident claim in 1894 that individuals could take control of their lives took on quite a different meaning in the interwar years.[89] Using the tactics that doctors advocated for healthy living—suggestion, emotion, and discipline—fascism mobilized support and challenged liberal governments, successfully in the case of Italy and Germany.

Many of the specifics of what end-of-the-century medical and social scientists learned no longer apply, or some elements fade in importance, while others move to the forefront. Turn-of-the-century doctors extended the symptoms of epilepsy, and their successors cut them back. They associated fugue with numerous conditions, including epilepsy, hysteria, and neurasthenia. Still officially a disorder, it is not now a widely recognized one. What began as railway spine now lives large as posttraumatic stress disorder. During the First World War, neurasthenia disappeared into shell shock, and its other symptoms reappeared in disorders such as depression, hypochondria, and paranoia. Hysteria, too, diminished as physicians reallocated its properties to other disorders.

But not everything disappeared or took on new forms. Of the emphasis on the physical over the metaphysical, the association of truth with empiricism, and the role of the human sciences—new then, established now—much remains. The current understanding of personality, memory, willpower, and morality owes a good deal to late nineteenth-century thinking. When they explain deviants, people continue to look to family background, mental health records, and unusual circumstances rather than to perverse character. They check for signs of imbalance and maladjustment; they consider the possibility of developmental delays and glitches. Traces of thinking shaped 125 years ago also remain in the banal. The technical vocabulary deployed by turn-of-the-century scientists reappears in playground taunts and stadium slurs. Italian put-downs include "imbecile," "idiota," "cretino," and "deficiente," a few examples from a rich and inventive lexicon of insults. French use *bête* (beast), idiot, imbécile, and crétin for stupid, or stupidity; dérangé (deranged), détraqué (off track), among others, for the mad.

Comparing the aftermaths of the First and Second World Wars, J.B. Priestley remembered, "If you were born in 1894, as I was, you suddenly saw a great jagged crack in the looking glass. After that your mind could not escape from the idea of a world which ended in 1914 and another one that began about 1919 with a wilderness of smoke and fury, outside the sensible time, lying between them." A crack distorts the reflection, but it does not eliminate it.

Notes

Chapter 1

1   Jan Goldstein, *Console and Classify: The French Psychiatric Profession in the Nineteenth Century* (Chicago and London: University of Chicago Press, 1987, 2001) and Robert A. Nye, *Crime, Madness, & Politics in Modern France: The Medical Concept of National Decline* (Princeton, NJ: Princeton University Press, 1984).

2   Alberto De Bernardi, "Malattia mentale e trasformazioni sociali. La storia della follia," in *Follia, psichiatria, e società*, ed. Alberto De Bernardi (Milan: Franco Angeli Editore, 1982), 11–32.

3   Janet Oppenheim, *"Shattered Nerves": Doctors, Patients, and Depression in Victorian England* (New York: Oxford University Press, 1991), 285, 286.

4   Ian R. Dowbiggin, *Inheriting Madness: Professionalization and Psychiatric Knowledge in Nineteenth-Century France* (Berkeley: University of California Press, 1991), 5. Dowbiggin summarized the position in "Degeneration and Hereditarianism in French Mental Medicine, 1840–90," in *The Anatomy of Madness: Essays in the History of Psychiatry*, eds. W. F. Bynum, Roy Porter, and Michael Shepherd (New York: Tavistock Publications, 1985), 188–232. See also Jan Goldstein, "'Moral Contagion': A Professional Ideology of Medicine and Psychiatry in Eighteenth-and Nineteenth-Century France," in *Professions and the French State, 1700–1900*, ed. Gerald L. Geison (Philadelphia: University of Pennsylvania Press, 1984), 181–222.

5   Vincenzo Accattatis, introduction to Enrico Ferri, *Sociologia criminale* (Milan: Feltrinelli, 1979), 14.

6   Accattatis, introduction to Enrico Ferri, *Sociologia criminale*, 16.

7   Cesare Lombroso, *Criminal Man*, trans. and with a new introduction by Mary Gibson and Nicole Hahn Rafter (Durham and London: Duke University Press, 2006), 23.

8   Daniel Pick, *Faces of Degeneration: A European Disorder, c. 1848–c. 1918* (Cambridge: Cambridge University Press, 1989).

9   Pick, *Faces of Degeneration*, 54.

10   Pick, *Faces of Degeneration*, 56.

11   Pick, *Faces of Degeneration*, 119–20.

12   Pick, *Faces of Degeneration*, 111.

13   Martine Kaluszynski, *La République à l'épreuve du crime: la construction du crime comme object politique, 1880–1920* (Paris: Maison des sciences de l'homme, 2002), 70, http://halshs.archives-ouvertes.fr/halshs-00343187/.

14   Kaluszynski, *La République à l'épreuve du crime*, 14.

15   Dominique Kalifa, *Crime et culture au XIXe siècle* (Paris: Perrin, 2005), 10.

16   Mark S. Micale, "Jean-Martin Charcot and *les névroses traumatiques*: From Medicine to Culture in French Trauma Theory of the Late Nineteenth Century," in *Traumatic Pasts: History, Psychiatry, and Trauma in the Modern Age, 1870–1930*, eds. Mark Micale and Paul Lerner (Cambridge: Cambridge University Press, 2001), 138.

17   Micale, "Jean-Martin Charcot and *les névroses traumatiques*," 138.

18   Michel Foucault, *The Archeology of Knowledge* and *The Discourse on Language*, trans. A. M. Sheridan Smith (New York: Pantheon Books, c. 1972) and *The Order of Things: An Archeology of the Human Sciences* (New York: Vintage Books, 1994, c. 1970).

19   Ian Hacking, *Mad Travelers: Reflections on the Reality of Transient Mental Illness* (Charlottesville and London: University Press of Virginia, 1998). See Lectures 3 and 4.

20   Jean-François Wagniart, *Le vagabond à la fin du XIXe siècle* (Paris: Belin, 1999); Bruno P. F. Wanrooij, *Storia del pudore: La questione sessuale in Italia, 1860–1940* (Venice: Marsilio Editori, 1990); Ann Jefferson, *Genius in France: An Idea and Its Uses* (Princeton, NJ: Princeton University Press, 2015).

21   David Forgacs, *Italy's Margins: Social Exclusion and Nation Formation since 1861* (Cambridge: Cambridge University Press, 2014).

22   Roy Porter, *Madness: A Brief History* (Oxford: Oxford University Press, 2002); Roy Porter, ed., *The Cambridge History of Medicine* (New York: Cambridge University Press, 2006); Edward Shorter, *A History of Psychiatry: From the Era of the Asylum to the Age of Prozac* (New York: John Wiley & Sons, Inc., 1997).

23   Enzo Bartocci, *Le politiche sociali nell'Italia liberale (1861–1919)* (Rome: Donzelli Editore, 1999) and Chiara Beccalossi, *Female Sexual Inversion: Same-Sex Desires in Italian and British Sexology, c. 1870–1920* (Basingstoke: Palgrave Macmillan, 2012).

24   Mary Gibson, *Born to Crime: Cesare Lombroso and the Origins of Biological Criminology* (Westport, CT: Praeger, 2002), 3.

25   Gibson, *Born to Crime*, 3.

26   Diomede Carito, *La Neurastenia nella vita e nel pensiero moderno: studio clinico e sociale* (Naples: Detken & Rocholl, 1907), 222–23.

27   Cesare Lombroso, *Delitti vecchi e delitti nuovi* (Turin: Fratelli Bocca, 1902), 316.

28   Pasquale Penta, *Pazzia e società* (Milan: Francesco Vallardi, [1893]), 45. He specified that asylums treated 17,566 in 1836; 18,367 in 1841; 46,357 in 1851; 84,181 in 1861; 93,952 in 1869.

29   Penta, *Pazzia e società*, 46, refers to Andrea Verga for the Italian figures, with no citation. Verga also recorded 54.14 in 1877; 61.25 in 1880; 61.75 in 1883.

30   Egisto De Nigris, *La Neurastenia* (Milan: Francesco Vallardi, 1896?), 6.

31   Paul-Émile Lévy, *L'éducation rationnelle de la volonté: son emploi thérapeutique*, 7th ed. (Paris: Félix Alcan, 1909), 147.

32   Henri Joly, *La France criminelle* (Paris: Librairie Léopold Cerf, 1889), 3, referring to the period from 1825 to 1888 and 11 for France.

33   Joly recorded an increase in crimes against morality between 1838 and 1888, 18. Illicit begging and vagrancy multiplied by 430 percent in the same period, 20.

34   Alfredo Niceforo, *Sull'aumento della delinquenza* (Rome, 1899), review by Cesare Lombroso in *Archivio di psichiatria, scienze penali ed antropologia criminale* 20 (1899): 646.

35   L. Roncoroni, "Influenza del sesso sulla criminalità in Italia," *Archivio di psichiatria, scienze penali ed antropologia criminale* 14 (1893): 1–14, 11.

36   Robin Walz, *Pulp Surrealism: Insolent Popular Culture in Early Twentieth-Century Paris* (Berkeley: University of California Press, 2000).

37   He was hung November 15, 1892. Angus McLaren, *A Prescription for Murder: The Victorian Serial Killings of Dr. Thomas Neill Cream* (Chicago: University of Chicago Press, 1993).

38   See Kalifa, *Crime*.

39 Napoleone Colajanni, *La sociologia criminale*, 2 vols. (Catania: Filippo Tropea, 1889), vol. 2, 478–79.

40 Colajanni, *La sociologia criminale,* vol. 2, 479. Of the 32,943 thefts prosecuted in the first half of 1882 in Paris, 57 percent were committed by vagrants. Of the 6,350 vagrants arrested in that period, 94 percent were repeaters, and of the 250 recidivists convicted at least five times, almost all of them began as vagrants, he reported.

41 Benjamin Ball, *La folie érotique* (Paris: L'Harmattan, 2001), 138. First edition was published in 1888.

42 Gabriel Tarde, *La criminalité comparée*, 7th ed. (Paris: Félix Alcan, 1910), 173. Only Norway escaped the pattern, he said. In France, the suicide rate increased 162 percent over the half century between 1838 and 1888, Henri Joly noted. Joly, *La France criminelle*, 20.

43 Albert Bournet, *De la criminalité en France et en Italie: étude médico-légale* (Paris: Librairie J.-B. Baillière et fils, 1884), 76–79. He reports that Italy, along with Spain and Russia, registered the lowest numbers. He dedicated the study to his teacher, the forensic doctor and criminologist Alexandre Lacassagne.

44 Ty Geltmaker, *Tired of Living: Suicide in Italy from National Unification to World War I, 1860-1915* (New York: Peter Lang, 2002), 2. He reviews contemporary statistics, concluding that they recorded a precipitous rise, 33–38.

45 Christoper Duggan, *The Force of Destiny: A History of Italy since 1796* (London: Allen Lane, 2007), 264.

46 Illiterate and poor males received the right to vote, almost tripling the electorate (from 3 million to 8.65 million). About half a million males did not have the vote. Italian women received the vote in 1945.

47 Bénédict Augustin Morel, *Traité des dégénérescences physiques, intellectuelles et morales de l'espèce humaine* (Paris: J.-B. Baillière, 1857; repr., New York: Arno Press, 1976), 125.

48 Morel, *Traité des dégénérescences physiques, intellectuelles et morales de l'espèce humaine,* 683.

49 Ribot received the agrégation from the École Normale Supérieure in 1866, his doctorate from the Sorbonne in 1873 with a thesis on heredity, and the appointment to the chair in 1889. He held that post until 1901.

50 Virginio Oddone, "La 'scuola' lombrosiana," in *La scienza e la colpa: crimini, criminali, criminologi: Un volto dell'Ottocento*, ed. Umberto Levra (Milan: Electa Editrice, 1985), 240. From 1900 to 1903 the title was Archives of Psychiatry, Penal Sciences and Criminal Anthropology.

51 Oddone, "La 'scuola' lombrosiana," 240.

52 *Archivio di psichiatria, antropologia criminale e scienze penali per servire allo studio dell'uomo alienato e delinquente*, vol. 21, fasc. I–II, 1900.

53 Other examples include *Annales médico-psychologiques* (The Bulletin of the Medico-Psychological Society), *Archivio delle psicopatie sessuali: Rivista quindicinale di psicologia, psicopatologia umana e comparata di medicina legale e de psichiatria forense ad uso dei medici, magistrati ed avvocati* (Archives of Sexual Psychopathologies: Biweekly Review of Psychology, Human and Comparative Psychopathology, Legal Medicine and Forensic Psychiatry for the Use of Doctors, Judges, and Lawyers), and *La Scuola Positiva* (The Positivist School).

54 *Revue philosophique de France et de l'étranger* 1 (January 1, 1876): 2.

55 For example, Series 1 included: C. Lombroso, *L'Uomo delinquente* (several editions); R. Garofalo, *Criminologia*, 2nd ed. (Turin: Fratelli Bocca, 1889), C. Lombroso, *L'Uomo di genio*, 6th ed. (Turin: Fratelli Bocca, 1894), S. Tonnino, *Le epilessie* (Turin: Fratelli Bocca, 1890); Silvio Venturi, *Le Degenerazioni psico-sessuali* (Turin: Fratelli Bocca, 1892); E. Ferri, *Omicidio-suicidio* (Turin: Fratelli Bocca, 1885); G. Mingazzini, *Il cervello in relazione coi fenomeni psichici* (Turin: Fratelli Bocca, 1895). Series 2 (some in the first series were also in the second) included G. Campili, *Il grande ipnotismo* (Turin: Fratelli Bocca, 1886); G. Ferrero, *I simboli* (Turin: Fratelli Bocca, 1893); Series 3 included R. Krafft-Ebing, *Le psicopatie sessuali* (Turin: Fratelli Bocca, 1889), M. A. Raffalovich, *L'uranismo: inversione sessuale* (Turin: Fratelli Bocca, 1896), and M. Nordau, *Degenerazione*, 2nd ed. (Turin: Fratelli Bocca, 1896).

56 See, for example, Harry Oosterhuis, "Richard von Krafft-Ebing's 'Step-Children of Nature': Psychiatry and the Making of Homosexual Identity," in *Science and Homosexualities*, ed. Vernon A. Rosario (New York: Routledge, 1997), 67–88.

57 Carlo Ginzburg, *The Night Battles: Witchcraft and Agrarian Cults in the Sixteenth and Seventeenth Centuries*, trans. John and Anne Tedeschi (New York: Penguin Books, 1985, c1966).

58 Henri-Barthélemy Géhin, *Contribution à l'étude de l'automatisme ambulatoire ou vagabondage impulsif* (Bordeaux: Imprimerie Centrale A. de Lanefranque, 1892), 70–75. Voisin's case came from his *Leçons sur l'hystérie* (Paris, 1891).

59 Porter, *Madness: A Brief History*, 62.

60 Porter, 63.

Chapter 2

1 Cesare Lombroso, *Genio e degenerazione: nuovi studi e nuove battaglie*, 2nd ed. (Milan: Remo Sandron, 1907), 270.

2 Le Dr [Edouard] Toulouse, *Emile Zola* (Paris: Ernest Flammarion, 1896), 39.

3 Michael Cowan, *Cult of the Will: Nervousness and German Modernity* (University Park: Pennsylvania State University Press, 2008).

4 Anson Rabinbach, *The Human Motor: Energy, Fatigue, and the Origins of Modernity* (Berkeley and Los Angeles: University of California Press, 1992).

5 Albert Regnard, "Génie et folie," *Annales médico-psychologiques*, 8th series, 7 (January–February 1898): 10–34; 7 (March–April 1898): 204–28; 9 (January–February 1899): 22–42; 9 (May–June 1899): 379–419, 21.

6 Eugenio Tanzi, *Trattato delle malattie mentali* (Milan: Società Editrice Libraria, 1905), 51.

7 Antonello La Vergata, "Lombroso e la degenerazione," in *Cesare Lombroso. Gli scienziati e la nuova Italia*, ed. Silvano Montaldo (Bologna: Il Mulino, 2010), 93.

8 Havelock Ellis, *A Study of British Genius*, revised and enlarged (London: Constable and Company, 1927), 7.

9 Max Nordau, *Psycho-physiologie du génie et du talent*, trans. Auguste Dietrich (Paris: Félix Alcan, 1897), 159.

10 Nordau, *Psycho-physiologie du génie et du talent*, 164.

11 Adolfo Padovan, *Che cosa è il genio?* 2nd ed. (Milan: Ulrico Hoepli, 1907), 28.

12 Giovanni Bovio, *Il genio* (Milan: Fratelli Treves, 1890), 32. Italics his. See also his *Il genio: un capitolo di psicologia* (Milan: Fratelli Treves, 1899).

13 Giuseppe Sergi, "Gli uomini di genio," *Nuova antologia*, 4th series, 85 (February 1, 1900): 405–32, 423.

14 Cesare Lombroso, "La pazzia ed il genio in Cristoforo Colombo," *Archivio di psichiatria, scienze penali ed antropologia criminale* 21 (1900): 29–48, 46.

15 Lombroso, "La pazzia ed il genio in Cristoforo Colombo," 48.

16 Adolfo Padovan, *I figli della gloria*, 2nd ed. (Milan: Ulrico Hoepli, 1906), 285.

17 Padovan, *I figli della gloria*, 287.

18 Padovan, *I figli della gloria*, 118.

19 J[acques-Joseph] Moreau (de Tours), *La psychologie morbide dans ses rapports avec la philosophie de l'histoire ou de l'influence des névropathies sur le dynamisme intellectuel* (Paris: Librairie Victor Masson, 1859), 8.

20 Moreau, *Psychologie*, 10.

21 Moreau, *Psychologie*, 33.

22 Moreau, *De la folie raisonnante envisagée sous le point de vue médico-légal* (Paris: Lacour et Compagnie, 1840), 49–50.

23 Lombroso, *L'Uomo di genio*, 6th ed. (Turin: Fratelli Bocca, 1894), xiii.

24 Lombroso, *The Man of Genius* (London: Charles Scribner's Sons, 1891), vii.

25 Lombroso, *L'Uomo di genio*, xxii.

26 Lombroso, *L'Uomo di genio*, 64–67.

27 Lombroso, *L'Uomo di genio*, 149.

28 Lombroso, *L'Uomo di genio*, 95.

29 Lombroso, *Genio e degenerazione*, 116.

30 Lombroso, *The Man of Genius*, 354–58.

31 Lombroso, *Genio e degenerazione*, 337.

32 Lombroso, *Genio e degenerazione*, 133.

33 Lombroso, *L'Uomo di genio*, 24.

34 Lombroso, *L'Uomo di genio*, 7–11.

35 Lombroso, *L'Uomo di genio*, 13–21.

36 Lombroso, *L'Uomo di genio*, 218–19.

37 Lombroso, *Genio e degenerazione*, 270.

38 Lombroso, *Genio e degenerazione*, 18–22.

39 Lombroso, *Genio e degenerazione*, xv.

40 Lombroso, *Genio e degenerazione*, 24.

41 Toulouse, *Emile Zola*, 49.

42 A. G. Bianchi, *La patologia del genio e gli scienziati italiani: inchiesta a proposito del caso de Guy de Maupassant* (Milan: Max Kantorowicz, 1892), 15. Many Italian psychiatrists supported Lombroso and many challenged him.

43 Bianchi, *La patologia del genio e gli scienziati italiani,* 33–34. See also Silvio Tonnini, an expert on epilepsies, who emphasized that epilepsy often accompanied genius, because the two asymmetries mirrored each other so well.

44 Sergi, "Gli uomini di genio," 418–19.

45 Augusto Tebaldi, *Napoleone: una pagina storico-psicologica del genio* (Padua: Angelo Draghi, 1895), 33.

46 Tebaldi, *Napoleone*, 29.

47 Tebaldi, *Napoleone*, 31.

48 Tebaldi, *Napoleone*, 124.

49 Tebaldi, *Napoleone*, 160.

50 Tebaldi, *Napoleone,* 164.

51 Lombroso, *Genio e degenerazione*, 116.

52 Lombroso, *Genio e degenerazione*, 118–32.
53 Lombroso, *Genio e degenerazione*, 132.
54 Rinaldo Nazzari, "L'uomo di genio per gli psichiatri e gli antropologi," *Rivista filosofica* 6 (November–December 1903): 628–63, focuses on Lombroso's overly broad definition.
55 Padovan, *Che cosa è il genio?*, 72.
56 Paolo Mantegazza, *Che cosa è il genio?* (Florence: Salvadore Landi, 1907), 3.
57 Toulouse, *Emile Zola*, 20.
58 Giovanni Gallerani, *Fisiologia del genio: analisi del prodotto geniale* (Bari: Pasquale De Ganosa, 1929), 19. First published by the Tipografia Savino Camerino in 1889. President of the Fascist Center of Culture and Professor at the University Adriatica "Benito Mussolini," he dedicated the 1929 edition to Mussolini.
59 Gallerani, *Fisiologia del genio*, 29.
60 Gallerani, *Fisiologia del genio*, 26–28, "perfection"; 14, "superior structure"; 16, "exquisite operation."
61 Bovio, *Il genio: un capitolo*, 78.
62 Bovio, *Il genio: un capitolo*, 206.
63 Bovio, *Il genio: un capitolo*, 149.
64 Bovio, *Il genio: un capitolo*, 162.
65 Regnard, "Génie et folie," vol. 7, 10–11.
66 Regnard, "Génie et folie," vol. 7, 13.
67 Regnard, "Génie et folie," vol. 9, 22–23.
68 Regnard, "Génie et folie," vol. 9, 403.
69 Regnard, "Génie et folie," vol. 9, 22–23.
70 Regnard, "Génie et folie," vol. 9, 384.
71 Regnard, "Génie et folie," vol. 9, 388–89.
72 Regnard, "Génie et folie," vol. 9, 416.
73 Toulouse, *Emile Zola*, 52.
74 Toulouse, *Emile Zola*, 54.
75 Toulouse, *Emile Zola*, 279.
76 Toulouse, *Emile Zola*, 166.
77 Toulouse, *Emile Zola*, 280.
78 Lombroso, *Genio e degenerazione*, 137–39.
79 Lombroso, *Genio e degenerazione*, 140–51.
80 Lombroso, *Genio e degenerazione*, 156.
81 Padovan, "Il genio," *Rivista d'Italia* 8 (January 1905): 117–20.
82 Padovan, *Che cosa è il genio?*, 112.
83 Padovan, *Che cosa è il genio?*, 65–69, 106.
84 Ellis received his medical degree in 1889 but practiced medicine only briefly.
85 Ellis, *A Study of British Genius*, 169. About 4.2 percent of his sample experienced mental illness compared to 1–2 percent of the general population. See also 172.
86 Ellis, *A Study of British Genius*, 207–8.
87 Sergi, "Gli uomini di genio," 429.
88 Lombroso, *Genio e degenerazione*, 270.
89 Gallerani, *Fisiologia del genio*, 16, 14.
90 Regnard, "Génie et folie," vol. 9, 22–23.
91 Bovio, *Il genio: un capitolo*, 49.
92 Padovan, *Le origini del genio* (Milan: Ulrico Hoepli, 1909).
93 Padovan, *Che cosa è il genio?* 43. That phrase also followed the title of the book *Che cosa è il genio?* in small italics.

94 Padovan, "Il genio," 118.

95 Padovan, *Che cosa è il genio?*, 44, 28.

96 Nazzari, "L'uomo di genio per gli psychiatri e gli antropologi," 629, summarizes his thesis: "genius [is] a degenerative psychosis and more exactly *an irritation of the cortex of the epileptic type, which changes* (at the moment of the seizure) *into psychic epilepsy.*" Italics his.

97 G[iuseppe] Antonini, "Donizetti," *Archivio di psichiatria, scienze penali, ed antropologia criminale* 21 (1900): 595–600, 597.

98 Antonini, "Donizetti," 598.

99 Lombroso, *L'Uomo di genio*, xxi.

100 Nordau, *Psycho-physiologie du génie et du talent*, 55.

101 Ellis, *A Study of British Genius*, 162.

102 Padovan, *Le origini del genio*, 76, 79.

103 Padovan, *Le origini del genio*, 51–53, 61.

104 Padovan, *Che cosa è il genio?*, 77, 124.

105 Bovio, *Il genio: un capitolo*, 49.

106 Bovio, *Il genio: un capitolo*, 128.

107 Bovio, *Il genio: un capitolo*, 137.

108 Lombroso, *L'Uomo di genio*, 167–70.

109 Lombroso, *L'Uomo di genio*, 179–95.

110 Lombroso, *L'Uomo di genio*, 229.

111 Ellis, *A Study of British Genius*, 66–80, 121–23, 92–101, 196.

112 Ellis, *A Study of British Genius*, 154.

113 Ellis, *A Study of British Genius*, 81, 83–84.

114 Ellis, *A Study of British Genius*, 212.

115 Valeria Paola Babini, *La questione dei frenastenici: alle origini della psicologia scientifica in Italia (1870–1910)* (Milan: FrancoAngeli, 1996), 9. Verga also founded the first specialized psychology review, *Archivio italiano per le malattie nervose e più particolarmente per le alienazioni mentali*, 12.

116 Sergi, "Gli uomini di genio," 414, says there was no debate on the matter.

117 B[enjamin] Ball, *Leçons sur les maladies mentales*, 2nd ed. (Paris: Asselin and Houzeau, 1890).

118 Ball, *Leçons sur les maladies mentales*, 813–14.

119 Ball, *Leçons sur les maladies mentales*, 826.

120 Paul Sollier, *L'Idiotie et l'imbécilité au point de vue nosographique* (Evreux: Imprimerie de Charles Hérissey, 1894), 3. Sollier was a student of Jean-Martin Charcot.

121 Sollier, *L'Idiotie et l'imbécilité au point de vue nosographique*, 5.

122 Sollier, *L'Idiotie et l'imbécilité au point de vue nosographique*, 2.

123 Sante de Sanctis, "Sui criteri e metodi per l'educabilità dei deficienti e dei dementi," *Rivista sperimentale di freniatria* 28 (1902): 354–409, 365–66. He identified three categories: major motor and minor mental impairment; minor motor and major mental impairment, and major impairment in both areas.

124 Ball, *Leçons sur les maladies mentales*, 832.

125 Ball, *Leçons sur les maladies mentales*, 833–35.

126 Ball, *Leçons sur les maladies mentales*, 840–41.

127 Morel, *Traité des dégénérescences physiques, intellectuelles et morales de l'espèce humaine*, 333–34.

128 G. B. Pellizzi, "Idiozia ed epilessia," *Archivio di psichiatria, scienze penali, ed antropologia criminale* 21 (1900): 409–25, 417–18.

129 Pellizzi, "Idiozia ed epilessia," 421–22, 428.

130 Moreau, *Psychologie*, 109.

131 Regnard, "Génie et folie," vol. 9, 418.

132 Sergi, "Gli uomini di genio," 418.

133 Ellis, *A Study of British Genius*, 206–7.

134 Lombroso, *L'Uomo di genio*, xvii.

135 Lombroso, *Genio e degenerazione*, 13–14.

136 Enrico Ferri, "Gli anormali," *La Scuola Positiva* 10 (June 1900): 321–33, 326. See also *I delinquenti nell'arte ed altre conferenze*, 2nd ed. (Turin: Unione Tipografico-Editrice Torinese, 1926).

137 Ferri, "Gli anormali," 326. See also Susan A. Ashley, "Marginal People: Degeneration and Genius," in *Proceedings of the Western Society for French History: Selected Papers*, ed. Barry Rothaus (Boulder CO: University Press of Colorado, (1997).

138 Ferri, "Gli anormali," 329–30.

139 Padovan, "Il genio," 120.

140 Venturi, *Le Degenerazioni psico-sessuali*, 419.

Chapter 3

1 Ball, *Leçons sur les maladies mentales*, 976.

2 Th[éodule-Armand] Ribot, *Les maladies de la volonté*, 32nd ed. (Paris: Librairie Félix Alcan, 1920), 177.

3 See W. F. Bynum, "The Nervous Patient in Eighteenth-and Nineteenth-Century Britain: The Psychiatric Origins of British Neurology," in *The Anatomy of Madness: Essays in the History of Psychiatry*, eds. W. F. Bynum, Roy Porter, and Michael Shepherd (New York: Tavistock Publications, 1985), 96. The neurological profession emerged in 1870–1890 in London hospitals. Jan Goldstein presents a particularly detailed and convincing analysis of the development of French psychiatry in *Console and Classify: The French Psychiatric Profession in the Nineteenth Century*. See also Ian Dowbiggin, "Degeneration and Hereditarianism in French Mental Medicine, 1840–90," in Bynum et al., on the establishment of two chairs in the Faculty of Medicine of Paris, one for mental diseases and one for diseases of the nervous system, 188–232.

4 Porter, *Madness: A Brief History*, 62.

5 *Archivio italiano per le malatie* [sic] *nervose e più particolarmente per le alienazioni mentali* 12 (1875): 244. Unsigned and untitled news item.

6 Lombroso, *Delitti vecchi e delitti nuovi*, 316.

7 Penta, *Pazzia e società*, 43. See also Ball, *Leçons sur les maladies mentales*, 372, who noted "an incontestable increase in Europe."

8 Penta, *Pazzia e società*, 44. He counted the insane, not the intellectually disabled. Other figures were 17.65 in Sweden; 9.71 in the United States; 9.27 in Belgium. He offered no source for the statistics.

9 Ball, *Leçons sur les maladies mentales*, 146–47.

10 Ball, *Leçons sur les maladies mentales*, 149.

11 Ball, *Leçons sur les maladies mentales*, 150.

12 Ball, *Leçons sur les maladies mentales*, 153.

13 Ball, *Leçons sur les maladies mentales*, 144.

14 Luigi Brajon, *Intorno alla follia morale: considerazioni medico-psicologiche* (Bologna: Tipografia Archivescovile, 1888), 7.

15 Francesco Bini, *Della pazzia morale in relazione alle esigenze sociali ed umanitarie* (Milan: Stabilmento dei Fratelli Rechiedei, 1881), 5.

16 See Michel Collée and Claude Quétel, *Histoire des maladies mentales* (Paris: Presses Universitaires de France, 1987), 69–76; Valeria Paola Babini, "La responsabilità nelle malattie mentali," in *Tra sapere e potere: la psichiatria nella seconda metà dell'Ottocento*, eds. Valeria Paola Babini, Maurizia Cotti, Fernanda Menuz, and Annamaria Tagliavini (Bologna: Il Mulino, 1982), 135–98; and Porter, *Madness: A Brief History*, 134–37.

17 See Robert Marmier, *Les perversions instinctives: origines et débuts de cette notion* (Paris: Librairie Médicale et Scientifique, 1912), 14–29.

18 By 1912, Marmier said the concept of moral insanity was "now almost universally admitted," 83. See also Ulysse Trélat's influential study of reasoning insanity. It described variants and provided cases used by others in diagnosis. *La folie lucide* (Paris: Frénésie Editions, 1988). Reprint of his 1861 edition entitled *La folie lucide étudiée et considérée au point de vue de la famille et de la société* (Paris: Adrien Delahaye, 1861).

19 Cesare Agostini, *Manuale de psichiatria per uso degli studenti e dei medici*, 3rd ed. (Milan: Dottor Francesco Vallardi, 1908), 369.

20 E[nrico] Morselli and Cesare Lombroso, "Epilessia larvata-pazzia morale," *Archivio di psichiatria, scienze penali ed antropologia criminale* 6 (1885): 29–43.

21 Eugenio Tanzi and Ernesto Lugaro, *Trattato delle malattie mentali*, 2nd ed., vol. 1 (Milan: Società Editrice Libraria, 1914), 377.

22 Bini, *Della pazzia morale in relazione alle esigenze sociali ed umanitarie*, 24.

23 Agostini, *Manuale de psichiatria per uso degli studenti e dei medici*, 365.

24 A. Tamburini and G. Guicciardi, "Ulteriori studi su un caso di imbecillità morale," *Rivista Sperimentale di Freniatria e di Medicina Legale* 13 (1887): 163, 170.

25 Tamburini and Guicciardi, "Ulteriori studi su un caso di imbecillità morale," 179.

26 Leonardo Cognetti di Martiis, *Pazzia morale, simulazione, mania* (Rome: Vochera Enrico, 1894), 24.

27 Ball, *Leçons sur les maladies mentales*, 154.

28 Jules Falret, *De la folie raisonnante ou folie morale: programme de questions à étudier* (Paris: E. Martinet, 1866), 5–8; and Jules Falret, *De la folie raisonnante ou folie morale: Réponse à M. Delasiauve* (Paris: E. Martinet, 1867), 1–2.

29 Falret, *De la folie raisonnante: Réponse*, 4.

30 Falret, *De la folie raisonnante: Réponse*, 4.

31 Falret, *De la folie raisonnante: Programme*, 20–37.

32 Falret, *De la folie raisonnante: Réponse*, 10–11.

33 Ernesto Bonvecchiato, *A proposito di un processo scandaloso: semi-imbecilli, mattoidi e folli morali* (Venice: C. Ferrari alla Posta, 1884), 83.

34 See also Tanzi and Lugaro, *Trattato delle malattie mentali*, 2nd ed., vol. 2, 737, who said it was a defect, not a sickness, one distinct from idiocy and insanity.

35 C[elso] Sighicelli and R[uggero] Tambroni, "Pazzia morale ed epilessia," *Rivista sperimentale di freniatria e de medicina legale* 13 (1887): 249–78, 249; and Lorenzo Ellero, *La psichiatria, la libertà morale e la responsabilità penale* (Padova: Angelo Draghi Editore, 1885), 156–57. Babini, in Babini et al., identifies this position with Arrigo Tamassia (1848–1917), a specialist in forensic medicine, and says it was the prevalent one.

36 Bini, *Della pazzia morale in relazione alle esigenze sociali ed umanitarie*, 29.
   He thought this was true especially of "moral imbecility" or the absence of moral faculties.

37 V[alentin] Magnan, *Leçons cliniques sur les maladies mentales* (Paris: Félix Alcan, 1897); Brajon, *Intorno alla follia morale*, 4; Eugenio Tanzi and Ernesto Lugaro, *Malattie mentali*, 3rd ed., vol. 1 (Milan: Società Editrice-Libraria, 1923), 377, for example.

38 Cesare Lombroso, *Atti del Quinto Congresso della Società Freniatrica Italiana*, Siena, September 19–25, 1886 (Milan: Fratelli Rechiedei, 1887), 224.

39 See Lombroso, "Identità dell'epilessia colla pazzia morale e delinquenza congenita," *Archivio di psichiatria, scienze penali, ed antropologia criminale* 6 (1885): 1–28, 27.

40 Agostini, *Manuale de psichiatria per uso degli studenti e dei medici*, 368–70.

41 Agostini, *Manuale de psichiatria per uso degli studenti e dei medici*, 368–69.

42 Lombroso, "Identità dell'epilessia colla pazzia morale e delinquenza congenita," 1–2, 11–13.

43 Sighicelli and Tambroni, "Pazzia morale ed epilessia," 271.

44 Sighicelli and Tambroni, "Pazzia morale ed epilessia," 272.

45 Sighicelli and Tambroni, "Pazzia morale ed epilessia," 277.

46 Lombroso, "Identità dell'epilessia colla pazzia morale e delinquenza congenita," 18–19. Refers in particular to Magnan, *Leçons sur l'épilepsie*, 1882, to Falret, *État mental des épileptiques*, 1861, and to Voisin, *Les épilepsies*.

47 Lombroso, "Identità dell'epilessia colla pazzia morale e delinquenza congenita," 26.

48 Morselli and Lombroso, "Epilessia larvata-pazzia morale," 43.

49 Lombroso, *Atti del Quinto Congresso*, 232. Tamburini made the point at the meeting.

50 See, for example, Ball, *Leçons sur les maladies mentales*, 144–45, who argued that organic immorality in the gravest cases could lead to murder and suicide.

51 Enrico Ferri, *L'omicida nella psicologia e nella psicopatologia criminale*, 2nd ed. and *L'omicidio-suicidio: responsabilità giuridica*, 5th ed. (Turin: Unione Tipografico-Editrice Torinese, 1925).

52 E[ugène] Billod, "Maladies de la volonté," *Annales médico-psychologiques* 10 (September 1847): 170–202, 180.

53 Billod, "Maladies de la volonté," 183.

54 Billod, "Maladies de la volonté," *Annales médico-psychologiques* 10 (July 1847): 15–35, 22.

55 Ribot, *Les maladies de la volonté* and Jules Payot, *L'éducation de la volonté*, 29th ed. (Paris: Félix Alcan, 1908).

56 Henry Maudsley, *Body and Will Being an Essay Concerning Will in Its Metaphysical, Physiological, and Pathological Aspects* (New York: D. Appleton and Company, 1884). See also Dominique-Joseph-Bertrand Rivière, *Contribution à l'étude clinique des aboulies et principalement de l'aboulie neurasthénique* (Paris: Henri Jouve, 1891). He provides a chronology of the discovery of abulia.

57 Fr[édéric] Paulhan, *La volonté* (Paris: Octave Doin, Editeur, 1903), 274.

58 Ribot, *Les maladies de la volonté*, 49.

59 See also V[ictor] Bourdin, "De l'impulsion," *Annales médico psychologiques* 54 (March 1896): 280.

60 Ribot, *Les maladies de la volonté*, 54.

61 Pierre Janet, *Névroses et idées fixes*, vol. 1, *Études expérimentales sur les troubles de la volonté, de l'attention, de la mémoire, sur les émotions, les idées obsédantes et leur traitement* (Paris: Félix Alcan, 1898), 2.

62 Janet, *Névroses et idées fixes*, 11–13, 36–37, 68.

63 See Georges Dequidt, *A propos d'un cas d'aboulie: réflexions cliniques et pathogéniques* (Paris: Henri Jouve, 1908), 11, for example. He labeled problems with execution "apraxie" and with decision making a form of "aboulie."

64 Ribot, *Les maladies de la volonté*, 63.

65 Ribot, *Les maladies de la volonté*, 77.

66 Ribot, *Les maladies de la volonté*, 128–38.

67 Lévy, *L'éducation rationnelle de la volonté*, 147.

68 Payot, *L'éducation de la volonté*, 88. See also Paulhan, *La volonté*, 112.

69 J[ules] Dallemagne, *Physiologie de la volonté* (Paris: Masson, [1898]), 17, and Ribot, *Les maladies de la volonté*, 3.

70 Billod, "Maladies de la volonté," 10 (July 1847): 22, 24. He combined will and willing in a way that doctors did not fifty years later. See also Dallemagne, *Physiologie de la volonté*, 13 who refers to the "je ne sais quoi" but does not see it as a separate faculty.

71 Dallemagne, *Physiologie de la volonté*, 67. See also Bourdin, "De l'impulsion," 219–20, who contended that not all willed acts are conscious and not all conscious acts are willed.

72 Paulhan, *La volonté*, 265 (quote) and 132–40.

73 In addition to Ribot and Dallemagne, Paulhan, *La volonté*, 24–25, 27–28, 167 used images of linked pieces. Barbara Tizard, "Theories of Brain Localization from Flourens to Lashley," *Medical History* 3 (1959): 138–40, emphasizes that the idea of the brain as composed of elementary particles interacting to perform complex functions constituted an important shift in perception.

74 Dallemagne, *Physiologie de la volonté*, 38.

75 Janet, *Névroses et idées fixes*, 13, 40–48. See also Paulhan, *La volonté*, 168. Ribot emphasized that volition drew together the layers of will, working out the conflicts among reflexes, appetites, desires, and ideas, 154.

76 Dallemagne, *Physiologie de la volonté*, 32, 37.

77 Maudsley, *Body and Will Being an Essay Concerning Will in Its Metaphysical, Physiological, and Pathological Aspects*, 114. Porter, *Madness: A Brief History*, 148, called Maudsley a "gloomy genius."

78 Leonardo Bianchi, *Trattato di psichiatria ad uso dei medici e degli studenti* (Naples: V. Pasquale, 1905), 370.

79 Alexander Bain, "The Feelings and the Will Viewed Physiologically," *The Fortnightly Review* 3 (1866): 578.

80 Ribot, *Les maladies de la volonté*, 87.

81 Ribot, *Les maladies de la volonté*, 155, referring to Hughlings Jackson, *Clinical and Physiological Researches on the Nervous System* (London: J. and A. Churchill, 1875), as the first to note the reverse process of disintegration. See also Tanzi and Lugaro, *Malattie Mentali*, 3rd ed., vol. 1, 375.

82 Ribot, *Les maladies de la volonté*, 123.

83 Janet, *Névroses et idées fixes*, 3. See also Paul Lapie, *Logique de la volonté* (Paris: Félix Alcan, 1902), 306–10, for an assessment of the case.

84 Billod, "Maladies de la volonté," 10 (September 1847), 173.

85 Ribot, *Les maladies de la volonté*, 53.

86 Ribot, *Les maladies de la volonté*, 173. Bianchi, *Trattato di psichiatria ad uso dei medici e degli studenti*, 366, argued that the richest and most complex circuits of the will produced the heroes of humanity.

87 Billod, "Maladies de la volonté," 10 (July 1847), 23.

88   Ribot, *Les maladies de la volonté*, 54.
89   Tanzi and Lugaro, *Malattie mentali*, 3rd ed., vol. 1, 420 and Paulhan, *La volonté*, 112. See also Payot, *L'éducation de la volonté*, 88.
90   Billod, "Maladies de la volonté," 10 (September 1847), 181; Janet, *Névroses et idées fixes*, 56–65.
91   Rivière, *Contribution à l'étude clinique des aboulies et principalement de l'aboulie neurasthénique*, 105–6.
92   Payot, *L'éducation de la volonté*, 172. See also 87–88, 154.
93   Lévy, *L'éducation rationnelle de la volonté*, 119–45.
94   Ball, *Leçons sur les maladies mentales*, 38.
95   Ellero, *La psichiatria, la libertà morale e la responsabilità penale*, 37.
96   Henry Maudsley, *The Pathology of Mind*, 3rd ed. of pt. 2 of *Physiology and Pathology of Mind* (London: Macmillan, 1879), 107.
97   Laurent Sueur, "La fragile limite entre le normal et l'anormal: lorsque les psychiatres français essayaient, au XIXe siècle, de reconnâitre la folie," *Revue historique* 292 (1994): 31–51, discusses the difficulties psychiatrists encountered in defining mental illness.
98   Gilbert Ballet, *Leçons de clinique médicale: psychoses et affections nerveuses* (Paris: Octave Doin, 1897), 12–13. The articles in J[ulien] Bogousslavsky, ed. *Following Charcot: A Forgotten History of Neurology and Psychiatry*. Frontiers of Neurology and Neuroscience, vol. 29. Basel: Karger, 2011, work out distinctions between neurology, psychology, and psychiatry. With boundaries still loose, neuropsychiatry applied to scientists such as Ballet who applied neurology to psychology.
99   Claudio Pogliano, "Localizzazione delle facoltà e quantificazione: frenologia e statistica medio-psichiatrica," in *Follia, psichiatria, e società*, ed. Alberto De Bernardi (Milan: Franco Angeli Editore, 1982), 330–49.
100 Ellero, *La psichiatria, la libertà morale e la responsabilità penale*, 44, saw psychiatry as a branch of the study of nervous disorders.
101 Agostini, *Manuale de psichiatria per uso degli studenti e dei medici*, 184. See also Lombroso, *L'uomo alienato: trattato clinico sperimentale delle malattie mentali* (Turin: Fratelli Bocca, 1913), xi. In 1898 he revised his earlier classification, recognizing two main groups: congenital (hereditary) and acquired. The first group he divided into (1) cretinism (cretinism, imbecility, mentally weak); (2) epilepsy (genius, epilepsy itself, hysteria, moral insanity, born criminality, bipolar disorder, transitory insanity, sexual psychopathologies, obsessions, raptus); and (3) paranoia (hypochondria, semi-insanities [*mattoidismo*], plaintiff madness [*follia querulante*], simple monomanias). In the second he identified insanity caused by (1) acute or chronic illnesses; (2) intoxications; and (3) physical and psychological traumas.
102 Agostini, *Manuale de psichiatria per uso degli studenti e dei medici*, 178–79.
103 Anne Harrington, "Beyond Phrenology: Localization Theory in the Modern Era," in *The Enchanted Loom: Chapters in the History of Neuroscience*, ed. Pietro Corsi (New York: Oxford University Press, 1991), 207–15, provides a useful summary. See also Robert M. Young, *Mind, Brain and Adaptation in the Nineteenth Century: Cerebral Localization and Its Biological Context from Gall to Ferrier* (Oxford: Oxford University Press, 1990).
104 Agostini, *Manuale de psichiatria per uso degli studenti e dei medici*, 11. See also 6–8, 10.
105 Bianchi, *Trattato di psichiatria ad uso dei medici e degli studenti*, 11. See also 10–18.
106 Charles Richet, *Essai de psychologie générale*, 8th ed. (Paris: Félix Alcan, 1910), 165.

107 Ball, *Leçons sur les maladies mentales*, 354. Collée and Quétal, *Histoire des maladies mentales*, 109–10, described Ball's two editions (1883 and 1890) of *Leçons sur les maladies mentales* as synthesizing psychiatric knowledge at the time.

108 Agostini, *Manuale de psichiatria per uso degli studenti e dei medici*, 22–26, for example.

109 Agostini, *Manuale de psichiatria per uso degli studenti e dei medici*, 35–39, 44–50.

110 Ball, *Leçons sur les maladies mentales*, 368.

111 Tanzi, *Trattato delle malattie mentali*, 2nd ed., vol. 1, 643. See also Penta, *Pazzia e società*, 51, who said "People with healthy constitutions do not become insane."

112 Agostini, *Manuale de psichiatria per uso degli studenti e dei medici*, 165.

113 Agostini, *Manuale de psichiatria per uso degli studenti e dei medici*, 135.

114 Ball, *Leçons sur les maladies mentales*, 976–77.

115 Porter, *Madness: A Brief History*, 112, reports a tenfold increase in patients in England between 1800 and 1900 (about 10,000 to 100,000). See also Goldstein, *Console and Classify*.

116 Pierre Morel, Jean-Pierre Bourgeron, and Elisabeth Roudinesco, *Au-delà du conscient: histoire illustrée de la psychiatrie et de la psychanalyse* (Paris: Editions Hazan, 2000), 50–51.

117 Porter, *Madness: A Brief History*, 112, from 8,000 to 40,000.

118 Renzo Villa, "'Pazzi e criminali': strutture istituzionali e pratica psichiatrica nei manicomi criminali italiani (1876–1915)," *Movimento operaio e socialista* 3 (1980): 369–93, 373–74.

119 Adda Lonni, "Pubblica sicurezza, sicurezza pubblica e malato di mente. La legge del 1904," in De Bernardi, 270. Article 47 of the Code.

120 Robert Castel, *The Regulation of Madness: The Origins of Incarceration in France*, trans. W. D. Halls (Berkeley: University of California Press, 1988), 11–13.

121 See, for example, Dowbiggin, *Inheriting Madness* and Mario Galzigna, *La malattia morale: alle origini della psichiatria* (Venice: Marsilio Editore, 1988), 130–31, 248.

122 Porter, *Madness: A Brief History*, 122.

123 Porter, *Madness: A Brief History*, 98–100.

124 Agostini, *Manuale de psichiatria per uso degli studenti e dei medici*, 153.

125 Penta, *Pazzia e società*, 68.

126 Carito, *La Neurastenia nella vita e nel pensiero moderno*, 226.

127 Penta, *Pazzia e società*, 69. See also De Nigris, *La Neurastenia*, 85 and Agostini, *Manuale de psichiatria per uso degli studenti e dei medici*, 152, for any patients with signs of degeneration.

128 Agostini, *Manuale de psichiatria per uso degli studenti e dei medici*, 151.

129 Richet, *Essai de psychologie générale*, 165.

130 Th[éodule-Armand] Ribot, *Les maladies de la personnalité*, 14th ed. (Paris: Félix Alcan, 1908), 55–56.

131 Ribot, *Les maladies de la personnalité*, 2–3.

132 Silvio Venturi, *Le pazzie dell'uomo sociale* (Milan: Remo Sandron, 1901), 8–10.

133 Castel, *The Regulation of Madness*.

134 Bain, "The Feelings and the Will Viewed Physiologically," 578. See also Bianchi, *Trattato di psichiatria ad uso dei medici e degli studenti*, 370, who identifies the will by the greater number of its circuits.

135 Renzo Dubbini, *Geography of the Gaze: Urban and Rural Vision in Early Modern Europe*, trans. Lydia G. Cochrane (Chicago: University of Chicago Press, 2002), 195.

136 Paulhan, *La volonté*, 277–94, worked out the analogy between society and individuals: both made decisions through the concurrence of different elements.

137 German E. Berrios, *The History of Mental Symptoms: Descriptive Psychopathology since the Nineteenth Century* (Cambridge: Cambridge University Press, 1996), 351, "a fashionable concept." Gregory A. Kimble, "Voluntary Behavior," in *International Encyclopedia of Psychiatry, Psychology, Psychoanalysis, and Neurology*, ed. Benjamin B. Wolman, vol. 11 (New York: Aesculapius Publishers, 1977), 406.

138 Robert Jean Campbell, *Psychiatric Dictionary*, 7th ed. (New York: Oxford University Press, 1996).

139 Lorraine J. Daston, "The Theory of Will versus the Science of Mind," in *The Problematic Science: Psychology in Nineteenth-Century Thought*, eds. William R. Woodward and Mitchell G. Ash (New York: Praeger, 1982), 88–115. She argues that doctors seized on the issue of the will, because it provided an appropriate testing ground for debates over a science of the mind.

140 Berrios, *The History of Mental Symptoms*, 357.

141 Payot, *L'éducation de la volonté*, xi.

Chapter 4

1 J[ules] Dallemagne, *Les théories de la criminalité* (Paris: Masson, 1896), 110–11.

2 Auguste Vial, *Dégénérescence mentale et neurasthénie* (Lyon: A. H. Storck, 1897), 29.

3 Lombroso, *Atti del Quinto Congresso della Società Freniatrica Italiana*, 230.

4 De Nigris, *La Neurastenia*, 6.

5 Paolo Mantegazza, *Il secolo nevrosico* (G. Barbèra, Florence, 1887; Pordenone: Edizioni Studio Testi, 1995), 20.

6 George Miller Beard, *A Practical Treatise on Nervous Exhaustion (Neurasthenia): Its Symptoms, Nature, Sequences, Treatment*, 4th ed., ed. and enlarged by A. D. Rockwell (New York: E. B. Treat & Company, 1901), 8. Italian edition: Giorgio M. Beard, *Trattato pratico dell'esaurimento nervoso (Neurastenia): sintomi, natura, conseguenze, trattamento*, ed. A. D. Rockwell and trans. by Gustavo Bonvecchiato (Milan: Dottor Francesco Vallardi, 1892).

7 Hacking, *Mad Travelers*.

8 Carito, *La Neurastenia nella vita e nel pensiero moderno*, ix.

9 Carito, *La Neurastenia nella vita e nel pensiero moderno*, 11. Bianchi, *Trattato di psichiatria ad uso dei medici e degli studenti*, 617, listed the races. Paul Blocq, *La neurasthénie et les neurasthéniques* (Paris: Imprimerie F. Levé, 1891), 8, added Jews to Americans and Slavs. See also Emile Laurent, *La neurasthénie et son traitement*, 2nd ed. (Paris: A. Maloine, 1897), 7.

10 Charcot's preface to Fernand Levillain, *La neurasthénie: maladie de Beard* (Paris: A. Malline, 1891), ix.

11 Levillain, *La neurasthénie*, on women, 32–34; L[éon] Bouveret, *La neurasthénie (épuisement nerveux)* (Paris: J.-B. Baillière et fils, 1890), 14–15, thought women were prone in times of emotional strain; Laurent just said it favored women, 7; Georges Martin, *Étude sur la neurasthénie et l'état mental des neurasthéniques* (Paris: A. Maloine, Editeur, 1898), 12, said it happened to men more often, because it resulted from mental exertion.

12 Clodomiro Bonfigli, *Idée fisse e nevrastenia: quattro lezioni preliminari di clinica psichiatrica* (Milan: Dottor Francesco Vallardi, 1898), 29 and J. H. Bourguignon, *La neurasthénie: ses causes, ses symptomes, son traitement*, 4th ed. (Paris: Laboratoire Bourguignon, 1911), 3. Both called it the "disease of the day."

13 George Miller Beard, *American Nervousness, Its Causes and Consequences: A Supplement to Nervous Exhaustion (Neurasthenia)* (New York: G. P. Putnam's Sons, 1881), vii–viii. See also the Italian edition, Giorgio M. Beard, *Il nervosismo americano: le sue cause e le sue conseguenze*, trans. Sofia Fortini Santarelli (Città del Castello: S. Lapi Tipografo Editore, 1888), vii–viii. The initial study, *A Practical Treatise on Nervous Exhaustion (Neurasthenia): Its Symptoms, Nature, Sequences, Treatment* (New York: Wood, 1880), went through several editions.

14 Levillain, *La neurasthénie*, 1; A[lbert] Mathieu, *Neurasthénie (épuisement nerveux)* (Paris: J.-B. Ballière et fils, 1890), 7–8; Laurent, *La neurasthénie et son traitement*, 2–3; Dr. [Lucien] Angelvin, *La neurasthénie, mal social* (Paris: Edouard Cornély, 1905), 19, agreed with Beard that it was a new disease. De Nigris, *La Neurastenia*, 7, believed it existed since ancient times but had greatly increased in his own day.

15 Levillain, *La neurasthénie*, 13, evaluated inpatients; Blocq, *La neurasthénie et les neurasthéniques*, 7–8, examined outpatients.

16 Bouveret, *La neurasthénie (épuisement nerveux)*, 1.

17 Levillain, *La neurasthénie*, 7. See also Carito, *La Neurastenia nella vita e nel pensiero moderno*, 77: "a group of well defined constant symptoms, which, always produced by the same source, constitute a genuine well determined pathological type."

18 This symptom was known as "Charcot's helmet."

19 Carito, *La Neurastenia nella vita e nel pensiero moderno*, 77–81; De Nigris, *La Neurastenia*, 59–69; Levillain, *La neurasthénie*, 76–108; Blocq, *La neurasthénie et les neurasthéniques*, 11–13; Laurent, *La neurasthénie et son traitement*, 12–22; Martin, *Étude sur la neurasthénie et l'état mental des neurasthéniques*, 8, for example.

20 Levillain, *La neurasthénie*, 66.

21 Carito, *La Neurastenia nella vita e nel pensiero moderno*, 82–89; De Nigris, *La Neurastenia*, 72–76, for example.

22 Blocq, *La neurasthénie et les neurasthéniques*, 14.

23 Bonfigli, *Idée fisse e nevrastenia*, 29; Bianchi, *Trattato di psichiatria ad uso dei medici e degli studenti*, detailed the psychoses which resulted from neurasthenia, 696–97; Martin, *Étude sur la neurasthénie et l'état mental des neurasthéniques*, 57, saw "neurasthenic folly" as one form of the disease.

24 De Nigris, *La Neurastenia*, 9–10, 78–79, for example.

25 De Nigris, *La Neurastenia*, 79.

26 Sante De Sanctis, *Sulla nevrastenia: studio clinico-nosografico* (Milan: Leonardo Vallardi, 1890), 12–14.

27 See, for example, Bouveret, *La neurasthénie (épuisement nerveux)*, 23.

28 Several use this term including Martin, *Étude sur la neurasthénie et l'état mental des neurasthéniques*, 7.

29 Mantegazza, *Il secolo nevrosico*, 79.

30 Carito, *La Neurastenia nella vita e nel pensiero moderno*, 14.

31 Mantegazza, *Il secolo nevrosico*, 57.

32 Bianchi, *Trattato di psichiatria ad uso dei medici e degli studenti*, 616.

33 Carito, *La Neurastenia nella vita e nel pensiero moderno*, 135. Charcot argued that children lacked the willpower to overwork themselves to that degree. Mathieu agreed in *Neurasthénie (épuisement nerveux)*, 22.

34 Mathieu, *Neurasthénie (épuisement nerveux)*, 16. See also Angelvin, *La neurasthénie, mal social*, 8.

35 Mathieu, *Neurasthénie (épuisement nerveux)*, 21.

36 Carito, *La Neurastenia nella vita e nel pensiero moderno*, 19.

37 De Nigris, *La Neurastenia*, 12.

38 Bouveret, *La neurasthénie (épuisement nerveux)*, 14–15.

39 Carito, *La Neurastenia nella vita e nel pensiero moderno*, 130.

40 Bianchi pointed to the importance of delivery and nursing in *Trattato di psichiatria ad uso dei medici e degli studenti*, 618; Carito, *La Neurastenia nella vita e nel pensiero moderno* referred to recent studies which showed the connections to syphilis and flu, 123–24; Angelvin, *La neurasthénie, mal social,* also refers specifically to both diseases.

41 De Nigris, *La Neurastenia*, 52; Bianchi, *Trattato di psichiatria ad uso dei medici e degli studenti*, 616.

42 De Nigris, *La neurasthenia,* 54–56.

43 Albert Blum, *De l'hystéro-neurasthénie traumatique (Railway-Spine)* (Paris: Asselin et Houzeau, 1893), 39. Blum took the case from [Charles-Albert] Vibert, *Étude médico-légale sur les blessures produites par les accidents de chemin de fer* (Paris: Librairie J.-B. Baillière et fils, 1888), 71–77.

44 Blum, *De l'hystéro-neurasthénie traumatique (Railway-Spine)*, 40.

45 Vibert, *Étude médico-légale sur les blessures produites par les accidents de chemin de fer*, 13; Blum, *De l'hystéro-neurasthénie traumatique (Railway-Spine),* 4–5; Carito, *La Neurastenia nella vita e nel pensiero moderno*, 119.

46 Blum, *De l'hystéro-neurasthénie traumatique (Railway-Spine)*, 5–6. See also Vibert, *Étude médico-légale sur les blessures produites par les accidents de chemin de fer*, 37.

47 Herbert W. Page, *Injuries of the Spine and Spinal Cord without Apparent Mechanical Lesion, and Nervous Shock in Their Surgical and Medical-Legal Aspects* (London: J. & A. Churchill, 1883), 157.

48 Blum, *De l'hystéro-neurasthénie traumatique (Railway-Spine)*, 16. He refers to the curative power of money.

49 Vibert, *Étude médico-légale sur les blessures produites par les accidents de chemin de fer*, 34–38, 14.

50 Page, *Injuries of the Spine and Spinal Cord without Apparent Mechanical Lesion, and Nervous Shock in Their Surgical and Medical-Legal Aspects*, 2–3. Erichsen, Page reported, published *Six Lectures on Certain Obscure Injuries of the Nervous System Commonly Met with as the Result of Shocks to the Body Received in Collisions on Railways* in 1866 and then another work *Concussion of the Spine, Nervous Shock, and Other Obscure Injuries*, published in a second edition in 1882; Vibert refers to Erichsen's *On Railway and Other Injuries of the Nervous System*, published in London in 1866.

51 Page, *Injuries of the Spine and Spinal Cord without Apparent Mechanical Lesion, and Nervous Shock in Their Surgical and Medical-Legal Aspects*, 158–66.

52 A[dolphe] Dutil, *Hystérie et neurasthénie associées (Railway-Spine et névrose traumatique)* (Paris: Librairie Octave Doin, 1889), 8. Dutil was born in 1862 and is thought to have died in 1899. See also Joseph Fabre, *De l'hystéro-neurasthénie devant la loi dans les accidents de chemin de fer* (Paris: Henri Jouve, 1893) and Blum, *De l'hystéro-neurasthénie traumatique (Railway-Spine)*, 2. For a modern summary of similar arguments, see Ralph Harrington, "The Railway Accident: Trains, Trauma, and Technological Crises in Nineteenth-Century Britain," in *Traumatic Pasts: History, Psychiatry, and Trauma in the Modern Age, 1870–1930*, eds. Mark S. Micale and Paul Lerner (Cambridge: Cambridge University Press, 2001), 31–56.

53 Jean-Martin Charcot, *Leçons du mardi à la Salpêtrière, professeur Charcot. Policlinique, 1887–1888*, vol. 1, 2nd ed. (Paris: Babé, 1892), 4th Lesson, Tuesday, December 13, 1887, 52–54. See also Dutil, *Hystérie et neurasthénie associées*, 8.

54 [Georges] Gilles de la Tourette, *Les états neurasthéniques: formes cliniques, diagnostic, traitement*, 2nd ed. (Paris: Librairie J.-B. Ballière et fils, 1900), 38. See also Levillain, *La neurasthénie*, 37 who identified hereditary neurasthenia when the condition was either directly or indirectly inherited.

55 Blum, *De l'hystéro-neurasthénie traumatique (Railway-Spine)*, 96.

56 Carito, *La Neurastenia nella vita e nel pensiero moderno*, 121.

57 Levillain, *La neurasthénie*, 18. Martin, *Étude sur la neurasthénie et l'état mental des neurasthéniques*, 11, said you could "often" see neurasthenia develop without any hereditary link. See also Veuillot, *La neurasthénie et les états neurasthéniformes*, 5, who said it was the only neurosis in which heredity might play no role.

58 Laurent, *La neurasthénie et son traitement*, 4–5. Levillain, *La neurasthénie*, 18–19, admitted he could accept that healthy people who became neurasthenic had a pathological inability to recover from strain or exhaustion.

59 Mathieu, *Neurasthénie (épuisement nerveux)*, 162. See also Vial who said not everyone favored including neuroses among degenerative diseases, 17.

60 Ch[arles] Féré, *La famille névropathique: théorie tératologique de l'hérédité et de la prédisposition morbides et de la dégénérescence* (Paris: Ancienne Librairie Germer Baillière, 1894), 103–4.

61 Gilles de la Tourette, *Les états neurasthéniques*, 36. See also Bourguignon, 3–4. Bourguignon and Fulgence Raymond, *Neurasthénie-syndrome (neurasthénie simple, acquise ou accidentelle), leçon faite à l'hospice de la Salpêtrière* (Paris: Imprimerie Typographique Jean Gainche, 1907) preferred to call "hereditary neurasthenia" "psychasthénie." Levillain used the words "accidental" or "original" neurasthenia, 38–39.

62 Fernand Veuillot, *La neurasthénie et les états neurasthéniformes: rôle de l'hérédité névropathique* (Paris: G. Steinheil, 1896), 7.

63 Gilles de la Tourette, *Les états neurasthéniques*, 46.

64 Bouveret, *La neurasthénie (épuisement nerveux)*, 141. See also Gilles de la Tourette, *Les états neurasthéniques*, 37–38 and Raymond, *Neurasthénie*, 6.

65 Mathieu, *Neurasthénie (épuisement nerveux)*, 183.

66 Levillain, *La neurasthénie*, 201.

67 Vial, *Dégénérescence mentale et neurasthénie*, 1.

68 Carito, *La Neurastenia nella vita e nel pensiero moderno*, 226–27.

69 Laurent, *La neurasthénie et son traitement*, 53. See also De Nigris, *La Neurastenia*, 86–87.

70 Bouveret, *La neurasthénie (épuisement nerveux)*, 16, listed "intellectual slowdown, the reduction of memory, an inaptitude toward intellectual work, insomnia, headaches, palpitations, nervous stomach."

71 Levillain, *La neurasthénie*, 14–15. See also Bianchi, *Trattato di psichiatria ad uso dei medici e degli studenti*, 608.

72 Blum, *De l'hystéro-neurasthénie traumatique (Railway-Spine)*, 2, noted that they looked at neurasthenia, hysteria, and hystero-neurasthenia as one illness, but outside France scientists saw them as distinct. See also Mark S. Micale, "Jean-Martin Charcot and *les névroses traumatiques*: From Medicine to Culture in French Trauma Theory of the Late Nineteenth Century," in Mark S. Micale and Paul Lerner, eds., *Traumatic Pasts*, 115–39.

73 Charcot, *Leçons*, 27–28.

74 Dutil, *Hystérie et neurasthénie associées*, 10–14, reported the case. The accident occurred the night of September 4–5, 1888, and Charcot visited the patient July 3, 1889.

75 Jean-Martin Charcot, *Clinique des maladies du système nerveux*, ed. Georges Guinon, vol. 1 (Paris: Progrès Médical, 1892), 302–6.

76 Bonfigli, *Idée fisse e nevrastenia*, 57. Bonfigli (1838–1909), a doctor, was named Director of S. Maria della Pietà, a psychiatric hospital in Rome in 1893 and was elected deputy in 1897.

77 Laurent, *La neurasthénie et son traitement*, 53–59.

78 Mantegazza, *Il secolo nevrosico*, 85, 102.

79 Diomede Carita, *La Neurastenia nella vita e nel pensiero moderno: studio clinico e sociale* (Naples: Detken & Rocholl, 1907), 113–14.

80 De Nigris, *La Neurastenia*, 15–16.

81 Beard, *American Nervousness*, vi.

82 Angelvin, *La neurasthénie, mal social*, 8, used the terms "little" and "big" to characterize the light and serious variants of neurasthenia.

83 Charcot, *Leçons*, 410. He entered the clinic December 12, 1888, and Charcot presented the lesson February 19, 1889.

84 Charcot, *Leçons*, 413–15.

85 Bonfigli, *Idée fisse e nevrastenia*, 30, 59–60, for example. The psychological effects of masturbation (the guilt) combined with the physical to promote neurasthenia.

86 Jules Voisin, *L'épilepsie* (Paris: Félix Alcan, 1897), 230.

87 S[alvatore] Ottolenghi, "Epilessie psichiche," *Rivista sperimentale di freniatria* 16 (1890): 189–219, 189. He was born in 1861 and died in 1934.

88 Silvio Tonnino, "Le epilessie," *Archivio di psichiatria, scienze penali ed antropologia criminale* 6 (1885): 370–415, 371–73, argues for the plural. (He signs the article Tonnino.) Voisin uses the singular; Ch[arles] Féré, *Les épilepsies et les épileptiques* (Paris: Félix Alcan, 1890), 2–3, the plural.

89 Voisin, *L'épilepsie*, 54–62; Féré, *Les épilepsies*, 88, said they appeared about half the time.

90 Féré, *Les épilepsies*, 95.

91 Féré, *Les épilepsies*, 128.

92 Féré, *Les épilepsies*, 403, 384–87, 398.

93 Féré, *Les épilepsies*, 422.

94 Bianchi, *Trattato di psichiatria ad uso dei medici e degli studenti*, 477. See also Agostino, *Manuale de psichiatria per uso degli studenti e dei medici*, 427.

95 Féré, *Les épilepsies*, 424, 422.

96 Féré, *Les épilepsies*, 424.

97 Voisin, *L'épilepsie*, 297–98 and Féré, *Les épilepsies*, 481.

98 Bianchi, *Trattato di psichiatria ad uso dei medici e degli studenti*, 476–77.

99 Voisin, *L'épilepsie*, 7.

100 Voisin, *L'épilepsie*, 31–35, on masturbation, menstruation, pregnancy; 40–41 on overwork and insomnia; 41 on trauma.

101 Voisin, *L'épilepsie*, 197–98.

102 Voisin, *L'épilepsie*, 196.

103 Féré, *Les épilepsies*, 421.

104 Cesare Lombroso, "Identità dell'epilessia colla pazzia morale e delinquenza congenita," *Archivio di psichiatria, scienze penali, ed antropologia criminale* 6 (1885): 1–28, 1–2.

105 Lombroso, *Atti*, 228.

106 Lombroso, *Identità*, 27.

107 Bianchi, *Trattato di psichiatria ad uso dei medici e degli studenti*, 481. According to Agostini, 428–29, the parallels between epilepsy, moral insanity, and congenital criminality applied only in the most serious cases of degeneration in epileptics.

108 A[ugusto] G[uido] Bianchi, Guglielmo Ferrero, and Scipio Sighele, *Il mondo criminale italiano, 1889–1892* (Milan: L. Omodei Zorini, 1893), 18. Writer, social reformer, and socialist, Ferrero collaborated closely with Lombroso and married his daughter, Gina, in 1901.

109 Bianchi et al., *Il Mondo*, 23.

110 Féré, *Les épilepsies*, 236–37.

111 Paul Richer, *Etudes cliniques sur la grande hystérie ou hystéro-épilepsie*, 2nd ed. (Paris: Adrien Delahaye et Emile Lecrosnier, 1885). See also Voisin, *L'épilepsie*, 236. Richer was born in 1849 and he died in 1933.

112 Richer, *Etudes cliniques sur la grande hystérie ou hystéro-épilepsie*, 39.

113 Richer, *Etudes cliniques sur la grande hystérie ou hystéro-épilepsie*, 148.

114 Voisin, *L'épilepsie*, 192.

115 Pierre Janet, *Les Névroses* (Paris: Ernest Flammarion, 1909), 371–78.

116 Féré, *Les épilepsies*, 350.

117 Janet, *Les Névroses*, 383. Micale, 35, calls the change from physical to psychologically based models of the mind "the great paradigm shift" in Euro-American psychological sciences.

118 Janet, *Les Névroses*, 387–89.

119 Janet, *Les Névroses*, 391–93.

120 Gilles de la Tourette, *Les États neurasthéniques*, and Raymond, *Neurasthénie*, thought true neurasthenia was a syndrome and the hereditary form was a disease.

121 Tonnino, "Le epilessie," 5, argued that as the "embodiment of asymmetry" epileptics deviated the most dramatically from normal balance and harmony.

122 Angelvin, *La neurasthénie, mal social*, 85.

123 Angelvin, *La neurasthénie, mal social*, 104–9.

124 Carito, *La Neurastenia nella vita e nel pensiero moderno*, 28.

125 Carito, *La Neurastenia nella vita e nel pensiero moderno*, 226.

126 Carito, *La Neurastenia nella vita e nel pensiero moderno*, 30.

127 Tonnino, "Le epilessie," 67.

128 Voisin, *L'épilepsie*, 280.

129 Janet Oppenheim, *"Shattered Nerves": Doctors, Patients, and Depression in Victorian England*, 80, argues that by the mid-nineteenth century, the British saw nervous energy as electrical. Beard, *American Nervousness*, 11–12, compared the stores of energy required to batteries. French and Italian doctors also began to refer to nervous impulses as electrical.

130 Beard, *American Nervousness,* 12, compares the neurasthenic to a man with a moderate income who must meet an unusual expense and finds himself insolvent. See also Oppenheim, *"Shattered Nerves,"* 85, for the British use of economic metaphors.

131 Bruna Bianchi, "Psychiatrists, Soldiers, and Officers in Italy during the Great War," in Micale and Lerner, eds., *Traumatic Pasts*, 234. She argues that Italian psychiatrists, in contrast to those in other countries, saw the problem less as a psychological one and more as one of willpower and self-control, especially after Caporetto.

132 Oppenheim, *"Shattered Nerves,"* 5–6.

133 Mayo Clinic, Depression (major depression), http://www.mayoclinic.com/health/depression/DS00175/DSECTION=symptoms (accessed May 16, 2013).

134 Laurent, *La neurasthénie et son traitement*, 21.

135 Laurent, *La neurasthénie et son traitement*, 22, used the word "depression," and in this context it meant slowdown.

136 Mark S. Micale, "On the 'Disappearance' of Hysteria: A Study in the Clinical Deconstruction of a Diagnosis," *Isis*, 84, no. 3 (September 1993): 496–526, 502.

137 Micale, "Disappearance," 514.

Chapter 5

1 Alexandre Bérard, "Le vagabondage en France," *Archives d'anthropologie criminelle* 13 (1898): 604.

2 A[uguste] Marie and Raymond Meunier, *Les vagabonds* (Paris: V. Giard & E. Brière, 1908), 67–68.

3 *The Rule of St. Benedict*, c. 530, number 48, Fordham University, Medieval Sourcebook, http://www.fordham.edu/halsall/source/rul-benedict.asp, Order of Saint Benedict (accessed March 15, 2010).

4 Joly, *La France criminelle*, 21.

5 A[rmand] Pagnier, *Le vagabond* (Paris: Vigot Frères, 1910), i.

6 Gordon Wright, *Between the Guillotine and Liberty* (New York: Oxford University Press, 1983), 154. See also Bérard, "Le vagabondage en France," 601.

7 Marie and Meunier, *Les vagabonds*, 248.

8 Bérard, "Le vagabondage en France," 601.

9 The French use the words *vagabond* and *vagabondage*, the Italians *vagabondo* and *vagabondaggio*. These terms applied to anyone without regular work or residence, and fears of vagabonds gave the term a negative connotation. To capture the sense given the terms at the time, I've used "vagrancy" and "vagrant" more often than "vagabond" and the little-used word "vagabondage." Italians distinguished between *vagabondi*, who were homeless and without work, and the *oziosi*, who had a place to live but did not work regularly. *Ozio* means sluggish or indolent; it also means free time or leisure. Applied to people without a trade or profession, it carried a tone of moral criticism. The term "idler" seemed an appropriate English equivalent.

10 Marie and Meunier, *Les vagabonds*, 80, believed that 200,000 underestimated the real number.

11 René Beck, *Contribution à l'étude des rapports du vagabondage et de la folie* (Lyon: Typographie et Lithographie Prudhomme, 1902), 7.

12 Jean-Pierre Deloux, *Vacher l'assassin: Un "serial killer" français au XIXe siècle* (Paris: Claire Vigne, 1995), 27.

13 Beck, *Contribution à l'étude des rapports du vagabondage et de la folie*, 7.

14 Joly, *La France criminelle*, 20, reported an overall increase of 430 percent.

15 Bérard, "Le vagabondage en France," 609.

16 Bérard, "Le vagabondage en France," 613. Eugenio Florian and Guido Cavaglieri, "I vagabondi," *La Scuola Positiva* 4 (May 1894): 393. Italian figures are based on the annual average of idlers and vagrants put under surveillance (*ammoniti*) for the periods 1872–1875, 25.4; 1883–1889, 7.8; 1890–1891, 1.5 and in France on vagrants brought before the courts, 1866–1870, 21.9; 1871–1880, 27.4; 1881–1889, 44.8.

17 Eugenio Florian and Guido Cavaglieri, *I vagabondi*, vol. 1 (Turin: Fratelli Bocca, 1897) and vol. 2 (Turin: Fratelli Bocca, 1900), 100.

18 Paul Collin, *Aperçu sur le vagabondage: Effets, causes, remèdes* (Paris: Marcel Rivière, 1907), 13. Article 70. Article 69 stated it was a crime.

19 Collin, *Aperçus sur le vagabondage*, 57–58. Article 277 increased punishment to 2–5 years for beggars or vagabonds found "travesti; porteur d'armes; muni de limes, crochets ou autres instruments propres à commettre des vols ou autres délits, ou à lui procurer le moyen d'entrer dans les maisons." Article 278 set six months to two years for beggars or vagabonds caught with goods valued at 100 francs who could not account for them. Article 279 gave two to five years for having committed or tried to commit acts of violence against anyone and reclusion if they were also found in any of the conditions defined in article 277.

20 After 1859 and until 1889, the Piedmontese criminal code applied everywhere in Italy except Tuscany. Article 450 of the Piedmontese code of 1839 specified three to six months in jail for vagrancy. This provision came, in turn, from the Albertine Code of 1839. The Piedmontese public security law of February 26, 1852, added special police surveillance for idlers and people suspected of rural theft and abusive pasturage. See Tommaso Bertolli, *Della ammonizione seconda la legge di pubblica sicurezza, 30 giugno 1889* (Turin: Unione Tipografico-Editrice, 1892), 2. See also Flavio Verona, *Oziosi e vagabondi nella legislazione penale dell'Italia liberale* (Pisa: ETS, 1984), 8.

21 Bertolli, *Della ammonizione seconda la legge di pubblica sicurezza*, 2. The practice of imposing the condition to find work was called *sottomissione*.

22 Verona, *Oziosi e vagabondi nella legislazione penale dell'Italia liberale*, 41, for the 1865 law.

23 Beck, *Contribution à l'étude des rapports du vagabondage et de la folie*, 10–13.

24 Ach[ille] Foville (fils), "Les aliénés voyageurs ou migrateurs: Étude clinique sur certains cas de lypémanie," *Annales médico-psychologiques: journal de l'aliénation mentale et de la médecine légale des aliénés* 14 (1875): 5–45, 41–45.

25 [Jean-Martin] Charcot, *Leçons du mardi à la Salpêtrière. Policliniques*, vol. 1, *1887–1888*, vol. 2, *1888–1889* (Paris: C. Tchou pour la Bibliothèque des Introuvables, 2002). Reference is to vol. 2, 358. He described the case in the lessons of January 31, 1888, vol. 1, 199–204 and February 12, 1889 in vol. 2, 357–87.

26 Charcot, *Leçons du mardi à la Salpêtrière*, vol. 1, 199.

27 Charcot, *Leçons du mardi à la Salpêtrière*, vol. 1, 206–07.

28 Charcot, *Leçons du mardi à la Salpêtrière*, vol. 2, lesson of February 12, 1889. Charcot reduced the dosage in May, in September Men … s stopped taking it, and from January 18 to 26, he had the attack.

29 Charcot, *Leçons du mardi à la Salpêtrière*, vol. 2, 384.

30 See Marie and Meunier, *Les vagabonds*, 27, 31.

31 A. Joffroy and R. Dupouy, *Fugues et vagabondage: étude clinique et psychologique* (Paris: Félix Alcan, 1909), 366–67; Armand Pagnier, *Du vagabondage et des vagabonds: étude psychologique, sociologique, et médico-legale* (Lyon: A. Storck, 1906), 39–45, 1906, 39–44; Géhin, *Contribution à l'étude de l'automatisme ambulatoire ou vagabondage impulsif*, 37; Victor-Charles Dubourdieu, *Contribution à l'étude de l'automatisme ambulatoire de la dromomanie des dégénérés* (Bordeaux: Imprimerie du Midi, 1894), 33.

32 Hacking, *Mad Travelers*, 26. He features the case in his lectures on fugue. In the epilogue, he reports that Tissié revealed Albert's full name for the first time in print in 1930 in an autobiographical piece he wrote for a journal he edited.

33 Philippe Tissié, *Les aliénés voyageurs: essai médico-psychologique* (Paris: Octave Doin, 1887), 56–108.

34 Tissié, *Les aliénés voyageurs*, 81–86.

35 Tissié, *Les aliénés voyageurs*, 105.

36 See Géhin, *Contribution à l'étude de l'automatisme ambulatoire ou vagabondage impulsif.*

37 Hacking, *Mad Travelers*, 25.

38 Tissié, *Les aliénés voyageurs*, 106–07.

39 Géhin, *Contribution à l'étude de l'automatisme ambulatoire ou vagabondage impulsif*; Pagnier, *Du vagabondage et des vagabonds*; Joffroy and Dupouy, *Fugues et vagabondage*, 145, identified the double personality.

40 Géhin, *Contribution à l'étude de l'automatisme ambulatoire ou vagabondage impulsif*, 84–87.

41 Géhin, *Contribution à l'étude de l'automatisme ambulatoire ou vagabondage impulsif*, 37.

42 Géhin, *Contribution à l'étude de l'automatisme ambulatoire ou vagabondage impulsif*, 88. See also Pagnier, *Du vagabondage et des vagabonds*, 51–57.

43 Géhin, *Contribution à l'étude de l'automatisme ambulatoire ou vagabondage impulsif*, 89.

44 Géhin, *Contribution à l'étude de l'automatisme ambulatoire ou vagabondage impulsif*, 97–98; Pagnier, *Du vagabondage et des vagabonds*, 51.

45 Joffroy and Dupouy, *Fugues et vagabondage*, 288. Alix Joffroy was born in 1844 and died in 1908.

46 Dubourdieu, *Contribution à l'étude de l'automatisme ambulatoire de la dromomanie des dégénérés*, quote from 57, reference from 58; Joffroy and Dupouy, *Fugues et vagabondage*, 225, refer to neurotic travelers, wandering Jews whose "scarcely appealing silhouette" Meige "so amusingly drew"; Tissié, *Les aliénés voyageurs*, 76, referred to Albert D … as "this new Wandering Jew"; Pagnier, *Du vagabondage et des vagabonds*, refers to Henry Meige, *Le Juif-Errant à la Salpêtrière* (Paris: Editions du Nouvel Objet, 1993), 10.

47 Meige, *Le Juif-Errant à la Salpêtrière*, the reference to culture, 23, and to neurosis, 26.

48 Meige developed a particularly striking example of neurasthenia's connection to impulsive wandering, one which also offers insight into racist sentiments at the time, 101.

49 Meige, *Le Juif-Errant à la Salpêtrière*, 22.

50 Meige, *Le Juif-Errant à la Salpêtrière*, 22.

51 Meige, *Le Juif-Errant à la Salpêtrière*, 50–55.

52 Géhin, *Contribution à l'étude de l'automatisme ambulatoire ou vagabondage impulsif*, 100. He and others drew on the work of Moriz Benedikt, who equated vagabondage and neurasthenia.

53 Beck, *Contribution à l'étude des rapports du vagabondage et de la folie*, 18.

54 Tissié, *Les aliénés voyageurs*, 22–23.

55 Tissié, *Les aliénés voyageurs*, 35.

56 Joffroy and Dupouy, *Fugues et vagabondage*, 98–102.

57 Dubourdieu, *Contribution à l'étude de l'automatisme ambulatoire de la dromomanie des dégénérés*, 35.

58 Pagnier, *Du vagabondage et des vagabonds*, 72–73, summarizes the links in a table.

59 Dubourdieu, *Contribution à l'étude de l'automatisme ambulatoire de la dromomanie des dégénérés*, 51, distinguishes between accidental and organic neurasthenia and focuses on the latter.

60 Dubourdieu, *Contribution à l'étude de l'automatisme ambulatoire de la dromomanie des dégénérés*, 58–59.

61 Dubourdieu, *Contribution à l'étude de l'automatisme ambulatoire de la dromomanie des dégénérés*, 61.

62 Joffroy and Dupouy, *Fugues et vagabondage*, 123–27.

63 Florian and Cavaglieri, *I vagabondi*, vol. 2, 14.

64 Florian and Cavaglieri, *I vagabondi*, vol. 2, 5. See also 3.

65 Florian and Cavaglieri, *I vagabondi*, vol. 2, 6–8. Reference to psychic atavism is on page 14.

66 Florian and Cavaglieri, *I vagabondi*, vol. 2, 9–12.

67 Florian and Cavaglieri, *I vagabondi*, vol. 2, 22–33, attributed some vagrancy to pathologies. They referred to the *automatisme ambulatoire* produced by neuroses and to vagrancy produced by delusions or obsessions, and by idiocy and imbecility.

68 Marie and Meunier, *Les vagabonds*, 10. Joffroy and Dupouy, *Fugues et vagabondage*, 223, called Florian and Cavaglieri's idea that vagrants returned to primitive instincts "very curious," and they said they had trouble accepting it. Auguste Marie lived from 1865 to 1934.

69 Beck, *Contribution à l'étude des rapports du vagabondage et de la folie*, 39–43.

70 Beck, *Contribution à l'étude des rapports du vagabondage et de la folie*, 53.

71 Pagnier, *Du vagabondage et des vagabonds*, 68–69.

72 Pagnier, *Du vagabondage et des vagabonds*, 62.

73 Pagnier, *Le vagabond*, 68.

74 Pagnier, *Du vagabondage et des vagabonds*, 12.

75 Marie and Meunier, *Les vagabonds*, 33.

76 Joffroy and Dupouy identified symptomatic vagrancy or real fugue; idiopathic vagrancy or conscious fugue; vagrancy caused by necessity or occasional vagrancy, and special vagrants such as gypsies, 114–15; Pagnier, *Le vagabond*, divided them into the insane and inferior and medium degenerates, superior degenerates, occasional vagrants, and specialized vagrants (gypsies).

77 Riccardo Scartezzini, "Sui 'vagabondi' di Florian e Cavaglieri," *Quaderni di sociologia* 2 (1980–1981): 216–35, 220.

78 Florian and Cavaglieri, *I vagabondi*, vol. 2, and "I vagabondi," 395–97.

79 Bérard, "Le vagabondage en France," 608.

80 Louis Rivière, *Mendiants et vagabonds* (Paris: Librairie Victor Lecoffre, 1902), viii.

81 Carlo Manes, *Capitalismo e criminalità* (Rome: Tipografia Editrice Nazionale, 1912), 192.

82 Florian and Cavaglieri, *I vagabondi*, vol. 1, 591.

83 Dino Carina, *Dell'ozio in Italia* (Lucca: P. Canovetti, 1870), 14.

84 Collin, *Aperçus sur le vagabondage*, 79.

85 Joly, *La France criminelle*, 302, 22.

86 Joly, *La France criminelle*, 24.

87 Marie and Meunier, *Les vagabonds*, 27.

88 Marie and Meunier, *Les vagabonds*, 199.

89 Marie and Meunier, *Les vagabonds*, 170. Marie and Meunier added ex-cons trying to escape their past or unable to find work, 202–6, and people seeking to escape deportation by feigning insanity, 207–12, to this group.

90 Florian and Cavaglieri, *I vagabondi*, vol. 2, 226. See also 240.

91 Rivière, *Mendiants et vagabonds*, also calls them "parasseux irreductibles," 195.

92 Pagnier, *Le vagabond*, 169–70.

93 Joffroy and Dupouy, *Fugues et vagabondage*, 223. They included Vacher in this category and also, referring to Meige's work, wandering Jews, 225.
94 Florian and Cavaglieri, *I vagabondi*, vol. 2, 219.
95 Marie and Meunier, *Les vagabonds*, 26, 90.
96 Marie and Meunier, *Les vagabonds*, 28–29.
97 Joffroy and Dupouy, *Fugues et vagabondage*, 43.
98 Marie and Meunier, *Les vagabonds*, 26, 90.
99 See also Colajanni, *La sociologia criminale*, 489.
100 Florian and Cavaglieri, *I vagabondi*, vol. 2, 66.
101 Florian and Cavaglieri, *I vagabondi*, vol. 2, 16.
102 Bérard, "Le vagabondage en France," 610.
103 Florian and Cavaglieri, *I vagabondi*, vol. 2, 15–16.
104 Pagnier, *Le vagabond*, 63–68.
105 Florian and Cavaglieri, *I vagabondi*, vol. 2, 34.
106 Florian and Cavaglieri, *I vagabondi*, vol. 2, 5.
107 Florian and Cavaglieri, *I vagabondi*, vol. 2, 56.
108 Pagnier, *Le vagabond*, 42. Marie and Meunier also invoked Vacher as an example of the pathological vagrant, as did Bérard, "Le vagabondage en France," 601.
109 Deloux, *Vacher l'assassin*, 150. The University of Lyon also received a sample.
110 Lombroso, *Delitti vecchi e delitti nuovi*, 99, 100.
111 Lombroso, *Delitti vecchi e delitti nuovi*, 105.
112 Lombroso, *Delitti vecchi e delitti nuovi*, 105.
113 Lombroso, *Delitti vecchi e delitti nuovi*, 101.
114 Lombroso, *Delitti vecchi e delitti nuovi*, 101, 104.
115 Florian and Cavaglieri, *I vagabondi*, vol. 2, 37.
116 Florian and Cavaglieri, *I vagabondi*, vol. 2, 37.
117 Pagnier, *Du vagabondage et des vagabonds*, 124–25.
118 Florian and Cavaglieri, *I vagabondi*, vol. 2, 2.
119 See Florian and Cavaglieri, *I vagabondi*, vol. 1, 121–23.
120 If a vagrant committed a crime, then all other vagrancy convictions counted toward the four.
121 Article 19 of the May 27 law. This substituted for police surveillance.
122 Articles 269 and 270 of the Penal Code. Law of May 27, 1885. "Sont considérés comme gens sans aveu et punis des peines édictées contre le vagabondage: tous individus qui, soit qu'ils aient ou non un domicile certain, ne tirent habituellement leur subsistance que du fait de pratiquer ou faciliter, sur la voie publique, l'exercice de jeux illicites ou la prostitution d'autrui sur la voie publique."
123 The law of April 3, 1903, punished only illicit gaming under vagrancy laws, Collin, *Aperçus sur le vagabondage*, 14.
124 Bertolli, *Della ammonizione seconda la legge di pubblica sicurezza*, 28, 88–89. The law specified not less than one year or more than three for the first violation and up to two years for a second. See Bertolli, *Della ammonizione seconda la legge di pubblica sicurezza*, 11.
125 Bertolli, *Della ammonizione seconda la legge di pubblica sicurezza*, 26–27.
126 Bertolli, *Della ammonizione seconda la legge di pubblica sicurezza*, 32, summarizes the 1889 public security law. Previously other groups qualified for *ammonizione*: those suspected of rural theft and abusive pasturage in 1854; plus "grassatori, ladri, truffatori, borsaiuoli e ricettatori" (highwaymen, thieves, swindlers, pickpockets, and fences) in 1859; plus camorristi (those who "habitually and illicitly" demanded money

from the profits of others) in 1865; plus "diffamati per crimini o per delitti contro le persone e le proprietà" (reputed to have committed crimes or felonies against people and property), listing especially "manutengoli, camorristi, maffiosi, contrabbanderi, accoltellatori" (receivers of stolen goods, members of the Camorra, members of the Mafia, smugglers, stabbers) in 1871, 3–4.

127 Joly, *La France criminelle*, 125–26, said he subscribed to this view; Collin, *Aperçus sur le vagabondage*, 59, and Florian and Cavaglieri, *I vagabondi*, vol. 2, 27, agreed.

128 Rivière, *Mendiants et vagabonds*, 44–45; Pagnier, *Le vagabond*, 181.

129 Joly, *La France criminelle*, 21, for the quote and 125–26.

130 Bérard, "Le vagabondage en France," 611–12.

131 Collin, *Aperçus sur le vagabondage*, 59.

132 Carlo Gatteschi, *Dell'ammonizione de pubblica sicurezza* (Florence: Fioretti, 1889), 211.

133 Marie and Meunier, *Les vagabonds*, 266.

134 Bérard, "Le vagabondage en France," 613.

135 Pagnier, *Le vagabond*, 168.

136 Marie and Meunier, *Les vagabonds*, 285. The sick "deserve private and public assistance." They thought that some of the insane could remain free but most should be put in asylums.

137 Beck, *Contribution à l'étude des rapports du vagabondage et de la folie*, 57–59.

138 Marie and Meunier, *Les vagabonds*, 287.

139 Marie and Meunier, *Les vagabonds*, 265.

140 Marie and Meunier, *Les vagabonds*, 285.

141 Marie and Meunier, *Les vagabonds*, 263. See also Florian and Cavaglieri, *I vagabondi*, vol. 2, 244: those with "real holes or disturbances of the psychic organism" needed medical attention.

142 Florian and Cavaglieri, *I vagabondi*, vol. 2, 240, 253.

143 Pagnier, *Le vagabond*, 52.

144 Florian and Cavaglieri, *I vagabondi*, vol. 2, 264.

145 Florian and Cavaglieri, *I vagabondi*, vol. 2, 274.

146 Pagnier, *Le vagabond*, 206.

147 Pagnier, *Le vagabond*, 207.

148 Pagnier, *Du vagabondage et des vagabonds*, 196.

149 Vittorio Codeluppi, "L'autobiografia di un vagabondo nato," *La Scuola Positiva* 12 (February 1902): 108–16, 108.

150 Also Auguste Pierret, clinical professor of mental illness and head doctor of the departmental asylum of Bron, and Fleury Rabael, director of a clinic.

151 Pagnier, *Le vagabond*, 195, estimated that 27–28 percent of the youth were repeat offenders.

152 Maurice [Moriz] Benedikt, "Le vagabond et son traitement: étude psychologique et sociologique," *Annales de l'hygiène publique et médecine légale*, 3rd series, no. 24 (1890), 495–96, argued that they all "by nature unbalanced" and required treatment by experts, especially alienists.

153 December 7, 1874, for children under sixteen.

154 Rivière, *Mendiants et vagabonds*, 108, estimated 89 percent of 5,545,000.

155 Rivière, *Mendiants et vagabonds*, 124–30. The 1889 law also gave courts the option of ending parental rights in certain conditions.

156 Bertolli, *Della ammonizione seconda la legge di pubblica sicurezza*, 165–66.

157 Collin, *Aperçus sur le vagabondage*, 4.

158 Florian and Cavaglieri, *I vagabondi*, vol. 2, 240.
159 Pagnier, *Le vagabond*, 56.
160 Florian and Cavaglieri, *I vagabondi*, vol. 1, 122.

Chapter 6

1 Gaspare Virgilio, *Sulla natura morbosa del delitto: saggio di ricerche* and *Passanante e la natura morbosa del delitto* (Turin: Fratelli Bocca, 1910), 123.
2 Kalifa, *Crime et culture au XIXe siècle*, 323.
3 Michelle Perrot cited in Wright, *Between the Guillotine and Liberty*, 153. Original in Perrot, "Délinquance et système pénitentiare en France au XIXe siècle," *Les ombres de l'histoire* (1975), 169–70.
4 Gibson, *Born to Crime*, 13–14.
5 Kalifa, *Crime et culture au XIXe siècle*, 10.
6 Kalifa, *Crime et culture au XIXe siècle*, 317, notes the paradox that more information increased rather than diminished the sense of danger.
7 G[abriel] Tarde, "Revue critique: la criminalité en France dans les vingt dernières années," *Archives d'anthropologie criminelle* 18 (March 15, 1903): 162–81.
8 E. Fornasari di Verce, "La criminalità e le vicende economiche d'Italia dal 1873 al 1890," *Archivio di psichiatria, scienze penali ed antropologia criminale* 14 (1893): 365–405; 536–55, 398. He notes that in 1876 amnesties reduced the number of criminals sentenced. L. Bodio, "La delinquenza italiana nel 1893," *La Scuola Positiva* 5 (September 1895): 174–84, 174–75 reported that criminal cases and violations of special laws brought to court increased from 526,000 in 1887 to 660,000 in 1893, an increase of 20 percent. Enrico Ferri, "Criminalità in Italia e sostituivi penali a rovescio," *La Scuola Positiva* 1 (June 1891): 102–17, 108, reported a steady increase in both reported crime and in convictions after 1886.
9 The annual average of cases before local magistrates (*pretori*) rose from 238,222 in 1880–1883 to 433,649 in 1896, Pietro Nocito, "La delinquenza in Italia nel 1896," *La Scuola Positiva* 8 (June 1898): 373–79, 373; those heard by the Assizes courts fell from an annual average of 8,018 cases a year in 1880–1883 to 5,815 in 1893 and 4,959 in 1896, 375. See also Eugenio Florian, "La statistica dei motivi determinanti al Reato," *La Scuola Positiva* 5 (October–November 1895): 207–54. Bruno Franchi "Delitti e contravvenzioni secondo le più recenti statistiche e nel loro carattere giuridico," *La Scuola Positiva* 12 (October 1902): 577–98; 12: (November 1902): 668–77; 12 (December 1902): 712–21, 580, reported that crimes increased from 526,300 in 1887 to 826,195 in 1899.
10 Enrico Ferri, "L'omicidio in Europa," *La Scuola Positiva* 3 (March 1893): 241–51. For every one million inhabitants, there were 96 convictions for murder in Italy, 76 in Spain, 40 in Rumania, 24 in Austria, 23 in Portugal, 16 in Switzerland, 15 in France and Russia, 14 in Belgium, 13 in Sweden, 12 in Denmark, 10 in Ireland and Germany, and 5 in Holland, England, and Scotland, 249. See also Bournet, *De la criminalité en France et en Italie*, 35.
11 Nocito, "La delinquenza in Italia nel 1896," 375, reported that the annual average of numbers of crimes reported per 100,000 people in 1890–1892 was 13.24 and in 1896 12.43; theft in 1890–1892 was 362.31 versus 395.81 in 1896; violence against public officials 44.87 versus 47.45; crimes against public order 1.70 versus 4.29. Convictions

for fraud increased from 14,277 in 1887 to 19,158 in 1895; for forgery (*i reati di falso*) from 12,886 in 1890 to 15,605 in 1893 according to a review by Lombroso in *Archivio di psichiatria, scienze penali, ed antropologia criminale* 20 (1899): 646, of A. Niceforo, *Sull'aumento della delinquenza* (Rome, 1899). See also Franchi, "Delitti e contravvenzioni" and Fornasari, 400.

12 Enrico Ferri, *I delinquenti nell'arte ed altre conferenze*, 2nd ed. (Turin: Unione Tipografico-Editrice Torinese, 1926), 2–3. A total of 4,404,808 persons appeared in the lower courts. He noted that between 1879 and 1888, French courts convicted 6,439,933 people, "the immense majority small fry," just as in Italy.

13 Joly, *La France criminelle*, 11.

14 Tarde, "Revue critique," 162. He became director in 1894.

15 Joly, *La France criminelle*, 5. Bournet agreed. Bodio, "La delinquenza italiana nel 1893," 177, reported 3,258 cases before the Assizes in 1880 and 2,939 in 1891; 119,481 before the Correctional Courts in 1880 versus 137,461 in 1891; and 351,351 in police courts in 1880 and 393,103 in 1891.

16 Joly, *La France criminelle*, 20, reported that in 1889 compared to 1838, violence increased by 51 percent, theft by 69 percent, suicide 162 percent, immorality 240 percent, and begging and vagrancy 430 percent.

17 Joly, *La France criminelle*, 18, reported an increase in property crimes between 1825 and 1882, and Bournet, 19–20, contended that, correcting for population growth, they decreased. Conversely, Joly noted a general decline in crimes against persons, 18, and Bournet, an increase, 18.

18 Joly, *La France criminelle*, 18, and Bournet, 65, reported that the number of rapes and of sexual assaults against children increased by a factor of six comparing 1826–1830 and 1876–1880.

19 Joly, *La France criminelle*, 21.

20 Tarde, "Revue critique," 180, based on statistics from the Société Generale des Prisons.

21 Tarde, "Revue critique," 168–69.

22 Tarde, "Revue critique," 165, 167. See also the comprehensive analysis of James M. Donovan, *Juries and the Transformation of Criminal Justice in France in the Nineteenth and Twentieth Centuries* (Chapel Hill: University of North Carolina Press, 2010). Kalifa discusses the security crisis of the early twentieth century in chapter 13.

23 Bournet, *De la criminalité en France et en Italie*, 38. See also 19–20.

24 Niceforo, *Sull'aumento della delinquenza*, 646.

25 Bournet, *De la criminalité en France et en Italie*, 31, 1875–1880 compared to 1850–1855.

26 A[lexandre] Lacassagne, *Des transformations du droit pénale et les progrès de la médicine légale de 1810 à 1912* (Lyon: A. Rey, Imprimeur-Editeur 1913), 19.

27 Cesare Lombroso, review of A. Niceforo, 646. It was 15 percent in 1870 and 41 percent in 1893–1894.

28 Kalifa, *Crime et culture au XIXe siècle*, 318, also points to monarchists who attacked the government for not ensuring security and radicals who complained about the Prefecture of the Police.

29 Kalifa, *Crime et culture au XIXe siècle*, 318.

30 Cesare Lombroso, "Prolusione al corso di medicina legale," in *Antologia Lombrosiana*, ed. Luigi Ferrio (Pavia: Società Editrice Pavese, 1962), 79–85, 85.

31 Fornarsari di Verce, "La criminalità e le vicende economiche d'Italia dal 1873 al 1890," 370.

32 Roncoroni, "Influenza del sesso sulla criminalità in Italia," 1–14, 3. For every 100 sentenced at the courts of first instance, 21.8 were women; at the Correctional Courts, 9.2, and the Assize Courts 6.0.

33 Lombroso, "Prolusione al corso di medicina legale," 84.

34 Lombroso published a collection of previous studies as *L'Uomo delinquente* in 1876 and then republished it in 1878 as *L'Uomo delinquente in rapporto all'antropologia, alla giurisprudenza, ed alle discipline carcerarie.*

35 Lombroso, *Criminal Man*, 53.

36 Lombroso, *Criminal Man*, 1st ed., 1876, 63–65.

37 Lombroso, *Criminal Man*, 1st ed., says "savages and the colored races," 91.

38 Lombroso, *Criminal Man*, 1st ed., 91.

39 Lombroso, *Criminal Man*, 1st ed., 51.

40 Lombroso, *Criminal Man*, 1st ed., 83.

41 Lombroso, *Criminal Man*, 1st ed., 82.

42 Lombroso, *Criminal Man*, 1st ed., 83.

43 Lombroso, *Criminal Man*, 1st ed., 80, "shoemaker, cook, domestic servant, and, perhaps, soldier."

44 Lombroso, *Criminal Man*, 2nd ed., 1878, 100, emphasizes this in the preface.

45 Enrico Ferri first used the term, and Lombroso adopted it in the third edition, 1889.

46 This edition was translated into English, the only translation until that of Mary Gibson and Nicole Rafter in 2006.

47 Gibson, *Born to Crime*, 48, n.58. The edition of 1876 had 256 pages; of 1878, 746 pages; of 1884, 610 pages; of 1889, 1,241 pages in two volumes; of 1896, 1,903 pages in three volumes plus a volume of tables.

48 Lombroso, *Criminal Man*, 2nd ed., 106.

49 Lombroso, *Criminal Man*, 4th ed., 1889, 268–71. He estimated 30 percent, an incidence thirty times greater than in the population outside prisons.

50 Lombroso, *Criminal Man*, 4th ed., 284–85.

51 Lombroso, *Criminal Man*, 4th ed., 289–90.

52 Lombroso, *Criminal Man*, 4th ed., 292–95; quote, 295.

53 Lombroso, *Criminal Man*, 3rd ed., 221–22.

54 Lombroso, *Criminal Man*, 4th ed., 247.

55 Lombroso, *Criminal Man*, 4th ed., 261.

56 Lombroso, *Criminal Man*, 4th ed., 247–48, 251.

57 Lombroso, *Criminal Man*, 4th ed., 254–56. See also the 1924 edition of *L'Uomo delinquente*, reprint of the last edition by Gina Lombroso (Turin: Fratelli Bocca, 1924), vol. 2, 155, 157–62.

58 Lombroso, *Criminal Man*, 4th ed., 265.

59 Lombroso, *Criminal Man*, 2nd ed., 127–34 also looked at age, sex, moral education, the size of the genitals, and the influence of imitation.

60 Lombroso, *Criminal Man*, 5th ed., 1896–97, 316–24.

61 Lombroso, *Criminal Man*, 5th ed., 322.

62 Lombroso, *Criminal Man*, 2nd ed., 188–92, quote 195. "They get angry, seek revenge, lie, are jealous, don't have a moral sense, are cruel, lack affection, are lazy, use jargon, are vain, and at the lower ends of society indulge in alcohol, gambling and obscene activities."

63 Lombroso, *Criminal Man*, 3rd ed., 221–22.

64 Gibson, *Born to Crime*, 2. See also R[affaele] Garofalo, *Criminologia*, 2nd ed. (Turin: Fratelli Bocca, 1891). First edition 1885.

65   Dallemagne, *Les théories de la criminalité*, 128.

66   Garofalo, *Criminologia*, 1–5.

67   Garofalo, *Criminologia*, 45, 51, 63.

68   Garofalo, *Criminologia*, 115–35.

69   Garofalo, *Criminologia*, 105.

70   Garofalo, *Criminologia*, 92–93.

71   Garofalo, *Criminologia*, 111–12.

72   Garofalo, *Criminologia*, 96.

73   Garofalo, *Criminologia*, 97.

74   Garofalo, *Criminologia*, 113.

75   Ferri, *Sociologia criminale*, 81. He titled the first and second editions in 1881 and
     1884, *I Nuovi orizzonti del diritto e della procedura penale*. The third (1892), fourth
     (1892), and fifth (1929–30) editions had the title *Sociologia criminale*. See Gibson,
     Born to Crime, 50, n.111.

76   Ferri, *Sociologia criminale*, 88.

77   Martine Kaluszynski, "The International Congresses of Criminal Anthropology," in
     Criminals and Their Scientists: The History of Criminology in International Perspective,
     eds. Peter Becker and Richard F. Wetzell, 301–16, describes the meetings in detail.

78   Marc Renneville, "La réception de Lombroso en France (1880–1890)," in *Histoire de
     la criminologie française*, ed. Laurent Mucchielli (Paris: Editions L'Harmattan, 1994),
     115–16.

79   For example, Gabriel Tarde, "Le type criminel," *Revue philosophique de France et de
     l'étranger* 19 (June 1, 1885): 593–627, 597. Tarde included the article in a collection of
     essays, *La criminalité comparée*, 7th ed. Lombroso wrote a response, "La fusion de la
     folie morale et du criminel né," *Revue philosophique de la France et de l'étranger* 20
     (June 15, 1885): 178–82. That article included a brief riposte from Tarde. See also
     G[abriel] Tarde, *La philosophie pénale*, 5th ed. (Paris: G. Masson, 1900), 227.

80   Féré, *Dégénérescence et criminalité*, 72.

81   Féré, *Dégénérescence et criminalité*, 76.

82   Tarde, "Le type criminel," 620.

83   Tarde, "Le type criminel," 606.

84   Tarde, "Le type criminel," 613–14.

85   Tarde, "Le type criminel," 19.

86   Paolo Mantegazza, "Gli atavismi psichici," *Archivio per l'antropologia e la etnologia* 18
     (1888): 69–82, 71, argued that atavism was too narrow an explanation. Pathology also
     produced anomalies, and regression in addition to atavism explained primitive traits.
     The defect of the school of criminal anthropology is to "want to open the door of
     science and of psychiatry with a single key." He reproached Lombroso for "not having
     used the scale and the metronome, primary instruments of any science."

87   Féré, *Dégénérescence et criminalité*, 42.

88   Féré, *Dégénérescence et criminalité*, 70.

89   Féré, *Dégénérescence et criminalité*, 63.

90   Féré, *Dégénérescence et criminalité*, 59.

91   Féré, *Dégénérescence et criminalité*, 88.

92   Dr. Emile Laurent, *Le criminel aux points de vue anthropologique, psychologique et
     social* (Paris: Vigot Frères, 1908).

93   Dallemagne, *Les théories de la criminalité*, 178.

94   Laurent, *Le criminel aux points de vue anthropologique, psychologique et social*,
     122, 130.

95 Laurent, *Le criminel aux points de vue anthropologique, psychologique et social*, 153, 154.

96 Laurent, *Le criminel aux points de vue anthropologique, psychologique et social*, 158–60.

97 Laurent, *Le criminel aux points de vue anthropologique, psychologique et social*, 132.

98 Laurent, *Le criminel aux points de vue anthropologique, psychologique et social*, 133.

99 Giuseppe Sergi, *Le degenerazioni umane* (Milan: Fratelli Dumolard, 1889), 3. Sergi (1841–1936) taught anthropology at the University of Bologna in 1880 and in Rome from 1884 to 1916.

100 Sergi, *Le degenerazioni umane*, 19.

101 Sergi, *Le degenerazioni umane*, 26, 51–52.

102 M. Angelo Vaccaro, *Genesi e funzioni delle leggi penali* (Rome: Fratelli Bocca, 1889).

103 Vaccaro, *Genesi e funzioni delle leggi penali*, 222.

104 Vaccaro, *Genesi e funzioni delle leggi penali*, 218–19.

105 Vaccaro, *Genesi e funzioni delle leggi penali*, 143, 145.

106 Vaccaro, *Genesi e funzioni delle leggi penali*, 154.

107 Achille Loria, *Le basi economiche della costituzione sociale*, 3rd ed. (Turin: Fratelli Bocca, 1902), 150–51. The quote is on 155. First edition was in 1886.

108 Loria, *Le basi economiche della costituzione sociale*, 155.

109 Napoleone Colajanni, *La sociologia criminale*, 2 vols. (Catania: Filippo Tropea, 1889), 294.

110 Colajanni, *La sociologia criminale*, 447–48.

111 Colajanni, *La sociologia criminale*, 461.

112 Colajanni, *La sociologia criminale*, 486–87.

113 Colajanni, *La sociologia criminale*, 672–73.

114 Colajanni, *La sociologia criminale*, 121.

115 Colajanni, *La sociologia criminale*, 188.

116 Tarde, "Le type criminel," 627.

117 Tarde, *La philosophie pénale*, 322.

118 Tarde, *La philosophie pénale*, 331–33.

119 Tarde, *La criminalité comparée*, 85.

120 Tarde, *La criminalité comparée*, 85.

121 Tarde, *La criminalité comparée*, 166.

122 A[lexandre] Lacassagne, *Cesare Lombroso (1836–1909)* (Lyon: A. Rey & Cie, 1909), 5–8.

123 Dallemagne, *Les théories de la criminalité*, 157.

124 Laurent Mucchielli, "Hérédité et milieu sociale: le faux-antagonisme franco-italien," in *Histoire de la criminologie française*, ed. Mucchielli, 189–214, 189. He refers to Darmon, *Médecins et assassins*, 1989.

125 Martine Kaluszynski, *La République à l'épreuve du crime: la construction du crime comme object politique, 1880–1920* (Paris: Maison des Sciences de l'Homme, 2002), 18. Mucchielli credits her with presenting new material that minimizes the division while herself accepting the division, 189.

126 Kalusznyski, *La République à l'épreuve du crime*, 18–20.

127 Kalusznyski, *La République à l'épreuve du crime*, 23.

128 Kalusznyski, *La République à l'épreuve du crime*, 42.

129 Lacassagne, *Des transformations*, 48.

130 Lacassagne, *L'homme criminel comparé à l'homme primitif* (Lyon: Association Typographique, 1882), 13–15.

131 Lacassagne, *L'homme criminel*, 6–7. Mucchielli, "Hérédité et milieu sociale," 190, notes his debt to Le Gall and phrenology, saying he was a "fervent partisan" his whole career.

132 Lacassagne, *L'homme criminel*, 15–16.

133 Lacassagne, *L'homme criminel*, 20–22.

134 Mucchielli, "Hérédité et milieu sociale," 191. See also Renneville, "La réception de Lombroso en France (1880–1890)," 114.

135 Mucchielli, "Hérédité et milieu sociale," points out that in an "exact reflection of reality" Garofalo in *Criminologie* (1888) identified Lacassagne and Bournet as supporters as did Lombroso in 1887 and Ferri in 1901, 200.

136 See Mucchielli, "Hérédité et milieu sociale," for the *Archives*, 198–99 and for a discussion of his followers, Alfred Bourne, Henry Coutagne, and Etienne Martin, 194–97.

137 Renneville, "La réception de Lombroso en France (1880–1890)," 115–17 observes that French reports of Lacassagne's challenge at the first congress exaggerated the weight of his interventions. He describes Lacassagne's "strategy of differentiation" as a failure, because others actually agreed with him about the role the social milieu played.

138 Renneville, "La réception de Lombroso en France (1880–1890)," 111.

139 Mucchielli, "Hérédité et milieu sociale," 199, 203. Gibson, *Born to Crime,* 248, points out that the differences between the French and the Italian schools over etiology were "more of emphasis than substance."

140 Mucchielli, "Hérédité et milieu sociale," 203.

141 Renneville, "La réception de Lombroso en France (1880–1890)," 124–26.

142 Amerigo Vespucci, *Giuseppe Musolino: il bandito calabrese* (Naples: F. Bideri, 1932). The editor's note dated December 1, 1900 says Vespucci based his account on the report of someone who knew Musolino.

143 Antonio De Leo, *Il brigante Musolino* (Rosarno: Virgiglio, 1996), 64. See also a sympathetic account by Aroldo Norlenghi, *Delinquenza presente e delinquenza futura: a proposito della condanna di Musolino* (Turin: Renzo Streglio, 1902).

144 Norlenghi, *Delinquenza presente e delinquenza future,* 12–13, details the judicial abuses evident at the trial including not letting witnesses who confirmed Musolino's story speak, not pursuing charges that two of the witnesses testified falsely, and allowing prison personnel to testify though they had no information on the crime itself.

145 Giuseppe Musolino, *S. Stefano in Aspromonte: storia e protagonisti* (Marigliano: Rexodes Magna Grecia, 1994), 361. He says Travia admitted to Enzo Magri that he shot at Zoccoli. Travia was arrested at the time, escaped from jail, and emigrated to America.

146 Dario Altobelli, *Indagine su un bandito: il caso Musolino* (Rome: Salvatorelli, 2006), 25–31 describes the escalating efforts. This is an excellent recent analysis of the case.

147 E[nrico] Morselli and Sante De Sanctis, *Biografia di un bandito: Giuseppe Musolino di fronte alla psichiatria ed alla sociologia* (Milan: Treves, 1903) reported there had not been that sort of interest in a trial in the last thirty years, 363.

148 A doctor from Lucca, M. Del Carlo, joined Morselli and De Sanctis, and Andrea Cristiani, director of the Insane Asylum of Lucca, served with the defense team.

149 M. L. Patrizi, *La fisiologia d'un bandito (Musolino): Esperimenti e commenti* (Turin: Fratelli Bocca, 1904), 205.

150 Patrizi, *La fisiologia d'un bandito*, 208–9.

151 Patrizi, *La fisiologia d'un bandito*, 207, 210.

152 Patrizi, *La fisiologia d'un bandito*, 210.

153 Patrizi, *La fisiologia d'un bandito*, 212.

154 Morselli and De Sanctis, *Biografia di un bandito*, 393.

155 Morselli and De Sanctis, *Biografia di un bandito*, 400–1.

156 Morselli and De Sanctis, *Biografia di un bandito*, 245.

157 Vespucci, *Giuseppe Musolino*, 139. Enzo Magrì, *Musolino: il brigante dell'Aspromonte* (Milan: Camunia, 1989) reported they withdrew at 12:02 and finished at 18:20. The date was June 11, 1902.

158 Cesare Lombroso, "L'ultimo brigante: Giuseppe Musolino," *Nuova antologia* 97 (February 1, 1902): 508–16. Also published as an appendix in Lombroso, *Delitti vecchi e delitti nuovi*.

159 Lombroso, *Delitti vecchi e delitti nuovi*, 326.

160 Lombroso, *Delitti vecchi e delitti nuovi*, 326, 327.

161 Lombroso, *Delitti vecchi e delitti nuovi*, 327 added that an uncle and three cousins on the mother's side were criminals, the maternal grandfather was stroke-prone, and the paternal grandfather was an alcoholic. The daughter of his aunt had epilepsy and his other sister, a serious nervous disorder.

162 Lombroso, *Delitti vecchi e delitti nuovi*, "pathological vanity," 328; "pathological epileptic base," 331.

163 Lombroso, *Delitti vecchi e delitti nuovi*, 335.

164 Lombroso, *Delitti vecchi e delitti nuovi*, 334–35.

165 Vincenzo Nisticò, *Giuseppe Musolino: galera o manicomio?* (Naples: A. Delle Donne, 1902), 9.

166 Nisticò, *Giuseppe Musolino*, 8.

167 Nisticò, *Giuseppe Musolino*, 8–12.

168 Nisticò, *Giuseppe Musolino*, 15–16.

169 Nisticò, *Giuseppe Musolino*, 19.

170 Nisticò, *Giuseppe Musolino*, 29.

171 Morselli and De Sanctis, *Biografia di un bandito*, 383.

172 Enrico Morselli, "Riepilogo del 'fenomeno Musolino,'" *Nuova antologia* 185 (December 16, 1902): 696–704.

173 Enrico Pessina, "La crisi del diritto penale nell'ultimo trentennio del secolo XIX," *Rivista giurdica e sociale* 3 (February 1906): 49–61, 52.

174 See Jean-Lucien Sanchez, "Les lois Bérenger (lois du 14 août 1885 et du 26 mars 1891)," *Criminocorpus, revue hypermédia* (2005), http://criminocorpus.revues .org/13; doi:10.4000/criminocorpus.132 (accessed January 28, 2013). The August 14, 1885, law provided that prisoners with sentences of less than six months in length were eligible for parole after having served time for at least three months. For sentences of longer than six months, they had to have served half the sentence. The law of March 26, 1891, allowed judges to suspend prison sentences or fines for first offenses. The law approved on November 15, 1892, subtracted time served before the trial, and the April 5, 1899, law increased the age of minors. See also Kalifa, *Crime et culture au XIXe siècle*, 282–3.

175 Ferri, *Sociologia criminale*, 93–95.

176 Ferri, *Sociologia criminale*, 101.

177 Ferri, *Sociologia criminale*, 106.

178 Italians separated reformatories from prisons in 1907, Gibson, *Born to Crime*, 189. The French prohibited punishments before age 18 in 1906 and in 1912 permitted trials only after age 13, Lacassagne, *Des Transformations*, 19.

179 Gibson, *Born to Crime*, 3, and Kalifa, *Crime et culture au XIXe siècle*, 264, 268.
180 Kalifa, *Crime et culture au XIXe siècle*, 257. He refers to "a veritable psychosis." See also Donovan on French efforts to sideline juries because of their sympathetic treatment of criminals.
181 Kalifa, *Crime et culture au XIXe siècle*, 288–97.
182 Enrico Ferri, "Difesa sociale e difesa di classe nella giustizia penale," *La Scuola Positiva* 9 (1899): 577–89, 580.
183 Ferri, "Difesa sociale e difesa di classe nella giustizia penale," 589.

Chapter 7

1 Dr. J[ulien] Chevalier, *L'inversion sexuelle: une maladie de personnalité* (Paris: G. Masson, 1893), vi–vii.
2 Chevalier, *L'inversion sexuelle*, xii–xiii.
3 Georges Vigarello, *Histoire du viol, XVIe–XXe siècle* (Paris: Seuil, 1998) reviews the terms of the 1810 Code, 136–49.
4 *Il Codice Penale del Regno d'Italia*, preamble to Titolo VIII, https://archive.org/details/ilcodicepenalep00crivgoog (accessed July 13, 2015).
5 *Il Codice Penale del Regno d'Italia*, articles 353–58.
6 "Atti di libidine contro nature," *Il Codice Penale del Regno d'Italia*, preamble to Titolo VIII.
7 Georges Lantéri-Laura, *Lecture des perversions: historie de leur appropriation médicale* (Paris: Masson, 1979), 20–23, discusses the role of the Church.
8 Lantéri-Laura, *Lecture des perversions*, 10.
9 A[nnunziato] La Cara, *La base organica dei pervertimenti sessuali e la loro profilassi sociale*, 2nd ed. (Turin: Fratelli Bocca, 1924), 1–2. First edition published in 1902.
10 Ch[arles] Féré, *L'instinct sexuel: évolution et dissolution* (Paris: Félix Alcan, 1899), 10–11. *Instinct sexuel* can be translated as sexual impulse.
11 Chevalier, *L'inversion sexuelle*, xxiv.
12 Marmier, *Les perversions instinctives*, 49.
13 Marmier, *Les perversions instinctives*, 48.
14 Marmier, *Les perversions instinctives*, 49–50.
15 Féré, *L'instinct sexuel*, 154.
16 Féré, *L'instinct sexuel*, 154.
17 Chevalier, *L'inversion sexuelle*, vi, ix.
18 Leonardo Bianchi, "Sulla impotenza neurastenica," *Archivio delle psicopatie sessuali* 1 (May–June 1896): 133–34.
19 Bianchi, "Sulla impotenza neurastenica," 138–39.
20 Bianchi, "Sulla impotenza neurastenica," 132, 139.
21 Bianchi, "Sulla impotenza neurastenica," 134–35.
22 Bianchi, "Sulla impotenza neurastenica," 137.
23 Bianchi, "Sulla impotenza neurastenica," 141.
24 Pasquale Penta, "Ancora sulla impotenza sessuale neurastenica—Note critiche ed osservazioni," *Archivio delle psicopatie sessuali* 1 (August 1–15, 1896): 206.
25 Bianchi, "Sulla impotenza neurastenica," 141.
26 Bianchi, "Sulla impotenza neurastenica," 142.
27 Penta, "Ancora sulla impotenza sessuale neurastenica," 212.
28 Emile Laurent, *L'amour morbide: étude de psychologie pathologique* (Paris: Société d'Editions Scientifiques, 1891), 57.

29 Benjamin Ball, *La folie érotique* (Paris: L'Harmattan, 2001), 86. The first edition was published in 1888 and the second in 1893. It is not clear which one is the basis for this work. He held the chair beginning in 1877.

30 Ball, *La folie érotique*, 69–78. See also Trélat, *La folie lucide*.

31 Ball, *La folie érotique*, 44.

32 Ball, *La folie érotique*, 17.

33 The following year the articles appeared in a collection titled *Études de psychologie expérimentale* (Paris: Doin, 1888). They are reprinted in Alfred Binet, *Le fétichisme dans l'amour* (Paris: Payot & Rivages, 2001).

34 Binet, *Le fétichisme dans l'amour*, 32.

35 Binet, *Le fétichisme dans l'amour*, 80–92.

36 Binet, *Le fétichisme dans l'amour*, 101.

37 [Jean-Martin] Charcot and [Valentin] Magnan, "Pathologie mentale: inversion du sens génital," *Archives de neurologie: Revue des maladies nerveuses et mentales* 4 (November–December 1882): 308–11.

38 Charcot and Magnan, "Pathologie mentale: inversion du sens génital," 320.

39 Ball, *La folie érotique*, 114.

40 William A. Peniston, *Pederasts and Others: Urban Culture and Sexual Identity in Nineteenth-Century Paris* (New York: Harrington Park Press, 2004).

41 Ambroise Tardieu, *Étude médico-légale sur les attentats aux moeurs* (Paris: J.-B. Baillìre et fils, 1858). Page references come from the Italian edition, *Delitti di libidine: Oltraggi pubblici al pudore, stupri, ed attentati al pudore, pederastia e sodomia* (Rome: Fratelli Capaccini, 1898). Translator is not identified.

42 Tardieu, *Étude médico-légale sur les attentats aux moeurs*, 245.

43 Tardieu, *Étude médico-légale sur les attentats aux moeurs*, 248.

44 Tardieu, *Étude médico-légale sur les attentats aux moeurs*, 269. He said it was "extremely rare" to see no signs in an avowed pederast, 270.

45 Tardieu, *Étude médico-légale sur les attentats aux moeurs*, 275–76.

46 Tardieu, *Étude médico-légale sur les attentats aux moeurs*, 265.

47 Tardieu, *Étude médico-légale sur les attentats aux moeurs*, 264.

48 Tardieu, *Étude médico-légale sur les attentats aux moeurs*, 321.

49 Carl Westphal, "Die conträre Sexualempfindung, Symptom eines neuropathischen (psychopathischen) Zustandes," *Archiv für Psychiatrie und Nervenkrankheiten* 2 (February 1870): 73–108 and "Zur conträren Sexualempfindung," *Archiv für Psychiatrie und Nervenkrankheiten* 6 (June 1876): 620–21. Some references to the first article erroneously date its publication in 1869. For an English translation of the first article, see Michael A. Lombardi-Nash, ed. and trans., *Sodomites and Urnings: Homosexual Representations in Classic German Journals* (New York: Harrington Park Press, 2006), 87–120.

50 Arrigo Tamassia, "Sull'inversione dell istinto sessuale," *Rivista sperimentale di freniatria e medicina legale delle alienazioni mentali* 4 (1878): 97–117.

51 Tamassia describes the case 103–9.

52 Tamassia, "Sull'inversione dell istinto sessuale," 110–11.

53 Charcot and Magnan, "Pathologie mentale: inversion du sens génital," 164.

54 Charcot and Magnan, "Pathologie mentale: inversion du sens génital," 43.

55 Charcot and Magnan, "Pathologie mentale: inversion du sens génital," 222–23, 227.

56 Charcot and Magnan, "Pathologie mentale: inversion du sens génital," 200–15.

57 Charcot and Magnan, "Pathologie mentale: inversion du sens génital," 304–5.

58 Charcot and Magnan, "Pathologie mentale: inversion du sens génital," 299.

59 Chevalier, *L'inversion sexuelle*, xix.

60 Chevalier, *L'inversion sexuelle*, 43.
61 Chevalier, *L'inversion sexuelle*, 379–80.
62 Chevalier, *L'inversion sexuelle*, 163–64.
63 Pasquale Penta, "Caratteri generali, origine e significato dei PERVERTIMENTI SESSUALI dimostrati colle autobiografie di Alfieri e di Rousseau e col dialogo 'Gli amori' di Luciano," *Archivio delle psicopatie sessuali* 1 (January 1, 1896): 2–3. This was a biweekly review of *Psicologia, psicopatologia umana e comparata di medicina legale e di psichiatria forense ad uso dei medici, magistrati ed avvocati*. Capitalization in the title is his.
64 Venturi, *Le degenerazioni psico-sessuali*, 125–26, argued that in some cases absent or defective moral sensibility caused prostitution.
65 Tardieu, *Étude médico-légale sur les attentats aux moeurs*, 25.
66 Tardieu, *Étude médico-légale sur les attentats aux moeurs*, 31. Ninety were between 13 and 15, eighty-four between 15 and 20, nine over 20, and fourteen not specified.
67 Cesare Lombroso, *Delitti di libidine*, 2nd ed. (Turin: Fratelli Bocca, 1886), 46. England reported 167 in 1830–1834; 972 in 1835–1839; 1395 in 1851–1855, 46–47.
68 Penta, "Caratteri generali," 221.
69 Penta, "Caratteri generali," 293.
70 Penta, "Caratteri generali," 1.
71 Chevalier, *L'inversion sexuelle*, xiii.
72 Ball, *La folie érotique*, 8–9.
73 Ball, *La folie érotique*, 131.
74 Ball, *La folie érotique*, 138.
75 Ball, *La folie érotique*, 156.
76 Ball, *La folie érotique*, 156.
77 Ball, *La folie érotique*, 149.
78 Féré, *L'instinct sexuel*, 4.
79 Féré, *L'instinct sexuel*, 31.
80 Ribot, *Les maladies de la personnalité*, 57–58. The first edition was published in 1884. Pasquale Penta, *I pervertimenti sessuali nell'uomo e Vincenzo Verzeni strangolatore di donne: studio biologico* (Naples: Luigi Pierro, 1893) also described the evolution of the sexual instinct from animals to primitives to civilized humans, 93–121.
81 Féré, *L'instinct sexuel*, 33.
82 Féré, *L'instinct sexuel*, 33, 36.
83 Bianchi, *Trattato di psichiatria ad uso dei medici e degli studenti*, 619–20. See also Pasquale Penta, "L'origine e la patogenesi della inversione sessuale, secondo Krafft-Ebing e gli altri autori," *Archivio delle psicopatie sessuali* 1 (February 15 and March 1, 1896), 53–70.
84 [Valentin] Magnan, *Des anomalies, des aberrations et des perversions sexuelles* (Paris: A. Delahaye & E. Lecrosnier, 1885), 7–8. Arnold I. Davidson, *The Emergence of Sexuality: Historical Epistemology and the Formation of Concepts* (Cambridge, MA: Harvard University Press, 2001), 11–12, contends that Magnan's effort to classify aberrations according to their anatomical sites was a marginal one, not taken up by others. But Lantéri argues that Magnan developed a unifying scheme that he considers the most authentic representation of the "positivist theory of perversions" at the end of the nineteenth century, 48–50. Davidson and Lantéri agree that Magnan reasoned by analogy, because he could not prove his theory.
85 Magnan, *Des anomalies, des aberrations et des perversions sexuelles*, 8–10.
86 Magnan, *Des anomalies, des aberrations et des perversions sexuelles*, 14–17.

87 Magnan, *Des anomalies, des aberrations et des perversions sexuelles*, 27.

88 Ball, *La folie érotique*, 67–68.

89 Ball, *La folie érotique*, 89. See 83–106 for the discussion.

90 La Cara, *La base organica dei pervertimenti sessuali e la loro profilassi sociale*, 9.

91 La Cara, *La base organica dei pervertimenti sessuali e la loro profilassi sociale*, 53.

92 La Cara, *La base organica dei pervertimenti sessuali e la loro profilassi sociale*, 61, 82–83, 84. He defends Mantegazza's theory that faulty wiring promoted pederasty.

93 Emile Laurent, "Prostitution et dégénérescence," *Annales médico-psychologiques*, 8th series, 10 (November 1899): 353–81, 353.

94 Michael L. Wilson, "'Je m'occupe de politique': The Male Prostitute in Belle Epoque Print Culture" (paper presented at the meeting of the Western Society for French History, Long Beach, CA, October 20, 2006). See also Peniston, *Pederasts and Others*, who details the increasing scrutiny applied to pederasts by the police in Paris at the end of the nineteenth century.

95 Peniston explains that the police saw and took pains to document the connection between pederasty and criminality, 35–42.

96 Wilson's paper establishes that commentators equated pederasty and male prostitution in this period in France and seeks to understand why.

97 Lombroso, *Delitti di libidine*, 48.

98 La Cara, *La base organica dei pervertimenti sessuali e la loro profilassi sociale*, 26. Tardieu, *Étude médico-légale sur les attentats aux moeurs*, 142, confirmed that "many men" especially of the lower classes believed in what he called "such an inconceivable and destructive mistake" ("un errore si inconcepibile e si funesto").

99 Domenico Rizzo, *Gli spazi della morale: buon costume e ordine delle famiglie in Italia in età liberale* (Rome: Biblink, 2004). See also Vigarello, who attributes the sharp increase in reports of attacks on children in urban areas (106 cases in 1830 compared to over 800 in the 1870s) to the greater popular condemnation of the act, 179–81.

100 Chevalier, *L'inversion sexuelle*, 199.

101 Tanzi, *Trattato delle malattie mentali*, 622.

102 Chevalier, *L'inversion sexuelle*, 269.

103 Chevalier, *L'inversion sexuelle*, 228–44.

104 Chevalier, *L'inversion sexuelle*, 221, 222.

105 Chevalier, *L'inversion sexuelle*, 245.

106 Chevalier, *L'inversion sexuelle*, 251.

107 Chevalier, *L'inversion sexuelle*, 268. He referred specifically to Diderot's *La religieuse*; Balzac's *Une passion au desert*; Flaubert's *Salambò*; Sarrazine's, *Illusions perdues*, *Dernière incarnation de Vautrin, Fille aux yeux d'or*; Gauthier's *Mlle. de Maupin*, 252–53.

108 La Cara, *La base organica dei pervertimenti sessuali e la loro profilassi sociale*, 130.

109 Venturi, *Le degenerazioni psico-sessuali*, 43.

110 Venturi, *Le degenerazioni psico-sessuali*, 47 (quote), 49.

111 Chevalier, *L'inversion sexuelle*, 127.

112 La Cara, *La base organica dei pervertimenti sessuali e la loro profilassi sociale*, 23–24.

113 See Féré, *L'instinct sexuel*, 238, for example.

114 Chevalier, *L'inversion sexuelle*, 191.

115 La Cara, *La base organica dei pervertimenti sessuali e la loro profilassi sociale*, 29–30.

116 La Cara, *La base organica dei pervertimenti sessuali e la loro profilassi sociale*, 28. Venturi, *Le degenerazioni psico-sessuali*, 9, argued it was natural for adolescent males, a way of awakening their sexuality.

117 Laurent, *Le criminel aux points de vue anthropologique, psychologique et social*.

118 Ball, *La folie érotique*, 149.

119 Penta, "Caratteri generali," 1.

120 Charcot and Magnan, "Pathologie mentale: inversion du sens génital," 296–97.

121 Charcot and Magnan, "Pathologie mentale: inversion du sens génital," 4, 322.

122 Chevalier, *L'inversion sexuelle*, 393.

123 Chevalier, *L'inversion sexuelle*, 42.

124 Chevalier, *L'inversion sexuelle*, 383–88.

125 Chevalier, *L'inversion sexuelle*, 390.

126 Tanzi, *Trattato delle malattie mentali*, 619.

127 Tanzi, *Trattato delle malattie mentali*, 622.

128 Tanzi, *Trattato delle malattie mentali*, 620.

129 Ribot, *Les maladies de la personnalité*, 73–74.

130 Laurent, "Prostitution et dégénérescence," 381.

131 Laurent, "Prostitution et dégénérescence," 356.

132 Tanzi and Lugaro, *Trattato delle malattie mentali*, 103–4. Lugaro was the head of the psychiatric clinic at the University of Turin.

133 Tanzi and Lugaro, *Trattato delle malattie mentali*, viii–ix.

134 Tanzi and Lugaro, *Trattato delle malattie mentali*, xi.

135 Tanzi and Lugaro, *Trattato delle malattie mentali*, 703.

136 Féré, *L'instinct sexuel*, 177.

137 Ball, *La folie érotique*, 147. See also Chevalier, *L'inversion sexuelle*, 317.

138 Chevalier, *L'inversion sexuelle*, 354.

139 Penta, *I pervertimenti sessuali nell'uomo e Vincenzo Verzeni strangolatore di donne*, 305–6.

140 Cesare Lombroso, "Del Tribadismo nei manicomi," *Archivio di psichiatria, scienze penali ed antropologia criminale* 6 (1885): 218–21, 219.

141 La Cara, *La base organica dei pervertimenti sessuali e la loro profilassi sociale*, 129, 133–34.

142 Féré, *L'instinct sexuel*, 52, 54.

143 Féré, *L'instinct sexuel*, 42.

144 Féré, *L'instinct sexuel*, 28.

145 Féré, *L'instinct sexuel*, 11.

146 Laurent, "Prostitution et dégénérescence," 371.

147 Binet, *Le fétichisme dans l'amour*, 75.

148 Wanrooij, *Storia del pudore*, 135–49.

Chapter 8

1   [Valentin] Magnan and [Paul-Maurice] Legrain, *Les dégénérés (Etat mental et syndromes épisodiques)* (Paris: Rueff et cie, Editeurs, 1895), 91.

2   Jean-Claude Schmitt, "L'histoire des marginaux," in *La nouvelle histoire*, eds. Jacques Le Goff, Roger Chartier, and Jacques Revel (Paris: CEPL, 1978), 345.

3   Schmitt, "L'histoire des marginaux," 346.

4   André Gueslin and Dominique Kalifa, eds., *Les exclus en Europe, 1830–1930* (Paris: Les Editions de l'Atelier, 1999), 466.

5   Gueslin and Kalifa, *Les exclus en Europe, 1830–1930*, 468.

6   Gueslin and Kalifa, *Les exclus en Europe, 1830–1930*. For example, Christian Topalov
    (Sociologist and director of studies at the School for Advanced Studies in the Social
    Sciences [EEHSS, Ecole des Hautes Etudes in Sciences Sociales], Paris), 469–70;
    Antoine Prost (Historian and professor emeritus at the University of Paris, 1), 471;
    Kalifa in his summary of the round table, 475.

7   Schmitt, "L'histoire des marginaux," 368.

8   Gueslin and Kalifa, *Les exclus en Europe, 1830–1930*, 460–61. André Gueslin
    explains the utility of the term to describe the poor and those not able to achieve
    fulfillment.

9   Gueslin and Kalifa, *Les exclus en Europe, 1830–1930*, 469–70.

10 Georges Canguilhem, *The Normal and the Pathological*, 2nd ed., trans. Carolyn R.
    Fawcett (New York: Zone Books, 1991). He explains the difference between anomalies
    and abnormalities, 132–43.

11 Bianchi, *Trattato di psichiatria ad uso dei medici e degli studenti*, 366. Bianchi saw
    the will as "a powerful conscious engine" which translated ideas and emotions into
    action.

12 Laurent, "Prostitution et dégénérescence," 354, 361.

13 Penta, *Pazzia e società*, 55. The book appeared in a popular series, *Il medico di casa*
    [The Family Doctor].

14 See, for example, Max Nordau, *Degeneration*, 7th ed. (New York: D. Appleton,
    1895), 537. He spoke of "the severe mental epidemic … [the] sort of black death of
    degeneration and hysteria …" which afflicted modern society. See also Robert A. Nye,
    "Sociology and Degeneration: The Irony of Progress," in *Degeneration: The Dark Side
    of Progress*, eds. J. Edward Chamberlain and Sander L. Gilman (New York: Columbia
    University Press, 1985) and Pick, *Faces of Degeneration*.

15 Max Nordau, "Signification biologique de la dégénérescence," in *L'Opera di Cesare
    Lombroso nella scienze e nelle sue applicazioni*, ed. Leonardo Bianchi (Turin: Fratelli
    Bocca, 1906), 251. Raffaele Brugia, *I problemi della degenerazione* (Bologna: Nicola
    Zanichelli, 1906), 11, said that Morel's theory was a "starting point." See also Magnan
    and Legrain, *Les dégénerés*, 12–13, 17–18.

16 Georges-Paul-Henri Genil-Perrin, *Histoire des origines et de l'évolution de l'idée de
    dégénérescence en médicine mentale* (Paris: Alfred Leclerc, 1913), 131–32 and Magnan
    and Legrain, *Les dégénerés*, 98–100.

17 Féré, *Les épilepsies*, 239.

18 Genil-Perrin, *Histoire des origines et de l'évolution de l'idée de dégénérescence en
    médicine mentale*, 279.

19 Agostini, *Manuale de psichiatria per uso degli studenti e dei medici*, 26.

20 Agostini, *Manuale de psichiatria per uso degli studenti e dei medici*, 25.

21 Albert Mathieu, *Neurasthénie (épuisement nerveux)* (Paris: J. Rueff et Cie, Editeurs,
    1892), 177.

22 Agostini, *Manuale de psichiatria per uso degli studenti e dei medici*, 427.

23 Bianchi, *Trattato di psichiatria ad uso dei medici e degli studenti*, 477.

24 Raymond, *Neurasthénie* identifies a simple or acquired neurasthenic syndrome which
    can be treated and a more serious psychic form which results from degeneration
    and never disappears completely. The second form Janet called "psychasthénie" and
    Charcot called organic neurasthenia ("neurasthenie constitutionelle"), 3–4.

25 Canguilhem, *The Normal and the Pathological*, 43.

26 Ribot, *Les maladies de la volonté*, 6 and *Les maladies de la personnalité*, 152.

27 Dallemagne, *Physiologie de la volonté*, 25–26.

28 Dallemagne, *Physiologie de la volonté*, 27–28.
29 Dallemagne, *Physiologie de la volonté*, 48.
30 Ribot, *Les maladies de la volonté*, 176.
31 For example, Enrico Ferri served in the Chamber of Deputies beginning in 1886, and Gabriel Tarde headed the division of criminal statistics in the Ministry of Justice.
32 Fulvio Cammarano, "The Professions in Parliament, in Society and the Professions in Italy, 1860–1914," in *Society and the Professions in Italy, 1860–1914*, ed. Maria Malatesta (Cambridge: Cambridge University Press, 1995), 281. Cammarano counts 246 in the 8th and 301 in the 24th legislatures.
33 Jack D. Ellis, *The Physician-Legislators of France: Medicine and Politics in the Early Third Republic, 1870–1914* (Cambridge: Cambridge University Press, 1990), 4. He reports that lawyers, notaries, and magistrates constituted about a third (227) of the total number of deputies in 1871, a level they maintained in the next ten legislatures, 3–4.
34 Ellis, *The Physician-Legislators of France*, 2. Between forty-three and seventy-one physicians served in the Chamber of Deputies between 1876 and 1914.
35 Cammarano, "The Professions," 281, reports that in the 21st through the 24th legislatures an average of 37 deputies were doctors. Doctors constituted 5.21 percent of the deputies (35) in the 8th and 7.07 percent or 37 in the 24th.
36 Fulvio Cammarano and Maria Serena Piretti, "I professionisti in Parlamento (1861–1958)" in *Storia d'Italia, Annali 10, I professionisti*, ed. Maria Malatesta (Turin: Giulio Einaudi editore, 1996), 521–89.
37 See Gibson, *Born to Crime*.
38 See, for example, Kalifa, *Crime et culture au XIXe siècle*.
39 Wilson, "'Je m'occupe de politique'".
40 Agostini, *Manuale de psichiatria per uso degli studenti e dei medici*, 135.
41 Penta, *Pazzia e società*, 68. He argued that excessive wealth or poverty weakened the organism and then the mental faculties either immediately or in the next generation.
42 Penta, *Pazzia e società*, 70–71.
43 Penta, *Pazzia e società*, 73.
44 Guglielmo Ferrero, "La morale primitiva e l'atavismo del delitto," *Archivio di psichiatria, scienze penali ed antropologia criminale* 17 (1896): 21. See Rabinbach, *The Human Motor* for a detailed analysis of the reasons behind such views.
45 Only in exceptional circumstances could those transported return to France after having served their term. See the text of the law of May 27, 1885, https://criminocorpus.org/sources/12941/, published July 7, 2006 (accessed May 27, 2014).
46 The law passed August 14, 1885, provided that convicted criminals having served three months of sentences of less than six months or half of sentences in excess of six months could be paroled. March 26, 1891, lawmakers allowed judges to suspend sentences of first-time offenders. See Kaluszynski, *La République à l'épreuve du crime*, 147.
47 See Giovanna Vicarelli, *Alle radici della politica sanitaria in Italia: Società e salute da Crispi al fascismo* (Bologna: Il Mulino, 1997); Anne Cova, "French Feminism and Maternity: Theories and Policies, 1890–1918," in *Maternity and Gender Policies: Women and the Rise of the European Welfare States, 1880s–1950s*, eds. Gisela Bock and Pat Thane (London and New York: Routledge, 1991), 119–37, for details about maternity laws.
48 See Bartocci, *Le politiche sociali nell'Italia liberale*.

49 Law on women's and children's work, June 18, 1902; the Maternity Fund (Cassa di Maternità), August 3, 1910; vote for all male citizens 30 or older and for males over 21 who had passed the 2nd elementary school exam, completed military service, or had a high personal income.

50 See Vicarelli, *Alle radici della politica sanitaria in Italia* and Susan A. Ashley, *Making Liberalism Work: The Italian Experience, 1860–1914* (Westport, CT: Praeger, 2003).

51 See, for example, Timothy B. Smith, *Creating the Welfare State in France, 1880–1940* (Montreal & Kingston: McGill-Queen's University Press, 2003).

52 Bérard, "Le vagabondage en France," 613.

53 Ball, *Leçons sur les maladies mentales,* 359.

54 Mantegazza, "Gli atavismi psichici," 69–82, 74.

55 Penta, *I pervertimenti sessuali nell'uomo e Vincenzo Verzeni strangolatore di donne,* 123.

56 Harrington, "Beyond Phrenology," 207–15.

57 Sergi, *Le degenerazioni umane,* 197.

58 Sergi, *Le degenerazioni umane,* 25.

59 Sergi, *Le degenerazioni umane,* 26.

60 Sergi, *Le degenerazioni umane,* 80.

61 Sergi, *Le degenerazioni umane,* 93.

62 Sergi, *Le degenerazioni umane,* 169.

63 See, for example, Venturi, *Le degenerazioni psico-sessuali* and Elie Reclus, *Les primitifs: études d'ethnologie comparée* (Paris: Librairie C. Reinwold, 1902), vi–vii.

64 Féré, *La famille névropathique,* 168–69. See also Magnan, *Leçons cliniques sur les maladies mentales,* 70, who emphasizes that *dégénerés* constitute a "famille morbide."

65 Maudsley, *The Pathology of Mind,* 108. See also Féré, *La famille névropathique,* 309 and Penta, *Pazzia e società,* 55.

66 See Rabinbach for a very useful discussion of the effects of the discovery of the first and second laws of thermodynamics on thinking about the body in the last decades of the nineteenth century.

67 Ribot, *Les maladies de la personnalité,* 170.

68 Ellero, *La psichiatria, la libertà morale e la responsabilità penale,* 155.

69 Ellero, *La psichiatria, la libertà morale e la responsabilità penale,* 64. See also Ribot, *Les maladies de la volonté.*

70 In the case of neurasthenia, convention applied the label "true" to the acquired and more curable type.

71 Venturi, *Le degenerazioni psico-sessuali,* 494–95.

72 Ferri, "Gli anormali," 322.

73 Ferri, "Gli anormali," 323.

74 Ferri, "Gli anormali," 326.

75 Ferri, "Gli anormali," 325.

76 Marie and Meunier, *Les vagabonds,* 195.

77 Marie and Meunier, *Les vagabonds,* 306.

78 Nordau, *Psycho-physiologie du génie et du talent,* 41.

79 Nordau, *Psycho-physiologie du génie et du talent,* 89.

80 Ferri, "Gli anormali," 325.

81 Ferri, "Gli anormali," 331.

82 Paolo Orano, "Cesare Lombroso," *La Scuola Positiva* 16 (May–June 1906): 291. Orano was born in 1875 and died in 1945.

83   Paulhan, *La volonté*, 298.
84   Tanzi, *Trattato delle malattie mentali*, 52.
85   Tanzi, *Trattato delle malattie mentali*, 55.
86   Ribot, *Les maladies de la volonté*, 173.
87   Padovan, *Che cosa è il genio?* 121.
88   Padovan, *Che cosa è il genio?* 121–22.
89   Payot, *L'education de la volonté*, xi.

Bibliography

Agostini, Cesare. *Manuale de psichiatria per uso degli studenti e dei medici*. 3rd ed. Milan: Dottor Francesco Vallardi, 1908.

Aisenberg, Andrew R. *Contagion: Disease, Government, and the "Social Question" in 19th Century France*. Stanford, CA: Stanford University Press, 1999.

Allocati, Luigi. *Delinquenza, pazzia morale, ed epilessia: identismo clinico*. Naples: Gennaro Cozzolino, 1906.

Altobelli, Dario. *Indagine su un bandito: il caso Musolino*. Rome: Salvatorelli, 2006.

"Anarchism." In *Rivista Penale, Collezione Legislativa*, Vol. 7. Turin: Unione Tipografico-Editrice, 1890–1894, 553–79.

Anfosso, Luigi. "Domicilio coatto." In *Enciclopedia Giuridica Italiana*, Vol. 4, Part 4, 665–88. Milan: Società Editrice Libraria, 1922.

Angelvin, Dr. *La neurasthénie, mal social*. Paris: Edouard Cornély, 1905.

Angiolini, A. "Il terzo volume di 'L'Uomo Delinquente.'" *La Scuola Positiva* 7 (September 1897): 536–41.

Antolisei, Francesco. "Sul concetto del pericolo." *La Scuola Positiva* 24 (January–February 1914): 22–46.

Antonini, G. "Donizetti." *Archivio di psichiatria, scienze penali, ed antropologia criminale* 21 (1900): 595–600.

Ashley, Susan A. "Marginal People: Degeneration and Genius." In *Proceedings of the Western Society for French History: Selected Papers*, edited by Barry Rothaus, 101–09. Boulder CO: University Press of Colorado, 1997.

Ashley, Susan A. *Making Liberalism Work: The Italian Experience, 1860–1914*. Westport, CT: Praeger, 2003.

Atti del Quinto Congresso della Società Freniatrica Italiana, Siena, September 19–25, 1886. Milan: Fratelli Rechiedei, 1887.

"Atti del Sesto Congresso della Società Freniatrica Italiana." In *Supplemento al fascicolo I dell'Archivio italiano per le malattie nervose e le alieni mentali*. Milan: Fratelli Rechiedei, 1890.

Audiffrent, Dr. [Georges]. "De l'hystérie." *Archives d'anthropologie criminelle, de criminologie, et de psychologie normale et pathologique* 18 (1903): 321–34.

Babini, Valeria Paola. *La questione dei frenastenici: Alle origini della psicologia scientifica in Italia (1870–1910)*. Milan: FrancoAngeli, 1996.

Babini, Valeria Paola, Maurizia Cotti, Fernanda Minuz, and Annamaria Tagliavini. *Tra sapere e potere: La psichiatria italiana nella seconda metà dell'Ottocento*. Bologna: Il Mulino, 1982.

Badaloni, Nicola, and Agostino Berenini. *Lotta di classe e la legge del domicilio coatto*. Milan: Ufficio della Lotta di Classe, 1894.

Bain, Alexander. "The Feelings and the Will Viewed Psychologically." *The Fortnightly Review* 3 (1866): 575–88.

Ball, B[enjamin]. *De la responsabilité partielle des aliénés*. Paris: Librairie J.-B. Baillière, 1886.

Ball, Benjamin. *La folie érotique*. Paris: L'Harmattan, 2001.

Ball, B[enjamin]. *Leçons sur les maladies mentales*. 2nd ed. Paris: Asselin et Houzeau, 1890.

Ballet, Gilbert. "Attitude extatique chez un douteur aboulique." *Revue neurologique* 13 (1905): 749–50.

Ballet, Gilbert. *Leçons de clinique médicale: Psychoses et affections nerveuses*. Paris: Octave Doin, 1897.

Banti, Alberto Mario. "Retoriche e idiomi: L'antiparlamentarismo nell'Italia de fine Ottocento." *Storica* 1 (1995): 7–41.

Bartocci, Enzo. *Le politiche sociali nell'Italia liberale (1861–1919)*. Rome: Donzelli Editore, 1999.

Beachy, Robert. "The German Invention of Homosexuality." *Journal of Modern History* 82 (December 2010): 801–38.

Beard, George Miller. *American Nervousness, Its Causes and Consequences: A Supplement to Nervous Exhaustion (Neurasthenia)*. New York: G. P. Putnam's Sons, 1881.

Beard, Giorgio M. *Il Nervosismo americano: Le sue cause e le sue conseguenze*. Translated by Sofia Fortini Santarelli. Città del Castello: S. Lapi Tipografo Editore, 1888.

Beard, Giorgio M. *Trattato pratico dell'esaurimento nervoso (Neurastenia): Sintomi, natura, conseguenze, trattamento*. Edited by A. D. Rockwell and translated by Gustavo Bonvecchiato. Milan: Dottor Francesco Vallardi, 1892.

Beaune, Jean-Claude. *Le vagabond et la machine: Essai sur l'automatisme ambulatoire, médicine, technique et société, 1880–1910*. Seyssel: Editions du Champ Vallon, 1983.

Beccalossi, Chiara. *Female Sexual Inversion: Same-Sex Desires in Italian and British Sexology, c. 1870–1920*. Basingstoke: Palgrave Macmillan, 2012.

Beccalossi, Chiara. "The Origin of Italian Sexological Studies: Female Sexual Inversion, ca. 1870–1900." *Journal of the History of Sexuality* 18 (No. 1) (January 2009): 103–20, http://www.jstor.org/stable/20542720 (accessed October, 28, 2013).

Beck, René. *Contribution à l'étude des rapports du vagabondage et de la folie*. Lyon: Typographie et Lithographie J. Prudhomme, 1902.

Becker, Peter and Richard F. Wetzell, eds. *Criminals and Their Scientists. The History of Criminology in International Perspective*. New York: Cambridge University Press, Washington DC: German Historical Institute, 2006.

Benedikt, Maurice [Moriz]. "Le vagabond et son traitement: étude psychologique et sociologique." *Annales de l'hygiène publique et médicine légale*, Series 3, no. 24 (1890): 493–501.

Bérard, Alexandre. "Le vagabondage en France." *Archives d'anthropologie criminelle* 13 (1898): 601–14.

Berrios, German E. *The History of Mental Symptoms: Descriptive Psychopathology since the Nineteenth Century*. Cambridge: Cambridge University Press, 1996.

Bertolli, Tommaso. *Della ammonizione secondo la legge di pubblica sicurezza, 30 Giugno 1889*. Turin: Unione Tipografico-Editrice, 1892.

Bianchi, A. G. *La patologia del genio e gli scienziati italiani: Inchiesta a proposito del caso di Guy de Maupassant*. Milan: Max Kantorowicz, 1892.

Bianchi, A. G., Guglielmo Ferrero, and Scipio Sighele. *Il mondo criminale italiano, 1889–1892*. Milan: L. Omodei Zorini, 1893.

Bianchi, Leonardo. "Sulla impotenza neurastenica." *Archivio delle psicopatie sessuali* 1 (May–June 1896): 129–47.

Bianchi, Leonardo. *Trattato di psichiatria ad uso dei medici e degli studenti*. Naples: V. Pasquale, 1905.

Billod, E. "Maladies de la volonté." *Annales médico-psychologiques* 10 (September 1847): 170–202.

Binet, Alfred. *Le fétichisme dans l'amour*. Paris: Payot & Rivages, 2001.

Bini, Francesco. *Della pazzia morale in relazione alle esigenze sociali*. Edited by Umanitarie. Milan: Stabilmento dei Fratelli Rechiedei, 1881.

Bland, Lucy, and Laura Doan. *Sexology in Culture: Labelling Bodies and Desires*. Chicago: University of Chicago Press, 1998.

Bloch, Iwan. *La vita sessuale dei nostri tempi nei suoi rapporti con la civiltà moderna*. 6th ed. Translation of the 10th ed. by Dottor Mario Carrara with the addition of three chapters by Cesare Lombroso on "L'amore nel suicidio, nel delitto e nella pazzia." Turin: Sten Editrice, 1921.

Blocq, Paul. *La neurasthénie et les neurasthéniques*. Paris: Imprimerie F. Levé, 1891.

Blum, Albert. *De l'hystéro-neurasthénie traumatique (Railway-Spine)*. Paris: Asselin et Houzeau, 1893.

Bodio, L. "La delinquenza italiana nel 1893." *La Scuola Positiva* 5 (September 1895): 174–84.

Bogousslavsky, J[ulien], ed. *Following Charcot: A Forgotten History of Neurology and Psychiatry*, Vol. 29. Frontiers of Neurology and Neuroscience. Basel: Karger, 2011.

Bolis, Giovanni. *La polizia in Italia e in altri stati d'Europa e le classi pericolose della società*. Bologna: Nicola Zanichelli, 1871.

Bonfigli, Clodomiro. *Idee fisse e nevrastenia: Quattro lezioni preliminari di clinica psichiatrica*. Milan: Dottor Francesco Vallardi, 1898.

Bonvecchiato, Ernesto. *A proposito di un processo scandaloso: Semi-imbecilli, mattoidi e folli morali*. Venice: C. Ferrari alla Posta, 1884.

Borgonovo, Giacomo. *Ammoniti, oziosi e traviate: Mali e remedi*. Genoa: Del Movimento, 1879.

Bourdin, V. "De l'impulsion." *Annales médico-psychologiques* 54 (March 1896): 317–39.

Bourguignon, J. H. *La neurasthénie: ses causes, ses symptomes, son traitement*. 4th ed. Paris: Laboratoire Bourguignon, 1911.

Bournet, Albert. *De la criminalité en France et en Italie: Étude médico-légale*. Paris: Librairie J.-B. Baillière et fils, 1884.

Bouveret, L. *La neurasthénie (épuisement nerveux)*. Paris: J.-B. Baillière et fils, 1890.

Bovio, Giovanni. *Il genio*. Milan: Fratelli Treves, 1890.

Bovio, Giovanni. *Il genio: un capitolo di psicologia*. Milan: Fratelli Treves, 1899.

Brajon, Luigi. *Intorno alla follia morale: Considerazioni medico-psicologiche*. Bologna: Tipografia Archivescovile, 1888.

Bravo, Anna. "Polizia." In *Storia d'Italia, vol. 2, Il Mondo Contemporaneo*, 885–96. Florence: La Nuova Italia, 1978.

Breger, Claudia. "Feminine Masculinities: Scientific and Literary Representations of 'Female Inversion' at the Turn of the Twentieth Century." *Journal of the History of Sexuality*, 14 (No. 1–2) (April 2005): 76–106, http://www.jstor.org/stable/3704710 (accessed June 8, 2014).

Bristow, Joseph. "Remapping the Sites of Modern Gay History: Legal Reform, Medico-Legal Thought, Homosexual Scandal, Erotic Geography." *Journal of British Studies*, 46 (No. 1) (January 2007): 116–42, http://www.jstor.org/stable/10.1086/508401 (accessed October 28, 2013).

Brown, Wendy. *Regulating Aversion: Tolerance in the Age of Identity and Empire*. Princeton and Oxford: Princeton University Press, 2006.

Brugia, Raffaele. *I problemi della degenerazione*. Bologna: Nicola Zanichelli, 1906.

Burgalassi, Marco M. *Itinerari di una scienza: La sociologia in Italia tra Otto e Novecento*. Milan: FrancoAngeli, 1996.

Buttafuoco, Annarita. "Motherhood as a Political Strategy: The Role of the Italian Women's Movement in the Creation of the *Cassa Nazionale di Maternità*." In *Maternity and Gender Policies: Women and the Rise of the European Welfare States, 1880s–1950s,* edited by Gisela Bock and Pat Thane, 178–95. London and New York: Routledge, 1991.

Bynum, W. F., Roy Porter, and Michael Shepherd, eds. *The Anatomy of Madness: Essays in the History of Psychiatry. Vol. 3, The Asylum and Its Psychiatry.* New York: Tavistock Publications, 1985.

Cammarano, Fulvio. "The Professions in Parliament, in Society and the Professions in Italy, 1860–1914." In *Society and the Professions in Italy, 1860–1914,* edited by Maria Malatesta, 277–312. Translated by Adrian Belton. Cambridge and New York: Cambridge University Press, 1995.

Cammarano, Fulvio, and Maria Serena Piretti. "I professionisti in Parlamento (1861–1958)." In *Storia d'Italia,* Annali 10, *I professionisti,* edited by Maria Malatesta, 521–89. Turin: Giuli Einaudi Editore, 1996.

Campbell, Robert Jean. *Psychiatric Dictionary.* 7th ed. New York: Oxford University Press, 1996.

Canguilhem, Georges. *The Normal and the Pathological.* 2nd ed. Translated by Carolyn R. Fawcett. New York: Zone Books, 1991.

Cappelletti, Vincenzo. "Evoluzione ed evoluzionismo: Nota storico-critica su un paradigma dominante." *Clio* 20 (1984): 213–32.

Castel, Robert. *The Regulation of Madness: The Origins of Incarceration in France.* Translated by W. D. Halls. Berkeley: University of California Press, 1988.

Celesia, Paolo. "Sulla inversione sessuale." *Archivio di psichiatria, scienze penali ed antropologia criminale* 21 (1900): 209–20.

Chamberlain, J. Edward, and Sander L. Gilman, eds. *Degeneration: The Dark Side of Progress.* New York: Columbia University Press, 1985.

Chaperon, Sylvie. "The Foundations of 19th-Century Psychiatric Approaches to Sexual Deviance." Translated by Kristina Valendinova. *Recherches en psychanalyse* 2010/2 (No. 10) (2010): 276–85. doi: 10.3917/rep. 010.0097 (accessed May 5, 2014).

Charcot, [Jean-Martin]. *Leçons du mardi à la Salpêtrière. Volume 1, Policliniques 1887–1888.* Paris: Tchou pour la Bibliothèque des Introuvables, 2002.

Charcot, Jean-Martin. *Leçons du mardi à la Salpêtrière, professeur Charcot. Volume 1, Policlinique 1887–1888.* 2nd ed. Course notes by MM. Blin, Charcot et H. Colin. Paris: Babé, 1892.

Charcot, [Jean-Martin], and [Valentin] Magnan. "Pathologie mentale: inversion du sens génital." *Archives de neurologie: Revue des maladies nerveuses et mentales* 3 (Part 1) (January–February 1882): 53–60 and (Part 2) (November–December 1882): 296–322.

Chauncey, George, Jr. "From Sexual Inversion to Homosexuality: Medicine and the Changing Conceptualization of Female Deviance." *Salmagundi* (No. 58/59) (Fall 1982–Winter 1983): 114–46, http://www.jstor.org/stable/40547567 (accessed October 28, 2013).

Chevalier, J[ulien] Dr. *L'inversion sexuelle: une maladie de la personnalité.* Paris: G. Masson, 1893.

Ciacci, Margherita, and Vittoria Gualandi, eds. *La costruzione sociale della devianza.* Bologna: Il Mulino, 1977.

Cionci, Venanzio. *La legge di polizia sulle persone sospette.* Rieti: Tipografia Trinchi, 1880.

Codeluppi, Vittorio. "L'autobiografia di un vagabondo nato." *La Scuola Positiva* 12 (February 1902): 109–16.

Cognetti de Martiis, Leonardo. *Pazzia morale, simulazione, mania.* Rome: Vochera Enrico, 1894.

Colajanni, Napoleone. *La sociologia criminale,* 2 vols. Catania: Filippo Tropea, 1889.

Collée, Michel, and Claude Quétel. *Histoire des maladies mentales*. Paris: Presses Universitaires de France, 1987.

Collin, Paul. *Aperçus sur le vagabondage: Effets, causes, remèdes*. Paris: Marcel Rivière, 1907.

Congrès international d'anthropologie criminelle, 2ième session, Paris 1889. *Compte rendu des travaux de la session* by Dr. E. Magitot. Lyon: Imprimerie de A. Storck, 1889.

Corridore, Francesco. *Nota sulla statistica degli ammoniti*. Rome: Tipografia delle Terme Diocleziane, 1907.

Cosenza, Vincenzo. "Degli ammoniti e dei diffamati arrestati in flagranza di contravvenzione." *La Scuola Positiva* 1 (September 15–30, 1891): 385–408.

Cotard, [Jules] le Dr. "De l'aboulie et de l'inhibition en pathologie mentale." Extract from *La Revue philosophique*, June 1886.

Cowan, Michael. *Cult of the Will: Nervousness and German Modernity*. University Park: Pennsylvania State University Press, 2008.

Crozier, Ivan. "La sexologie et la définition du 'normal' entre 1860 et 1900." Translated by Oristelle Boni. *Cahiers du Genre* 34 (No. 1) (2003):17–37. doi: 0.3917/cdge.034.0017 (accessed January 31, 2013).

Crozier, Ivan. "Nineteenth-Century British Psychiatric Writing about Homosexuality Before Havelock Ellis: The Missing Story." *Journal of the History of Medicine and Allied Sciences* 63 (No. 1) (January 2008): 65–102, http://muse.jhu.edu/journals/jhm/summary/v063/63.1crozier.html (accessed May 31, 2014).

Curcio, Giorgio. *Delle persone sospette in Italia*. Milan: Tipografia Editrice Lombarda, 1874.

Dallemagne, J. *Les theories de la criminalité*. Paris: Masson, 1896.

Dallemagne J. *Pathologie de la volonté*. Paris: Masson, [1898].

Dallemagne, J. *Physiologie de la volonté*. Paris: Masson, [1898?].

Dandeker, Christopher. *Surveillance, Power and Modernity: Bureaucracy and Discipline from 1700 to the Present Day*. New York: St. Martin's Press, 1990.

Daston, Lorraine J. "The Theory of Will versus the Science of Mind." In *The Problematic Science: Psychology in Nineteenth-Century Thought*, edited by William R. Woodward and Mitchell G. Ash, 88–115. New York: Praeger, 1982.

Davidson, Arnold I. *The Emergence of Sexuality: Historical Epistemology and the Formation of Concepts*. Cambridge, MA: Harvard University Press, 2001.

De Bernardi, Alberto, ed. *Follia, psichiatria, e società*. Milan: FrancoAngeli Editore, 1982.

De Leo, Antonio. *Il brigante Musolino*. Rosarno: Virgiglio, 1996.

De Nava, Giovanni. *Musolino: Il bandito D'Aspromonte*. Florence: Casa Editrice G. Nerbini, 1961.

De Nigris, Egisto. *La Neurastenia*. Milan: Francesco Vallardi, 1896?.

De Rocchi, L. "La legislazione penale nella sua funzione sociale." *La Scuola Positiva* 5 (July 1895): 29–32.

De Sanctis, Sante. "Sui criteri e metodi per l'educabilità dei deficienti e dei dementi." *Rivista sperimentale di freniatria* 28 (1902): 354–409.

De Sanctis, Sante. *Sulla nevrastenia: studio clinico-nosografico*. Milan: Leonardo Vallardi, 1890.

Dean, Carolyn J. "The Productive Hypothesis: Foucault, Gender, and the History of Sexuality." *History and Theory* 33 (1994): 271–296.

Dean, Carolyn J. *Sexuality and Modern Western Culture*. New York: Twayne Publishers, 1996.

Deloux, Jean-Pierre. *Vacher l'assassin: Un* Serial Killer *français au XIXe siècle*. Paris: Claire Vigne, 1995.

Demoor, Jean, Jean Massart, and Émile Vandervelde. *L'évolution régressive en biologie et en sociologie*. Paris: Félix Alcan, 1897.

Dequidt, Georges. *À propos d'un cas d'aboulie: Réflexions cliniques et pathogéniques*. Paris: Henri Jouve, 1908.

Di Stasio, Guglielmo. *Su l'accattonaggio: Studio in economia sociale*. 2nd ed. Naples: Priore, 1913.

Donovan, James M. *Juries and the Transformation of Criminal Justice in France in the Nineteenth and Twentieth Centuries*. Chapel Hill: University of North Carolina Press, 2010.

Dowbiggin, Ian R. *Inheriting Madness: Professionalization and Psychiatric Knowledge in Nineteenth-Century France*. Berkeley: University of California Press, 1991.

Dubbini, Renzo. *Geography of the Gaze: Urban and Rural Vision in Early Modern Europe*. Translated by Lydia G. Cochrane. Chicago: University of Chicago Press, 2002.

Dubourdieu, Victor-Charles. *Contribution à l'étude de l'automatisme ambulatoire de la dromomanie des dégénérés*. Bordeaux: Imprimerie du Midi, 1894.

Duggan, Christopher. *The Force of Destiny: A History of Italy since 1796*. London: Allen Lane, 2007.

Dutil, A. *Hystérie et neurasthénie associées (Railway-Spine et Névrose traumatique)*. Paris: Librairie Octave Doin, 1889.

Ellero, Lorenzo. *La psichiatria, la libertà morale e la responsabilità penale*. Padua: Angelo Draghi Editore, 1885.

Ellis, Havelock. *Studies in the Psychology of Sex. Volume 2, Sexual Inversion*. 3rd ed. Philadelphia: F. A. Davis Company, 1927.

Ellis, Havelock. *A Study of British Genius*. London: Constable and Company, 1927. Revised and enlarged edition.

Ellis, Jack D. *The Physician-Legislators of France: Medicine and Politics in the Early Third Republic, 1870–1914*. Cambridge: Cambridge University Press, 1990.

Elwitt, Sanford. *The Third Republic Defended: Bourgeois Reform in France, 1880–1914*. Baton Rouge and London: Louisiana State University Press, 1986.

Fabre, Joseph. *De l'hystéro-neurasthénie traumatique devant la loi dans les accidents de chemin de fer*. Paris: Henri Jouve, 1893.

Falret, Jules. *De la folie raisonnante ou folie morale: programme de questions à étudier*. Paris: E. Martinet, 1866.

Falret, Jules. *De la folie raisonnante ou folie morale: Réponse à M. Delasiauve*. Paris: E. Martinet, 1867.

Federn, Karl. *La verità sul processo contro la contessa Linda Murri-Bonmartini*. Bari: Giuseppe Laterza, 1908.

Féré, Ch[arles]. *Contribution à l'étude de la descendance des invertis*. Extract from Archives de neurologie, no. 28, 1898. Published by Progrès Médical.

Féré, Charles. *Dégénérescence et criminalité: essai physiologique*. Paris: Félix Alcan, 1888.

Féré, Charles. *L'instinct sexuel: évolution et dissolution*. Paris: Félix Alcan, 1899.

Féré, Ch[arles]. *La famille névropathique: Théorie tératologique de l'hérédité et de la prédisposition morbides et de la dégénérescence*. Paris: Ancienne Librarie Germer Baillière, 1894.

Féré, Charles. *Les épilepsies et les épileptiques*. Paris: Félix Alcan, 1890.

Ferrero, Ernesto. *La mala Italia: Storie nere di fine secolo*. Milan: Rizzoli, 1973.

Ferrero, Guglielmo. "La morale primitiva e l'atavismo del delitto." *Archivio di psichiatria, scienze penali ed antropologia criminale* 17 (1896): 1–37.

Ferri, Enrico. "Criminalità in Italia e sostituivi penali a rovescio." *La Scuola Positiva* 1 (June 1891): 102–17.

Ferri, Enrico. "Difesa sociale e difesa di classe nella giustizia penale." *La Scuola Positiva* 9 (October 1899): 577–89.

Ferri, Enrico. "Gli anormali." *La Scuola Positiva* 10 (June 1900): 321–33.

Ferri, Enrico. *I delinquenti nell'arte ed altre conferenze.* 2nd ed. Turin: Unione Tipografico-Editrice Torinese, 1926.

Ferri, Enrico. *L'omicida nella psicologia e nella psicopatologia criminale.* 2nd ed. Turin: Unione Tipografico-Editrice Torinese, 1925.

Ferri, Enrico. "L'omicidio in Europa." *La Scuola Positiva* 3 (March 1893): 241–51.

Ferri, Enrico. *L'omicidio-suicidio: Responsabilità giuridica.* 5th ed. Turin: Unione Tipografico-Editrice Torinese, 1925.

Ferri, Enrico. *Socialismo e criminalità: appunti.* Turin: Fratelli Bocca, 1883.

Ferri, Enrico. *Socialismo e scienza positiva (Darwin-Spencer-Marx).* Rome: Casa Editrice Italiana, 1894.

Ferri, Enrico. *Sociologia criminale.* Milan: Feltrinelli, 1979.

Ferri, Enrico. *Studi sulla criminalità.* 2nd ed. Turin: Unione Tipografico Editrice Farinesi, 1926.

Fiessinger, Ch. *Les maladies des caractères: Étude de physiologie morale.* Paris: Perrin et Cie, 1916.

Filippi, [Angiolo]. "L'epilessia procursiva." *Lo Sperimentale: Giornale italiano di scienze mediche* 59 (October 1887): 433–37.

Florian, Eugenio. "La statistica dei motivi determinanti al reato." *La Scuola Positiva* 5 (October–November 1895): 207–54.

Florian, Eugenio, and Guido Cavaglieri. *I Vagabondi,* 2 vols. Turin: Fratelli Bocca, 1897, 1900.

Fontana, Alessandro. *Il vizio occult: Cinque saggi sulle origini della modernità.* Ancona: Transeuropa, 1989.

Forgacs, David. *Italy's Margins: Social Exclusion and Nation Formation since 1861.* Cambridge: Cambridge University Press, 2014.

Fornasari di Verce, E. "La criminalità e le vicende economiche d'Italia dal 1873 al 1890." *Archivio di psichiatria, scienze penali ed antropologia criminale* 14 (1893): 365–405, 536–55.

Foucault, Michel. *The Archeology of Knowledge* and *The Discourse on Language.* Translated by A. M. Sheridan Smith. New York: Pantheon Books, c. 1972.

Foucault, Michel. *The Birth of the Clinic: An Archaeology of Medical Perception.* Translated by M. Sheridan Smith. New York: Vintage Books, 1994.

Foucault, Michel. *Discipline and Punish: The Birth of the Prison.* Translated by A. M. Sheridan. New York: Vintage, 1979.

Foucault, Michel. *Mental Illness and Psychology.* Translated by Alan Sheridan. Berkeley: University of California Press, 1987.

Foucault, Michel. *The Order of Things: An Archeology of the Human Sciences.* New York: Vintage Books, 1994, c. 1970.

Foville, Ach[ille], fils, "Les aliénés voyageurs ou migrateurs: étude clinique sur certains cas de lypémanie." *Annales médico-psychologiques: Journal de l'aliénation mentale et de la médicine légale des aliénés* 14 (1875): 5–45.

Franchi, Bruno. "Delitti e contravvenzioni secondo le più recenti statistiche e nel loro carattere giuridico." *La Scuola Positiva* 12 (October 1902): 577–98; 12 (November 1902): 668–77; and 12 (December 1902): 712–21.

Franchi, Bruno. "Intorno al principio della 'difesa sociale.'" *La Scuola Positiva* 11 (May 1901): 257–70.

"Frenocomio di Reggio-Emilio." *Archivio italiano per le malattie nervose e più particolarmente per le alienazioni mentali* 13 (1876): 112–14.

Gallerani, Giovanni. *Fisiologia del genio: Analisi del prodotto geniale.* Bari: Pasquale De Ganosa, 1929.

Galzigna, Mario, ed. *La follia, la norma, l'archivio: prospettive storiografiche e orientamenti archivistici.* Venice: Marsilio Editori, 1984.

Galzigna, Mario. *La malattia morale: Alle origini della psichiatria.* Venice: Marsilio Editore, 1988.

Garnier, P[aolo]. *Nevrastenia sessuale: Cause e rimedi.* Revised by G. Ambron. Milan: R. Quintieri, 1915.

Garofalo, R[affaele]. *Criminologia.* 2nd ed. Turin: Fratelli Bocca, 1891.

Garofalo, Raffaele. "Influenza sul diritto penale degli studii di antropologia e sociologia criminale." *La Scuola Positiva* 3 (September 15–30, 1893): 771–80.

Garofalo, Raffaele. "La detenzione preventiva." *La Scuola Positiva* 2 (March 15, 1892): 199–215.

Gatteschi, Carlo. *Dell'ammonizione de pubblica sicurezza.* Florence: Fioretti, 1889.

Géhin, Henri-Barthélemy. *Contribution à l'étude de l'automatisme ambulatoire ou vagabondage impulsif.* Bordeaux: Imprimerie Centrale A. de Lanefranque, 1892.

Geltmaker, Ty. *Tired of Living: Suicide in Italy from National Unification to World War I, 1860–1915.* New York: Peter Lang, 2002.

Genil-Perrin, Georges-Paul-Henri. *Histoire des origines et de l'évolution de l'idée de dégénérescence en médicine mentale.* Paris: Alfred Leclerc, 1913.

Gervasoni, Marco. "Cultura della degenerazione tra socialismo e criminologia alla fine dell'Ottocento in Italia." *Studi Storici* 38 (No. 4) (October–December, 1997): 1087–119, http://www.jstor.org/stable/20566866 (accessed May 30, 2014).

Giacobini, Giacomo, and Gian Luigi Panattoni. *Il Darwinismo in Italia.* Turin: Tipografico-Editrice Torinese, 1983.

Gibson, Mary. *Born to Crime: Cesare Lombroso and the Origins of Biological Criminology.* Westport, CT: Praeger, 2002.

Gilles de la Tourette, [Georges]. *Les états neurasthéniques: formes cliniques, diagnostic, traitement.* 2nd ed. Paris: Librairie J.-B. Baillière et fils, 1900.

Gilman, Sander L. *Diseases & Diagnoses: The Second Age of Biology.* New Brunswick and London: Transaction Publishers, 2010.

Goetz, Christopher G., Michel Bonduelle, and Toby Gelfand. *Charcot: Constructing Neurology.* New York: Oxford University Press, 1995.

Goldstein, Jan. *Console and Classify: The French Psychiatric Profession in the Nineteenth Century.* Chicago and London: University of Chicago Press, 1987, 2001.

Goldstein, Jan. "'Moral Contagion': A Professional Ideology of Medicine and Psychiatry in Eighteenth-and Nineteenth-Century France." In *Professions and the French State, 1700–1900*, edited by Gerald L. Geison, 181–222. Philadelphia: University of Pennsylvania Press, 1984.

Goldstein, Jan. "The Wandering Jew and the Problem of Psychiatric Anti-Semitism in Fin-de-Siècle France." *Journal of Contemporary History* 20 (No. 4) (October 1985): 521–52. http://www.jstor.org/stable/260396 (accessed October 28, 2013).

Goode, Erich, and Nachman Ben-Yehuda. *Moral Panics: The Social Construction of Deviance.* Cambridge, MA: Blackwell Publishers, 1994.

Guarnieri, Patrizia. *A Case of Child Murder: Law and Science in 19th Century Tuscany.* Cambridge: Polity Press, 1993.

Gueslin, André. *Gens pauvres, pauvres gens dans la France du XIXe siècle*. Paris: Aubier, 1998.

Gueslin, André, and Dominique Kalifa, eds. *Les exclus en Europe, 1830–1930*. Paris: Les Editions de l'Atelier, 1999.

Gurrieri, R., and E. Fornasari. *I sensi e le anomalie somatiche nella donna normale e nella prostituta*. Turin: Fratelli Bocca, 1893.

Hacking, Ian. *Mad Travelers: Reflections on the Reality of Transient Mental Illness*. Charlottesville and London: University Press of Virginia, 1998.

Hacking, Ian. *The Social Construction of What?* Cambridge, MA and London, England: Harvard University Press 1999.

Harrington, Anne. "Beyond Phrenology: Localization Theory in the Modern Era." In *The Enchanted Loom: Chapters in the History of Neuroscience*, edited by Pietro Corsi, 207–15. New York: Oxford University Press, 1991.

Herzen, A. [Gertsen, Aleksandr Aleksandrovi]. *Physiologie de la volonté*. Translated from the Italian by Ch. Letoureau. Paris: Librairie Germer Baillière, 1874.

Huysmans, J.-K. *Against Nature*. Translated by Robert Baldick. Middlesex: Penguin Books, 1959.

Janet, Pierre. *Les Névroses*. Paris: Ernest Flammarion, 1909.

Janet, Pierre. *Névroses et idées fixes*. Vol. 1 in *Études expérimentales sur les troubles de la volonté, de l'attention, de la mémoire, sur les émotions, les idées obsédantes et leur traitement*, Paris: Félix Alcan, 1898.

Jefferson, Ann. *Genius in France: An Idea and Its Uses*. Princeton, NJ: Princeton University Press, 2015.

Jodelet, Denise. *Madness and Social Representations: Living with the Mad in One French Community*. Translated by Tim Pownall and edited by Gerard Duveen. Berkeley: University of California Press, 1991.

Joffroy, A[lix], and R[aoul] Dupouy. *Fugues et vagabondage: étude clinique et psychologique*. Paris: Félix Alcan, 1909.

Joly, Henri. *La France criminelle*. Paris: Librairie Léopold Cerf, 1889.

Jordanova, Ludmilla. *Sexual Visions: Images of Gender in Science and Medicine between the Eighteenth and Twentieth Centuries*. New York: Harvester Wheatsheaf, 1989.

Kalifa, Dominique. *Crime et culture au XIXe siècle*. Paris: Perrin, 2005.

Kaluszynski, Martine. *La République à l'épreuve du crime: la construction du crime comme object politique, 1880–1920*. Paris: Maison des sciences de l'homme, 2002. http://halshs .archives-ouvertes.fr/halshs-00343187/ (accessed June 12, 2014).

Kimble, Gregory A. "Voluntary Behavior." In *International Encyclopedia of Psychiatry, Psychology, Psychoanalysis, and Neurology*, Vol. 11, edited by Benjamin B. Wolman. New York: Aesculapius Publishers, 1977.

Kershaw, Alister. *Murder in France*. London: Constable & Company, 1955.

Krafft-Ebing, R[ichard] von. *Psychopathia Sexualis: With Special Reference to the Antipathic Sexual Instinct: A Medico-Forensic Study*. 12th ed. Brooklyn, NY: Physicians and Surgeons Book Company, 1932.

La Cara, A[nnunziato]. *La base organica dei pervertimenti sessuali e la loro profilassi sociale*. 2nd ed. Turin: Fratelli Bocca, 1924.

La Vergata, Antonello. "Lombroso e la degenerazione." In *Cesare Lombroso. Gli scienziati e la nuova Italia*, edited by S[ilvano] Montaldo, 55–93. Bologna: Il Mulino, 2010.

Lacassagne, A[lexandre]. *Cesare Lombroso (1836–1909)*. Lyon: A. Rey & Cie, 1909.

Lacassagne, A[lexandre]. *Des transformations du droit pénale et les progrès de la médicine légale de 1810 à 1912*. Lyon: A. Rey Imprimeur-Éditeur, 1913.

Lacassagne, A[lexandre]. *L'homme criminel comparé à l'homme primitif.* Lyon: Association Typographique, 1882.

Lacassagne, A[lexandre]. *Vacher L'Eventreur et les crimes sadiques.* Lyon. A. Storck and Paris: Masson, 1899.

Lalli, Pina di, ed. *Immagini dal manicomio: Le fotografie storiche del "S. Lazzaro" di Reggio Emilia, 1892–1936.* Reggio Emilia: AGE Grafico-Editoriale, 1993.

Lantéri-Laura, Georges. *Lecture des perversions: Histoire de leur appropriation médicale.* Paris: Masson, 1979.

Lapie, Paul. *Logique de la volonté.* Paris: Félix Alcan, 1902.

Laurent, Émile. *L'amour morbide: étude de psychologie pathologique.* Paris: Société d'Editions Scientifiques, 1891.

Laurent, Émile. *La neurasthénie et son traitement.* 2nd ed. Paris: A. Maloine, 1897.

Laurent, Émile. *Le criminal aux points de vue anthropologique, physiologique et social.* Paris: Vigot Frères, 1908.

Laurent, Émile, Dr. "Prostitution et dégénérescence." *Annales médico-psychologiques* Série 8, 10 (November, 1899): 353–81.

Le Bon, Gustave. *Lois psychologiques de l'évolution des peuples.* 10th ed. Paris: Félix Alcan, 1911.

Leggiardi-Laura, C. "Ancora sul cervello di Vacher." *Archivio di psichiatria, scienze penali ed antropologia criminale* 21 (1900): 484–86.

Leggiardi-Laura, C. "Il cervello di Vacher." *Archivio di psichiatria, scienze penali ed antropologia criminale* 21 (1900): 283–84.

Leps, Marie-Christine. *Apprehending the Criminal: The Production of Deviance in Nineteenth-Century Discourse.* Durham and London: Duke University Press, 1992.

Levillain, Fernand. *La neurasthénie: maladie de Beard.* Paris: A. Malline, 1891.

Levra, Umberto, ed. *La scienza e la colpa: crimini, criminali, criminologi: Un volto dell'Ottocento.* Milan: Electa Editrice, 1985.

Lévy, Paul-Émile. *L'éducation rationnelle de la volonté: Son emploi thérapeutique.* 7th ed. Paris: Félix Alcan, 1909.

Lioy, Paolo. "Piccole miserie d'uomini grandi." *Nuova antologia* 17 (September 1888): 312–25.

Locatelli, G. *Il vagabondaggio e dei mezzi per prevenirlo e reprimerlo.* Padua: Stabilmento Prosperini, 1885.

Lombroso, Cesare. *Criminal Man.* Translated and with a new introduction by Mary Gibson and Nicole Hahn Rafter. Durham and London: Duke University Press, 2006.

Lombroso, Cesare. "Del tribadismo nei manicomi." *Archivio di psichiatria, scienze penali ed antropologia criminale* 6 (1885): 218–21.

Lombroso, Cesare. *Delitti di libidine.* 2nd ed. Turin: Fratelli Bocca, 1886.

Lombroso, Cesare. *Delitti vecchi e delitti nuovi.* Turin: Fratelli Bocca, 1902.

Lombroso, Cesare. *Delitto, genio, follia: Scritti scelti.* Edited by Delia Frigessi, Ferruccio Giacanelli and Luisa Mangoni. Turin: Bollati Boringhieri, 1995.

Lombroso, Cesare. *Genio e degenerazione: Nuovi studi e nuove battaglie.* 2nd ed. Milan: Remo Sandrion, 1907.

Lombroso, Cesare. "Identità dell'epilessia colla pazzia morale e delinquenza congenita." *Archivio di psichiatria, scienze penali, ed antropologia criminale* 6 (1885): 1–28.

Lombroso, Cesare. "L'Ultimo brigante: Giuseppe Musolino." *Nuova antologia* 97 (February 1902): 508–16.

Lombroso, Cesare. *L'Uomo alienato: Trattato clinico sperimentale delle malattie mentali.* Preface by Leonardo Bianchi and reordered by Gina Lombroso. Turin: Fratelli Bocca, 1913.

Lombroso, Cesare. *L'uomo bianco e l'uomo di colore: Letture sull'origini e la varietà delle razze umane.* 2nd ed. Turin: Fratelli Bocca, 1892.

Lombroso, Cesare. *L'uomo delinquente.* Turin: Fratelli Bocca, 1924.

Lombroso, Cesare. *L'Uomo di genio.* 6th ed. Turin: Fratelli Bocca, 1894.

Lombroso, Cesare. *La funzione sociale del delitto.* 2nd ed. Milano-Palermo: Remo Sandron, 1898.

Lombroso, Cesare. "La Fusion de la folie morale et du criminel-né." *Revue philosophique de la France et de l'étranger* 20 (1885): 178–82.

Lombroso, Cesare. "La pazzia ed il genio in Cristoforo Colombo." *Archivio di psichiatria, scienze penali ed antropologia criminale* 21 (1900): 29–48.

Lombroso, Cesare. *The Man of Genius.* London: Charles Scribner's Sons, 1891.

Lombroso, Cesare. "Prolusione al corso di medicina legale." In *Antologia Lombrosiana,* edited by Luigi Ferrio, 79–85. Pavia: Società Editrice Pavese, n.d.

Lombroso, Cesare. Review of *Sull'aumento della delinquenza* by A. Niceforo. *Archivio di psichiatria, scienze penali, antropologia criminale* 20 (1800): 646.

Lombroso, Cesare, and A. G. Bianchi. *Il Caso Olivo.* Milan: Libraria Editrice Nazionale, 1905.

Lombroso, [Cesare], and [Augusto Guido] Bianchi. *Misdea e la nuova scuola penale.* Turin: Fratelli Bocca, 1884.

Lombroso, Cesare, and G. Ferrero. *La donna delinquente: La prostituta e la donna normale.* 2nd ed. Turin: L. Roux, 1894.

Longhi, Silvio. "Del concetto giuridico di 'contravvenzione' in contrapposizione a quello di delitto." *La Scuola Positiva* 8 (July 1898): 385–408.

Lonni, Ada. "Dalla prassi alla norma. Criteri di definizione e di repressione delle azioni proibite (Secoli XVIII–XIX)." In *Emarginazione, criminalità e devianza in Italia fra '600 e '900,* edited by Alessandro and Paolo Sorcinelli, 85–101. Milan: FrancoAngeli, 1990.

Loria, Achille. "Socialismo giurdico." *La Scienza del diritto privato* 1 (September 1893): 519–27.

Loria, Achille. *Le basi economiche della costituzione sociale.* 3rd ed. Turin: Fratelli Bocca, 1902.

Luzzatto, Oscar. "Intorno al concetto di normalità." *Archivio di psichiatria, scienze penali ed antropologia criminale* 21 (1900): 251–73.

Magnan, [Valentin]. *Des anomalies, des aberrations et des perversions sexuelles.* Paris: A. Delahaye & E. Lecrosnier, 1885.

Magnan, V[alentin]. *Leçons cliniques sur les maladies mentales.* Paris: Félix Alcan, 1897.

Magnan, V[alentin], and [Paul-Maurice] Legrain. *Les dégénérés (Etat mental et syndromes épisodiques).* Paris: Rueff et Cie, Editeurs, 1895.

Magrì, Enzo. *Musolino: Il brigante dell'Aspromonte.* Milan: Camunia, 1989.

Malagreca, Miguel Andrés. *Queer Italy: Contexts, Antecedents, and Representation.* New York: Peter Lang, 2007.

Manes, Carlo. *Capitalismo e criminalità.* Rome: Tipografia Editrice Nazionale, 1912.

Mangoni, Luisa. *Una crisi fine secolo: La cultura italiana e la Francia fra Otto e Novecento.* Turin: Giulio Einaudi, 1985.

Mantegazza, Paolo. *Che cosa è il genio?* In *Archivio per l'antropologia e la etnologia.* Florence: Salvadore Landi, 1907.

Mantegazza, Paolo. "Gli atavismi psichici." *Archivio per l'antropologia e la etnologia* 18 (1888): 69–82.

Mantegazza, Paolo. *Il secolo nevrosico.* Pordenone: Edizioni Studio Testi, 1995.

Marie, A., and Raymond Meunier. *Les vagabonds.* Paris: V. Giard & E. Brière, 1908.

Mario, Jessie White. "Il sistema penitenziaria e il domicilio coatto." *Nuova antologia* 64 (July 1896):16–35; 65 (September 1896): 313–35; 68 (April 1897): 680–707; 70 (August 1897): 503–19.

Marmier, Robert. *Les perversions instinctives: Origines et débuts de cette notion*. Paris: Librairie Médicale et Scientifique, 1912.

Marro, [Antonio], and [Cesare] Lombroso. *I germi della pazzia morale nei fanciulli*. Turin: Tipografia Celanza, 1883.

Martin, Georges. *Étude sur la neurasthénie et l'état mental des neurasthéniques*. Paris: A. Maloine, Editeur, 1898.

Martin, Randy, Robert J. Mutchnick, and W. Timothy Austin. *Criminological Thought: Pioneers Past and Present*. New York: Macmillan, 1990.

Mathieu, A. *Neurasthénie (épuisement nerveux)*. Paris: J.-B. Baillière et fils, 1890.

Matlock, Jann. *Scenes of Seduction: Prostitution, Hysteria, and Reading Difference in Nineteenth-Century France*. New York: Columbia University Press, 1994.

Maudsley, Henry. *Body and Will, Being an Essay Concerning Will in Its Metaphysical, Physiological, and Pathological Aspects*. New York: D. Appleton and Company, 1884.

Maudsley, Henry. *The Pathology of Mind*. 3rd ed. London: Macmillan, 1879.

Mayo Clinic. "Depression: Major Depression." http://www.mayoclinic.com/health/depression/DS00175/DSECTION=symptoms (accessed May 16, 2013).

McLaren, Angus. *A Prescription for Murder: The Victorian Serial Killings of Dr. Thomas Neill Cream*. Chicago: University of Chicago Press, 1993.

Meige, Henry. *Le Juif-Errant à la Salpêtrière*. Paris: Editions du Nouvel Objet, 1993.

Merlino, Francesco Saverio. *L'Italia qual è; Politica e magistratura dal 1860 ad oggi in Italia: Fascismo e Democrazia*. Edited by Nicola Tranfaglia. Milan: Feltrinelli, 1974.

Micale, Mark S. "On the 'Disappearance' of Hysteria: A Study in the Clinical Deconstruction of a Diagnosis." *Isis* 84 (September 1993): 496–526.

Micale, Mark S. "The Salpêtrière in the Age of Charcot: An Institutional Perspective on Medical History in the Late Nineteenth Century." *Journal of Contemporary History* 20 (No. 4) (October 1985): 703–31. http://www.jstor.org/stable/260396 (accessed November 21, 2003).

Micale, Mark S., and Paul Lerner, eds. *Traumatic Pasts: History, Psychiatry, and Trauma in the Modern Age, 1870–1930*. Cambridge: Cambridge University Press, 2001.

Montaldo, Silvano, ed. *Cesare Lombroso. Gli scienziati e la nuova Italia*. Bologna: Il Mulino 2010.

Moreau (de Tours), Jacques-Joseph. *De la folie raisonnante envisagée sous le point de vue médico- légal*. Paris: Lacour et Compagnie, 1840.

Moreau (de Tours), Jacques-Joseph. *La psychologie morbide dans ses rapports avec la philosophie de l'histoire ou de l'influence des névropathies sur le dynamisme intellectuel*. Paris: Librairie Victor Masson, 1859.

Moreau (de Tours), Paul. *De la contagion du suicide: à propos de l'épidémie actuelle*. Paris: A. Parent, 1875.

Moreau (de Tours), Paul. *De la démence dans ses rapports avec l'état normal des facultés intellectuelles et affectives*. Paris: Asselin, 1878.

Moreau (de Tours), Paul. *Des aberrations du sens génésique*. Paris: Asselin et Cie, 1880.

Morel, Bénédict Augustin. *Traité des dégénérescences physiques, intellectuelles et morales de l'espèce humaine*. Paris: J.-B. Baillière, 1857. Reprint, New York: Arno Press, 1976.

Morel, Pierre, Jean-Pierre Bourgeron, and Elisabeth Roudinesco. *Au-delà du conscient: histoire illustrée de la psychiatrie et de la psychanalyse*. Paris: Editions Hazan, 2000.

Morel, Pierre, and Pierre Bouvery. *Aspects anthropologiques et sociopathiques de dix assassins guillotinés au XIXe siècle, dans la région lyonnaise*. Paris: Masson, 1964.

Morselli, Enrico. *Antropologia generale: L'uomo secondo la teoria dell'evoluzione: lezioni*. Turin: Unione Tipografico-Editrice Torinese, 1911.

Morselli, Enrico. *Linda e Tullio Murri: Studio psicologico e psichiatrico*. Genoa: Libreria Moderna, 1905.

Morselli, Enrico. "Riepilogo del 'Fenomeno Musolino.'" *Nuova antologia* 185 (December 1902): 696–704.

Morselli, E[nrico], and C[esare] Lombroso. "Epilessia larvata-pazzia morale." *Archivio di psichiatria, scienze penali, ed antropologia criminale* 6 (1885): 29–43.

Morselli, E[nrico], and Sante De Sanctis. *Biografia di un bandito: Giuseppe Musolino di fronte alla psichiatria ed alla sociologia*. Milan: Treves, 1903.

Mosse, George L. *Nationalism and Sexuality: Respectability and Abnormal Sexuality in Modern Europe*. New York: Howard Fertig, 1985.

Musolino, Giuseppe. *S. Stefano in Aspromonte: storia e protagonisti*. Marigliano: Rexodes Magna Grecia, 1994.

Nazzari, Rinaldo. "L'uomo di genio per gli psichiatri e gli antropologi." *Rivista filosofica*. (Fascicolo 5) Anno 5 (No. 6) (November–December, 1903): 628–63.

Neppi Modona, Guido. "Legislazione penale." In *Il Mondo contemporaneo, storia d'Italia*, Vol. 2, edited by Fabio Levi, Umberto Levra, and Nicola Tranfaglia, 584–607. Florence: La Nuova Italia, 1978.

Newman, Graeme. *Comparative Deviance: Perception and Law in Six Cultures*. New York: Elsevier Scientific Publishing Company, 1976.

Nisticò, Vincenzo. *Giuseppe Musolino: Galera o manicomio?* Naples: A. Delle Donne, 1902.

Nocito, Pietro. "La delinquenza in Italia nel 1896." *La Scuola Positiva* 8 (June 1898): 373–79.

Nordau, Max. *Degeneration*. 7th ed. New York: D. Appleton, 1895.

Nordau, Max. *Psycho-physiologie du génie et du talent*. Translated by Auguste Dietrich. Paris: Félix Alcan, 1897.

Nordau, Max. "Signification biologique de la dégénérescence." In *L'Opera di Cesare Lombroso nella scienze e nelle sue applicazioni*, edited by Leonardo Bianchi, 245–56. Turin: Fratelli Bocca, 1906.

Norlenghi, Arnoldo. *Delinquenza presente e delinquenza futura: a proposito della condanna di Musolino*. Turin: Renzo Streglio, 1902.

Nye, Robert A. *Crime, Madness & Politics in Modern France: The Medical Concept of National Decline*. Princeton, NJ: Princeton University Press, 1984.

Oppenheim, Janet. *"Shattered Nerves": Doctors, Patients, and Depression in Victorian England*. New York: Oxford University Press, 1991.

Orano, Paolo. "Cesare Lombroso." *La Scuola Positiva* 16 (March–April 1906): 138–48; (May–June 1906): 286–92.

Ottolenghi, S. "Epilessie psichiche." *Rivista sperimentale di freniatria* 16 (1890): 189–219.

Padovan, Adolfo. *Che cosa è il genio?* 2nd ed. Milan: Ulrico Hoepli, 1907.

Padovan, Adolfo. *I figli della gloria*. 2nd ed. Milan: Ulrico Hoepli, 1906.

Padovan, Adolfo. "Il genio." *Rivista d'Italia* 8 (January 1905): 117–20.

Padovan, Adolfo. *Le origini del genio*. Milan: Ulrico Hoepli, 1909.

Page, Herbert W. *Injuries of the Spine and Spinal Cord without Apparent Mechanical Lesion, and Nervous Shock, in Their Surgical and Medical-Legal Aspects*. London: J. & A. Churchill, 1883.

Pagnier, Armand. *Du vagabondage et des vagabonds. Étude psychologique, sociologique, et médico-legale.* Lyon: A. Storck, 1906.

Pagnier, A[rmand]. *Le vagabond.* Paris: Vigot Frères, 1910.

Patriarca, Silvana. *Italian Vices: Nation and Character from the Risorgimento to the Republic.* Cambridge: Cambridge University Press, 2010.

Patrizi, M. L. *La fisiologia d'un bandito (Musolino): esperimenti e commenti.* Turin: Fratelli Bocca, 1904.

Paulhan, Fr. *La volonté.* Paris: Octave Doin, Editeur, 1903.

Pavarini, Massimo. "Il 'socialmente pericoloso' nell'attività di prevenzione." *Rivista italiana di diritto e procedura penale* 18 (April–June 1975): 396–454.

Payot, Jules. *L'éducation de la volonté.* 29th ed. Paris: Félix Alcan, 1908.

Pellizzi, G. B. "Idiozia ed epilessia." *Archivio di psichiatria, scienze penali, ed antropologia criminale* 21 (1900): 409–25.

Peniston, William A. *Pederasts and Others: Urban Culture and Sexual Identity in Nineteenth-Century Paris.* New York: Harrington Park Press, 2004.

Penta, Pasquale. "Ancora sulla impotenza sessuale neurastenica—Note critiche ed osservazioni." *Archivio delle psicopatie sessuali* 1 (August 1–15, 1896): 204–22.

Penta, Pasquale. "Caratteri generali, origine e significato dei PERVERTIMENTI SESSUALI dimostrati colle autobiografie di Alfieri e di Rousseau e col dialogo 'Gli amori' di Luciano." *Archivio delle psicopatie sessuali* 1 (January 1, 1896): 1–9; (January 15, 1896): 17–21.

Penta, Pasquale. *I pervertimenti sessuali nell'uomo e Vincenzo Verzeni strangolatore di donne: studio biologico.* Naples: Luigi Pierro, 1893.

Penta, Pasquale. "L'origine e la patogenesi della inversione sessuale, secondo Krafft-Ebing e gli altri autori." *Archivio delle psicopatie sessuali* 1 (February 15 and March 1, 1896): 53–70.

Penta, Pasquale. *Pazzia e società.* Milan: Dottor Francesco Vallardi, [1893].

Pessina, Enrico. "La crisi del diritto penale nell'ultimo trentennio del secolo XIX." *Rivista giuridica e sociale* 3 (February 1906): 49–61.

Pick, Daniel. *Faces of Degeneration: A European Disorder, c.1848–c.1918.* Cambridge: Cambridge University Press, 1989.

Porter, Roy, ed. *The Cambridge History of Medicine.* New York: Cambridge University Press, 2006.

Porter, Roy. *Madness: A Brief History.* Oxford: Oxford University Press, 2002.

Proal, Louis. "La responsabilité légale des aliénés." *Annales médico-psychologiques,* 7th series, 12 (July 1890): 84–107.

Rabinbach, Anson. *The Human Motor: Energy, Fatigue, and the Origins of Modernity.* Berkeley and Los Angeles: University of California Press, 1992.

Rafter, Nicole. *The Criminal Brain: Understanding Biological Theories of Crime.* New York and London: New York University Press, 2008.

Rafter, Nicole Hahn. *Creating Born Criminals.* Urbana and Chicago: University of Illinois Press, 1997.

Raymond, Fulgence. *Neurasthénie-syndrome (neurasthénie simple, acquise ou accidentelle), leçon faite à l'hospice de la Salpêtrière.* Paris: Imprimerie Typographique Jean Gainche, 1907.

Réclus, Élie. *Les primitifs: Études d'ethnologies comparées.* Paris: Librairie C. Reinwald, 1903.

Regnard, Albert. "Génie et folie." *Annales medico-psychologiques,* 8th series, 7 (January–February 1898): 10–34; (March–April 1898): 176–95; (May–June 1898): 353–70;

8 (July–August 1898): 5–25, (September–October 1898): 204–28; 9 (January–February 1899): 22–42; (May–June 1899): 379–419.

Regno d'Italia. *Il Codice Penale per il Regno d'Italia*, 1899. https://archive.org/details/ilcodicepenalep00crivgoog (accessed July 13, 2015).

Ribot, Th[éodule]. *Diseases of Memory: An Essay in the Positive Psychology*. Translated by William Huntington Smith. New York: D. Appleton and Company, 1887.

Ribot, Th[éodule]. *Les maladies de la personnalité*. 14th ed. Paris: Félix Alcan, 1908.

Ribot, Th[éodule]. *Les maladies de la volonté*. 32nd ed. Paris: Librairie Félix Alcan, 1920.

Ribot, Th[éodule]. *Psychologie de l'attention Paris*. 11th ed. Paris: Félix Alcan, 1910.

Richer, Paul. *Études cliniques sur la grande hystérie ou l'hystéro-épilepsie*. 2nd ed. Paris: Adrian Delahaye et Émile Lecrosnier, 1885.

Richet, Charles. *Essai de psychologie générale*. 8th ed. Paris: Félix Alcan, 1910.

Rivière, Dominque-Joseph-Bertrand. *Contribution à l'étude clinique des aboulies et principalement de l'aboulie neurasthénique*. Paris: Henri Jouve, 1891.

Rivière, Louis. *Mendiants et vagabonds*. Paris: Librairie Victor Lecoffre, 1902.

Rizzo, Domenico. *Gli spazi della morale: buon costume e ordine delle famiglie in Italia in età liberale*. Rome: Biblink, 2004.

Roncoroni, L. "Influenza del sesso sulla criminalità in Italia." *Archivio di psichiatria, scienze penali ed antropologia criminale*. 14 (1893): 1–14.

Sanchez, Jean-Lucien. "Les lois Bérenger (lois du 14 août 1885 et du 26 mars 1891)." *Criminocorpus*, 2005. http://criminocorpus.revues.org/132;doi:10.4000/criminocorpus.132 (accessed January 28, 2013).

Scartezzini, Riccardo. "Sui 'vagabondi' di Florian e Cavaglieri." *Quaderni di sociologia* 2 (1980–1981): 216–35.

Schmitt, Jean-Claude. "L'histoire des marginaux." In *La nouvelle histoire*, edited by Jacques Le Goff, Roger Chartier, and Jacques Revel, 344–69. Paris: CEPL, 1978.

Sedgwick, Eve Kosofsky. *Epistemology of the Closet*. Berkeley and Los Angeles: University of California Press, 1990.

Seidman, Steven, Nancy Fischer, and Chet Meeks. *Handbook of the New Sexuality Studies*. London and New York: Routledge, 2006.

Sergi, Giuseppe. "Gli uomini di genio." *Nuova antologia*, 4th series, 85 (February 1, 1900): 405–32.

Sergi, Giuseppe. "Il temperamento scientifico: Un contributo alla teoria dell'uomo di genio." *Nuova antologia* 125 (October 1, 1906): 345–55.

Sergi, Giuseppe. *Le degenerazioni umane*. Milan: Fratelli Dumolard, 1889.

Sérieux, P., and J. Capgras. *Les folies raisonnantes: le délire d'interprétation*. Paris: Félix Alcan, 1909.

Shephard, Ben. *A War of Nerves: Soldiers and Psychiatrists 1914–1994*. London: Pimilco, 2002.

Shorter, Edward. *A History of Psychiatry: From the Era of the Asylum to the Age of Prozac*. New York: John Wiley & Sons, Inc., 1997.

Sibalis, Michael. "High-heels or Hiking Boots? Masculinity, Effeminacy and Male Homosexuals in Modern France." In *French Masculinities: History, Culture, and Politics*, edited by Christopher E. Forth and Bertrand Taithe, 172–89. Basingstoke: Palgrave Macmillan, 2007.

Sighele, Scipio. *La folla delinquente*. Edited by Clara Gallini. Venice: Marsilio Editori, 1985.

Sighicelli, C., and R. Tambroni. "Pazzia morale ed epilessia." *Rivista sperimentale di freniatria e di medicina legale* 13 (1887): 249–78.

Smith, Timothy B. *Creating the Welfare State in France, 1880–1940*. Montreal and Kingston: McGill-Queen's University Press, 2003.

Sollier, Paul. *L'Idiotie et l'imbécilité au point de vue nosographique*. Évreux: Imprimerie de Charles Hérissey, 1894.

Starr, Douglas. *The Killer of Little Shepherds: A True Crime Story and the Birth of Forensic Science*. New York: Alfred A. Knopf, 2010.

Sueur, Laurent. "La fragile limite entre le normal et l'anormal: lorsque les psychiatres français essayaient, au XIXe siècle, de reconnâitre la folie." *Revue historique* 292 (1994): 31–51.

Sullivan, Nikki. *A Critical Introduction to Queer Theory*. Washington Square, NY: New York University Press, 2003.

Tamassia, Arrigo. "Sull'inversione dell'istinto sessuale." *Rivista sperimentale de freniatria e medicina legale delle alienazioni mentali* 4 (1878): 97–117.

Tamburini, A., and G. Guicciardi. "Ulteriori studi su un caso di imbecillità morale." *Rivista sperimentale di freniatria e di medicina legale* 13 (1887): 153–98.

Tanzi, Eugenio. *Trattato delle malattie mentali*. Milan: Società Editrice-Libraria, 1905.

Tanzi, Eugenio, and Ernesto Lugaro. *Malattie mentali*. 3rd ed., Vol. 1. Milan: Società Editrice Libraria, 1923.

Tanzi, Eugenio, and Ernesto Lugaro. *Trattato delle malattie mentali*. 2nd ed., Vol. 1. Milan: Società Editrice Libraria, 1914. Vol. 2, 1916.

Tarde, Gabriel. *La criminalité comparée*. 7th ed. Paris: Félix Alcan, 1910.

Tarde, G[abriel]. "La criminalité en France dans les vingt dernières années." *Archives d'anthropologie criminelle, de criminologie, et de psychologie normale et pathologique* 18 (March 15, 1903): 162–81.

Tarde, G[abriel]. *La philosophie pénale*. 5th ed. Paris: G. Masson, 1900.

Tarde, Gabriel. "Le type criminel." *Revue philosophique de France et de l'étranger* 19 (June 1885): 593–627.

Tardieu, A[mbroise]. *Étude médico-légale sur les attentats aux moeurs*. Paris: J.-B. Baillière et fils, 1858.

Tebaldi, Augusto. *Napoleone: Una pagina storico-psicologica del genio*. Padua: Angelo Draghi Editore, 1895.

Temkin, Oswei. *The Falling Sickness: A History of Epilepsy from the Greeks to the Beginnings of Modern Neurology*. 2nd ed. revised. Baltimore: Johns Hopkins Press, 1971.

Tissié, Phillipe. *Les aliénes voyageurs: essai médico-psychologique*. Paris: Octave Douin, 1887.

Tizard, Barbara. "Theories of Brain Localization from Flourens to Lashley." *Medical History* 3 (1959): 132–45.

Tonnino, [Silvio]. "Le epilessie." *Archivio di psichiatria, scienze penali ed antropologia criminale* 6 (1885): 370–415.

Toulouse, Édouard. *Emile Zola: Enquête médico-psychologique sur la supériorité intellectuelle*. Paris: Ernest Flammarion, 1896.

Tranfaglia, Nicola. "Un delitto di gente perbene. Il processo Murri (1902–1905)." In *Storia d'Italia, vol. 12, La criminalità*, edited by Luciano Violante, 525–52. Turin: Giulio Einaudi: 1997.

Trélat, Ulysse. *La folie lucide*. Paris: Frénésie Editions, 1988.

Vaccaro, M. Angelo. *Genesi e funzioni delle leggi penali*. Rome: Fratelli Bocca, 1889.

Venturi, Silvio. *Le degenerazioni psico-sessuali*. Turin: Fratelli Bocca, 1892.

Venturi, Silvio. *Le pazzie dell'uomo sociale*. Milan: Remo Sandron, 1901.

Verona, Flavio. *Oziosi e vagabondi nella legislazione penale dell'Italia liberale*. Pisa: ETS, 1984.

Vespucci, Amerigo. *Giuseppe Musolino: Il bandito calabrese*. Naples: F. Bideri, 1932.

Veuillot, Fernand. *La neurasthénie et les états neurasthéniformes: rôle de l'hérédité névropathique*. Paris: G. Steinheil, 1896.

Vial, Auguste. *Dégénérescence mentale et neurasthénie*. Lyon: A. H. Storck, 1897.

Vibert, [Charles-Albert]. *Étude médico-légale sur les blessures produites par les accidents de chemin de fer*. Paris: Librairie J.-B. Baillière et fils, 1888.

Vicarelli, Giovanna. *Alle radici della politica sanitaria in Italia: Società e salute da Crispi al fascismo*. Bologna: Il Mulino, 1997.

Vidler, Anthony. "Psychopathologies of Modern Space: Metropolitan Fear from Agrophobia to Estrangement." In *Rediscovering History: Culture, Politics, and the Psyche*, edited by Michael S. Roth, 11–29. Stanford, CA: Stanford University Press, 1994.

Vigarello, Georges. *Histoire de viol, XVIe–XXe siècle*. Paris: Seuil, 1998.

Villa, Renzo. "'Pazzi e criminali': strutture istituzionali e practica psichiatrica nei manicomi criminali italiani (1876–1915)." *Movimento operaio e socialista* 3 (1980): 369–93.

Virgilio, Gaspare. *Sulla natura morbosa del delitto: saggio di ricerche* and *Passanante e la natura morbosa del delitto*. Turin: Fratelli Bocca, 1910.

Voisin, Jules. *L'épilepsie*. Paris: Félix Alcan, 1897.

Walz, Robin. *Pulp Surrealism: Insolent Popular Culture in Early Twentieth-Century Paris*. Berkeley: University of California Press, 2000.

Wanrooij, Bruno P. F. *Storia del pudore: La questione sessuale in Italia, 1860–1940*. Venice: Marsilio Editori, 1990.

Weeks, Jeffrey. *Sexuality and Its Discontents: Meanings, Myths & Modern Sexualities*. London, Melbourne, and Henley: Routledge & Kegan Paul, 1985.

Weininger, Otto. *Sex and Character*. New York: Howard Fertig, 2003. Originally published by New York: G. P. Putnam's Sons, 1906.

Weissbach, Lee Shai. *Child Labor Reform in Nineteenth-Century France: Assuring the Future Harvest*. Baton Rouge: Louisiana University Press, 1989.

Wetzell, Richard F. *Inventing the Criminal: A History of German Criminology, 1880–1945*. Chapel Hill and London: The University of North Carolina Press, 2000.

Willson, Perry, ed. *Gender, Family and Sexuality: The Private Sphere in Italy, 1860–1945*. Basingstoke: Palgrave Macmillan, 2004.

Wilson, Michael L. "'Je m'occupe de politique': The Male Prostitute in Belle Epoque Print Culture" (paper presented at the meeting of the Western Society for French History, Long Beach, CA, October 20, 2006).

Wright, Gordon. *Between the Guillotine and Liberty*. New York: Oxford University Press, 1983.

Xiberras, Martine. *Théories de l'exclusion: Pour une construction de l'imaginaire de la déviance*. Paris: Méridiens Klincksieck, 1994.

Young, Robert M. *Mind, Brain, and Adaptation in the Nineteenth Century: Cerebral Localization and Its Biological Context from Gall to Ferrier*. Oxford: Oxford University Press, 1990.

Zerboglio, Adolfo. "Contro il domicilio coatto." *Rivista popolare di politica, lettere, e scienze sociali* 3 (November 15, 1897): 169–73.

Index